Wittgenstein: Understandi

Part II: Exegesis §§1

Other volumes of this Commentary

Wittgenstein: Rules, Grammar and Necessity, Volume 2 of An Analytical Commentary on the *Philosophical Investigations*
Essays and Exegesis of §§185–242

G. P. Baker and P. M. S. Hacker,
second, extensively revised edition by P. M. S. Hacker

Wittgenstein: Meaning and Mind, Volume 3 of An Analytical Commentary on the *Philosophical Investigations*
Part I: Essays

P. M. S. Hacker

Wittgenstein: Meaning and Mind, Volume 3 of An Analytical Commentary on the *Philosophical Investigations*
Part II: Exegesis §§243–427

P. M. S. Hacker

Wittgenstein: Mind and Will, Volume 4 of An Analytical Commentary on the *Philosophical Investigations*
Part I: Essays

P. M. S. Hacker

Wittgenstein: Mind and Will, Volume 4 of An Analytical Commentary on the *Philosophical Investigations*
Part II: Exegesis §§428–693

P. M. S. Hacker

Epilogue:
Wittgenstein's Place in Twentieth-Century Analytic Philosophy

P. M. S. Hacker

Companion to this volume

Wittgenstein: Understanding and Meaning, Volume 1 of An Analytical Commentary on the *Philosophical Investigations*
Part I: Essays

G. P. Baker and P. M. S. Hacker
second, extensively revised edition by P. M. S. Hacker

Volume 1
of An Analytical Commentary on
the *Philosophical Investigations*

Wittgenstein:
Understanding and Meaning

Part II: Exegesis §§1–184

G. P. Baker and P. M. S. Hacker

Fellows of St John's College · Oxford

Second, extensively revised edition

by

P. M. S. Hacker

WILEY-
BLACKWELL

This edition first published 2009
© 2009 G. P. Baker and P. M. S. Hacker

This edition and *Wittgenstein: Understanding and Meaning. Part I: Essays* originally published
together as *Wittgenstein — Understanding and Meaning* in 1980.
First published in two volumes 1983
Second, extensively revised edition published 2005 by Blackwell Publishing Ltd

Blackwell Publishing was acquired by John Wiley & Sons in February 2007. Blackwell's
publishing program has been merged with Wiley's global Scientific, Technical, and Medical
business to form Wiley-Blackwell.

Registered Office
John Wiley & Sons Ltd, The Atrium, Southern Gate, Chichester, West Sussex, PO19 8SQ,
United Kingdom

Editorial Offices
350 Main Street, Malden, MA 02148-5020, USA
9600 Garsington Road, Oxford, OX4 2DQ, UK
The Atrium, Southern Gate, Chichester, West Sussex, PO19 8SQ, UK

For details of our global editorial offices, for customer services, and for information about how
to apply for permission to reuse the copyright material in this book please see our website at
www.wiley.com/wiley-blackwell.

The right of G. P. Baker and P. M. S. Hacker to be identified as the authors of this work has
been asserted in accordance with the Copyright, Designs and Patents Act 1988.

Wiley also publishes its books in a variety of electronic formats. Some content that appears in
print may not be available in electronic books.

Designations used by companies to distinguish their products are often claimed as trademarks.
All brand names and product names used in this book are trade names, service marks,
trademarks or registered trademarks of their respective owners. The publisher is not associated
with any product or vendor mentioned in this book. This publication is designed to provide
accurate and authoritative information in regard to the subject matter covered. It is sold on the
understanding that the publisher is not engaged in rendering professional services. If
professional advice or other expert assistance is required, the services of a competent
professional should be sought.

Library of Congress Cataloging-in-Publication Data

Wittgenstein : understanding and meaning / G. P. Baker & P. M. S. Hacker.
— Second, extensively rev. ed. / by P. M. S. Hacker.
p. cm. — (Analytical commentary on the Philosophical investigations ; v. 1)
Includes bibliographical references and index.
ISBN 978-1-4051-9925-4 (pbk. : pt. 2 : alk. paper)
1. Wittgenstein, Ludwig, 1889–1951. Philosophische Untersuchungen.
2. Philosophy.   3. Language and languages — Philosophy.
4. Semantics (Philosophy)   I. Hacker, P. M. S. (Peter Michael Stephan)
II. Title II. Series: Baker, Gordon P. Analytical commentary
on the Philosophical investigations (2000); v. 1.
B3376.W563P5323 2004
192—dc21
2004007861

A catalogue record for this book is available from the British Library.

Set in 10/12pt Bembo by Graphicraft Limited, Hong Kong
Printed in Singapore

1   2009

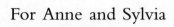

For Anne and Sylvia

The Editors

G. P. Baker was a Fellow of St John's College, Oxford from 1967 until his death in 2002. He is the co-author with P. M. S. Hacker of the first two volumes of the four-volume *Analytical Commentary on the Philosophical Investigations* (Blackwell, 1980–96), author of *Wittgenstein, Frege and the Vienna Circle* (Blackwell, 1988) and, with Katherine Morris, of *Descartes' Dualism* (1996). He also wrote numerous articles on Wittgenstein, Frege, Russell, Waismann and Descartes.

P. M. S. Hacker is the leading authority on the philosophy of Wittgenstein. He is author of the four-volume *Analytical Commentary on the Philosophical Investigations*, the first two volumes co-authored with G. P. Baker (Blackwell, 1980–96) and of *Wittgenstein's Place in Twentieth-century Analytic Philosophy* (Blackwell, 1996). His recent works include *The Philosophical Foundations of Neuroscience* (Blackwell, 2003) and *History of Cognitive Neuroscience* (Wiley-Blackwell, 2008), both co-authored with M. R. Bennett. Most recently he has published *Human Nature: The Categorial Framework* (Blackwell, 2007), the first volume of a trilogy on human nature. Together with Joachim Schulte, he has produced the 4th edition and extensively revised translation of Wittgenstein's *Philosophical Investigations* (Wiley-Blackwell, 2009).

Contents

Acknowledgements

Dr Erich Ammereller, Dr Hanoch Benyami, Professor Hans-Johann Glock, Professor Oswald Hanfling, Edward Kanterian, Dr Joachim Schulte, Dr Jonathan Witztum and Professor Eike von Savigny read and commented upon one or more chapters of exegesis. They saved me from a multitude of errors and oversights. I am most grateful to them for their generosity and for their constructive criticisms.

I owe thanks to Professor Brian McGuinness, Dr Joachim Schulte and the late Professor Georg Henrik von Wright, who have done so much to clarify the history of Wittgenstein's masterpiece, for reading and giving me their comments upon the essay entitled 'The history of the composition of the *Philosophical Investigations*' and upon the exegesis of the 'prelims' to Wittgenstein's book.

St John's College has, as always, been generous in its support of research and scholarship. I am, as I have now so often been, most grateful to Jean van Altena for her admirable copy-editing.

P. M. S. H.

Thoughts reduced to paper are generally nothing
more than the footprints of a man walking in
the sand. It is true that we see the path he
has taken; but to know what he saw on the way,
we must use our own eyes.

Schopenhauer

Introduction to Part II:
Exegesis §§1–184

The exegesis of the second edition of Volume 1 is constructed on the same principles as that of the first edition. The text of the *Investigations* §§1–184, as before, is divided into six chapters. There is nothing sacrosanct about the chosen division — other ways of segmenting the text can readily be imagined and justified. The divisions were chosen partly for convenience of exposition, and because we thought, and I still think, that they correspond to fairly evident thematic changes (the exception is chapter 5, §§134–42, which is a bridging sequence of remarks). They enable readers to pause for breath, as it were, and to gain their bearings in the landscape.

Each chapter of exegesis is preceded by an introduction, which surveys the argumentative development of the sequence of Wittgenstein's numbered *Bemerkungen* (referred to as 'sections' to avoid ambiguity) and explains the structure of the argument. This is supplemented by tree diagrams that represent the relationships between the various sections. At the end of each such introduction, there is a table of sources. In the first edition, we were satisfied to correlate the numbered sections of the text with TS 220 (the Early Draft (*Frühfassung* (FF))), and TS 226$_R$, which is Rhees's 1938/9 translation of it up to §116, although, of course, the exegesis of individual sections made reference to many more texts. Subsequent volumes of the Commentary were more thorough in their attempts to track down sections to their manuscript sources. Now, with the publication of the Bergen edition of the *Nachlass* in electronic form, and the consequent availability of a search engine, I have endeavoured to give all the relevant sources of a given section in the tables of sources annexed to each introduction to a chapter of exegesis. Of course, an element of judgement is involved in thus selecting sources, and no doubt there are some passages that I decided not to be worth registering which another person might, with equal right, think to be relevant.

As it was decided to publish this volume of the Commentary in two parts *ab initio*, rather than, as hitherto, waiting on the publication of the paperback edition, I have followed the practice of the paperback editions and indicated in a text box the appropriate locus, relative to the exegesis, of each essay, and have specified, in the inserted box, the section headings of the relevant essay. This will indicate to anyone using the exegesis for the study of Wittgenstein's book that corresponding to a particular place in it, there is a comprehensive discussion of Wittgenstein's treatment of a topic in an essay printed in Part I of this volume of Commentary.

I observed in the Introduction to Part I that my reasons for wishing to write a second edition of this volume included the fact that much new material by way of both primary sources (manuscripts, diaries and letters) and derivative primary sources (students' lecture notes, dictations) has been published in the last quarter of a century. These materials often shed light on the interpretation of individual sections of Wittgenstein's text. Furthermore, many debates over the interpretation of individual remarks have been illuminating and have sometimes led me to revise the interpretations we gave in the 1970s. I am especially indebted to Professor Eike von Savigny's methodical criticisms in his *Wittgensteins 'Philosophische Untersuchungen': Ein Kommentar für Leser*, 2nd edn (Klostermann, Frankfurt am Main, 1994). I do not *always* agree with his strictures or with the interpretations he advocates, but I always learnt a great deal from his criticisms and discussions. It would be tedious and unbearably lengthy to list all the significant changes I have made throughout the text of the exegesis, for I have rewritten, compressed and revised it extensively. But the 'chapter' that has undergone the most transformation and supplementation is the exegesis of §§89–133 on philosophy and philosophical methodology. The interpretations here are importantly different from those offered in the first edition, and are supported with a great deal of new evidence. The upshot is that, despite compression, this chapter of exegesis is almost twice as long as the previous text, and sheds a great deal more light on Wittgenstein's criticisms of the *Tractatus* and on his new conception of philosophy, its aims and methods.

In this second edition, I have added a preliminary essay entitled 'The history of the composition of the *Philosophical Investigations*' that summarizes what has been learnt over the past half-century by various scholars working closely on the editing of Wittgenstein's texts. I have also added an essay, 'An overview of the structure and argument of the *Philosophical Investigations*', in which I have tried to survey the argument of the whole book, from §1 to §693. It is not easy to see how it all hangs together, and why the various discussions are located where they are. So I have tried to remedy this.

The structure of the exegesis of the sections is in essence the same as before. Each section is discussed separately, as are the boxed remarks in the 4th edition of the *Investigations* that correspond to the *Randbemerkungen* in the first three editions. Different paragraphs in each section are referred to by lower-case letters (e.g. '§27(a)' refers to the first paragraph of §27). Five different kinds of comments are marked out by marginal numbers: 1, 1.1, 2, 2.1 and 3. The first, i.e. 1, consists of commentary on the section as a whole. 1.1 consists of comments on individual lines, phrases and words, as well as suggestions for rectification of mistranslations. 2 discusses parallel remarks from Wittgenstein's other writings, which sometimes offer elaborations of the thought expressed concisely in the *Investigations*, and sometimes contrast with the final text and therefore shed light on the development of his ideas. 2.1 consists of parallel lines or phrases in Wittgenstein's other works which amplify or illuminate matters of detail. 3, used infrequently, is reserved for any other business. Lower-case roman numerals are used when an enumeration of points is necessary. Enumeration within enumeration has sometimes forced recourse to arabic numerals or lower-case letters. Since these conventions were chosen for their perspicuity, I have, as before, not hesitated to transgress them where, for some reason, they impeded clarity.

To save space, I have much reduced the quotations in the original German, which, in the first edition, accompanied our translations from the *Nachlass*. Since the whole of the *Nachlass* is now available on CD-rom, the translations can readily be checked against Wittgenstein's original.

P. M. S. Hacker
St John's College, Oxford
October 2003

Note to the paperback edition 2009

Since the publication of the hardback edition of this volume of the Commentary, the 4th edition of the *Philosophische Untersuchungen* has been published, together with a much modified translation (2009). I have therefore adapted this paperback edition of Volume 1 of the Commentary to the new translation. This has involved many small changes to quotations, and a slight change to the title of essay XIII. It was entitled 'Turning the examination around: the recantation of a metaphysician' and, in conformity with the slightly different translation of §108, is now called 'Turning the inquiry round: the recantation of a metaphysician'. I have also deleted corrections to the old translation that have now been incorporated into the 4th edition.

What were *Randbemerkungen* (footnote remarks) in previous editions of the *Investigations* are now 'boxed remarks'. These are located in the body of the text of the 4th edition. Here they are referred to by the antecedent numbered remark ('boxed remark following §n', abbreviated 'b.r.f. §n'). Their page number in the first two editions is added in parentheses (e.g. b.r.f. §22 (p. 18n.)).

What was referred to previously as 'Part II' is now published in the same volume as the *Philosophical Investigations*, 4th edition, but under the title *Philosophy of Psychology — A Fragment*, with numbered remarks from §1 to §372. This text is now referred to by the abbreviation 'PPF' followed by section number, with the page number of the first two editions in parentheses.

I have also made a very few substantial changes to Exg. §1, 1.1; §6, 3; §92, 1; §108 (since §108(b)−(d) are now a separate boxed remark following §108); 110, 1.1; §140.

P. M. S. H.

Abbreviations

1. Wittgenstein's published works

The following abbreviations, listed in alphabetical order, are used to refer to Wittgenstein's published works.

BB   *The Blue and Brown Books* (Blackwell, Oxford, 1958).

BlB   Occasionally used to refer to the Blue Book.

BrB   Occasionally used to refer to the Brown Book.

BT   *The Big Typescript*: TS 213, tr. and ed. C. G. Luckhardt and M. A. E. Aue (Blackwell, Oxford, 2005).

C   *On Certainty*, ed. G. E. M. Anscombe and G. H. von Wright, tr. D. Paul and G. E. M. Anscombe (Blackwell, Oxford, 1969).

CL   *Cambridge Letters*, ed. Brian McGuinness and G. H. von Wright (Blackwell, Oxford, 1995).

CV   *Culture and Value*, ed. G. H. von Wright in collaboration with H. Nyman, tr. P. Winch (Blackwell, Oxford, 1980).

EPB   *Eine Philosophische Betrachtung*, ed. R. Rhees, in *Ludwig Wittgenstein: Schriften 5* (Suhrkamp, Frankfurt, 1970).

GB   'Remarks on Frazer's "Golden Bough"', tr. J. Beversluis, repr. in *Ludwig Wittgenstein: Philosophical Occasions 1912–1951*, ed. J. Klagge and A. Nordmann (Hackett, Indianapolis and Cambridge, 1993), pp. 118–55.

LPE   'Wittgenstein's Notes for Lectures on "Private Experience" and "Sense Data"', ed. R. Rhees, repr. in *Ludwig Wittgenstein: Philosophical Occasions 1912–1951*, ed. J. Klagge and A. Nordmann (Hackett, Indianapolis and Cambridge, 1993), pp. 202–88.

LW I   *Last Writings on the Philosophy of Psychology*, vol. I, ed. G. H. von Wright and H. Nyman, tr. C. G. Luckhardt and M. A. E. Aue (Blackwell, Oxford, 1982).

LW II   *Last Writings on the Philosophy of Psychology*, vol. II, ed. G. H. von Wright and H. Nyman, tr. C. G. Luckhardt and M. A. E. Aue (Blackwell, Oxford, 1992).

NB   *Notebooks 1914–16*, ed. G. H. von Wright and G. E. M. Anscombe, tr. G. E. M. Anscombe, 2nd edn (Blackwell, Oxford, 1979).

PG   *Philosophical Grammar*, ed. R. Rhees, tr. A. J. P. Kenny (Blackwell, Oxford, 1974).

PI   *Philosophical Investigations*, ed. P. M. S. Hacker and Joachim Schulte,
         tr. G. E. M. Anscombe, P. M. S. Hacker and Joachim Schulte, revised
         4th ed. (Wiley-Blackwell, Oxford, 2009).

PO   *Ludwig Wittgenstein: Philosophical Occasions 1912–1951*, ed. J. Klagge
         and A. Nordmann (Hackett, Indianapolis and Cambridge, 1993).

PPF   *Philosophy of Psychology — A Fragment*, published in *Philosophical
         Investigations*, ed. P. M. S. Hacker and Joachim Schulte, tr. G. E. M.
         Anscombe, P. M. S. Hacker and Joachim Schulte, revised 4th ed.
         (Wiley-Blackwell, Oxford, 2009).

PR   *Philosophical Remarks*, ed. R. Rhees, tr. R. Hargreaves and R. White
         (Blackwell, Oxford, 1975).

PTLP   *Proto-Tractatus: An Early Version of Tractatus Logico-Philosophicus*, ed.
         B. F. McGuinness, T. Nyberg and G. H. von Wright, tr. D. F. Pears
         and B. F. McGuinness (Routledge and Kegan Paul, London, 1971).

RC   *Remarks on Colour*, ed. G. E. M. Anscombe and G. H. von Wright,
         tr. L. L. McAlister and M. Schättle (Blackwell, Oxford, [1977]).

RFM   *Remarks on the Foundations of Mathematics*, ed. G. H. von Wright, R.
         Rhees and G. E. M. Anscombe, rev. edn (Blackwell, Oxford, 1978).

RLF   'Some Remarks on Logical Form', *Proceedings of the Aristotelian
         Society*, suppl. vol. 9 (1929), pp. 162–71.

RPP I   *Remarks on the Philosophy of Psychology*, vol. I, ed. G. E. M.
         Anscombe and G. H. von Wright, tr. G. E. M. Anscombe
         (Blackwell, Oxford, 1980).

RPP II   *Remarks on the Philosophy of Psychology*, vol. II, ed. G. H. von Wright
         and H. Nyman, tr. C. G. Luckhardt and M. A. E. Aue (Blackwell,
         Oxford, 1980).

TLP   *Tractatus Logico-Philosophicus*, tr. D. F. Pears and B. F. McGuinness
         (Routledge and Kegan Paul, London, 1961).

Z   *Zettel*, ed. G. E. M. Anscombe and G. H. von Wright, tr. G. E. M.
         Anscombe (Blackwell, Oxford, 1967).

Reference style: all references to *Philosophical Investigations* are to sections (e.g. PI §1), except those to boxed remarks (previously *Randbemerkungen* (notes below the line)) on various pages. Reference to these is 'boxed remark following §n' followed in parentheses by the page number of the *Randbemerkung* in the first two editions. References to *Philosophy of Psychology — A Fragment* are to the numbered sections in the 4th edition, followed in parentheses by the page number in the first two editions. References to other printed works are either to numbered remarks (TLP) or to sections signified '§' (Z, RPP, LW); in all other cases references are to pages (e.g. LFM 21 = LFM, page 21) or to numbered letters (CL); references to *The Big Typescript* are to the original pagination of the typescript as given in the Bergen electronic edition of *Wittgenstein's Nachlass* (Oxford University Press, Oxford, 2000), and in the margins of the Luckhardt/Aue edition.

2. Derivative primary sources

AWL   *Wittgenstein's Lectures, Cambridge 1932–35, from the Notes of Alice Ambrose and Margaret MacDonald*, ed. Alice Ambrose (Blackwell, Oxford, 1979).

LA   *Lectures and Conversations on Aesthetics, Psychology and Religious Beliefs*, ed. C. Barrett (Blackwell, Oxford, 1970).

LFM   *Wittgenstein's Lectures on the Foundations of Mathematics, Cambridge 1939*, ed. C. Diamond (Harvester Press, Hassocks, Sussex, 1976).

LPP   *Wittgenstein's Lectures on Philosophical Psychology 1946–47*, notes by P. T. Geach, K. J. Shah and A. C. Jackson, ed. P. T. Geach (Harvester Wheatsheaf, Hemel Hempstead, 1988).

LWL   *Wittgenstein's Lectures, Cambridge 1930–32, from the Notes of John King and Desmond Lee*, ed. Desmond Lee (Blackwell, Oxford, 1980).

M   G. E. Moore's notes entitled 'Wittgenstein's Lectures in 1930–33', repr. in *Ludwig Wittgenstein: Philosophical Occasions 1912–1951*, ed. J. Klagge and A. Nordmann (Hackett, Indianapolis and Cambridge, 1993), pp. 46–114.

PLP   *The Principles of Linguistic Philosophy*, by F. Waismann, ed. R. Harré (Macmillan, London, and St Martin's Press, New York, 1965).

RR   *Discussions of Wittgenstein*, by R. Rhees (Routledge and Kegan Paul, London, 1970).

VoW   *The Voices of Wittgenstein*, transcribed and edited by Gordon Baker, tr. Gordon Baker, Michael Mackert, John Connolly and Vasilis Politis (Routledge, London, 2003).

WWK   *Ludwig Wittgenstein und der Wiener Kreis*, shorthand notes recorded by F. Waismann, ed. B. F. McGuinness (Blackwell, Oxford, 1967). The English translation, *Wittgenstein and the Vienna Circle* (Blackwell, Oxford, 1979), matches the pagination of the original edition.

3. Nachlass

All references to other material cited in the von Wright catalogue (G. H. von Wright, *Wittgenstein* (Blackwell, Oxford, 1982), pp. 35ff.) are by MS or TS number followed by page number ('r' indicating recto, 'v' indicating verso) or section number '§', as it appears in the Bergen electronic edition of *Wittgenstein's Nachlass*.

In the case of the first manuscript draft of the *Investigations*, MS 142 (the so-called *Urfassung*), references are to Wittgenstein's section number ('§'), save in the case of references to pp. 77f., which are redrafts of PI §§1–2 and to pp. 78–91, which Wittgenstein crossed out and redrafted on pp. 91ff., subsequently assigning them section numbers in the redrafts alone.

Manuscripts
MSS 105–22 are eighteen large manuscript volumes written between 2 February 1929 and 1944. These were numbered by Wittgenstein as Vols I–XVIII.

In the first edition of this commentary they were referred to by volume number, followed by page number (e.g. 'Vol. XII, 271'). Since then it has become customary to refer to them by von Wright number alone. Here they are referred to on their first occurrence in a discussion by their von Wright number, followed by volume number in parentheses, followed by page number in the Bergen edition (e.g. 'MS 116 (Vol. XII), 271'). In the subsequent occurrence of a reference to the same volume in the same discussion, the volume number is dropped.

'MS 114 (Vol. X) Um.' refers to Wittgenstein's pagination of the *Umarbeitung* (reworking) of the *Big Typescript* in MS 114. The *Umarbeitung* begins on folio 31v of MS 114 (Vol. X), and is paginated consecutively 1–228.

Typescripts

B i   *Bemerkungen I* (TS 228), 1945–6, 185 pp. All references are to numbered sections (§).

B ii   *Bemerkungen II* (TS 230), 1945–6, 155 pp. All references are to numbered sections (§).

All other typescripts are referred to as 'TS', followed by the von Wright number and pagination as in the Bergen edition.

The successive drafts of the *Investigations* are referred to as follows:

TS 220 is the typescript of the Early Draft (*Frühfassung* (FF)) of the *Investigations*, referred to in the first edition of this Commentary as 'PPI' (*Proto-Philosophical Investigations*), dictated from MS 142 (the *Urfassung* (UF)).

TS 226$_R$ is Rhees's pre-war translation of TS 220, §§1–116, referred to in the 1st edn of this Commentary as PPI(R).

TS 227a and 227b are the two surviving carbon copy typescripts of the *Investigations* (the top copy having been lost).

TS 238 is a reworking of TS 220, §§96–116, with renumberings, deletions, corrections and additions in Wittgenstein's hand, referred to in the 1st edn of this Commentary as PPI(A).

TS 239 (the *Bearbeitete Frühfassung* (BFF)) is a reworking of TS 220.

ZF is the reconstructed Intermediate Draft (*Zwischenfassung*) of the *Investigations*, previously known as the Intermediate Version, and referred to in the 1st edn of this Commentary as PPI(I).

In transcriptions from the *Nachlass* I have followed Wittgenstein's convention of enclosing alternative draftings within double slashes '//'.

4. *Reference style to the other volumes of* An Analytical Commentary on the *Philosophical Investigations*

G. P. Baker and P. M. S. Hacker, *Wittgenstein: Rules, Grammar and Necessity, Volume 2 of an Analytical Commentary on the* Philosophical Investigations, 2nd, extensively revised ed. by P. M. S. Hacker (Wiley-Blackwell, Oxford, 2009).

P. M. S. Hacker, *Wittgenstein: Meaning and Mind, Volume 3 of an Analytical Commentary on the* Philosophical Investigations (Blackwell, Oxford and Cambridge, Mass., 1990).

P. M. S. Hacker, *Wittgenstein: Mind and Will, Volume 4 of an Analytical Commentary on the* Philosophical Investigations (Blackwell, Oxford and Cambridge, Mass., 1996).

References to these are of the form 'Volume', followed by the volume number, the quoted title of an essay in the designated volume, and the section number of that essay. Occasionally reference to specific pages in an essay is made, in which case it is the paperback edition that is referred to. References to the exegesis are flagged 'Exg.', followed by section number prefixed with '§'.

References to Part I of this volume of the Commentary are given by essay title and section number or page number.

5. Abbreviations for works by Frege

BLA i   *The Basic Laws of Arithmetic*, vol. i (1893); references to the preface by roman numeral indicating the original page number, all other references by section number (§).

BLA ii   *The Basic Laws of Arithmetic*, vol. ii (1903); all references by section number (§).

CN   *Conceptual Notation and Related Articles*, tr. and ed. T. W. Bynum (Clarendon Press, Oxford, 1972).

CP   *Collected Papers on Mathematics, Logic, and Philosophy*, ed. B. F. McGuinness (Blackwell, Oxford, 1984). To refer to individual articles in this volume, the following abbreviations are used:

        CO   'Concept and Object'
        CT   'Compound Thoughts'
        FC   'Function and Concept'
        FG   'Foundations of Geometry'
        N   'Negation'
        SM   'Sense and Meaning'
        T   'Thought'

All page references to these articles are to the original German pagination, as it occurs in the margins of the English translation, followed by the page number in CP.

FA   *The Foundations of Arithmetic*, tr. J. L. Austin, 2nd edn (Blackwell, Oxford, 1959).

NS   *Nachgelassene Schriften*, ed. H. Hermes, F. Kambartel and F. Kaulbach (Felix Meiner, Verlag, Hamburg, 1969).

PW   *Posthumous Writings*, ed. H. Hermes, F. Kambartel and F. Kaulbach, tr. P. Long and R. White (Blackwell, Oxford, 1979).

6. Abbreviations for works by Russell

AM   *The Analysis of Mind* (Allen and Unwin, London, 1921).

IMP   *Introduction to Mathematical Philosophy* (Allen and Unwin, London, 1919).

IMT   *An Inquiry into Meaning and Truth* (Allen and Unwin, London, 1940).

OK   *Our Knowledge of the External World as a Field for Scientific Method in Philosophy*, rev. edn (Allen and Unwin, London, 1926).

PLAt   'The Philosophy of Logical Atomism', repr. in *The Philosophy of Logical Atomism and Other Essays 1914–1919*, ed. J. G. Slater, in *The Collected Papers of Bertrand Russell*, vol. 8 (Allen and Unwin, London, 1986), pp. 157–246.

PM   *Principia Mathematica*, vol. i (with A. N. Whitehead), 2nd edn (Cambridge University Press, Cambridge, 1927).

PrM   *The Principles of Mathematics*, 2nd edn, rev. (Allen and Unwin, London, 1937).

PP   *The Problems of Philosophy* (Oxford University Press, London, 1967; originally published 1912).

TK   *Theory of Knowledge: The 1913 Manuscript*, ed. E. R. Eames in collaboration with K. Blackwell, in *The Collected Papers of Bertrand Russell*, vol. 7 (Allen and Unwin, London, 1984).

The history of the composition of the
Philosophical Investigations

As Wittgenstein wrote in the preface to the *Investigations* that he dated January 1945, and which was used, with minor amendments, in the published version, the thoughts he was presenting were the precipitate of his philosophical investigations over the previous sixteen years, i.e. dating back to 1929. His efforts to compose a book incorporating his new ideas can be divided into different phases.[1]

1. **The Big Typescript**. The first phase began in 1929. The first work to emerge was the typescript later published as *Philosophische Bemerkungen* (1964), compiled primarily to present to the Council of Trinity College in order to obtain a grant that would enable Wittgenstein to continue his work, and subsequently submitted as a Fellowship dissertation. It is doubtful whether this compilation of early 1930 was ever intended as a draft for a book. Concurrently, he was co-operating with Friedrich Waismann in writing the first volume of the Vienna Circle's series of publications *Schriften zur Wissenschaftliche Weltauffassung*. This was duly advertised as *Logik, Sprache, Philosophie*, for which Moritz Schlick wrote a preface. But the project never reached completion, and effectively collapsed with Schlick's murder in 1936. It was published under Waismann's name in English translation in 1965 as *The Principles of Linguistic Philosophy* (PLP).[2] These years of the early 1930s, however, were mainly dedicated to writing a book dismantling the edifice of the *Tractatus*, laying the foundations for Wittgenstein's new philosophical method, and applying it to the philosophy of logic and language, and to the philosophy

---

[1] For the historical data in the following discussion I am indebted to the bibliographical research of Georg Henrik von Wright, Joachim Schulte, Alois Pichler and Brian McGuinness, to the research of Stephen Hilmy and Anthony Kenny on *The Big Typescript*, and to the biographical research of Brian McGuinness and Ray Monk. (P. M. S. H.)

[2] The German text *Logik, Sprache, Philosophie* (Reclam, Stuttgart), ed. G. P. Baker and B. F. McGuinness, was published only in 1976, together with Schlick's preface. For the history of this ill-begotten co-operative project between Wittgenstein and Waismann, see G. P. Baker, 'Verehrung and Verkehrung: Waismann and Wittgenstein', in *Wittgenstein: Sources and Perspectives*, ed. C. G. Luckhardt (Cornell University Press, Ithaca, NY, 1979), pp. 243–85. The copious dictations that Wittgenstein gave to Waismann were published in 2003 in a bilingual edition as *The Voices of Wittgenstein* (Routledge, London), ed. G. P. Baker.

of mathematics. The fruits of this endeavour are evident in *The Big Typescript* (TS 213), a 768-page untitled typescript, with an eight-page annotated table of contents, made in 1933. It is divided into 19 chapters and 140 numbered sections. The typescript was based on MSS 105–114 (Vols I–X),[3] which had been sifted into preliminary typescripts TSS 208–11, on which *The Big Typescript* is based. He immediately began reworking *The Big Typescript*, initially by making extensive handwritten modifications and additions, on both recto and verso, as well as inserting handwritten pages. He then reverted to fresh manuscript composition based on the modified typescript and on the pocket notebooks MS 156(a) and (b), and wrote the *Umarbeitung* ('Revision') in the second part of MS 114 (Vol. X) beginning on 31v, and paginated 1–228, and continuing in MS 115 (Vol. XI), 1–117, written in late 1933 and early 1934. This too was unsatisfactory, and in 1934 he tried a second reworking (the *Zweite Umarbeitung* ('Second Revision')) in MS 140 (the *Grosses Format* ('Large Format')) — a 39-page attempt to mould the material afresh.[4] This too was abandoned, although *The Big Typescript* was to be quarried again later.

2. ***Revision of the Brown Book (EPB)***. The next attempt at the composition of a book was in Norway in autumn 1936. Wittgenstein had dictated the Brown Book to Francis Skinner and Alice Ambrose in Cambridge 1934/5. In August 1936 he travelled to Norway with the intention of continuing his philosophical work in solitude. The first effort was directed at the text of the Brown Book, which, at the end of August, Wittgenstein began translating into German[5] and reworking (up to BrB, p. 154) under the title 'Philosophische Untersuchungen, Versuch einer Umarbeitung' ('Philosophical Investigations: attempted revision') in MS 115 (Vol. XI), 118–292. In early November, he abandoned the attempt, writing 'Dieser ganze "Versuch einer Umarbeitung" von Seite 118 bis hierher ist NICHTS WERT' ('This whole "attempted revision" from page 118 to here is COMPLETELY WORTHLESS' (MS 115 (Vol. XI), 292)). As he wrote to Moore, 'I found it all, or nearly all, boring and artificial. For having the English version before me had cramped my thinking.' So, he continued, 'I therefore decided to start all over again and not to let my thoughts be guided by anything but themselves' (CL 169 (20 Nov. 1936)).

---

[3]   Underlying these large MS volumes were first draft writings in small pocket notebooks. Only four of these survive from this period: MS 153a, which is a source for MSS 110–12 (Vols. VI–VIII); MS 153b, a source for MSS 112–13 (Vols VIII–IX); MS 154, a source for MS 113 (Vol. IX); and MS 155, a source for MS 112 (Vol. VIII).

[4]   The published volume *Philosophical Grammar* (PG), ed. R. Rhees, is an editorial compilation from *The Big Typescript* and its various revisions. PG §§1–13, 23–40, and the final two paragraphs of 42 are derived from the second revision of BT, i.e. MS 140 (the *Grosses Format*). §§14–22, 41–2, 43–141 are derived from the first revision, i.e. MSS 114–15 (Vols X–XI). Most of the rest is derived from BT, but appendices 1–3 are from TS 214, and appendix 4b is from MS 116 (Vol. XII). For detailed information, see A. J. P. Kenny, 'From the Big Typescript to the *Philosophical Grammar*', repr. in his *The Legacy of Wittgenstein* (Blackwell, Oxford, 1984), pp. 24–37.

[5]   Now published as *Eine Philosophische Betrachtung* (EPB).

3. **The Proto-Draft *and* Early Draft** *(UF and FF)*. The new attempt was
MS 142, the manuscript of the first, pre-war, version of the *Investigations* that
corresponds roughly to §§1–189(a) of the published book. This is a 167-page
manuscript, written as consecutive paragraphed prose, with the title *Philosophische
Untersuchungen*. It was compiled during two separate periods. Pages 1–76 were
composed between early November and early December 1936. Pages 77–167
were written sometime between February and May 1937. Wittgenstein presented the unfinished manuscript volume to his sister Margarete for Christmas
1936, with the inscription 'Gretl von Ludwig zu Weihnachten 1936 ein schlechtes
Geschenk' ('Gretl from Ludwig for Christmas 1936 a poor gift'), but he obviously took the volume back with him to Norway in the new year. Pages 77–8
are a revision of the opening two pages, and pages 78 (bottom)–91 are crossed
out and reworked on pp. 91ff. Though the manuscript is much amended, it
was (initially) a 'clean copy' manuscript. This has now been published as the
Urfassung (the Proto-Draft (UF)).[6] Its surviving immediate sources are the pocket
notebooks MSS 152, 157(a), 157(b), the reworked version of the Brown Book
in MS 115 (Vol. XI), and MS 140 (the *Grosses Format*). It was, it seems, typed
in two stages: pages 1–76, and pages 91 to the end. The typing was completed
by either May or December 1937.[7] The result was the 137-page typescript
TS 220.

Wittgenstein returned to Norway in mid-August 1937, and began working
on the sequel to TS 220. TS 220 had ended with the remark corresponding
to *Philosophical Investigations* §189(a). On 11 of September, he began MS 117
(a 'clean copy' manuscript) by copying out the last sentence from TS 220.
The next 97 pages are the basis of the first 67 pages of the subsequent dictation of TS 221 (for further detail, see below pp. 36–9). He continued working
on themes in philosophy of mathematics until mid-October, after which he
switched to other topics, and also mined *The Big Typescript* for usable remarks
which he transcribed into MS 116 (Vol. XII).[8] He left Skjolden in mid-December
to return to Vienna. The first 117 pages (out of 134)[9] of TS 221 were dictated in Cambridge sometime in mid-1938, the final 17 pages apparently in
winter 1938/9. The first-level materials for this second part of the early
version include MSS 118, 119 (for pp. 1–119), MS 115 (for pp. 120–30),
MS 121 and MS 162(a) (for pp. 130–5). Wittgenstein had the 'Preface' to this
early version of the *Investigations* typed (and dated) in August in Cambridge.

---

[6]   In *Ludwig Wittgenstein, Philosophische Untersuchungen, Kritisch-genetische Edition*, ed. J. Schulte
(Suhrkamp, Frankfurt, 2001), but without the deleted pp. 78–91 that were redrafted on pp. 91ff.
[7]   There is some dispute about the dating of the two parts (cp. J. Schulte, 'Einleitung', ibid.,
pp. 18f. with B. F. McGuinness, 'Manuscripts and Works of the 1930s', repr. in his *Approaches
to Wittgenstein* (Routledge, London, 2002), pp. 278–80, and Schulte's reply in his 'Historisch-
philologische Nachbemerkungen', p. 1098).
[8]   See exegesis of the Preface, p. 38, n. 15.
[9]   Numbered as a sequel to TS 220, so the first page is numbered 138.

TSS 220–1 are published as the *Frühfassung* (Early Draft (FF)). It was with this typescript that Wittgenstein approached Cambridge University Press in August or early September 1938 with a view to publication in German with a parallel English translation, under the title 'Philosophical Remarks'. The Syndics agreed to this proposal on 30 September. On Moore's recommendation, Wittgenstein asked Rush Rhees to essay the translation. In consultation with Wittgenstein, Rhees worked on it throughout Michaelmas Term 1938 (TS 226$_R$). By January 1939 he had reached §116 (corresponding to PI §107),[10] at which point he had to leave Cambridge for the USA on account of his father's death. Wittgenstein, together with Yorick Smythies, revised Rhees's translation by hand.[11] Dissatisfied with it and with TS 221, he shelved the publication project for the time being.[12]

4. **The Revised Early Draft *(TS 239, BFF)*.** The next attempt consisted in a revision of the two typescripts. One of the copies of TS 220 was extensively revised by hand (TS 239) prior to late 1942 or early 1943. It has been printed as the *Bearbeitete Frühfassung* (the Revised Early Draft (BFF)). Sometime between 1939 and 1943, TS 221 was extensively reworked, cut up and rearranged. The result, TS 222, has been printed as Part I of the *Remarks on the Foundations of Mathematics*. It was with the former of these texts, or with both texts, in mind that Wittgenstein approached the Press again in September 1943 with the suggestion of publishing a book entitled *Philosophical Investigations*, to be printed together with a reprint of the *Tractatus*. This idea, as he explained in the final Preface, had occurred to him in the course of rereading the *Tractatus* with Nicholas Bachtin. The Syndics agreed on 14 January 1944, but Wittgenstein again moved on to something else.

5. **The Intermediate Draft *(ZF)*.** The next phase is exhibited in the *Zwischenfassung* (Intermediate Draft). This has been reconstructed by von Wright. It was a 195-page typescript, consisting of 300 numbered remarks, corresponding roughly to PI §§1–421. It is for this version that Wittgenstein, in late 1944, wrote the new drafts of a Preface (in MSS 128 and 129, see 'Preface', p. 42) dated January 1945. It consists of the reworked version of TS 220 (i.e. TS 239 (BFF)), roughly corresponding to PI §§1–189, together with eight pages from TS 221 (corresponding to PI §§189–97), followed by new material. The new material consists of 104 numbered remarks derived immediately from TS 241, mediately from MSS 129 and 124, and more remotely from MSS 130, 165, 179 and 180(a). It is possible that with this draft we see

[10] Curiously, although TS 220 is *not* typed in the form of *Bemerkungen* (i.e. spaced remarks), Rhees typed his translation in this form.

[11] His corrections are often of interest and sometimes of importance, especially when he corrects a translation proposed by Rhees which happens to coincide with Anscombe's 1953 translation.

[12] He was already having doubts in October, for the Minutes of the Syndics for 21 Oct. refer to Wittgenstein's uncertainty about publishing his 'Philosophical Remarks'.

the abandonment of the idea of including the mathematical materials in the book.[13] How did this come about?

In February 1944, Wittgenstein left Newcastle, where he had been assisting in research on wound shock with Drs Grant and Reeve (and briefly with their successor, Dr Bywaters). He returned briefly to Cambridge and then went to stay in Swansea, where Rhees lived, from March until September. After some further work on philosophy of mathematics, he abandoned that subject[14] in favour of reflections on a private language, on thinking, imagining, calculating in the head and consciousness (i.e. themes in the philosophy of psychology that bear directly or indirectly on meaning and understanding). These form the main topics of MS 129 (begun on 17 August 1944), which is a major source of these remarks in the Intermediate Draft. They were dictated, either in Wales or on his return to Cambridge, to form the 33-page TS 241. His new ideas led him to a fundamental change in his conception of the book. The material on following a rule, originally intended to lead into a fundamental investigation into philosophy of mathematics, was now to lead into an equally fundamental examination of the conceivability of a private language and associated themes in the philosophy of psychology that shed light on the nature of language, and on the relation between language and thought.

The fact that Wittgenstein dated the new Preface 'January 1945', even though it was written in late 1944, suggests that he was thinking of approaching Cambridge University Press again with a finished typescript early in the new year. He does not appear to have done this, however. Rather, he turned to a massive expansion of the Intermediate Draft.

6. *The* **Late Draft** *(SF)*. On 13 June 1945, Wittgenstein wrote to Rhees, 'I am dictating some stuff, remarks, some of which I want to embody in my first volume (if there'll ever be one). This business of dictating will take roughly another month, or even six weeks.'[15] The dictation in question is a typescript Wittgenstein called 'Bemerkungen I', consisting of 698 remarks. These are derived from post-war sources (the fourth part of MS 116 (Vol. XII), MSS 129–30)) and pre-war sources (MSS 115–17, 119). He selected 400 remarks from 'Bemerkungen I' to be included in his book,[16] and on this basis dictated the last typescript draft, TS 227, in the course of the academic year 1945/6. The

---

[13] This is uncertain, precisely because the 1945 draft of the Preface mentions the foundations of mathematics as one of the topics discussed in the book. It is unclear whether this signals an intention to continue, as before, with materials on mathematics, which would follow the new discussions of a private language and associated psychological concepts, or whether it is an oversight — as it evidently is in the final published version of the Preface.

[14] He never returned to his work on the philosophy of mathematics, although it is evident (see below, p. 28) that he intended a book, entitled 'Beginning Mathematics', as a sequel to the *Philosophical Investigations*.

[15] Quoted in G. H. von Wright, 'The Origin and Composition of the *Investigations*', in his book *Wittgenstein* (Blackwell, Oxford, 1982), p. 127.

[16] Seventeen of the boxed remarks are also from 'Bemerkungen I'.

Intermediate Draft had been 195 pages long. TS 227 is 324 pages long. The final typescript contains no remarks the manuscript sources of which post-date June 1945, but Wittgenstein made minor handwritten alterations to the typescript over the next few years.

On Wittgenstein's death in 1951, his literary executors found themselves responsible for his literary remains. The *Philosophical Investigations* was edited by Anscombe and Rhees, and published by Blackwell in 1953 in German with a facing English translation by Anscombe. The translation underwent various revisions for the second edition of 1958, and again for the third edition in 2001. The fourth edition, published in 2009, ed. by P. M. S. Hacker and Joachim Schulte, incorporates an extensively revised translation.

The first three editions included what was referred to as Part II of the *Investigations*, printed from a now lost typescript based on MS 144, a collection of 372 unnumbered remarks, divided into fourteen unnumbered sections, selected from manuscripts written between May 1946 and May 1949. Was this typescript intended to be part of the same book? The editors, G. E. M. Anscombe and R. Rhees, wrote: 'Part II was written between 1947 and 1949. If Wittgenstein had published his work himself, he would have suppressed a good deal of what is in the last thirty pages or so of Part I and worked what is in Part II, with further material, into its place.' There are good reasons for doubting this judgement.[17] Accordingly, the editors of the 4th edition (2009) published what was called 'Part I' as the *Philosophical Investigations*, and renamed what was called 'Part II' *Philosophy of Psychology — A Fragment*. The four volumes (seven books) of this Analytical Commentary are concerned only with the *Philosophical Investigations*.

———————————◆———————————

[17] See G. H. von Wright, 'The Troubled History of Part II of the *Investigations*', *Grazer Philosophische Studien*, 42 (1992), pp. 186f.

An overview of the structure and argument of the *Philosophical Investigations*

In the preface to the *Investigations* Wittgenstein recounts how he made several unsuccessful attempts to weld the results of his philosophical work into a seamless whole, in which the thoughts would proceed from subject to subject in a natural order and without breaks. In the end, he had to rest satisfied with an 'album of sketches' — a collection of philosophical remarks on many different subjects, arranged in sequences that occasionally jump abruptly from one topic to another. It is sometimes difficult to see the rhyme and reason for the ordering. But since Wittgenstein worked hard and long on the arrangement of his *Bemerkungen*, there is a presumption that it has a rationale. In this essay I shall try to give a synoptic view of the developing argument of the whole of the *Investigations*. It will, I hope, make clear the degree of unity and integrity of the book.

It was Wittgenstein's desire that the *Investigations* be published together with the *Tractatus* in a single volume, for it seemed to him that his new thoughts could be seen aright only by contrast with and against the background of his old way of thinking (Preface, p. x). The *Tractatus* belongs to the sublime, metaphysical tradition of Western philosophy. It had, in the view of its author, brought that tradition to its culmination and to a turning point. The *Investigations*, however, breaks even more radically with the great tradition. The sublime conception of philosophy that informs the *Tractatus* is abandoned, and the conception of analysis of logical form that the *Tractatus* prescribed for future philosophy is rejected. The *Investigations* advances a different conception of philosophy, a new way of understanding philosophical problems, and novel methods for tackling them. It is therefore unsurprising that the first quarter of the *Investigations* is contrapuntal. On the one hand, Wittgenstein criticizes, implicitly or explicitly, the fundamental commitments that underlay his first philosophy; on the other hand, he replaces them with a quite different way of tackling the problems. The central theme of the book is the nature of language and linguistic meaning. Here Wittgenstein goes over much the same ground as he had covered in the *Tractatus* account of the nature of the proposition, propositional representation and intentionality, but with very different results. His discussions, however, ramify into philosophical investigations of understanding, meaning something by a word or sentence, interpreting, following a rule,

subjective experience, thinking and imagining, which are barely mentioned in
the *Tractatus*, even though it presupposed a particular, misguided conception
of them. Conversely, the themes of the nature and status of logic and logical
necessity that were so central to the *Tractatus* are only briefly touched on here.
Presumably they were to be discussed in his book on the philosophy of mathematics and logic that was never completed.

Wittgenstein opens the *Investigations* with a quotation from Augustine's
Confessions, in which Augustine sketches how he thinks he learnt language as
a child. In this description Wittgenstein detected a picture of the essence of
language: namely, that words name objects and that sentences are combinations of names. This primitive picture of naming as the foundation of language
displays the seed from which numerous philosophical conceptions of language
and linguistic meaning grow. From Augustine's non-philosophical picture
Wittgenstein extracts a particular *philosophical* conception of linguistic meaning: every word has a meaning, the meaning is correlated with the word, it
is the object the word stands for. Sentences are essentially complex, composed
of words in appropriate combination. Subsequently he makes it clear that central to this Augustinian conception is also the idea that language is connected
with reality, i.e. that words (names) are endowed with meaning by means of
word–world connections. So ostensive definition of primitive terms is conceived to be the fundamental form of explanation of word-meaning, and it is
taken to be the point at which names are linked to things. Wittgenstein held
this philosophical conception of language and its relation to reality to be of
great importance. Elements or aspects of it affect and infect much traditional
philosophy, including the *Tractatus*. It has had a pervasive influence not
only upon philosophy of language and logic, but also upon metaphysics and
epistemology, philosophy of psychology and philosophy of mathematics.
Eradicating its influence upon philosophical thought is one of the aims of the
Investigations and of Wittgenstein's writings on psychology and mathematics.

§§1–27(a) are a preliminary exploration of the Augustinian conception of
language. Its purpose is both to shake the grip of the idea that the essence of
words is to name things and the attendant conception of sentences as necessarily complex expressions (e.g. composed of subject and predicate or function-
name and argument-expression) the essence of which is to be assertable. We
should not think that the distinctions we draw between kinds of words turn
on the kinds of things the words stand for. Rather they turn on the different kinds of use the words have. Sentences are not *essentially* complex. The
assertoric form does not enjoy any special priority relative to other forms of
sentence. Nor does it conceal in its depth grammar a truth-value-bearing
component (a sentence-radical) that is common to assertions, commands and
questions. (So the concepts of truth and truth-condition cannot have the
pivotal role in a proper account of meaning that is commonly allocated to
them.) In this opening 'chapter' Wittgenstein introduces some of the pivotal
themes of the book: the diversity of uses of words, the analogy between words

and tools, the role of explanations of word-meaning and their diversity, the concept of a sample and the function of samples in explanations of meaning, language-games and the use of the method of language-games in philosophical elucidation.

§§27(b)–64 examine misconceptions concerning names and naming associated with philosophical analyses operating under the aegis of the Augustinian conception of language. Throughout history, philosophers and linguists alike have been tempted to think of naming as the foundation of language. Names, it was thought, are either complex and definable or simple and indefinable. Indefinable names stand for simple objects in reality that are their meanings. They are unambiguously linked to their meanings by ostensive definition. But, Wittgenstein argues, it is not only simple and indefinable names that can be explained ostensively. Ostensive definition does not 'connect language and reality' in the requisite sense, for it is not a *description* at all, and the object pointed at is typically a sample that *belongs to the means of representation*. Ostensive definition is one rule among others for the use of a word, and it is no less capable of being misunderstood than any other form of explanation. Understanding an ostensive explanation of a word presupposes a degree of linguistic competence, e.g. a grasp of the category of expression that is being explained. So ostensive definition does not lay the foundations of language. In *this* sense, language has no foundations.

The idea that 'real names', *logically proper* names, are simple and indefinable, that they stand for objects in reality that are simple and indestructible, is a mythology of symbolism. What was held (by Russell) to be the paradigmatic name (i.e. 'This') is not a name at all. The destruction of the bearer of a name does not deprive a name of its meaning, for the bearer of a name is not its meaning. The meaning of a word is not an object of *any* kind, but *the use of the word*, which is explained by an explanation of meaning — which is a rule for its use. What look as if they have to exist as a condition of significant thought and language are not sempiternal simples but rather samples. The conception of simples, conceived as the ultimate constituents of reality (Platonic simple elements, Cartesian simple natures, *Tractatus* simple objects, Russellian individuals) is confused, because it takes 'simple' and 'complex' to be absolute, predicative expressions, whereas they are in fact relative, attributive ones. What counts as simple or complex has to be introduced separately and be defined for each kind of thing. So the conception of analysis that underpinned logical atomism is chimerical. Such analytic paraphrase may, for some purposes, be of elucidatory use, but the idea that it penetrates to the ultimate logical structure of the world is an illusion. The world has no *logical* structure.

§§65–88 investigate a conception of linguistic meaning and explanation of meaning that is a correlate of the conception of simple names linked to simple objects that are the ultimate constituents of reality. It is the thought that the proper form of explanation for complex concept-words (by contrast with simple names that cannot be defined by analysis) is analytic definition. This is typically definition by specification of characteristic marks the possession of which is necessary and sufficient for an object to fall under the concept. Analytic definitions specify the *essence* of the definiendum, and the philosophical quest for analytic definitions that originates with Socrates and Plato *is a quest for the essence of things*. According to this conception, philosophy is a sublime, supra-scientific, investigation into the essence of the world.

Wittgenstein opens this sequence of remarks with the observation that in undermining the presuppositions of analysis into simples, he has avoided what had once seemed to him to be the deepest and most important of questions, namely, 'What is the nature or essence of language?' In the *Tractatus* he had argued that language is the totality of propositions that can be generated from elementary propositions by means of the operation of joint negation. The essence of a proposition, he had argued, is given by the general propositional form, i.e. 'Es verhält sich so–und–so' ('This is how things stand'). This encapsulates the thoughts that all propositions are truth-functions of elementary proposi-tions, that an elementary proposition is a picture of a state of affairs, that a state of affairs is a possible concatenation of simple objects, and that the actualiza-tion of a state of affairs is an atomic fact. The elementary proposition itself, he had argued, consists of simple names that stand for simple objects that are their meanings. Here in the *Investigations* he has repudiated the conception of simple names and that of simple objects that constitute the substance of the world. He has rejected the idea that the meaning of a name is the object it stands for. He has denied that ostensive definition links words to world, constitut-ing, as it were, the 'exit' from language. With the rejection of analysis as pre-viously conceived, he has also undermined a pivotal idea of the *Tractatus*: namely, that propositions are necessarily isomorphic with what they truly or falsely depict. What, then, *is* the nature of language (even if, strictly speaking, it has no *essence*)?

Eschewing a direct approach, Wittgenstein focuses first upon the dogmatic demand for analytic definitions of all non-primitive terms. He now denies that a concept-word applies to all things that fall under it in virtue of their pos-session of common properties. It need not be so, and in the case of family-resemblance concepts, it is not so. The unity of such concepts consists in the overlapping similarities between members of the family. We do not explain what a game is by giving a definition specifying the necessary and sufficient conditions for an activity to be a game. Rather, we explain what the word 'game' means by reference to paradigmatic examples together with a similarity-rider: 'and other things like that'. It is a distinctive feature of family-resemblance concepts that they are *not closed*, but allow for the addition of new members (e.g. new categories of game) without any alteration in the concept. Furthermore, the concept of a game neither has nor needs sharp boundaries. It functions fruitfully as a paradigm for a family-resemblance concept here, since Wittgenstein has in effect been arguing that a language is a motley of language-*games*, and the concept of a language, like the concept of a pro-position or of a number, is a family-resemblance one.

The introduction of the idea of family resemblance provides the springboard for criticism of the conception of determinacy of sense that characterized both Frege's philosophy of logic and the *Tractatus*. Determinacy of sense seemed to be required by logic. For if concepts have indeterminate boundaries, one cannot argue with respect to any and every object that either it falls under such-and-such a concept or it does not. So, it seems, the law of excluded middle will not apply to propositions incorporating such vague concepts. Frege's strategy had been, on the one hand, to ensure that in his concept-script every expression *was* sharply defined, and, on the other, to dismiss words in natural languages that are not sharply defined as not genuine concept-words. This he could do, since he considered natural languages to be logically imperfect. Wittgenstein, by contrast, had considered every language to be all right as it is, since otherwise it would not express any sense and would not *be* a language. For in his view logic was not an ideal towards which natural languages strive and with respect to which they fall short. On the contrary, logic was a transcendental condition of the possibility of expressing any sense at all. So his strategy was quite different from Frege's. He argued that although sentences of natural language may appear to be vague, that is merely appearance. On analysis, every indeterminacy is determinately indeterminate, i.e. analysable into a disjunction of propositions each of which has a determinate sense. Now he criticizes this *Tractatus* conception. A language is not a calculus with rigid rules that provide for all possible circumstances. There are many vague concepts in natural language. Whether they cause trouble on a given occasion depends on whether we are dealing with objects that fall within the penumbra of indeterminacy or not, and on whether that matters for our purposes. Sometimes we positively *want* a vague concept, and the indeterminacy is unproblematic. But if trouble is generated, then we may make a *decision* in the particular case, for a specific purpose, drawing a boundary where there was none before. Exclusion of mere vagueness, however, does not amount to determinacy of sense. The latter requires the exclusion of the very possibility of vagueness. That is incoherent. Like a signpost, a rule (including a rule for the use of a word) is in order if it fulfils its function satisfactorily. A rule can always be supplemented by another rule to prevent actual misunderstandings. But the thought that we can lay down rules that will exclude all *possible* misunderstandings is incoherent. For there is no such totality.

The discussion of vagueness and determinacy of sense raised the Fregean and *Tractatus* fear that if there are any vague concept-words, the laws of logic will not apply to them. As just noted, Frege and the young Wittgenstein had very different conceptions of what logic is. Now, in the discussion of the nature of philosophy in §§89–133, the mature Wittgenstein reconsiders these questions. §§89–108 are criticisms of the deepest methodological principles that had guided the *Tractatus*, and a repudiation of the 'sublime' conception of philosophy and of logical investigation that had informed it. It was a misconception to suppose that logic is sublime — the mirror of the logical structure of the world. Philosophical investigation is grammatical, and its task is not to penetrate the objective, language-independent nature of all things, but to clear away certain kinds of misunderstandings caused by misleading analogies between different kinds of expression. The essence of language, i.e. its function and structure, is not hidden, to be dug out by analysis. It is in full view in our linguistic practices. Misunderstandings incline us to think that propositions *do* something extraordinary — they not only depict how things are, they also depict, when false, how things are not. Thought does not stop anywhere short of the fact — when we think truly that *p*, what we think is precisely what is in fact the case. Yet we can also think what is *not* the case — as we do when what we think is false. These truisms *can* seem mysterious and problematic, and did so seem to the author of the *Tractatus*. Wittgenstein defers discussion of these puzzles about intentionality, and full explanation of what seems mysterious and problematic, until §§428–65. Here he merely notes that they lead us to lay demands upon propositions and words, demands that *have* to be met, it seems, if propositions are to be able to do what they do. So we sublimate our ordinary concepts of name and proposition. The *real* names and the *real* elementary propositions, we think, are to be found only by analysis. We demand determinacy of sense, and if it cannot be found in surface grammar, then it must be present in depth grammar. Otherwise the unshakable adamantine demands of logic will not be met. But this was an illusion. It rested, among other things, on a misconception about the nature of logic itself. And it led to fundamental distortions of the very phenomena under scrutiny. The whole inquiry needs to be turned round. Logic is not the depth grammar that we have discovered to underlie all possible languages, but a grid we impose upon arguments to test and demonstrate their validity. Names, propositions, language, do not have an essential form to be disclosed by analysis — they are families of structures open to view, to be clarified by description.

§§109–33 outline Wittgenstein's new conception of philosophy and its methods. The sublime conception of the subject having been rejected, the impressiveness of philosophy now retreats to the illusions, including the metaphysical illusion of its sublimity. Philosophical problems are forms of misunderstanding or lack of understanding, that are resolved or dissolved by descriptions of the uses of words. There is no room in philosophy for explanatory (hypothetico-deductive) theory, on the model of science, or for dogmatic (essentialist) thesis, on the model of metaphysics. Its task is grammatical clarification that dissolves conceptual puzzlement and gives an overview or surveyable representation of a segment of the grammar of our language — an overview tailored to the puzzlement at hand. Its methods are descriptive, not hypothetical. It describes the familiar uses of words and arranges them so that the patterns of their use become surveyable, and our entanglement in the web of grammar becomes perspicuous. It does not add to the sum of knowledge, but contributes to the enlargement of human understanding, on the one hand, and to the dispelling of conceptual illusions and misunderstandings, on the other.

§§133–42 make the transition from the Janus-faced methodological discussion of philosophy to the subsequent investigation of understanding. The theme of the general propositional form that was at the heart of the picture theory of representation and of the conception of the propositions of logic as senseless has already been raised a number of times. For it was a crucial part of the *Tractatus* essentialism. Now Wittgenstein briefly examines and rejects the whole idea. He has already argued that *proposition* is a family-resemblance concept. So it does not have an essence that is given by the form 'This is how things stand'. So what exactly is that 'form'? Whence did Wittgenstein derive it? And if it is not the general form of the proposition, what is it? In fact, it is no more than a propositional variable used for purposes of anaphoric reference. Can one not define a proposition as whatever can be true or false? Not informatively, for all that means is that we call 'a proposition' only what can be true or false. 'True' *belongs* to our concept of proposition, it does not *fit* it.

Wittgenstein uses the terms 'fitting' and 'belonging' to introduce his next theme, a theme that must be examined in order to block an objection to, and an unclarity in, the conception of linguistic meaning that he is now advancing. The meaning of a word, he has argued, is its use. We typically grasp what a word, as used in a sentence, means at a stroke. But the complex use of a word in all its variety of combinations and contexts is something that is manifest only over time. How can what we grasp in an instant *fit* the use. Is what we grasp not the use? Is the meaning, after all, distinct from the use, something from which the use *follows*? The meaning of a word is what is given by an explanation of meaning. But such an explanation, a rule for the use of the word, does not always come to mind when one hears and understands the word. So how *can* one grasp the meaning of a word or utterance at a stroke, and yet the meaning *be* the use? To answer this, the concept of understanding must first be investigated.

§§143–84 do so. The negative purpose is to undermine the idea that understanding is a state that, in some sense, contains the use or application of a word (or the application of an algebraic formula of an arithmetical series) in advance of its being used, so that the use flows from this mental state like water from a reservoir. The positive purpose is to clarify the categorial status of understanding. Understanding is not a mental state at all. It lacks the 'genuine duration'[1] that characterizes mental states (such as feeling cheerful or depressed, being in pain, or concentrating). Nor is it a state of an apparatus of the mind, such as the brain or some abstract structure presupposed by a mind-model in psychology. Understanding is akin to knowing, and consequently bears a kinship to an ability. To understand or know what a word means is to be able to do certain things — for example, use it correctly, explain what it means, and respond appropriately to its use by others. Doing those things are, indeed, criteria of understanding.

---

[1] For explanation of this term of art, see 'Understanding and ability', sect. 4(c).

§189 marks the end of the Early Draft (FF), TS 220, composed in 1936–7. Wittgenstein had originally continued with the discussions in TS 221 that, now rearranged, form Part I of the *Remarks on the Foundations of Mathematics*. But with the Intermediate Draft (ZF) of 1944, Wittgenstein decided to abandon the mathematical sequel, and continue the book in the direction of the private language arguments that had preoccupied him again in 1944 and had led to such illuminating and original results. How two such different continuations could grow from the same trunk is explained in Volume 2 of this Commentary, in the essay entitled 'Two fruits upon one tree'.

§§185–242 complement the previous sequence of remarks and clarify the relationship between understanding an expression, the meaning or use of the expression, and the explanation of what it means (which is a rule for its use). As in the examination of understanding, here too the example with which Wittgenstein works is that of a rule for an arithmetical series. This may be because he originally meant to continue these sections with the mathematical discussions of TS 221. But it may also be because the conceptions of accord with a rule, of following a rule, and of something's following from a rule that he is combating are at their most powerful in such an arithmetical example. A rule for an arithmetical series, like an explanation of the meaning of a word, does not *contain* its applications *in nuce*. It is correct that acting thus-and-so counts as applying the rule correctly. But the rule is not a magical device from which the correct applications unfold. Any rule, given by a rule-formulation, can be misunderstood, interpreted wrongly, and hence misapplied. Correct application of a rule (or explanation of meaning) is a criterion of understanding. But what makes a given application of a rule correct? Not intuition; not, save trivially, accord with what the teacher meant; not, save by begging the question, doing the same as one was shown in a previous example; and not, save at the cost of a futile regress, an interpretation. In one sense, nothing *makes* it correct. But that is no mystery. Rather, the question is misleading. There is an internal relation between a rule and its extension. If a rule requires one to *V* in circumstances *C*, then *V*-ing in *C* is what is *called* 'obeying the rule'. The internal relation is forged by the existence of a practice, a regularity in applying the rule, and the normative behaviour (of justification, criticism, correction of mistakes, etc.) that surrounds the practice. Only when such complex forms of behaviour are in play does it make sense to speak of *there being* a rule at all, and of rule-following behaviour that accords with it. For the mere signs, the rule-formulation, are not magic. They express a rule only if they are *used* as the expression of a rule, a norm of correctness, a justification for acting thus-and-so, an explanation of action, in the context of a persistent practice.

The conclusion of the lengthy discussion of following a rule is brought to bear on language and linguistic meaning. Human beings agree in the language they use, they agree in what *counts* as applying a given rule (in particular a given explanation of meaning) correctly. Such agreement does not decide what is true and what is false. It determines shared concepts and mutual understanding. But empirical truth is determined by how things are, not by how we agree they are. Nevertheless, if linguistic communication is to be possible, there must be agreement not *only* in definitions, i.e. in what words mean, but *also*, over a wide range, in judgements. For correct application of an expression is a criterion of understanding. Chaotic disagreement in judgement (e.g. over the colours of things, or over measurements, or over arithmetical calculations) would mean disintegration of common language and mutual understanding.

§§243–315 incorporate the private language arguments. A 'private language' is a language the individual (non-logical, non-syncategorematic) words of which refer to the private sensations (or, more generally, experiences) of the speaker. Sensations or experiences, as conceived by the dominant philosophical tradition, are, Wittgenstein points out, in effect both *privately owned* and inalienable, i.e. no one other than their subject can have them, and *epistemically private*, i.e. only their 'owner' can really know that he has them. So, if the words of such a language have the subjective experiences of the speaker as their meanings, or if such subjective experiences function as defining samples for the basic vocabulary of the language (cf. the simple ideas of the empiricist tradition), then it is *radically private*, inasmuch as it cannot, in principle, be understood by anyone else. Is such a language possible?

Why does Wittgenstein raise the matter at this point? §§185–242 concluded with the assertion that language, if it is to be a means of communication, requires agreement both in definitions and in judgements. But empiricists and rationalists alike in the Idealist tradition had unwittingly committed themselves to a conception of language as consisting of names that signified ideas in the mind of the speaker, and had conceived of ideas as privately owned and epistemically private. Moreover, the temptation to conceive of 'ideas' or 'mental representations' as the gold-backing for the paper currency of words is powerful and deep. Accordingly, there *could* not be agreement in definitions. And if there is no agreement in definitions, there can be no agreement in judgements either. Of course, those who succumb to this temptation do not think that these commitments exclude the possibility of communication by means of language. They typically have an elaborate story to explain how communication is effected. But, if Wittgenstein is right, this story is incoherent. So in addressing this question, Wittgenstein is also taking issue with mainstream philosophical tradition and striving to dispel a perennial illusion.

Furthermore, the exclusion of this foundationalist, Idealist conception of a language as resting on names of subjective experiences is necessary for the vindication of Wittgenstein's own *normative* conception of language and linguistic meaning. Words, he insisted, are *deeds*. Speaking a language is a *normative practice* accessible to all, rooted in the form of life of a culture, moulded by human abilities, needs and interests, and conditioned by the circumstances of human life, our apprehension of them, and our natural reactions to them.

Wittgenstein opens by arguing that the ideas of private ownership of experience and of epistemic privacy are incoherent. Different people can and often do have the very same pain (as their hair may have the very same colour) — not qualitatively the same or numerically the same, but just the same. One *can* know whether another is in pain — if he displays pain-behaviour in appropriate circumstances. For that is neither inductive nor analogical evidence. Pain-behaviour is a *logical criterion* for being in pain. The primitive use of 'I have a pain' is as a replacement for natural pain-behaviour. It is typically an utterance that manifests or *expresses* the speaker's pain (rather than *describing* how things are with him). It no more has grounds than groaning has, and its utterance is itself an acculturated form of pain-behaviour and a criterion for others to ascribe pain to the speaker. In our own case, we are prone to confuse the grammatical fact that it makes no sense for us to doubt whether we are in pain for the nonsense that when we are in pain we *know* that we are. 'I know' can function as an informative sentence-forming operator on a sentence only if it serves to exclude the possibility of my not knowing. In the case of the sentence 'I am in pain' it is redundant, for there is no such possibility to exclude (and in the mouth of a philosopher, presenting the putative epistemic proposition as an example of an empirical certainty that constitutes the foundations of knowledge, it is nonsense).[2]

The conceptual nexus between pain and pain-behaviour is precisely what is precluded by the conception of a private language. I know I am in pain by introspection, or just by having a pain. So my mastery of the concept of 'pain' must be independent of grasping the behavioural grounds for its other-ascription. So the word 'pain' must be given its meaning either by association with the private sensation of pain, or it must be defined by a private ostensive definition in which the sensation of pain and its mnemonic reproduction function as a defining sample. But this, Wittgenstein demonstrates, is incoherent. A sensation (or a mnemonic reproduction of one) cannot fulfil the role of a sample. So the ceremony of private ostensive definition is empty. It cannot produce a rule that could possibly guide or warrant the application of a word. So not only can others not understand the private language, the speaker cannot either. Words cannot be defined by reference to private mental samples in the imagination. So there can be no such thing as a private language in this sense. Applying the predicate 'pain' (and many other psychological expressions) to oneself rests on no criteria at all, but the very possibility of such groundless applications of such predicates presupposes mastery of the third-person use that rests on public behavioural criteria.

Wittgenstein labours to make it clear that he is not arguing, as a behaviourist might, that there is no pain without pain-behaviour, but rather

---

[2] 'I know I am in pain' is to be seen here as being on the same level as 'I know that it seems to me just as if I were perceiving . . .', or 'I know that it sensibly seems to me just as if . . .', these being cast in the role of the foundations of empirical knowledge.

that it makes sense to ascribe pain to a creature only if it is the kind of creature that *can* (logically) exhibit pain in its behaviour. More generally, only to human beings and to what behave like human beings can one ascribe psychological predicates. Hence it is senseless to ascribe them to the mind or to the body or to parts of the body (such as the brain). Wittgenstein is not denying that pain is distinct from pain-behaviour. What he is arguing against is a misconception of the *grammar* of 'pain', the tendency to construe its grammar on the model of name and object signified. (Here again the Augustinian conception of meaning is under attack.)

§§316–62, and the subsequent investigation of the imagination in §§363–97, may give the misleading impression of abandoning investigations into language and linguistic meaning in favour of themes in the philosophy of mind. But Wittgenstein has to include an examination of such psychological concepts as thinking and imagining (as well as understanding and meaning something). When he wrote the *Tractatus*, he took a particular conception of thinking, meaning and understanding for granted, and neglected their analysis. He had thought that this was the proper business of psychology, not of philosophy. That had been mistaken, for what he had there assumed to belong to psychology was in fact metapsychological, and demanded philosophical elucidation as part of the general enterprise of clarifying the nature of linguistic representation. Misconceptions about thinking, images and the imagination have distorted reflection on the nature of language from the dawn of philosophy to the present day.

The primary targets of the investigation into thinking are the ideas that thinking is an inner process that informs speech, so that thoughtful speech is speech accompanied by a process of thinking, and that thinking is itself a kind of language, so that overt speech is a translation from thought into words. Wittgenstein concedes that one can speak without thinking and think without speaking, but thoughtful speech does not consist of a pair of concurrent processes, and to say what we think is not to translate our thoughts into words of spoken language. To do something with thought, one need neither say something aloud nor say something to oneself. Speech with and without thought is comparable to playing a piece of music with and without thought. What a being *can* think is what that being *can express* in its behaviour. We say of a being that it thinks on the grounds of its behaviour (including speech). Although our ability to say what we think does not rest on our observing what we are doing, a condition for us having such an ability is that we *can* display or give expression to our thought in our behaviour. The limits of what can be thought by a creature are the limits of what it can express in its behaviour. We do not say that machines can think, for we say only of a human being and what behaves like a human being that it thinks — and that is not an opinion. It is a conceptual, grammatical, truth, indicative of the place that the concept of thinking occupies in the weave of life.

The discussion of thinking leads naturally to the examination of mental images and the imagination. Its relevance to the overall concern is threefold. The

supposition that for a word to have a meaning is for it to stand for an idea or
mental image in the mind dominated empiricist thought, and is incompatible
with the conception of meaning that Wittgenstein is advancing. The misguided
thought that imaginability determines the bounds of sense, that imaginability
is a criterion of logical possibility, has tempted many empiricist philosophers.
And the fact that we can conjure up mental images of things inclines one to
suppose that one can think without words — in images. The brief sketches
that Wittgenstein offers us here do not deal systematically with all of these
questions, but they shed enough light on the concepts of a mental image and
of the imagination to enable one to fend for oneself.

§§398–427 deal all too briefly with great themes: the 'subjective world' of
sense-experience and the imagination, the 'self' and self-reference, the concepts
of consciousness and self-consciousness. The antecedent discussion of imagination leads to the thought of the privacy of 'the world of representations'
(*Vorstellungswelt*)[3] — the inalienable ownership of the 'visual room' of subjective experience. But this Idealist illusion is rooted in a misinterpretation of
grammatical forms. The role of the first-person pronoun is not to refer to a
subject (let alone to a mental substance or 'owner of experience'), but to
index an utterance. The discussion of the 'visual room' leads naturally to a
brief examination of consciousness, of the illusion of an 'unbridgeable gulf'
between consciousness and brain processes, and of the misconception that one's
consciousness is an object of indubitable introspective knowledge. Here the
connection with the central themes of the book seems to be lost, and the insights,
though as deep as hitherto, are all too fragmentary.

It is noteworthy that §421 marks the end of the Intermediate Draft (ZF)
that Wittgenstein composed in 1944. The sequel was added in 1945 and displays less coherent ordering than its antecedents.

§428 abruptly opens a fresh line of inquiry. It is directly linked with §§93–5
and §110, where the idea that a proposition is a remarkable or queer thing is
identified as the source of the sublimation of the whole philosophical investigation. That discussion alluded to the picture theory of representation in the
Tractatus, which proposed a metaphysical answer to the problems of intentionality.
It had explained how a proposition can be false but meaningful, how it can
describe not only what is the case (if it is true) but also what is *not* the case
(if it is false). It explained how it can be that the proposition reaches right up
to reality, so that when one thinks the sense of the proposition, and one thinks
truly, then what one thinks is what is the case (even though when one thinks
falsely, what one thinks is *not* what is the case, and yet what one thinks in
both instances is nevertheless the same). The explanation offered involved
a complex metaphysics, ontology and logico-linguistic analysis that postulated
a pre-established harmony between thought, proposition and world. Now
Wittgenstein turns to demolish and replace his early solution to the problems

---

[3] This, perhaps, is an echo of Schopenhauer.

of intentionality. This is his deepest and most far-reaching criticism of the picture theory of representation. It was, perhaps, a tactical error to bury it here,
so far from the criticisms of the *Tractatus* in the first quarter of the book, and
with no explicit connection indicated between this discussion and the picture
theory that is undoubtedly part of its target. Indeed, its connection with the
Tractatus is concealed by the fact that the problems of intentionality, there discussed in association with what he had called 'the mystery of negation', are
here handled in connection with expectation and its fulfilment, desire and its
satisfaction, and an order and its execution, which were not even mentioned
in the *Tractatus*. It is the most comprehensive and profound discussion of the
problems of intentionality, but it is woefully over-compressed.

Having clarified the concepts of understanding, thinking and imagining,
Wittgenstein can now, in §§428–65, turn to the misconceived idea, which
informed not only the *Tractatus* but also much of the prevailing tradition, that
the meaning of signs, their ability to represent whatever they represent, is para-
sitic on mental processes of thinking ('thinking' being construed here to include
meaning, imagining, believing, expecting, etc.). The intentionality of thoughts
was held to involve either an internal relation between a thought and the reality that corresponds to it, which was explained in terms of a pre-established
metaphysical harmony between thought and reality (as the *Tractatus* had
argued), or an external, causal relation, as empiricists (including Russell) had
argued. Both conceptions are now assailed. If the relationship between desire
and its satisfaction were external and causal, then the object of desire would
be whatever makes the feeling of desire disappear (such as a punch in the
stomach) — which is absurd. The relationship is indeed internal. But an internal relation is merely a reflection of an intra-grammatical nexus, not the result
of a relation between language and reality. Grammar is not 'the great mirror'.
It does not *reflect* the essences of things. On the contrary, it is autonomous. It
determines the essences of things. That the thought that *p* is the thought that
is made true by the fact that *p* is a *grammatical* proposition, not a metaphysical
truth. It merely says that the expression 'the thought that *p*' is intersubstitutable
with the expression 'the thought made true by the fact that *p*'. So what satisfies
the belief, expectation or desire that *p* is not a state of affairs or event that *fits*
it (and the obtaining or occurrence of which is *guaranteed* to fit it by a metaphysical pre-established harmony between thought, language and reality), but
rather one that *belongs* to it. For what we *call* 'the expectation that *e*' is the
expectation that is satisfied by the occurrence of *e*. So expectation and its
fulfilment make contact *in language*. It is not thinking that is the life of the
sign, it is its rule-governed use in a practice, in the application that a living
being, who has mastered the technique of its use, makes of it.

§§466–90 are a brief discussion of the problem of the justification of inductive reasoning. There is no obvious reason why it should be located here. Nor
is there any obvious reason why it should be in the book at all, save for the
fact that Wittgenstein is keen to repudiate foundationalism in all its forms. The

thought that inductive reasoning *needs* a foundation that will validate it is, he argues, an illusion. It makes no sense to search for a justification of inductive reasoning.

§§491–570 revert to an examination of meaning, touching on a multitude of related problems in a relatively disorderly manner. Wittgenstein opens by considering causal theories of meaning of the kind defended by Russell and Ogden and Richards. But the concept of a language cannot be defined by reference to extraneous purposes that a language fulfils, and the rules of grammar are rules constitutive of meaning, not technical (instrumental) norms specifying how words must be used if such-and-such purposes are to be fulfilled (e.g. to produce such-and-such effects on hearers). A language is a normative, rule-governed practice. The rules of grammar are not right or wrong, correct or incorrect, in so far as they accord with reality. The rules of grammar are, in this sense, 'arbitrary', and are not answerable to reality for truth or correctness.

The bounds of sense are not determined by the intrinsic limitations of the human powers of meaning this or that, or by the limitations of our powers of thinking or imagining. Nor are they determined by the objective combinatorial possibilities of the meanings of words (conceived — on the Augustinian model — as objects for which words stand). What is logically possible is determined by, not reflected in, what the rules of grammar permit. But the rules of grammar do not exclude or prohibit any possibilities — a logical impossibility is not a possibility that is impossible. What they exclude are meaningless concatenations of words — phrases to which we have assigned no sense. The rules themselves are autonomous; and the meanings of words are immanent.

These general conclusions are brought to bear on Wittgenstein's conception of meaning as use in the special cases of the meaning of negation (§§547–57) and of 'is' (§§558–70), both to illustrate the idea of the autonomy of meaning and to qualify the identification of meaning and use. Synonymy and ambiguity of words are context-dependent and purpose-relative, often requiring decisions rather than discernment of elusive facts. This reflects a degree of indeterminacy in the notions of sameness and difference of use, as well as the fluctuating criteria of what is essential and what accidental about the use of a word.

§§571–693 explore a group of psychological concepts: expecting, hoping and believing (§§571–93), followed by remembering and recognizing, and concluding with conative concepts such as willing, intending and meaning (*meinen*). All are subject to related forms of misconstrual and misunderstanding, which Wittgenstein is keen to expose. Expecting, opining, hoping, believing, knowing, etc. look as if they are verbs signifying states; seeing, hearing, thinking and feeling look as if they signify processes. Willing, wanting and intending look grammatically like verbs of action. In each case, for a variety of different reasons, appearances are deceptive. It is evident that Wittgenstein became interested in a multitude of local problems in these domains that have only an indirect bearing on the main themes of the book. These discussions are fascinating digressions, in which Wittgenstein's genius is evident again and again. The methodology of investigation in philosophy of psychology is exhibited and briefly discussed here, although, of course, it is further elaborated and applied in Wittgenstein's subsequent writings on that subject (RPP I and II, LW I and II). It is only with the concluding examination of meaning something that we are brought back to a central concern of the investigation that commenced with Augustine's picture of meaning. It is, to be sure, supported by the antecedent examination of intending.

§§611–28 are a brief but powerful discussion of the will and voluntary action. It is difficult to see any rationale for it, save that it provides the backcloth for the subsequent investigation of intending, which in turn is preparatory to the concluding examination of meaning something. However, it is evident that Wittgenstein is here revisiting a Schopenhauerian puzzlement of his youth, evident in the *Notebooks 1914–16* (NB 86–9), which he is now in a position to dissolve. When one acts voluntarily, does something because one wants to do it (and not accidentally or involuntarily), one's willing or wanting is not, contrary to the empiricist tradition, an experience — something that happens to one. But nor is it something one *does*. What one *does* when one raises one's arm voluntarily is *to raise one's arm*, not to will and thereby *bring about* the movement of one's arm. What we bring about are the causal consequences of what we do voluntarily. Willing (or wanting) is not an act one performs at all — it is not something one *does*. So neither the raising of one's arm nor the rising of one's arm are something one brings about when one voluntarily raises one's arm.

The brief discussion of voluntary action leads smoothly into a discussion of intentions and intentional action (§§629–60). This is executed with great subtlety through an examination of remembering what one was about to do or say prior to being interrupted. To remember one's intention is not to remember a mental phenomenon, an event, state or experience, that was the intending. Nor is it the upshot of interpreting whatever mental phenomena that may have occurred or obtained at the time at which one intended. Intentions, like so many instantiations of other psychological concepts, are embedded in the context in which they arise. The *Urphänomene* here is not an experience or event that is reported in the utterance 'I was going to . . .', but the language-game. The roots of the language-game with expressions of intention lie in the behaviour of incipient purposive action. The primitive language-game is the use of 'I'm going to . . .' to herald an action. If one uses this utterance to announce an action, *one must go on to perform the action*. 'I was going to . . .' is not a report of an episode that one recollects, but a memory-utterance or avowal distinctive of those who have mastered the use of 'I'm going to . . .'. Remembering that one was going to do something is akin to remembering that one could have gone on. So remembering an intention is akin to remembering having understood. This thought provides the link to the final discussion in the book — the examination of meaning something, a subject that is complementary to the antecedent investigations into understanding and thinking.

The subject of meaning something by a word or sentence has cropped up recurrently throughout the book. It is a residue of misconceptions that underlay Wittgenstein's first philosophy, where meaning something by an expression was conceived to be the method of projection linking words and world, sentences and their senses. But it is also a crucial component in a misguided picture of language and communication that has been a major target throughout the whole of the *Investigations*: namely, the conception of the signs of language as being given 'life' by acts of meaning (on the side of the speaker) and of interpreting, as a prerequisite for understanding (on the side of the hearer). According to that conception, language, linguistic meaning and communication by means of language should be reducible to, or be capable of being explained in terms of, the psychological concepts of meaning, intending and thinking, on the one hand, and interpreting and understanding, on the other. This would imply that, contrary to Wittgenstein's account, the normativity of language is merely a superficial phenomenon, reducible to the underlying psychological bedrock of acts and activities of meaning, interpreting and understanding. But this is an illusion, resting on misconstruals of these psychological concepts. 'Following according to a rule', as Wittgenstein remarked elsewhere, 'is FUNDAMENTAL to our language-game' (RFM 330), and the attempt to dig down below the level of the normative practices of speaking a language leads only to further illusion and confusion. For below the level of normativity the intentionality of language disintegrates. For the explanation of the manifold characteristic features of intentionality is wholly grammatical and normative (cf. §§428–65). So, to foreclose the temptations of reduction of the normative to the psychological, it is still necessary to demythologize the notion of meaning something by one's words.

§§661–93 do just that. The negative points to be established are that meaning something is not a mental act, activity or process. Nor is meaning something a form of thought. In particular, having meant someone or something by what one said is not the same as having thought of him or it while one said what one said. Meaning, like intending, has no experiential content, and does not belong to the category of experience. Meaning something by one's words is neither something one does nor something that happens to one. Far from meaning being a mental act possessing intrinsic intentionality, which endows the signs of language that one uses with derivative intentionality, the intentionality of meaning something by one's words is a partial function of the meanings of those words, and dependent upon one's mastery of the technique of their use.

The *Investigations* terminates at this point. It is possible that Wittgenstein thought that the demystification of *meaning something* brings the investigation of language and linguistic meaning full circle. The misconceptions concerning the nature of language and its relationship to reality, on the one hand, and to thinking, on the other, that opened with the quotation from St Augustine have been fully unravelled. A conception of language and linguistic meaning, of grammar and its autonomy, of intentionality, of thinking and understanding, have been presented to take the place of the extirpated misunderstandings. A method of tackling philosophical problems has been exemplified again and again, and a radical conception of philosophy and of what it can achieve has been advanced. Although presented as an album of sketches, the *Investigations* gives us a comprehensive picture of the wide landscape traversed. If we have followed Wittgenstein's footsteps, and also used our own eyes, we should now know our way around it.

THE EXEGESIS

The Title

W. contemplated various titles for the book he was attempting to write. In 1931, at the stage of composition of *The Big Typescript*, he toyed first with 'Philosophische Betrachtungen' ('Philosophical Reflections' (or 'Observations')) — (MS 154, 1r). In MS 110 (Vol. VI), 214, under 24 June 1931, he wrote: 'Mein Buch soll/kann/heissen: Eine Philosophische Betrachtung (Als Haupt-, nicht als Untertitel)' ('My book should/could/be called: Philosophical Reflection (as the main, not the subtitle)'). In early July, he toyed with 'Philosophische Grammatik' ('Philosophical Grammar'): 'Mein Buch könnte auch heissen: Philosophische Grammatik. Dieser Titel hätte zwar den Geruch eines Lehrbuchtitels aber das macht nichts, da das Buch hinter ihm steht' ('My book could also be called: Philosophical Grammar. This title, of course, has the smell of a textbook title, but that doesn't matter, since the book stands behind it'). Analogous titles were used for his large manuscript volumes throughout the early 1930s: 'Philosophische Bemerkungen' ('Philosophical Remarks') for Vols I, III, IV, VI; 'Bemerkungen' ('Remarks') for Vol. V; 'Bemerkungen zur Philosophie' ('Remarks on Philosophy') for Vol. VII; 'Bemerkungen zur Philosophischen Grammatik' ('Remarks towards a Philosophical Grammar') for Vol. VIII; 'Philosophische Grammatik' ('Philosophical Grammar') for Vols IX, X.

The first occurrence of the title 'Philosophische Untersuchungen' is as the heading of his reworking of the Brown Book in MS 115 (Vol. XI), 118–292 (published as *Eine Philosophische Betrachtung* (EPB)). It also occurs on the title-page of MS 142, the *Urfassung* (Proto-Draft) that he began writing in early November 1936, which is the first manuscript draft of the opening 188 sections of the *Investigations*. It then occurs on the title-pages of the subsequent typescript drafts of the book. However when W. approached the Syndics of Cambridge University Press in 1938 with the suggestion of publishing his book, it was referred to (in the Syndics' Minutes) as 'Philosophical Remarks'. But when he again contacted the Press in September 1943 with the idea of publishing it together with the *Tractatus* in a single volume, it was referred to in the Minutes under the title 'Philosophical Investigations'.

It is interesting that when W. was dictating 'Bemerkungen I' in June 1945, he wrote to Rhees: 'I am dictating some stuff, remarks, some of which I want to embody in my first volume (if there'll ever be one).'[1] It is evident that he was referring to the work he was doing transforming the Intermediate Draft (ZF) of January 1945 into the Final Draft (SF) of the *Investigations*. [1] What is the other volume that is referred to by implication? It is plausible to conjecture that it is a volume on the philosophy of mathematics presumably corresponding to, or based on, a further enlargement of TS 221 or its re-arranged successor, TS 222(= RFM I). It is noteworthy that in MS 169, 36v (1949?), W. wrote: 'Ich will die Betrachtung über Mathematik die diesen <<meinen>> Philosophischen Untersuchungen angehören ~~"infantile Mathematik" nennen~~ // "Anfänge der Mathematik" nennen //' ('I want to call the enquiries into mathematics that belong to these <<my>> Philosophical Investigations ~~"infantile mathematics"~~ // "Beginnings of Mathematics" //'). This suggests that as late as 1949 he still thought of a volume on the philosophy of mathematics as a sequel to the *Investigations*.

The folder containing TS 227 bears the words 'Philosophie der Psychologie' in W.'s handwriting. It is conceivable that typescripts of his later writings on the philosophy of psychology had been kept in this folder. One may speculate whether a third book of that title was contemplated.

———◆◆◆———

[1] Quoted in G. H. von Wright, 'The Origin and Composition of the *Investigations*', in his book *Wittgenstein* (Blackwell, Oxford, 1982), p. 127.

The Motto

1   The quotation from Nestroy comes from *Der Schützling* (*The Protégé*), Act
IV, scene 10. In its original context it expresses such negative views on progress
as would harmonize with W.'s own repudiation of this aspect, and this ideal,
of European culture (cf. Foreword to PR and its earlier drafts, MS 109 (Vol. V),
204ff., and also CV 56).

Es gibt so viele Ausrottungs- und Vertilgungs-mittel, und doch ist noch so wenig
Übles ausgerottet, so wenig Böses vertilgt auf dieser Welt, dass man deutlich sieht,
sie erfinden eine Menge, aber doch's Rechte nicht. Und wir leben doch in der Zeit
des Fortschrittes. Der Fortschritt ist halt wie ein neuentdecktes Land; ein blühendes
Kolonialsystem an der Küste, das Innere noch Wildnis, Steppe, Prärie. **Überhaupt hat
der Fortschritt das an sich, dass er viel grösser ausschaut, als er wirklich ist**.

(There are so many ways of extirpating and eradicating, and nevertheless so little evil
has yet been extirpated, so little wickedness eradicated from this world, that one clearly
sees that people invent a lot of things, but not the right one. And yet we live in the
era of progress, don't we? I s'pose progress is like a newly discovered land; a flourishing
colonial system on the coast, the interior still wilderness, steppe, prairie. **The trouble
about progress is that it always looks much greater than it really is.**)

What is Nestroy's remark intended to convey as a motto for the *Investigations*?
It might be suggested that it intimates that the advance made over the *Tractatus*
is less than it appears. This seems to me to be improbable. The shift from the
method of truth to the method of sense (MS 106 (Vol. II), 46) could hardly
be greater; nor could there be greater philosophical advance than from the
Wesensschau of the *Tractatus* to the quiet weighing of linguistic facts of the
Investigations (cf. Z §447), after the inquiry has been turned round (PI §108).
A more plausible hypothesis is that the motto is meant to echo the Preface to
the *Tractatus*: 'the value of this work . . . is that it shows how little is achieved
when these problems are solved'.

1.1   'Überhaupt hat der Fortschritt das an sich, . . .': W. already quoted this, with
admiration, in a letter to Schlick dated 18 September 1930:[1]

[1]   Cited in David Stern's 'Nestroy, Augustine and the opening of the *Philosophical Investigations*',
in *Wittgenstein and the Future of Philosophy: A Reassessment after 50 Years, Proceedings of the 24th International
Wittgenstein Symposium*, ed. R. Haller and K. Puhl (Öbr & hpt. Vienna, 2002).

Und ich wollte Sie könnten Ihre — so wohlgemeinten — Fanfarenstösse mildern. Es ist ja doch kein Grund zum Triumph; aus 1000 Gründen nicht. Und vergessen Sie, bitte, nicht das herrliche Wort Nestroys (ich kann es nicht wörtlich zitieren): Der Fortschritt hat es so an sich, dass er immer grösser ausschaut, als er ist.

And I wish you could tone down your so well-meant fanfares. There is indeed no ground for triumph; for a thousand reasons none. And please don't forget Nestroy's marvellous saying (I can't quote it word for word): The thing about progress is that it always looks greater than it is.

It would be rash, however, to assume that the purpose to which the quotation was put in a letter in 1930 — namely, repudiation of triumphalism at the philosophical advances made over the previous eighteen months — is the same as its purpose in the late 1940s.

2   W. toyed with various mottoes for 'the book' between 1930 and 1947. These are given in inverse temporal order:

(i)   The quotation from Nestroy was written into the final typescript sometime after 25 April 1947,[2] replacing an earlier motto from Hertz's introduction to his *Principles of Mechanics*: 'Sind diese schmerzenden Widersprüche entfernt, so ist nicht die Frage nach dem Wesen beantwortet, aber der nicht mehr gequälte Geist hört auf, die für ihn unberechtigte Frage zu stellen.'[3] ('When these painful contradictions are removed, the question as to the nature of force will not have been answered; but our minds, no longer vexed, will cease to ask illegitimate questions.') W. long admired this essay, which he had read in his youth. He refers to it in BB 26, 169, and also occasionally in his notebooks.

(ii)   In 1946 (MS 130, 121), while he was still evidently searching for something more resonant than the quotation from Hertz, W. jotted down as a motto (apparently from memory, since there is an error in transcription) a quotation from Goethe's 1820 poem 'Allerdings': 'Natur hat weder Kern noch Schale. Du frage Dich . . .' ('Nature has neither core nor husk. Just ask yourself . . .'). This poem is a polemical reply to Haller, whom Goethe quotes: 'Ins Innre der Natur / Dringt kein erschaffner Geist' and 'Glückselig, wenn sie nur / Die äussre Schale weist' ('No created spirit penetrates to the innermost heart of nature' and 'One is in bliss even if it displays only the outer husk'). Goethe, who detested the idea of a hidden reality beneath phenomena, to be inferred by a *theory*, responds:

Das hör ich sechzig Jahre wiederholen
Und fluche drauf, aber verstohlen,
Sage mir tausendmale:
Alles gibt sie reichlich und gern,
Natur hat weder Kern
Noch Schale,
Alles ist sie mit einemmale
Dich prüfe du nur allermeist,
Ob du Kern oder Schale seist.

---

2   The quotation, under the heading 'Motto', is entered in MS 134, 152, on 25 April 1947.
3   H. Hertz, *Die Prinzipien der Mechanik*, Einleitung (Barth, Leipzig, 1910), p. 9.

(I have heard this reiterated for sixty years —
And cursed at it, on the quiet.
I tell myself a thousand times:
Nature gives everything amply and gladly,
She has neither core
Nor husk,
She is everything at once.
Just ask yourself,
Whether you are core or husk.)

The aptness of these lines as a motto for the *Investigations* consists in the parallels between Goethe's conception of knowledge of nature and W.'s conception of philosophical understanding.

(iii)   In MS 162(b), 54r (sometime shortly before 10 April 1940), W. noted as a possible motto for his book, 'Ein Schuft der mehr gibt als er hat' ('A rascal who gives more than he has').

In 1931 W. considered two mottoes:

(iv)   In MS 109 (Vol. V), 288, he wrote: 'Ich könnte als Motto meines Buch wählen: ein Narr kann mehr fragen, als zehn Weise beantworten können. Eigentlich müsste es hier heissen "zehn Gescheite"' ('I could choose as the motto for my book: A fool can ask more than ten wise men can answer. Actually it should run "ten clever men"'). The proposed motto here is a German proverb.

(v)   In MS 110 (Vol. VI), 180 (19 June 1931) he jotted down 'as a motto for this book' three lines from Matthias Claudius's poem 'Abendlied': 'Seht ihr den Mond dort stehen? / Er ist nur halb zu sehen, / Und ist doch rund und schön'. The stanza runs thus:

Seht ihr den Mond dort stehen?—
Er ist nur halb zu sehen
   Und ist doch rund und schön!
So sind wohl manche Sachen,
Die wir getrost belachen
   Weil unsre Augen sie nicht sehn.

(Do you see the moon there?
Only half of it is visible
Yet it is round and beautiful!
Rather like that are many things,
At which we feel able to laugh
For our eyes do not see them.)

(vi)   On the opening page of MS 105 (Vol. 105), the very first of his large MS ledgers that begins on 2 February 1929, he wrote a motto adapted from Johann Nestroy's play *Heimliche Liebe — Heimliches Geld* (*Secret Love — Secret Money*): 'Motto: "Hier hilft dem Dummen die Dummheit allein"' ('Motto: "Here only stupidity can help the stupid"'). He later erased this and wrote over it 'Band I. Philosophische Bemerkungen'.

Recollections of pupils provide another pair of possible mottoes:

(vii)   M. O'C. Drury[4] relates that W. once thought of using as a motto a quotation from *King Lear*: 'I'll teach you differences'. This is line 94 in Act I, scene iv.

(viii)   G. Kreisel[5] reports that W. would have liked to use Bishop Butler's tag 'Everything is what it is, and not another thing' but for the fact that Moore had used it as the motto for *Principia Ethica*.

(ix)   In MS 120 (Vol. XVI), 20 April 1938, W. wrote:

Longfellow: In the elder days of Art
                    Builders wrought with greatest care,
                    Each minute and unseen part,
                    For the gods are everywhere.
(könnte mir als ein Motto dienen.)

The stanza comes from Longfellow's poem 'The Builders'. (Unless the alteration is intentional — which it may be — the last line should read 'For the gods see everywhere'.) But it is probable that the sense of the parenthesis is that these verses could serve as a motto, not for the book, but for W. *himself*.

It is striking that the mottoes display a kind of family resemblance. The images of husk and core, appearance and reality, the revealed and the concealed, naive and over-sophisticated vision, run through them like overlapping threads.

2.1   W. chose as the motto for the *Philosophical Remarks* a quotation from Augustine's *Confessions* I, 9: 'Et multi ante nos praestruxerant aerumnosas vias per quas transire cogebamur multiplicato dolore filiis Adam.' ('Countless long since forgotten had built up this stony path for us to tread and we were made to pass along it, adding to the toil and sorrow of the sons of Adam'.)

---

[4]   M. O'C. Drury, *Ludwig Wittgenstein: The Man and His Philosophy*, ed. K. T. Fann (Dell, New York, 1967), p. 69.
[5]   G. Kreisel, 'The Motto of "Philosophical Investigations" and the Philosophy of Proofs and Rules', *Grazer Philosophische Studien*, 6 (1978), pp. 15ff.

The Preface

1   The dating of the Preface is deceptive. It suggests that the published version of the *Investigations* was completed in January 1945. This is incorrect (see
'The history of the composition of the *Philosophical Investigations*' above). The
first surviving typescript of *this* Preface (TS 243) — by contrast with the draft
Prefaces written in 1938 (see 2 below) — is based on drafts in MS 129, 1v–10r,
themselves based on drafts written in MS 128, 40ff., written in the autumn of
1944 for the Intermediate Draft (ZF), i.e. prior to the insertion of more than
400 remarks from 'Bemerkungen I'. TS 243 was therefore evidently typed in
January 1945. The version that was typed into TS 227 (SF) on the opening
page of the text below the Hertz motto incorporated handwritten corrections
to TS 243. Further amendments were entered by hand in TS 227. I shall comment on the Preface paragraph by paragraph ((a)–(j)).

   (a) The *Investigations* is the precipitate of sixteen years' work, i.e. from 1929
to 1945. The process of precipitation out of manuscripts and typescripts was
complex. Of the subjects W. mentions here, it is noteworthy that the foundations of mathematics is *not* discussed.

   (b) W. connects his repeated failure to fulfil the requirement of a natural
sequential ordering mentioned in (a) with the nature of the investigation. (In
1937 he more explicitly blamed himself as well, rather than his material alone.
Waismann's *Logik, Sprache, Philosophie* (*The Principles of Linguistic Philosophy*),
which attempted to achieve a natural sequential ordering for W.'s work in the
early and mid-thirties, is not obviously defective in the organization of the
material.) The metaphor of travelling 'over a wide field of thought criss-cross
in every direction' was exchanged in his lectures for the simile of a London
guide: 'I have to take you through the city from north to south, from east to
west, from Euston to Embankment and from Piccadilly to the Marble Arch.
After I have taken you many journeys through the city, in all sorts of directions, we shall have passed through any given street a number of times —
each time traversing the street as part of a different journey. At the end of this
you will know London; you will be able to find your way about like a born
Londoner.'[1]

---

[1]   D. A. T. Gasking and A. C. Jackson, 'Wittgenstein as a Teacher', repr. in K. T. Fann, *Wittgenstein,
the Man and his Philosophy* (Dell, New York, 1967), p. 50.

(c) The metaphor of an album of sketches (a late addition to the final draft of the Preface, derived from MS 130, 22) is important. It signifies a confessed failing in the book, reaffirmed in the final paragraph of the Preface. The *Investigations* is, as it were, a sketchbook of a master-artist who could not produce a finished canvas.

The number of 'rejects' was huge, and W. often expressed doubts about his judgement concerning his selection of remarks (e.g. MS 119 (Vol. XV), 65, 84). As we shall see, numerous remarks become fully intelligible only when their original surroundings are restored. Similarly, the 'cutting down' of individual remarks frequently achieves economy of expression at the cost of perspicuity.

(d) The reference of 'bis vor Kurzem (until recently)' is unclear. These words also occur in the 1938 drafts of a Preface, which also emphasized his need, in response to plagiarized versions of his ideas, to publish the results of his work for the sake of his own peace of mind (see 2(v), e). Probably he is referring to a decision made in early 1938, a period which, by 1945, was no longer recent at all. The thought of postponing publication until after his death was mooted in September 1937 (see 2(ii) below). The question of what made him change his mind in mid-1938 is intriguing. His biographer, Brian McGuinness, has conjectured that the event that made a difference was the arrival, in 1938, of Friedrich Waismann in Cambridge.[2] Waismann both lectured on philosophy (circulating what seemed to W. watered-down or mangled versions of his own ideas) and proposed to publish, both in German and English, *Logik, Sprache, Philosophie* (PLP), which he, Waismann, conceived of as a survey of 'our philosophy' (meaning the views he thought of as shared by W., Schlick and himself). In the event, of course, Waismann did not publish this book in his lifetime, and W. postponed publication of *his* book until after his death. W. remarked to Malcolm in 1949 that the book was not in a completely finished state, but that he did not think that he could give it the final polish in his lifetime. He would, he said, like to have it mimeographed for his friends. Then he could add in parenthesis after a remark 'This is not quite right' or 'This is fishy'.[3]

The mention of watered-down or mangled results may allude to publications by W.'s students and acquaintances.[4] Braithwaite had been called to task in a letter to *Mind*.[5] Carnap had incurred W.'s wrath for plagiarizing his ideas on ostensive definition, hypotheses, physicalism, etc.[6] Waismann had angered

---

[2] B. F. McGuinness, 'Manuscripts and Works in the 1930s', repr. in his *Approaches to Wittgenstein* (Routledge, London, 2002), p. 282.

[3] N. Malcolm, *Ludwig Wittgenstein: A Memoir*, 2nd edn (Oxford University Press, London, 1984), p. 75.

[4] For further details, see ibid., pp. 48ff.

[5] 'Letter to the Editor', *Mind* 42 (1933), pp. 415f., repr. PO 156f.

[6] See letter to Schlick dated 20 Aug. 1932, in *Wittgenstein: sein Leben in Bildern und Texten*, ed. M. Nedo and M. Ranchetti (Suhrkamp, Frankfurt, 1983), pp. 254f.

W. with 'Über den Begriff der Identität'[7] and other writings, and Alice
Ambrose with 'Finitism in Mathematics'.[8] Certainly Schlick's 'Meaning and
Verification'[9] had mangled W.'s ideas. But W. may also be referring to lectures
by such people, especially Waismann's lectures in Cambridge, and to the prospective publication of *Logik, Sprache, Philosophie*.

(e) W. read the *Tractatus* together with Nicholas Bachtin (a linguist and
classical scholar). In TS 243 W. refers to the rereading as occurring *two years*
earlier (i.e. in 1943). If that is the correct date (as suggested by von Wright),
then the suggestion in the text that this occurred in 1941 is a slip.[10] The idea
of publishing the two books in the same volume occurred in this context.
He also mentioned this idea to Dr Basil Reeves (one of the two doctors
with whom he investigated wound shock in Newcastle), saying that he liked
the idea of publishing a refutation of ideas in the *Tractatus* side by side with
that text itself.[11] As noted already, when W. reopened negotiations with
Cambridge University Press in late 1943, the Syndics agreed to this condition.
The idea of so publishing the two works is scrawled on the final page of
MS 128.

(f) The 'grave mistakes' that W. was forced to recognize in the *Tractatus*
are sometimes explicitly mentioned or obvious in the *Investigations* (e.g. §§23,
46, 55, 57, 60, 81, 96f., 99, 108, 114, 136), but many, as will be shown, are
implicit and unobvious (e.g. the deep criticism of the picture theory in the
discussion of intentionality in §§428–65).

Details of discussions with Ramsey and Sraffa have not been published.
The mention of discussions with Ramsey during the last *two* years of his life
is erroneous. W. returned to Cambridge on 18 January 1929, and Ramsey died
on 19 January 1930.

(g) It is unclear what other reasons there are for points of contact apart from
W.'s influence and teaching. Conceivably he is alluding to common sources
of problems in Frege and Russell.

(h) W.'s anxieties about publication are marked throughout his later work,
and were written into all drafts of the 'Preface'. His detestation of contemporary civilization, his cultural pessimism and sense of alienation (cf. Foreword
to PR and draft Foreword, CV 6f.) inclined him to doubt whether he would
be understood. In 1930 (MS 110 (Vol. VI), 18) he remarked that his (projected) book is only for a small circle of people (who are not the élite of mankind, are not better or worse than others, but just different). They belong to
his cultural circle, and are, as it were, his countrymen, in contrast to others,

[7]   F. Waismann, 'Über den Begriff der Identität', *Erkenntnis* 6 (1936), pp. 56–64.

[8]   A. Ambrose, 'Finitism in Mathematics', *Mind* 44 (1935), pp. 186–203, 317–40.

[9]   M. Schlick, 'Meaning and Verification', *Philosophical Review* 45 (1936), pp. 339–69.

[10]   The dates are apparently problematic. W. had numerous meetings with Bachtin in 1936, but
his pocket diaries for 1942/3 show only a couple of meetings scheduled with Bachtin. I am indebted
to Brian McGuinness for this information.

[11]   See R. Monk, *Ludwig Wittgenstein: The Duty of Genius* (Jonathan Cape, London, 1990), p. 457.

who are alien to him. Drury reports his saying: 'My type of thinking is not
wanted in this present age, I have to swim so strongly against the tide. Perhaps
in a hundred years people will really want what I am writing.'[12] In his 1939
lectures he lamented: 'The seed I'm most likely to sow is a certain jargon'
(LFM 293). Still later (1947–8), he expressed his hesitations about publication,
his fear that the work would fall into hands other than those he would wish,
his hope that 'the philosophical journalists' would forget it quickly, and that it
would be preserved for a better kind of reader (MS 136, 81: 'Zum Vorwort').

(i) In MS 112 (Vol. VIII), 226, W. remarked: 'Ich soll nur der Spiegel sein,
in welchem mein Leser sein eigenes Denken mit allen seinen Unförmigkeiten
sieht und mit dieser Hilfe zurecht richten kann.' ('I should be merely the mirror in which my reader sees his own thought with all its distortions and with
this help can set it aright.')

(j) W. was never satisfied with the book, despite the numerous redraftings.[13]
By the standards to which he aspires, it has defects.

2   The 'Preface' went through uncountable drafts — uncountable because W.
sometimes redrafts a single sentence up to a dozen times in the context of
a single attempt to write a preface. I shall list the various sources chronolo-
gically and pick out their significant features.

(i)   MS 152 (C8), 13: written in late 1936, it contains a two-paragraph preface. The context is the discussion of reading (an ancestor of PI §§156–78).
It is unclear whether this is draft material for the attempt to rework the Brown
Book in MS 115 (Vol. XI), 118ff. (EPB), or for MS 142 (UF). It is only later
in MS 152 that we find draft material that occurs in MS 142 and *not* in *Eine
Philosophische Betrachtung*. So it is perfectly possible that this is a draft Preface
for the reworked Brown Book, written before it was abandoned.

The draft Preface bears only a remote resemblance to the final version.
Paragraph (a) says that the book presents W.'s philosophical thought as it had
developed over the previous eight years, and that, although he has done as
well as he could, it is in many ways defective. He mentions here, and in (b),
some of the defects: e.g. it is often too long, many of the examples could be
better, and the structure is frequently poor. It has other defects too, W. concludes, but what he means *thereby* will be seen only by a reader who *really*
understands something, and to him W. need not explain.

(ii)   MS 118 (Vol. XIV), 90r, under 16 September 1937: to see this draft
aright, its context must be clarified. The manuscript volume was begun on
13 August 1937 at Mjömna in Norway, continued on the boat to Skjolden,
and then used at Skjolden as a notebook and coded diary until its completion

---

[12]   M. O'C Drury, 'Some Notes on Conversations with Wittgenstein' in *Essays in Honour of
G. H. von Wright*, Acta Philosophica Fennica 28, ed. J. Hintikka (North Holland, Amsterdam,
1976), p. 25.
[13]   Cf. W.'s letters to Malcolm in 1945 (*Ludwig Wittgenstein: A Memoir*, pp. 42f.).

on 24 September, when MS 119 (Vol. XV) was started. It is evident that, though not a pocket notebook, MS 118 is nevertheless a first-level notebook (mediate) source of TS 221, the mathematical continuation of MS 142.

On 11 September W. was writing the remarks on propositions of logic being in a sense laws of thought, on surprises in mathematics, and on mathematicians being inventors not discoverers (cf. RFM I). Towards the bottom of p. 88v, he drew a line, and underneath it copied the final sentence from MS 142, i.e. what is now *Investigations* §189(a), and proceeded to develop this theme along roughly the same lines as those now familiar to us from §§189ff. and RFM I. At the bottom of p. 89v he wrote: 'Habe heute angefangen an dem grossen Manuskript weiterzuschreiben. Möge es gehen! Geht es aber nicht, so soll ich nicht unglücklich werden. Ich fürchte mich davor in meinem Buch in einem geschraubten und schlechten Stil zu schreiben.' ('Today I began to continue writing the large manuscript. May it go [well]! But if it doesn't, I mustn't become unhappy. I am afraid of writing in a stilted and bad style in my book.') The next day, 12 September, he wrote:

Ich schreibe jetzt an meinem Buch, oder versuche zu schreiben, und schreibe tropfenweise und ohne jeden Zug; von der Hand in den Mund. Es ist unmöglich, dass so etwas Gutes herauskommt. Ich bin vor allem viel zu unfrei im Schreiben. Wenn ich *so* schreiben muss, da ist es besser, kein Buch zu schreiben, sondern mich darauf zu beschränken Bemerkungen *tant bien que mal* zu schreiben, die nach meinen Tode vielleicht veröffentlicht werden.

(I am now writing my book, or trying to write, and am writing drop by drop and without any vigour; from hand to mouth. It is impossible that anything good come out of it thus. I am above all too unfree in writing. If I have to write *thus*, then it is better not to write a book, but to limit myself to writing remarks *tant bien que mal*, which may perhaps be published after my death.)

Two days later W.'s spirits sank even lower:

Es ist grauenhaft, dass ich die Arbeitsfähigkeit, d.h. die philosophische Sehkraft von einem Tag auf den andern verliere . . .
Ich hatte gestern Hoffnung, dass es mit dem Schreiben gehn wird. Heute aber ist meine Hoffnung wieder gesunken.
Und leider *brauche* ich die Arbeit, denn ich bin noch nicht resigniert, sie aufzugeben . . .
'Fang etwas Anderes an!' Aber ich will nicht! Wie soll ich Kraft haben jetzt etwas anderes anzufangen? Es sei denn, dass ich gezwungen werde, wie durch einen Krieg.

(It is dreadful, that I lose the ability to work, i.e. the power of philosophical insight, from one day to the next . . .
I had hopes yesterday that the writing would go all right. Today my hope has sunk again.
And unfortunately I *need* the work, for I am not yet resigned to giving it up . . .
'Do something else!' But I don't want to! How should I find the strength to do something different now? Unless I were being forced, as in a war.)

On 15 September he remarked that when he thinks 'for himself', as it were, without having the composition of a book in mind, he circles around a topic ('so springe ich um das Thema herum').[14] This is his natural way of thinking; to be forced to think sequentially ('In einer Reihe gezwungen fortzudenken') is torture for him. Is it worth trying? He is wasting untold toil on an arrangement of his thoughts, which, he writes, may be worthless.

The next day, 16 September 1937, he wrote a short 'Vorwort':

Dieses Buch besteht aus Bemerkungen die ich im Lauf von 8 Jahren über den Gegenstand der Philosophie geschrieben habe. Ich habe oft vergebens versucht sie in eine befriedigende Ordnung zu bringen oder am Faden *eines* Gedankenganges aufzureihen. Das Ergebnis war künstlich und unbefriedigend, und meine Kraft erwies sich als viel zu gering es zu Ende zu führen. Die einzige Darstellung, deren ich noch fähig bin, ist die, diese Bemerkungen durch ein Netz von Zahlen so zu verbinden, dass ihr, äusserst komplizierter, Zusammenhang sichtbar wird.

Möge dies statt eines Besseren hingenommen werden, — was ich gerne geliefert hätte.

(This book consists of remarks on the subject of philosophy which I have written in the course of the last eight years. I have often tried, in vain, to put them into a satisfactory order or to thread them together in *one* string of thoughts. The result was artificial and unsatisfactory, and my strength turned out to be far too slight to pursue the matter to its conclusion. The only presentation of which I am still capable is to connect these remarks by a network of numbers which will make evident their extremely complicated connections.

May this be taken instead of something better — which I should have liked to produce.)

Where had he begun to continue to write the 'large manuscript' ('dem grossen Manuscript') to which he is referring, and what is the 'book'? It is plausible to suppose that he is speaking of MS 117 (Vol. XIII), which he began on 11 September, 1937. It is presumably this to which he was referring in his diary entry (see above) in MS 118 (Vol. XIV) on the very same date.[15] It is

---

[14] He had remarked on this tendency in his thought earlier, in MS 118 (Vol. XIV), 77r–v: 'I generally approach a question not like this: x → · but like this x ⟋⟍. I shoot again and again past it, but always from a closer position.' ('Ich schiesse immer wiede an ihr vorbei, aber in immer näherem Abstand'.)

[15] It might be suggested that it is the large manuscript volume 116 (Vol. XII). But this possibility can be excluded. MS 116 is *not* an attempt to compose a book, but a repository of usable remarks for the composition of a book. It seems that transcription into it began on 23 Oct., when he wrote in MS 119, 79r, that he had begun reviewing what he called 'my old typescript' in order to separate the wheat from the chaff. On 24 Oct. he has the idea of 'setting up a flat for household effects in which I bring objects from a rubbish dump, try them out and attempt to clean them up'. MS 116 is the flat, and *The Big Typescript* is the rubbish dump. The next day he spent reading his 'old remarks' — most of them struck him as 'indifferent', very many as feeble; the best are those which simply state a problem. On 26 Oct. he gave up fresh work in order to

surely this volume to which he refers the following day ('I am now writing my book, or trying to write . . .'). For MS 117 is clearly a 'second-level', clean copy composition (one first-level source of which was indeed MS 118 itself). It is patently a composition intended to be a draft for the continuation of the book begun in MS 142 and typed up as TS 220 sometime between December 1936 and either May or December 1937 (see p. 3 above, n. 7). For it opens with the last sentence of that typescript (i.e. PI §189(a)), and the first 97 manuscript pages are the basis of the dictation of the first 67 pages of TS 221 (paginated 138–204). The 'book', it is evident, is the Early Draft of the *Investigations* that he was now struggling to continue. The reference to remarks written over the last eight years is warranted inasmuch as MS 142 made use of materials from *The Big Typescript* some of which do indeed date back to 1930. So the fragmentary Preface seems to signal W.'s abandonment of the effort to arrange the new material sequentially (which he presumably thought he had achieved in TS 220), opting instead for a numbering system for the mathematical continuation which would display a network of connections rather than a linear development of thought. This projected 'network of numbers' is discussed below.

(iii)   MS 159, 34r–41r: this pocket notebook contains what appears to be the first rough draft of the 1938 Preface. The manuscript contains no date. It is conjectured that it was written early in 1938. The draft Preface resembles the 'clean copy' drafts in MS 117 (Vol. XIII).

(iv)   MS 117 (Vol. XIII), 110–26, contains three drafts of a Preface, the first dated '27.6.' and the last concluding with the words 'Cambridge im August 1938'. The first and second drafts are prefaced by the dedication 'Meinen Freunden gewidmet' ('Dedicated to my friends'). These, and MS 159, differ from each other and from the final 1938 TS Preface only marginally, and so will be discussed in (c) below.

(v)   TS 225 is the typescript of the 1938 Preface. Comparing it with the final 1945 Preface reveals interesting differences.

Paragraph (a) added to the list of the topics to be discussed sense-data and the contrast between Idealism and Realism.

(b) differs in the following respects:

(1) It begins: 'Vor etwa 4 Jahren machte ich den ersten Versuch so einer Zusammenfassung. Das Ergebnis war ein unbefriedigendes, und ich machte weitere Versuche. Bis ich endlich (einige Jahre später) zur Überzeugung

---

concentrate on the selection (making marginal marks). There is much thought behind the remarks, he writes, but few are usable for a book without reworking. He has, he writes, done a quarter so far, and he should finish within six days. But the next day he starts fresh writing again. The first 135 pages of MS 116 are a revised selection from BT 1–196 (transcribed without any attempt at reordering), but pp. 51–6, 118, 124–7, and 130 are derived from MS 119, from remarks dated 30 Oct. to 12 Nov. 1937. MS 116, pp. 136–258, are transcribed from remarks in MSS 119–20 (Vols. XV–XVI), in which they date from 13 Nov. 1937 to 15 July 1938.

gelangte, dass es vergebens sei; und ich alle solche Versuche aufzugeben hätte.'
('Some four years ago I made the first attempt at such a collection. The result
was unsatisfactory, and I made further attempts. Until I finally (some years later)
was forced to the conclusion that it was in vain, and I had to give up all such
attempts.') (In the MS 117 (Vol. XIII) drafts, W. wrote not '(some years later)',
but 'after more than two years'; this he crossed out in the third draft, altering
it to the later variant.)

(2) Instead of 'Und dies hing freilich mit der Natur der Untersuchung'
('And this was, of course, connected with the very nature of the investiga-
tion'), W. wrote: 'Dies hing allerdings auch mit der Natur des Gegenstands'
('And this was, to be sure, also connected with . . .').

(3) The penultimate sentence continues '. . . durchreisen; dass die
Gedanken in ihm in einen verwickeltern Netz von Beziehungen zueinander
stehen' ('. . . direction; so that the thoughts in it stand to each other in an
intricate network of relationships'). This metaphor prepares the way for the
sequel.

(c) is quite different here.

Ich beginne diese Veröffentlichung mit dem Fragment meines letzten Versuchs, meine
philosophischen Gedanken in eine Reihe zu ordnen. Dies Fragment hat vielleicht
den Vorzug, verhältnismässig leicht einen Begriff von meiner Methode vermitteln zu
können. Diesem Fragment will ich eine Masse von Bemerkung in mehr oder weniger
loser Anordnung folgen lassen. Die Zusammenhänge der Bemerkungen aber, dort, wo
ihre Anordnung sie nicht erkennen lässt, will ich durch eine Numerierung erklären.
Jede Bemerkung soll eine laufende Nummer und ausserdem die Nummern solcher
Bemerkungen tragen, die zu ihr in wichtigen Beziehungen stehen.

(I start this book with the fragment of my latest attempt to arrange my philosophical
thoughts sequentially. This fragment has, perhaps, the virtue of making it compar-
atively easy to obtain a grasp of my method. I want to continue this fragment with a
mass of more or less loosely ordered remarks. But the links between these remarks,
where the arrangement does not make them evident, I shall clarify by means of a
numbering system. Each remark will have a serial number, and apart from that, the
numbers of those remarks which are related to it in important ways.)

What is the 'fragment' alluded to? It is characterized as W.'s *latest attempt*
to arrange his thoughts sequentially (in consecutive prose), even though, as
noted in the first paragraph, they had originally been written down as
'Bemerkungen' (remarks, in W.'s sense, hence separated one from another by
a line space). This is evidently a reference to TS 220 (and MS 142), both of
which are consecutive, paragraphed prose. This is patently W.'s latest attempt
to arrange his thoughts sequentially. MS 142 *was* derived largely from materials originally written as 'remarks', and yet was itself written as standard prose.
It is, indeed, noteworthy that the marginal numerals in the MS were inserted
later, as is evident from the absence of any numbering on pp. 78–91, which

were crossed out and redrafted on pp. 91ff. (where numbers are again inserted). So the numbering was added *after* the redrafting of these pages. Consequently, it is plausible to take this as being the 'fragment' alluded to. If so, then it seems that his idea was to publish TS 220 as a fragment of a 'conventional' book, and for it to continue into the materials of (what is now) TS 221, which would not be presented as (paragraphed) consecutive prose, but as sequences of numbered remarks, each also prefixed by a set of numbers indicating connections in a network, and separated from the next remark by a blank line.

Against this conjecture speaks the fact that there exists no MS or TS of the continuation of TS 220 that contains any such system of numbering. Further, TS 220 seems far too long to be called a 'fragment'. Both objections can be countered. First, there is no oddity in referring to TS 220 as 'ein Fragment', since the German word 'Fragment' signifies an unfinished (fragmentary) work that breaks off before completion, whether large or small; thus, for example, Goethe's *Wilhelm Meisters theatralische Sendung* is referred to as a 'Fragment'. Secondly, there is no reason to suppose that the reticular numbering mooted in the 1938 Preface had already been executed. The 'Vorwort' of 16 September 1937 (MS 118 (Vol. XIV)), as we have seen, suggested the same idea, and it is certain that *that* was *prospective*, since it was a solution to W.'s painful doubts and hesitations about producing a sequential ordering of his remarks on philosophy of mathematics expressed in the previous few days. It would, after all, be quite natural to leave that task until the writing was absolutely finished. Alternatively, it is possible that W. executed such a numbering on separate sheets of paper[16] (since only the final numbering would be entered in the TS), and that he later destroyed these, since once the idea was abandoned, such lists of interconnections would have little value.

(d) differs from the final Preface: 'Ich wollte, alle diese Bemerkungen wären besser, als sie sind. — Es fehlt ihnen — um es kurz zu sagen — an Kraft und an Präzision. Ich veröffentliche diejenigen hier, die mir nicht zu öde erscheinen.' ('I wish that all these remarks were better than they are. They are lacking — to put it briefly — in power and precision. I publish those here which do not seem to me too barren.')

(e) differs slightly. The final sentence runs as follows: 'Hierdurch wurde meine Eitelkeit aufgeregt und sie drohte mir immer wieder die Ruhe zu rauben, wenn ich die Sache nicht (wenigstens für mich) durch eine Publikation erledigte. Und dies schien auch in anderer Beziehung das Wünschenswerteste.' ('This stung my vanity and again and again threatened to rob me of peace of mind, unless I settled the matter (at least for myself) by a publication. And this seemed in other respects too the most desirable thing to do.') See 1 above for commentary.

---

[16] Compare TS 231, a concordance of correlations between B i and B ii.

(f)–(i) do not differ materially from the printed Preface, but its final paragraph does not occur.

(vi)   MS 128, 40ff., contains material for the Preface. It is clear that by this date (1944/5) W. had given up the idea of presenting a fragment in consecutive prose followed by a sequence of interrelated remarks connected by a system of enumeration. He refers to the book as containing a 'conglomerate' ('Konglomerat') of remarks written over a sixteen-year period. In the end, he remarks, he had to order them in some way, no matter how loosely, and this conglomerate is what he proposes to publish. This drafting gives way to various elaborations of the 'sketches of a landscape' metaphor.

MS 128, 49, has the only draft of the final paragraph of the 1945 Preface: 'Dass dieses Buch nicht gut ist, weiss ich. Aber ich glaube dass die Zeit in der es von mir verbessert werden könnte vorüber ist, und diese Überzeugung hat mich zu seiner Veröffentlichung bewogen.' ('That this book is not good, I know. But I believe that the time is past in which I could improve it, and this conviction has moved me to publish it.') This version was typed into TS 243, and thence into the final typescript, TS 227, where it was further altered in pen.

(vii)   MS 180(a), 15f., has a further draft, not significantly different from those of MS 129 that succeed it.

(viii)   MS 180(b), 24v–25r, contains some redrafts of the second and third sentences of paragraph (a). W. toyed with adding to 'They concern many subjects' the addendum 'that preoccupy the philosophy of our time' ('die die Philosophie unserer Zeit beschäftigen').

(ix)   MS 129 contains numerous drafts written on special index sheets at the beginning of this volume. The first date in the MS volume proper is 17 August 1944, but the drafts may well have been entered later. They are very close to the final version, and display how much care went into the composition. It is here that mention of Realism and Idealism, and of sense-data, as topics to be discussed, is dropped. W. refers to his first attempt to weld his results together as occurring ten years before, i.e. 1934–5. Other variations in the redraftings are largely stylistic.

(x)   MS 130, 22, contains the draft of the album metaphor.

(xi)   MS 136, 81, contains a paragraph headed 'Zum Vorwort' (see 1(h) above).

Chapter 1

The Augustinian conception of language (§§1–27(a))

INTRODUCTION

§§1–27(a) introduce some of the main themes of the book. The central pre-occupation of PI is the nature of language and linguistic meaning, and associated philosophical perplexities. The book opens with a quotation from Augustine's *Confessions*, which W. saw as articulating a picture that is a source of important misconceptions concerning thought and language, words and sentences, meaning and use. The purpose of the first twenty-seven remarks is to sketch the ideas that stem from this picture of the essence of language, and to subject it to preliminary scrutiny and criticism.

The 'chapter' divides into three parts.

Part A runs from §1 to §7. It introduces Augustine's picture of language: words name objects, and sentences are combinations of words. In this apparently innocuous description one can find the roots of the *idea* (which we shall call 'the Augustinian conception of language') that every word has a meaning, and that the meaning of a word is the object correlated with the word, for which it stands. W. raises a variety of questions concerning: (i) word-meaning; (ii) the word/sentence distinction; (iii) diversity of types of word; (iv) different methods of explaining the meaning of a word (and their bearing on different 'parts of speech'); (v) the nature of understanding and the relation between the meaning of an expression and the criteria for understanding that expression. In each case the Augustinian conception is shown to breed confusion and error. In the course of the discussion various key notions occur, the significance of which emerges only later: the use and criteria of application of words, phrases and sentences, as well as their role and purpose. Key distinctions are briefly introduced: (i) the contrast between training and explanation; (ii) the distinction between ostensive teaching and ostensive definition (exemplifying the first contrast); (iii) the difference between a complete and an incomplete language or language-game. Finally, crucial methodological notions are introduced: the concept of a language-game (§7) and the language-game method of elucidation.

The structure of Part A:

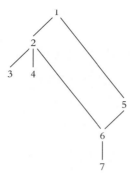

Part B runs from §8 to §17. It opens with an extension of language-game (2) in preparation for examining the idea that the essential role of words is to signify objects. This expanded language-game contains different kinds of word or 'parts of speech' over and above the names of building stones in (2): namely, demonstratives, colour-names and numerals. According to the Augustinian conception, every word signifies something, and to know what it means is to know what it stands for. This idea forces the diversity of uses of words into a vacuous strait-jacket (language-game (8) illustrates this point). The discussion introduces the analogies between words and tools, and between words and levers. Finally, W. characterizes the logical status of the colour samples in language-game (8), recommending that they be counted as 'instruments of language'.

The structure of part B:

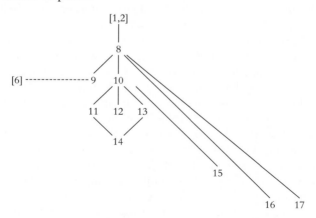

Part C runs from §18 to §27(a). It is parallel to Part B and explicitly linked with §§2 and 8. It explores the other main ingredient of Augustine's picture: namely, sentences. W. makes a number of controversial claims: (i) that a language might consist only of commands or questions and answers; (ii) that such a language would not be incomplete; (iii) that the distinction between assertions, questions, commands, etc. turns neither on the grammatical forms of sentences nor on any mental acts accompanying their utterance, but on their uses or applications; (iv) that Frege's conception of assertion and constituent assumption is mistaken; (v) that uttering sentences and responding to their utterance must be seen as part of a whole pattern of activity; and (vi) that what each of the words of a sentence signifies (if anything) does not fix the use of the whole sentence (as is obvious from considering one-word sentences, which may be used to report, order or query).

The structure of Part C:

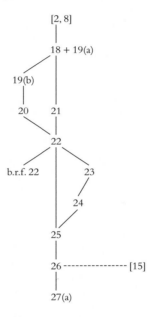

§§26 and 27(a) link the preliminary investigation of the Augustinian conception with the more thorough discussion of naming and ostensive definition in §§27(b)–64 (Chapter 2).

Sources

The following table of correlations does not itemize individual paragraph cor- <
relations within remarks, but only the numbered remarks of PI. Some of the /
correlations, therefore, are correlations only of individual paragraphs within the
numbered remark.

PI§	BT	MS 115[1]	MS 142§/ TS 220§	TS 226$_R$§	Other
1	25	79f., 118	1–2	1f.	111, 15; 114 Um., 35–7, 179; 140, 40; 141, 1; 152, 38–40, 87; BrB 77
2	25	118	3	3f.	111, 16; 114 Um., 36, 179; 141, 1; 152, 40; BrB 77
3	26r	118	4	5f.	111, 17; 114 Um., 36f.; 141, 1
4	26r–27		5	7	111, 18; 114 Um., 37
5		80, 88, 119, 121	6	8	141, 1; 152, 41
6		118f.	7	9	141, 1; BrB 77
7		118, 126	8	10	141, 1f.; BrB 77
8		120f., 124	9	11	141, 1f.; BrB 79–84
9		121	10	12	141, 1; BrB 79f.
10			11	13	152, 43; BrB 82
11			11f.	14f.	
12		28	12	16	107, 232; 114 Um., 38
13			12	17	
14			12	18	
15			13	19	BlB 69
16		130f.	14	20	107, 226; 141, 3; BrB 84f.
17	29	128	15	21	140, 17; 141, 3; BrB 83f.
18	209		16	22	141, 2; BlB 19
19		88, 119f.	16f.	22f.	141, 2
20		119f.	18f.	23–5	BrB 78; 110, 188
21			20	26	
22	206–9	85–7	21–3	27–9	109, 199; 113, 50r; 116, 345
b.r.f. 22	244–6	58f.			113, 29r; Bi §432

PI§	BT	MS 115[1]	MS 142§/ TS 220§	TS 226ᵣ§	Other
23	208v	87f., 129	24	30	152, 47; BlB 67f.
24		89f.,	25	31	147, 45r–v
25	209	90	26	32	
26	209r–v	90	26	33	
27(a)	202r	90f.	26	34	

[1] MS 115 (Vol. XI), pp. 118–292, dated end of August 1936, is Wittgenstein's translation and reworking of BrB, which has been published in German as *Eine Philosophische Betrachtung*. Up to p. 117, MS 115 is a continuation of the *Umarbeitung* of BT that began in MS 114 (Vol. X), p. 31v.

I. The Augustinian conception of language
   1. Augustine's picture
   2. The Augustinian family
       (a) word-meaning
       (b) correlating words with meanings
       (c) ostensive explanation
       (d) metapsychological corollaries
       (e) sentence-meaning
   3. Moving off in new directions
   4. Frege
   5. Russell
   6. The *Tractatus*

EXEGESIS §§1–27(a)

SECTION 1

1   The book opens with a quotation from St Augustine, from which W. extracts a 'particular picture of the essence of human language'. This picture is held to inform philosophical thought. It is the seedbed of *the Augustinian conception* (or *idea*) of the essence of language (see 'The Augustinian conception of language', sect. 1). One task of the *Investigations* is to show how it leads to error.

Why did W. choose to open his book with this quotation? The reasons he gave (see 2 below) are that: (a) this pre-theoretical picture is, for most of mankind, the natural way to think about the nature of language; (b) it exhibits the roots from which the philosophical concept and conception of the meaning of a word grow; and (c) it is the source of his own misconceptions about the meaning of words in the *Tractatus*, misconceptions that he took over from Frege and Russell.

The context of the passage in the *Confessions* is as follows:

Little by little I began to realize where I was and to want to make my wishes known to others, who might satisfy them. But this I could not do, because my wishes were inside me, while other people were outside, and they had no faculty which could penetrate my mind. So I would toss my arms and legs about and make noises, hoping that such few signs as I could make would show my meaning, though they were quite unlike what they were meant to mime. And if my wishes were not carried out, either because they had not been understood or because what I wanted would have harmed me, I would get cross with my elders . . . simply because they did not attend to my wishes; and I would take my revenge by bursting into tears. By watching babies I have learnt that this is how they behave, and they, quite unconsciously, have done more than those who brought me up and knew all about it to convince me that I behaved in just the same way myself.[1]

Augustine's remarks that immediately precede the passage are:

. . . later on I realized how I had learnt to speak. It was not my elders who showed me the words by some set system of instruction, in the way they taught me to read not long afterwards; but, instead, I taught myself by using the intelligence which you, my God, gave to me. For when I tried to express my meaning by crying out and making various sounds and movements, so that my wishes should be obeyed, I found that I could not convey all that I meant or make myself understood by everyone whom I wished to understand me.[2]

---

[1]   Augustine, *Confessions*, Bk I, §6, tr. R. S. Pine-Coffin (Penguin, London, 1961), pp. 25f.
[2]   Ibid. I, §8.

Augustine's reflections, of course, are not *recollections* of childhood, but his inferences from his observations of children. These remarks, which W. does not quote, contain the following central points: (i) an 'inner' and 'outer' picture of the mind; (ii) a presumption of pre-linguistic self-consciousness, and *a fortiori* a presumption of the intelligibility of self-knowledge of mental states (sensations, wishes, thoughts); (iii) a conception of language according to which it is necessary only for communication, but not for thinking; (iv) a conception of meaning something that assumes meaning (*meinen*) to be antecedent to mastery of a public language. These, though not mentioned here by W., are later assailed. Repudiation of (i) and (ii) are central in W.'s philosophy of mind (see Volume 3, *passim*). That he associated Augustine with these conceptions is evident in PI §32(b), as well as by a passing jotting in MS 149, 7: 'Augustin [*sic*], about expressing [t]he wishes within him', which is followed by a discussion of whether a child has a private language before it learns our public one. Repudiation of (iii) is a recurrent theme of his philosophy of language. Rejection of (iv) is a *leitmotiv* (§§19, 20, 22, 33, 35, p. 18n., §§81, 186–8, 358, 504–13, 592) that culminates in the last 32 remarks of the book (see Volume 4, 'The mythology of meaning something'). Here, however, he is concerned only with the points explicit in the quotation in §1(a), from which he selects two: (v) words name objects; (vi) sentences are combinations of names.

Augustine makes three further points with which W. must agree. First, he stresses gestures ('ihren Gebärden' is W.'s translation, although the Latin has 'motu corporis', i.e. bodily movements) as 'the natural language of all people', and as a pre-condition of language and language-acquisition, a point W. himself emphasizes (PI §§185, 206–7, etc.). Secondly, he insists that the child's learning required hearing words 'uttered in their assigned places in various sentences', and hence that meaning and understanding generally presuppose mastery of combinatorial possibilities of expressions. Thirdly, he holds that language, although it is learnt in a certain sense, cannot be taught.[3] W. similarly noted that 'Every way of making a language intelligible already presupposes a language. And the use of a language, in a certain sense, cannot be taught' (MS 108 (Vol. IV), 103 = PR 54;[4] cf. PG 40). But W., unlike Augustine, held that this initial language-learning was training.

W. does not take Augustine to be expounding a 'theory', or a philosophical account, of meaning. What interests W. is what he takes to be Augustine's pre-philosophical *picture* (*Bild*) of the working of language. For, as he remarked (MS 111 (Vol. VII), 15), this conception (*Auffassung*) is significant

---

[3]   See the above quotation from *Confessions* I, §8.
[4]   This remark is part of W.'s comment on what was right and what was wrong about TLP 3.263. If one explains the meaning of 'A' by saying 'This is A', this can be understood as a statement, in which case it presupposes knowledge of the meaning of 'A'. Or it can be understood as a definition, in which case it presupposes a grasp of the grammatical category of 'A'. In this sense, every way of making language intelligible already presupposes a language. What this amounts to, W. concludes, is that one cannot exit language with language.

for us precisely because it belongs to a naturally clear-thinking person, temporily far removed from us, who does not belong to our cultural milieu.[5] Whether Augustine's account is as unreflective and pre-theoretical as W. evidently assumes is debatable (for Augustine had various Platonist and theological axes to grind[6]), but of little importance as far as the purpose of the quotation here is concerned.

The picture of the essence of language, extracted in (b) *from the quotation*, involves the following main contentions: (i) words name objects; (ii) sentences are combinations of (such) names. This simple pair of apparent truisms is at the root of a more sophisticated idea or conception (*the Augustinian conception*) according to which, in addition, (iii) every word has a meaning; (iv) a word is correlated with its meaning; (v) the meaning of a word is the object for which it stands. These last three contentions provide the main themes of §§1–59. §§1–27(a) explore (iii); §§27(b)–38 examine the primary candidate for the correlating mechanism of (iv); §§38–59 examine the ramifications of (v). Although the Augustinian conception thereafter sinks from sight, it continues to constitute, as it were, a muted *leitmotiv* throughout the book (and RFM I — originally conceived as a sequel to TS 220). For this conception distorts reflections not only in philosophy of language, but also in philosophy of mathematics and of psychology (see Volume 2, 'Two fruits upon one tree').

In (c), W. notes that Augustine's description fails to distinguish different parts of speech. Its primary focus is upon personal names and common nouns ('table', 'chair', 'loaf' or 'bread'). Names of actions and properties, and other types of words, are neglected. Elsewhere (MS 111 (Vol. VII), 16; AWL 46; MS 141, 1; BrB 77), W. lists other types of words — demonstratives ('here', 'there'), token reflexives ('now', 'today'), connectives and quantifiers ('but', 'not', 'or', 'all'), and modal adverbs ('perhaps') — that must not be assimilated to the category of names. They cannot correctly be deemed to be names at all.

(d) illustrates differences between nominals by highlighting different ways in which one might operate with three kinds of word, each of which *can* be called 'a name': a common noun, a colour-adjective and a number-word. 'Five', 'red' and 'apple' are words each one of which belongs to a type the use of which is fundamentally different from that of the others. To say that 'apple' is the name of a fruit, 'red' the name of a colour, and 'five' the name of a number is not incorrect (cf. PI §§28, 38(b)) — 'we call very different things "names"; the word "name" is used to characterize many different kinds of use

---

[5] Malcolm reports that W. told him that he had decided to begin the book with the quotation from Augustine, not because he could not find the conception there expressed as well stated by other philosophers, but because the conception *must* be important if so great a mind held it (N. Malcolm, *Ludwig Wittgenstein: A Memoir*, 2nd edn. (Oxford University Press, London, 1984), pp. 59f.).

[6] See M. Burnyeat, 'Wittgenstein and Augustine *De Magistro*', *Proceedings of the Aristotelian Society*, supp. vol. 61 (1987), pp. 1–24.

of a word' — but it masks important logico-grammatical differences beneath superficial similarities. So even when we restrict attention to expressions that can be called 'names', and disregard the multitude of expressions in a language that cannot be so called, we have still not penetrated to the 'essence of language' by claiming that individual words of a language name objects, since the differences between these kinds of name are great, and they cannot all be said to stand for an object.[7] These differences are made salient by the distinct operations carried out in each case, and the ordering of the operations. First, objects of a given type (apples) are identified; subsequently, a sensible characteristic (red) is matched with a sample; finally, a 1:1 correlation of objects and number-words is carried out. It would be senseless to recite the series of number-words before identifying a range of objects. Now it is evident that calling all these words 'names', and saying that naming is the essence of language, tells us nothing about the fundamentally different *uses* of these distinct parts of speech (sortal noun, colour-adjective and number-word).

Each of the three words in 'five red apples' has a different use, and this can be described without answering questions such as 'Of what is "five" the name?', 'What does "five" stand for?', or 'What is the meaning of the word "five"?' — where 'meaning' is conceived to be a correlative entity. There is no need to answer what, on the Augustinian conception of language, is the fundamental question (cf. PLP 156–8).

Note that it is unimportant that greengrocers do not actually go through this rigmarole, red items being identified without the aid of a sample, and small numbers such as '5' being applied visually. What matters is that the different operations illuminate the categorial differences between sortal nouns, colour-predicates and number-words respectively. W.'s description deliberately highlights the greengrocer's operations in order to drive home the point that the different parts of speech fulfil different functions, and are integrated in different ways into human action. It would make no difference to the tale (but only complicate it) if the order were for 25 reels of ultramarine cotton thread or 17 swatches of eau-de-nil silk (here the colour identification would typically require a colour chart, and the number requires counting).

How the shopkeeper knows what operation to carry out in each case is brushed aside as irrelevant. W.'s typical grounds for this move are twofold. First, that genesis of knowledge, as of any ability, is a matter of empirical fact. Being contingent, it stands in no logical or normative relation to exercise of the ability or manifestation of the knowledge. Second, justifications come to an end somewhere: *this* is what is called 'red', *the number of these* is called 'five'.

---

[7] Regarding the term 'object', W. held it incorrect to characterize colours (MS 111 (Vol. VII), 113) and numbers (MS 117 (Vol. XIII), 197) as objects, and thought that Frege's willingness to call the simultaneous occurrence of an eclipse of the moon and a court case 'an object' was misleading (MS 107 (Vol. III), 14).

1.1   (i)   The German translation of the Latin quotation appears to be W.'s own.[8]
It is a very free translation, with an informality that W. needed in order to
convey the idea that Augustine's ruminations are autobiographical reflections
rather than philosophical speculations. It is important to be aware of the fact
that W. is not *criticising* Augustine for mistakes. Had he wished to do that —
which he did not — he could and should have looked elsewhere for
Augustine's philosophy of language, for example in *De Magistro*, where a quite
different picture is to be found. What W. used the quotation for was to impress
upon the reader just how natural it is to think of language acquisition as a
matter of learning names and their sentential combination, and then using those
names to express one's wishes. If a mind as great as Augustine's could naturally
entertain such ideas, then the misconceptions which they readily imply when
elaborated in what we are calling the Augustinian conception of language are
surely of great importance.

(ii)   'Wortarten': W. preferred 'parts of speech' (TS 226$_R$ §1; PG 56n.).
See Exg. §17.

(iii)   'No such thing was in question here': W. corrected this to read 'There
was no question of such an entity "meaning" here' (TS 226$_R$ §2). This makes
it clear *what* concept of meaning is under attack.

2   (i)   W. considered various ways of opening his second book. On 19 June
1931, when writing his notes on Frazer's *Golden Bough*, he contemplated beginning his new book with remarks about metaphysics as a kind of magic. The
depth of magic would have to be preserved. 'Indeed, here the elimination of
magic has itself the character of magic.' Importantly, he then alludes to the
Tractatus: 'For, back then, when I began talking about the "*world*" (and not
about this tree or table), what else did I want but to bind something higher
in a spell' (MS 110 (Vol. VI), 177f.; PO 116f.).

He rapidly abandoned this idea in favour of something much closer to talking about 'this tree or table'. On 30 June, he wrote that he should begin his
book with an analysis of an ordinary sentence such as 'A lamp is standing on
my table', since everything should be derivable from this. This idea, he adds,
expresses something he has long felt: namely, that he should start his book
with a description of a situation from which the material for all that follows
can be obtained (MS 110, 243).

He did not do so, however, in *The Big Typescript* and its redraftings. It opens
with a discussion of understanding, which emphasizes that meaning something
(*meinen*) drops out of consideration, and that understanding is the correlate of
explanation. The concept of meaning (*Bedeutung*) is only broached in Chapter
2, the first section heading of which is 'The concept of meaning stems from
a primitive philosophical conception of language [var.: 'a primitive philosophy of language']', alluding to the philosophical conception of the meaning

---

[8]   E. von Savigny has checked all the German translations between 1840 and 1940 (see his
Wittgensteins 'Philosophische Untersuchungen': ein Kommentar für Leser, 2nd edn, vol. 1 (Klostermann,
Frankfurt, 1994), p. 36.

of a word as a correlative entity. The section opens with a discussion of
Augustine's description of language-learning (BT 25). This ordering is main-
tained in the *Umarbeitung* (MS 114 Um.) and the *Grosses Format* (MS 140). It
is only with the Brown Book and its reworking (EPB) that the discussion of
Augustine's picture of language shifts to the beginning of W.'s projected book.
It remains in this position in MS 142 and all subsequent drafts.

(ii)   Why did W. choose this passage from Augustine as the opening of his
book? He made various revealing remarks about it.

(a) For most of mankind the conception articulated by Augustine is the most
natural way to think about the nature of language (MS 141, 1). Presumably
this is because it reflects a prominent aspect of teaching children to speak, and
incorporates the most common auxiliary device: namely, pointing at something and saying 'That is . . .'.

(b) In the rough notes of redrafts in MS 152, 40, W. remarks that
Augustine's words are a picture of the approach in which the '*meaning* of words'
is seen as the foundation of language. This concept (or conception) of the 'meaning of a word', *as we attempt to use it in philosophy*, or — this *philosophical con-
cept(ion)* of the meaning of words — is seen as the foundation of language. On
p. 87 W. has 'the philosophical idea of the meanings of words'.

(c) Why that is important is stated in MS 111 (Vol. VII), 18: Augustine's
description of learning a language can show us from what primitive picture
or 'world-picture' (*Weltbild*) this conception of language derives.

(d) This primitive picture informed W.'s own conception of language
in the *Tractatus* and that of his predecessors (Frege and Russell). MS 114
(Vol. X) Um., 35, immediately prior to the examination of Augustine, has:
'The philosophical concept [or conception] of meaning that I *took over* in
my philosophical discussions derives from a primitive philosophy of language'
(emphasis added).[9] 'Bedeutung', W. notes, comes from 'deuten'. Augustine,
when he talks of language-learning, talks only of how we assign names to things,
or understand the names of things. Naming appears here to be the foundation
and essence of language.

In BT 27 (derived from MS 111, 19, and repeated in MS 114 Um., 38),
immediately following the discussion of Augustine, W. writes: 'Here also belongs
the following', and interpolates a discussion of the roots of his own misleading
expression 'a fact is a complex of objects' [more accurately, 'a combination of
objects'] — see Exg. §4.

AWL 43 notes that the word 'meaning' plays a great role in philosophy, as
is evident in discussing the nature of mathematics. So, Frege ridiculed people
for not seeing that what is important is the *meaning* of numerals and number-
words, i.e. something they stand for and that corresponds to them, as Smith
corresponds to the name 'Smith'. The question 'What is the number 1?' is

---

[9]   Apropos the error of identifying the meaning (*Bedeutung*) of a name with its bearer, Waismann
remarks (PLP 313) that 'Wittgenstein, in the *Tractatus*, took over this opinion of Frege's'. It is
unlikely that he would have written this unless he heard it from Wittgenstein.

misleading. It is correct to say that there is no object corresponding to '1' as Smith corresponds to his name; but then we look for an object in *another* sense. So, when [like Frege] we confront the question 'What is a number?', we are prone to think of an aethereal object. We should not try to give a definition, and should avoid such talk of meanings. Rather, we should investigate the *uses* of words. (It is striking that in the corresponding discussion in BB 4, W.'s criticism of Frege focuses on his conception of sense, as giving life to a sign (rather than of meaning, as an entity corresponding to the numeral).) In similar vein, W., in a dictation to Waismann (VoW (F 94)), remarked:

> We shall see that Frege's definition of number does not at all capture the concept of a number. But now we grasp what dragged him into his mistaken line of enquiry. The question 'What is a number if it is not a sign?' arises from a mistaken grammatical background; for to this 'What?' we imagine a 'This', or we expect some 'This' in answer. Even the tone of the question recalls the tone of Augustine's question 'What is time?' A substantive misleads us into looking for a substance.

The Russellian association with the Augustinian conception is evident in PI §46 (cf. BrB 81).

MS 156b, 33v–34r, notes that our philosophers say that things are classes of sense-perceptions, as if one could define 'table' as a class of sense-impressions. They imagine that if there is a connection with sense-impressions, it can be only that. For they do not think of the *use* of words in their countless forms, but only of a word as the name of a thing.

2.1   (i) 'picture': elsewhere 'idea' (*Idee* (MS 140, 40)), conception (*Auffassung* (MS 111 (Vol. VII), 15f.; MS 141, 1)) or 'approach // way of considering things' (*Betrachtungsweise* (BT 25)). MS 152, 38, says that Augustine's words are a picture of an approach (*Bild der Betrachtungsweise*) that conceives of the meaning of words as the foundation of language.

(ii) 'picture of the essence of language': MS 111 (Vol. VII), 15f., states that Augustine's conception makes it appear as if naming is the foundation and essence of language ('Hier scheint also das Benennen Fundament und Um-und-Auf der Sprache zu sein'). This, W. continues, is equivalent to the conception according to which the form of explanation 'This is' is conceived to be fundamental.

BT 25 notes that when Augustine discusses language-learning, he speaks exclusively of how we *assign names to things* or *understand names*. Here naming appears to be the foundation and essence of language.

(iii) 'primarily of nouns': MS 111, 16, links this to Plato, who, W. notes, said that sentences consist of nouns and verbs (cf. *Sophist* 261–2).

(iv) 'operates with words': BB 16 uses the same green grocery example in order to sidestep the unhelpful question 'What are signs?' (Presumably to avoid the answers: 'They are marks or sounds with meanings' or, even worse, 'that have meanings associated with them' or 'attached to them'.) Instead W. examines this simple case of 'operating with words'.

BrB 79 elaborates the introduction of numerals into this game. It stresses the different *training* and *method of application* of each type of word. Mastering the use of numerals from 1 to 10, unlike learning the use of the words 'brick', 'cube', 'slab', etc., requires learning an ordered series by heart. As with other words, teaching is demonstrative; but the same numeral, e.g. '3', may be taught by pointing to slabs, bricks or columns. On the other hand, different numerals will be taught by pointing to *different groupings* of stones of the *same shape*. The demonstrative gesture and uttering of the word are the same in all cases. But the way the gesture is used differs, and the difference is not captured by saying 'In the one case one points at a shape, in the other at a number'.

⊂ §2 ?.   SECTION 2   §2

1   The philosophical conception of the meaning of a word as an entity correlated with it is rooted in a primitive (i.e. crude) idea, or picture (TS 226$_R$), ᵃ/ . of the functioning of language: namely, that words are names, and sentences combinations of names. A primitive idea, in this sense, is one that over-simplifies the phenomena. But, 'one can also say that it is the idea of a language more primitive than ours'. To shake the grip of the picture, and to demolish the philosophical misconception of meaning, W. describes such a language more primitive (i.e. simpler) than ours. Its further exploration will show that this concept of meaning (i.e. the concept rooted in Augustine's picture) is worthless.

(b) describes a language (subsequently referred to as a 'language-game') for which Augustine's *description* (as W. interprets it) of the way he learnt to speak Latin (viz. 'I gradually learnt to understand what objects [the words] signified, and . . . I used [the words] to express my own desires') *is* apt. The words are indeed all names. The building materials severally correspond to the names. To understand a name is to know what object corresponds to it. The speaker uses one of the four expressions to express his desire for one of the materials. The assistant responds with understanding (cf. PI §6(c)) in handing the speaker the right object. Note that it is *not* contended that *the Augustinian conception* of the nature of language (i.e. the conception rooted in Augustine's picture) is right for this proto-language (see 1.1(i) below).

The description of the language specifies a context (building activities), speakers (builder and assistant), a vocabulary ('block', 'pillar', 'slab', 'beam'), criteria of understanding (bringing the requested stones in the appropriate order), and a use of the vocabulary (the words are called out when the corresponding stones are wanted). However, the 'language' (i) has no syntax; (ii) contains no rules for sentence-formation, *a fortiori* none for formation of complex sentences (and so no logical connectives); (iii) is incapable of express-ing generality; (iv) has only one discourse function, namely: ordering. But W. tells us to conceive of it as a *complete* primitive (i.e. proto-) language.

Is W. right to call this 'a language'? One might think that syntax is essential to language, since it is a prerequisite for the creative powers of language that distinguish arbitrary signs from symbols in a language. Equally, truth and falsehood are often supposed to be essential to anything that can be deemed a language, but are absent here. Philosophers frequently assume that assertion is the most fundamental speech-function, and that non-assertoric speech-functions must be explained in terms of the assertoric. But this 'language' contains no possibility of assertion. It is held that the distinction between sense and nonsense is essential to language, but it has no grip here. Finally, one might suppose that it is essential to language that it express thought.

A general reply to these qualms is given in §494. It may be that we would be inclined to withhold the term 'language' from this activity. But it is a rudimentary system of communication and is, in important ways, analogous to language. It is a primitive *language-game* (cf. §37). Qua object of comparison it highlights features of language to which W. wanted to draw attention. It is tailored to Augustine's description, so obviously contains no more than is warranted thereby. It is a language-game only of giving orders and obeying them (the first language-game on the list in PI §23) — but that does not show it to be incomplete (PI §18). It must be remembered that this scenario is an expository device constructed for a specific purpose. It is not a piece of armchair anthropology.

Other scattered remarks deal with the more specific objections. Whether this language-game lacks sentences, whether 'Slab' is a word or a sentence, is raised in PI §§19f. (cf. §49). Absence of syntax, logical connectives and quantifiers no more disqualifies it from counting as a 'primitive language' than does the fact that it consists only of orders (PI §§18ff.). In so far as the sense/nonsense distinction depends on trangressing combinatorial rules, it obviously has no place here. But another kind of nonsense *can* be found even here: e.g. calling out the names of building materials when there are none present at all. Z §§98f., MS 132, 204, MS 136, 53a–b, discuss a range of issues. Would one call the sounds produced by the builder 'a language' under *all* circumstances? Certainly not. But what makes the context appropriate for calling it a language is *not* that the sounds have a certain mental accompaniment. One might say that language-game (2) describes a *degenerate* language (i.e. a limiting case of a language). Is W. just tacitly assuming that these people *think*, that they are like us in this respect, that they do not play the language-game mechanically? If they were just making noises mechanically, W. concedes, he would *not* call it the use of a rudimentary language. (So he is *not* viewing this language-game as *merely* causally interactive behaviour, akin to primitive animal cries and causally determined responses (cf. PI §493).) It is true that the life of these men must be like ours in many respects, W. continues, and that he had said nothing about this similarity. But the important thing is that their language, and their thinking too, may be rudimentary, that there is such a thing as 'primitive thinking', which is to be described via primitive behaviour. RFM 343 discusses the notion of *explaining* language-game (2), and RFM 433 examines the question of whether it incorporates *concepts*. C §§396, 564–6, discuss the applicability of the concept of knowledge to the users of such a proto-language.

1.1   (i) 'the idea of a language more primitive than ours': But the referential conception of meaning is incorrect even for this primitive language. If a pillar breaks, the meaning of a word has not broken, and if all pillars are destroyed, the word 'pillar' does not lack meaning (it can be used when new ones are made). Similarly, the conception of the essence of language is mistaken here too. The words are indeed names, but the essential *use* of the names is *to order*.

     (ii) 'a complete primitive language': not, of course, one that cannot be extended (cf. BrB 77). No language is, as it were, incomplete *from within* — it is what it is. If it provides no means for a certain type of discourse, then so be it. Our language was not incomplete before the introduction of the terminology and notation of chemistry. The fact that an extension of a system of communication is conceivable does not prove that in its unextended form it contains gaps (see also Exg. §18).

2   (i) In all the early occurrences of this example, it is not presented as an imaginary language-game. MS 111 (Vol. VII), 16, observes: 'this game does really occur in reality. Suppose I wanted to build a house from building materials that another would hand to me . . .'. Here the example is not meant to describe an imaginary speech community or primitive language-game, but merely to isolate a fragment of our own activities. This is maintained in BT and MS 114 (Vol. IX) Um., 36, which notes that the game Augustine describes is 'part of language'. It is only in BrB 77 that W. shifts towards an imaginary language-game in an imaginary context.

     (ii) Z §§98ff. discusses thinking in connection with §2. The builders may do their job thoughtfully or thoughtlessly, for thinking is not an inner quasi-verbal accompaniment of external activity.

2.1   (i) 'That philosophical notion of meaning': BT §7, which contains this, has as the section heading 'The notion of meaning [i.e. as designation and object] stems from a primitive philosophy of language'. MS 152, 40, has 'the notion of the "meaning of words" as we attempt to employ it in philosophy', and also 'the philosophical notion of the meaning of words — as the foundation of all languages'.

     (ii) 'is at home': AWL 46 observes that we can criticize Augustine's view of the way he learnt Latin (namely, by learning the names of things) in either of two ways: (a) that it is wrong, or (b) that it describes something simpler. PI §5 explains why W. focuses upon the simpler phenomena.

     (iii) 'more primitive than ours': MS 111, 16 (and BT) say that Augustine describes the game as being simpler than it is. MS 114 (Vol. IX) Um., 36, repeats this and adds, 'But the game that Augustine describes is at any rate part of language'. MS 141, 1, says that one could call Augustine's description incomplete or gappy — akin to describing a forest of deciduous trees, conifers, bushes and ferns as consisting of pines. But it is important that we can think of a language, a system of communication, for which his description *is* appropriate.

(iv)   'a complete primitive language': AWL 46 asserts: 'With language-games such as this there is no standard of completeness, but we may as well say it is complete since we cannot say merely by looking at it that something is lacking. What we are doing is like taking chess and making a simpler game involving simpler operations and a smaller number of pawns.'

SECTION 3

1.1   'Augustine, we might say, does describe a system of communication': what description is alluded to, of learning a language or of the essence of language? The former (see 2.1 below).

2.1   (i)   MS 111 (Vol. VII), 18 (cf. MS 114 Um., 37) follows this with a draft of PI §2(a), and then: '(Someone who describes chess as simpler than it is (with simpler rules) nevertheless describes a game, but a different one.) I originally wanted to say: the way Augustine describes learning a language can show us whence this conception derives. (From which primitive picture, world picture.)' The 'conception' in question is the one spelled out on the previous page, i.e. of language as having its foundations and essence in naming, and of the form of explanation 'This is . . .' as fundamental.

(ii)   'Augustine . . . does describe a system of communication . . .': MS 111, 17, has 'describe a calculus, only not everything we call language is this calculus'. This is later dropped, as the calculus model is rejected.

SECTION 4

1   The analogy parodies Augustine's picture. The misinterpretation of the script fails to distinguish the radically different *functions* of letters (sounds, emphasis, punctuation). So Augustine's picture assimilates the functions of, e.g., 'red', 'run', 'perhaps', 'three', 'here', to that of words like 'cat', 'table', 'tree'.

2   BT 27 (from MS 111 (Vol. VII), 19) interpolates after this the following (paraphrase): Here also belongs: one can speak of combinations of colours and shapes (e.g. of red and blue with square and circular). Here we have the root of my misleading expression (MS 114 Um., 37, has 'the bad expression ('schlechten Ausdruck')): a fact is a complex of objects. One compares a man's being ill with a combination of two things, a man and an illness. We mustn't forget that it is only a simile. (MS 111, 19, has 'we should beware of this

simile', and adds 'Philosophy is rejecting false arguments'). A paragraph later, W. observes that what we call 'meaning' must be connected with primitive gesture-language (ostensive language). If I am arranging guests around a dinner table according to a plan, then it makes sense to point at a person when reading out a name. But if I am comparing a description of a picture with the picture (e.g. of two people kissing), I wouldn't know what to point at as the correlate of kissing. Or, if one person is taller than another, what to point at for 'taller'. At any rate, I cannot point at anything that corresponds to the word in the sense in which I can point at person A in the picture. Of course, there is such a thing as an act of 'directing one's attention to the height of a person' or to his actions, and in this sense one can also collate the kissing and the relation of size. This shows how the general notion of meaning arises. Something analogous to confusing colour with pigment is going on here.[10] And the use of 'collate' is as fluctuating as that of 'meaning'. Words obviously have altogether different functions in a sentence, and these functions are manifest in the rules for the use of the words.

This discussion too makes it clear that W. was thinking of the errors of the *Tractatus* in connection with Augustine's picture.

SECTION 5

1.1   (i) 'the general concept': i.e. the philosophers' concept of the meaning of a word as an object correlated with it.

(ii) 'can clearly survey the purpose and functioning of the words': in the primitive shopping case the different roles of the different kinds of words is evident.

(iii) 'phenomena of language in primitive kinds of application': see 'Explanation', sect. 1, and 'The language-game method', sect. 3.

2   MS 115 (Vol. XI), 80, has an early version beginning: 'The word "meaning", when it is systematically applied, has a dangerous after-taste of the occult. That is why it is good to study the phenomena of language in primitive forms of application of language. In the forms and applications of language as it is used by a child when he starts to talk.'

2.1   'It disperses the fog': BB 17 advocates the study of the language-games of children who are beginning to talk, since it disperses the mental mist that seems to enshroud our ordinary use of language. We see activities and reactions that are clear-cut and transparent. These simple forms of language are not sharply separated from our more complicated ones, and we can build up the more complicated ones by gradually adding new forms. This claim is withdrawn in MS 115, 81, which insists rather that we should just let the language-games

---

[10]   An allusion to Frege, BLA ii §150.

stand as they are, and have a clarifying effect on our problems (cf. PI §130 and Exg.).

II. Explanation
   1. Training, teaching and explaining
   2. Explanation and meaning
   3. Explanation and grammar
   4. Explanation and understanding

SECTION 6

1   §6(a) is connected with the last sentence of §2. Two points are stressed: (i) that the language of §2 can be conceived to be the whole language of a group; (ii) that the use of the four words is integrated into everyday actions and reactions.

§6(b) introduces the primitive correlate of ostensive explanation or definition — 'ostensive teaching of words' ('demonstrative teaching' (BrB 77)). W. applies the distinction between training and explaining. Ostensive teaching is part of the training in the use of words, but does not amount to an explanation, since the child cannot yet ask for the name.

Ostensive teaching is an important part of training — with *human beings*. It could be imagined otherwise. First, were we born with the ability to speak (as opposed to the ability to learn to speak), ostensive teaching of language would not exist (cf. BB 12, 97; PI §495(b)). But ostensive *definition*, as an explanation of the meaning of expressions, would still obtain in so far as giving an appropriate definition would constitute a criterion of understanding, and agreement in definitions (cf. PI §242) could still be established by ostensively explaining what one meant by a word 'W'. Secondly, ostensive teaching involves pointing at objects, thereby directing the child's attention. It is part of our nature to look in the direction of the gesture, and not (like cats) at the gesturing limb (PG 94; PI §185). Were this not so, the instruction would be different. We might go up to the object and tap it, or smell it, etc.; or we might use illustrated tables (cf. PLP 107, in a section entitled 'Must there be ostensive definition in every language?'). Samples can be introduced other than by pointing, and ostensive definition (as W. terms it) of proper names can be replaced by other kinds of explanation (cf. 'Ostensive definition and its ramifications', sect. 2).

Ostensive teaching establishes an association between word and object. But what is the nature of the association? One conception, widespread among philosophers and psychologists, is that hearing the word will, by associative habit, call up a picture of the object in the mind of the hearer. So the training is conceived of as designed to inculcate such an associative habit.

It could be that such associative habits are generated. It could even be that the production of such associations is part of the purpose of an utterance, in which case uttering words *would be* like striking a note on the keyboard of the imagination. But it is not the purpose in the language of §2, which is rather to produce a behavioural response: namely, to bring a slab or a pillar to the builder, or, if one becomes a builder, to learn to utter these words when one wishes one's assistant to bring the correlated object. Bringing a slab, using 'Slab!' in order to get another to bring a slab (as well as naming a slab, cf. §7 below) are the *criteria* for understanding the expression. (So does 'Slab' here mean the same as 'slab' in our language? — see §20.)

The mechanical analogy of §6(d) emphasizes the fact that ostensive teaching *alone* does not bring about understanding. Only in the context of a particular training and circumstances will it be efficacious. There is a parallel to this for ostensive definition and explanation (and the lever analogy is invoked to illuminate a grammatical, not a causal point (cf. §12; PB 59)).

2.1   (i)   'Uttering a word is like striking a note on the keyboard of the imagination': PG 152ff. (MS 114 (Vol. X) Um., 219) elaborates this metaphor. In NB and TLP language was indeed conceived to mediate between thought and the reality which it is about, and communication was pictured as playing on the keyboard of the mind to produce the appropriate 'psychical constituents' of the language of thought.

(ii)   'It may . . . be discovered': It is an empirical question whether the calling up of mental images is involved in the use of language; also whether mental images facilitate the learning of a language or increase the accuracy with which it is applied. The conclusions of such inquiries would be 'hypotheses' about the psychical mechanism underlying the use of language (BB 12).

(iii)   'given the whole mechanism': PB 59 notes that a lever is a lever only in use, i.e. when connected to the mechanism. This is a gloss on Frege's dictum 'A word has a meaning only in the context of a sentence'.

3   It is striking that Coleridge used a similar keyboard image in explaining what poets mean by 'the soul'. The soul, he suggested, is conceived as a 'being inhabiting our body and playing on it like a musician enclosed in an organ whose keys were placed inwards.' *Letters*, i, 278.

III. The language-game method
  1. The emergence of the game analogy
  2. An intermediate phase: comparisons with invented calculi
  3. The emergence of the language-game method
  4. Invented language-games
  5. Natural language-games

Section 7

1   §7(b) introduces the notion of a language-game. The following points
are stressed: 'language-game' refers to the complex consisting of activity and
language-use. The training activity and instruction antecedent to the language-
game of §2 is itself a language-game. The use of language in §2 can be considered a form of initial language-learning.

   Exploiting the classification of the essay 'The language-game method' we
can anatomize the language-game of §2. (i) Ordering (in the building activity) and naming or repeating (in the learning activity) are distinguishable. So
'slab' has a use as a name in the naming activity and as an order in the building activity. (ii) The context of the game: (a) the participants are builder and
assistant, adult and learner; (b) the essential activities are building activities;
(c) the essential objects are the building materials; (d) the goal is making
buildings (not further specified). (iii) The game is to be considered complete.
(iv) The learning and training are described. (v) Other than in teaching, the
use of the elementary expressions of §2 is exclusively imperative.

1.1   (i) 'the practice of the use of language'/'the following process': the contrast
is between the use of language in the actual language-game and its similar
use in training, where no 'moves in the language-game' (other than in the
language-game of teaching itself) are effected.

   (ii) 'beides sprachähnliche Vorgänge': W. altered this to 'both of these
exercises already [being] primitive uses of language' (TS 226$_R$ §10).

   (iii) 'Spiele': 'games' in English is more restricted, see Exg. §66.

   (iv) 'games like ring-a-ring o' roses': W. preferred 'nursery rhymes' (TS
226$_R$ §10).

Section 8

1   The expansion of the language-game of §2 diversifies the parts of speech
of the language by adding (i) primitive numerals, (ii) demonstratives, (iii) colour
samples. Consequently, a primitive syntax can be built up. Thus, 'd-slab-there',
uttered while showing a colour sample, and pointing to a place when saying
'there', is grammatical. But 'slab-pillar-a-b-c-this-there', uttering 'there' without pointing, or showing a colour sample when saying 'there', is nonsense.

   The diversity of parts of speech introduces a further diversity of operations
performed by the speaker, i.e. producing samples and pointing. The amplified
language-game now contains (i) an enlarged vocabulary; (ii) syntactical structure; (iii) novel activities, i.e. matching objects to samples and pointing; (iv)
new instruments, i.e. colour samples, gestures (in BrB 79 numerals are also
called instruments). Consequently, there are new criteria of understanding for
the new parts of speech and resultant sentences.

1.1   (i)   ' "there" and "this" . . . that are used in connection with a pointing gesture': brings out the interpenetration of speech and non-linguistic activity (cf. §7).

(ii)   'samples': see 'Ostensive definition and its ramifications', sect. 4.

2   (i)   BrB 79ff.: what in PI §8 is treated in one stage is treated as a series of extensions, and each stage is discussed in detail. PLP 93f. discusses a series of four language-games. The first is the slab game of §2, and the final one corresponds exactly to the extension here.

SECTION 9

1   Parallel to the novel operations in language-game (8) are novel training techniques. So, memorizing the ordered series of number-words is an essential part of learning to count. Is there a role for ostension here? W. distinguishes two cases: first, where the number of objects can be taken in at a glance, and, second, where counting is necessary. In the first case, ostensive teaching of the number-words is similar to ostensive teaching of the names in language-game (2) in so far as pointing is involved, but unlike it in its being indifferent *which* group of *n* objects is pointed at in teaching a given number-word, although *different* number-words will be taught by pointing to groups of the *same kind* of object (BrB 79). In the second case, however, one does not point at a group of objects, but at each object of a kind successively, each ostension being accompanied by utterance of a number-word (in the appropriate order).

The role of ostension in training in the use of demonstratives again differs, because the ostensive gesture is *itself* part of the demonstrative *use* of 'this' or 'there', and not merely part of teaching their use (cf. BrB 80). When the child learns the use of 'slab', one exercise is to learn to *name* building elements which the teacher points out. But in learning the demonstrative use of 'this' and 'there', he is not learning to name anything. (Cf. Exg. §38 and 'Indexicals'.)

1.1   'Not merely in learning': W. changed this to read 'not merely in teaching' (TS 226$_R$ §12).

2   BrB 79 notes that by introducing numerals an entirely different kind of instrument is introduced into the language. The difference in kind is easier to see in this simple language-game than in ordinary language, with innumerable kinds of words all looking more or less alike in the dictionary.

2.1   (i)   'the first five or six': PLP 105 distinguishes between the categories of 'visual number' and 'inductive number', arguing that ostensive definition of numerals is possible only for the first class.

(ii)   'pointing occurs in the *use*': PLP 95f. notes that 'the gesture of pointing is part of the expression of the command, it is essential to its sense, i.e.

the words of the command without the gesture would be incomplete'. The *words* 'a-slab-there!' do not express the whole sense of A's command to put a slab in a particular place.

SECTION 10

1   The moral of the two language-games is drawn. Augustine claimed that in observing his elders using words, 'he learnt to understand what things they *signified*'. But the question 'What do the words signify?' is answered by describing the kind of use they have, not by citing a kind of entity they name. If descriptions of use are strait-jacketed into the general form 'This word signifies such-and-such', that will create an illusion of uniformity among expressions with wholly different uses. So too one may invoke the general form ' "W" is the word *for* this ☞', i.e. specifying what the word signifies, saying, for example, that 'table' is the word for (signifies) a piece of furniture of *this* kind, that 'red' is the word for (signifies) *this* colour, that 'however' is the word for (signifies?) expressing a contrast between a pair of successive assertions. But this masks profound differences in the logico-grammatical character of diverse expressions — i.e. differences in their use — under a homogenizing form of representation.

   There is, to be sure, *a* use for this canonical form: namely, to distinguish *between* different types of expression, e.g. ' "a", "b", and "c" signify (are words for) numbers not building-blocks', or to distinguish *within* categories, e.g. ' "c" signifies 3 not 4'. But in both kinds of case a general grasp of the use of the type of expression is presupposed, and not explained, by the canonical form.

1.1 'so the expression "This word signifies *that*" would have to become part of our description'; i.e. it would simply be part of the *form* of representation of descriptions of word-use.

2   BrB 82 argues that just as we are tempted by the canonical form 'The word "W" signifies . . .', so too we are tempted by the canonical form ' "W" is the name of a . . .'; e.g. we talk of names of numbers, colours, materials, nations. W. suggests two sources. One is an illusion of uniformity of function — we imagine that the function of every word is more or less like the function of proper names or common nouns. The other, more subtle, stems from noticing the *differences* in function between say 'chair' and 'Jack', both of which are deemed names, and between 'east' and 'Jack', and so noticing the analogy in the lack of analogy, which seemingly warrants conceiving of 'east' as the name of a direction.

SECTION 11

1   The salient point of the tool analogy is diversity of function, despite similarities and interconnections. A screwdriver looks similar to an auger, but one

makes a hole, the other screws a screw into a hole. Both are connected with screws (screws cannot be used without screwdrivers), but their roles are quite different. So too with words (cf. MS 116 (Vol. XII), 217).

(b) connects §11 with §§10 and 12. The uniform spatial or temporal sequence of written or spoken words makes them look alike, and does not make evident the differences in their use. Contrast this uniform appearance of our symbols with the language-game of §8, or the example of §1, where difference between kinds of word (or parts of speech) *is* manifest in their application (cf. BrB 79 in Exg. §9, 2).

1.1   (i)   'Werkzeuge': 'tools'. It is unnatural in English to refer to nails, screws and glue as tools. Not so in German: to classify e.g. glue as belonging to *Werkzeug* (used as a mass-noun) is quite normal. By using the plural, 'Werkzeuge', W. indicates that what is part of your *Werkzeug* is also one of your *Werkzeuge*. He did, however, transfer this German usage to English (LA 1).

(ii)   'the uniform appearance of words': e.g. 'pin' looks like 'pain', 'true' like 'blue', 'and' like 'sand', 'four' like 'for', but in each case the uses are wholly different.

2.1   (i)   'tools in a toolbox': MS 114 (Vol. X) Um., 35, remarks of a similar analogy that the toolbox is grammar and its rules.

(ii)   'uniform appearance of words': AWL 46 remarks that words are brought together in a dictionary, where they look as similar to each other as [various] tools do in a toolbox. But the uses of words can differ from each other as beauty differs from a chair, and can be as incomparable as things we buy, e.g. a sofa and a right to a seat in the theatre. We tend to talk of words and their meanings as if this were comparable to money and the things it buys, rather than to money and its uses. The thing we buy with money is not its use, just as the bearer of a name is not its meaning. MS 156b, 45v, observes that 'A sentence consists of nouns, verbs and adjectives' corresponds to 'All tools are hammers, nails or pliers'.

SECTION 12

1   Words are deceptively uniform in appearance. This is comparable to the handles in a locomotive cabin. They look alike, since they are made to be handled, as words are suited to being spoken or written; but their functions differ profoundly, and they are used differently (one is pushed, another pulled, a third pumped back and forth).

2   (i)   Other favoured analogies for this functional diversity of words are (a) lines on a map, which may indicate rivers, roads, borders, railways, isotherms, contours, etc., despite the fact that they look alike (PG 58); (b) chessmen, which are all similar pieces of carved wood, but have different roles (PG 59).

(ii)   PR 59 invokes the lever analogy (a) to exemplify, as here, the diverse functions of words; (b) to exemplify the contextual dictum that a word has a meaning only in the context of a sentence (a rod is a lever only in use, when connected to the mechanism; cf. PI §6(d)); (c) to illuminate what it is to understand a proposition as a member of a system of propositions.

(iii)   PG 58 juxtaposes this with the following:

A man who reads a sentence in a familiar language experiences the different parts of speech in quite different ways. (Think of the comparison with meaning-bodies.) We quite forget that the written and spoken words 'not', 'table', 'green' are similar to each other. It is only in a foreign language that we see clearly the uniformity of words. (Compare William James on the feelings that correspond to words like 'not', 'but', and so on.)

This latter theme (experiencing the meaning of a word) is deferred in PI. The analogy holds, nevertheless. One might say of the locomotive driver that to him the brake feels different from the pump, the crank, the valve-lever, etc. Not so to the child who clambers up to play. The different experience is an epiphenomenon of the ability to use the levers (words) correctly.

Section 13

1   The assertion 'Every word in the language [i.e. in the language of §8] signifies something', derived from the canonical form 'The word "W" signifies such-and-such' (cf. Exg. §10), is vacuous. No principle of distinction (contrast) is drawn by this statement, unless it is between words of the language of §8 and nonsense words like 'Tra-la-la'. The assertion is not criticized as false. For the words can be put into this strait-jacket: e.g. 'red' signifies a colour, 'three' signifies a number, 'this' signifies whatever one points at.

2   PLP 157 rejects the dictum (taken out of any context) as false, since 'Oh dear!' cannot be put into the canonical form, yet it would be false to say that it is meaningless, or has no significance. It is used as a 'vocal vent'. Similarly, a full stop has a use, but does not signify an object. This reflects W.'s early moves against the calculus model of language (cf. discussion of 'perhaps' and 'Oh!' (PG 64, 66)).

Section 14

1   'All tools serve to modify something' is analogous to 'All words signify something'. Both are altogether uninformative, and involve the imposition of a form of description of uses that serves only to represent differences in use in the guise of uniformities.

1.1   'This assimilation of expressions': the expressions 'knowing a thing's length', 'keeping the temperature of the glue constant', and 'ensuring the solidity of a box' are incorrectly characterized as 'descriptions of ways of modifying something'. We use a ruler to find out the length of a thing — but the function of a ruler is misdescribed as being to modify our knowledge (its function is to measure). Analogously, assimilating the descriptions of the uses of words (§10) by imposing the form of description 'The word "W" signifies such-and-such' serves only to obscure the diversity of uses of words.

SECTION 15

1   'Signify' is used most straightforwardly perhaps when the sign for a thing is actually written on it. We commonly *mark things* with their name, or containers with the name of what they contain.

The introduction, into the primitive language-game, of names of tools that are marked on the tool is envisaged (rather curiously) in §41 as introducing proper names into the game. This new instrument enables the builder to give an instruction to his assistant in a new way: namely, by showing him the mark (compare this with the word 'apple' in §1).

1.1   (i)   'Am direktesten ist das Wort "bezeichnen" vielleicht da angewandt . . .': W. translated 'The expression "the name of an object" is very straightforwardly applied where the name is actually a mark on the object itself' (TS 226$_R$ §19).

(ii)   'in more or less similar ways': this kind of naming is one centre of variation.

2.1   'naming something is like attaching a name tag to a thing': In BB 69 we are to imagine that 'objects' are labelled with names that we use to refer to them. Some of these words would be proper nouns, others would be generic names, others names of colours, shapes, etc. This diversity makes it clear that 'a label would only have a meaning to us in so far as we made a particular use of it'. But one can readily see that the fact that everything is labelled may so impress us that we forget that what gives the words on the labels their meaning is not that they are stuck on objects, but their use.

SECTION 16

1   This discusses the status of the samples in §8. Whenever A issues an order of the type 'd-slab-there', he shows B a colour sample, and B then selects slabs of this colour from the building materials. The samples are used in issuing orders, not to introduce colour-words; indeed, there are no colour-words in this language-game. W. recommends including these samples among the instruments of the language. This is a first step towards undermining the misconception

that ostensive definitions, in explaining expressions by reference to samples, connect language with reality, symbols (signs) with what they symbolize (signify).

In certain respects W.'s proposal is entirely natural. If I send someone a sample when placing an order for cloth of a certain colour, this sample is obviously part of my communication (PR 73). It is a symbol, not something symbolized or described (cf. PLP 109, 277f.). Language-game (8) could be enriched by introducing colour-words explained by reference to samples, and thereafter these words could displace the samples. It would be counter-intuitive to deny that a colour sample is a symbol if it can be replaced by a word without affecting what is communicated. Hence it is natural to call any sample playing a role in communication an instrument of *communication*.

Does this mean that it belongs to the *language* or that it is *an instrument of language*? Of course, colour samples are not words, and words in use are not objects for comparison as samples are. Further, a sample used *ad hoc* for a particular communication is not governed by standing rules. Nevertheless, one might extend the term 'language' to include 'everything that serves the end of expression and communication', hence everything that counts as a sign (PLP 93f., 109). This is apparent in W.'s contrasting language (*Sprache*) with spoken language (*Wortsprache*). Samples are signs used in communication, and are part of the means of representation, not something represented.

W. counters the objection to his extension of 'language' with an analogical argument. We count as a word, and hence as part of a sentence, a *mentioned* word used as a sample sound to be repeated (e.g. 'Pronounce the word "the"'). This argument is not compelling: it shows that a word can function as a sample, but not that something that functions as a vocal sample is therefore a symbol (e.g. 'Say "juwiwallera"'). More compelling is the above consideration that a word can take over the communicative role of a sample. Furthermore, in a more developed language a colour sample, together with a gesture and a 'this colour', can take over the communicative role of a word, as in 'The curtains are *this* ☞ ■ colour'.

1.1   (i)   'Zur Wortsprache gehören sie nicht': W. preferred 'they do not belong to our spoken language' (TS 226$_R$ §20).

(ii)   '((Remark on the reflexive pronoun "*this* sentence"))': The reference is probably to MS 107 (Vol. III), 226f. (PR 207f.; Z §691); but see also MS 124, 66 and MS 163, 31. What connection did W. have in mind? There are two clues: first, the phrase '*this* sentence', which occurs in W.'s discussion of the Cretan Liar Paradox, and secondly, the context, viz. the discussion of samples and of their being counted as instruments of language. This suffices for a reasonable conjecture.

In language-game (8) A uses colour samples to tell B what colour stone to bring. This language-game might be extended by introducing the demonstrative expression 'this ☞ colour', to be used in conjunction with an ostensive gesture at a colour sample, or by introducing colour-words explained ostensively in terms of samples. In the first case, uttering 'this colour', together with a gesture and a sample, takes the place of showing a colour sample in the primitive game. In the second, the colour-words might be said to be *representatives* of the samples (cf. PG 89). To call them 'representatives' implies that they can, at least in certain cases, do the job as well as the principal. Conversely, what is represented must be capable of replacing the representative. And so indeed it is with colour samples (together with 'this ☞ colour') and colour-words.

W. applied the same idea to the phrase 'this sentence'. If correctly used, it must *represent* some sentence; i.e. it must hold the place of a sentence, as a card with 'Mr Jones' written on it represents Mr Jones by holding his place at a dinner table (PLP 312). Therefore, it must be possible to replace this indexical phrase by the sentence that it represents. In some cases, this is unproblematic. 'This sentence contains five words' allows such replacement ('The sentence "This sentence contains five words" contains five words') and expresses a truth, and 'This sentence is written in Gothic script' does too and expresses a falsehood (B i §735). But what about the paradoxical sentence 'This sentence is false'? If it has a meaning, then the phrase 'this sentence' must represent some sentence and hence be replaceable by it. But what sentence? The answer cannot be simply to repeat that it refers to *this* sentence — it must take the form of uttering a complete sentence which will take the place of the phrase '*this* sentence' in 'This sentence is false' (Z §691). This cannot be done, for in this context 'This sentence is false' cannot be substituted once for all for the phrase 'this sentence', since the same question crops up again, viz. what sentence is represented in the new, more complex sentence by the phrase '*this* sentence'. The fundamental error lies in thinking that the phrase 'this sentence' can refer to a sentence without having to represent it. That idea is comparable to the thought that a sample (coupled with a demonstrative) used to explain a colour-word could not take the place of this word in communication.

2.1   (i)   'It is most natural': MS 141, 3 (cf. BrB 84) remarks that it is natural for us to count ostensive gestures as introduced in language-game no. 4 of BrB 80, that accompany the use of 'there' and are part of the practice of communication itself, as belonging to language. But also the pictures in language-game no. 7 (viz. a table with pictures of a table, a chair, a teacup, etc. with written signs opposite them) — these too are linguistic instruments. Samples and words have different functions. One compares things to samples, but not to words (but if a word is employed onomatopoeically, it could be called a sample). This distinction does not point to an ultimate logical duality but only singles out two characteristic kinds of instruments, between which there is no sharp boundary, from the variety of instruments in our language. 'One', 'two', 'three' are called words, ' | ', ' || ', ' ||| ' are called samples; but if a language had the number-words 'one', 'one one', 'one one one', should we call 'one' a word or a sample? The same linguistic element can function here both as word and as sample.

SECTION 17

1   Augustine, in his description of child language-learning, did not speak of
there being different kinds of word (or *parts of speech*, as W. preferred to say
in English), although he was evidently thinking primarily of common nouns
and proper names. In language-game (2) all the words belong to the same part
of speech (BrB 83). Language-game (8) added new kinds of expression. So
here we can distinguish between different parts of speech, such as names of
material objects (building elements), numerals and demonstratives, according
to their function, which is vividly displayed in this simple language-game. For
there are more affinities between the uses of 'slab' and 'block' than between
those of 'slab' and 'd'. But, W. stresses, our classification is purpose-relative,
and also depends on our inclination.

      Elsewhere W. notes that this conception is at odds with 'the simple and
rigid rules which logicians give for the construction of propositions' (BrB 83),
and 'how much less rigid the function of words in a sentence is than logicians
for the most part suppose' (MS 141, 3). Moreover, it is at odds with the standard construction of categories according to the criterion of substitutability *salva
significatione* that was presupposed in the *Tractatus* account of formal concepts
(TLP 4.126–4.128). Categories so constructed are sharp. By contrast, W. now
envisages classifying words by affinity of functions. This will allow the shad-
ing off of one category into another, i.e. non-transitivity of the relation 'belongs
to the same category as'.

1.1   (i) 'verschiedene *Wortarten*': different parts of speech, by contrast with
samples, that are instruments of language, but not parts of *speech*.

      (ii) 'different points of view according to which one can classify tools . . .
or chess pieces': chess pieces: by their powers; the directions of their permitted
movements; their order of value; their size, constitutive material, colour, etc.
(cf. BB 84). The usefulness of a given grouping depends on our purposes and
inclinations (ivory chess pieces are more costly than plastic ones). Tools: PLP
97 notes that tools too have different kinds of similarity, and can be grouped
differently (the hammer with the nails, or with the axe; the axe with the
hammer, or with the chisel, or with the saw; the screwdriver with the screw,
or with the auger).

2   BrB 83 (cf. MS 141, 3) notes that what in one language-game is effected
by word-order (e.g. 'Slab, column, brick') might be effected in another by
ordinals (e.g. 'Second, column; first, slab; third, brick!'). This highlights the
variety of functions of words in propositions. If we classify parts of speech
according to the similarities of the functions of words, it is evident that
many different classifications are possible. One could imagine a reason for
not classifying 'one' together with 'two' and 'three'; e.g. if only one slab is
needed, the builder simply calls out 'Slab', and if more are needed, he uses

number-words 'two', 'three', etc. If he were then introduced to 'one', he might well not classify it together with 'two' and 'three'. Compare this with our reasons for and against classifying '0' among the cardinals, or black and white among colours.

PLP 96ff. comments on 'kinds of words'. The test of substitutability *salva significatione* makes the construction of categories pointless. It has some initial plausibility: e.g. the order 'Put the ξ in the corner!' allocates 'surface of the table' and 'table' to different categories. But this evaporates once we note that it would segregate 'black' from 'green', 'red' and 'white' (e.g. 'The signal light flashed . . .'), and each numeral from every other (e.g. '1' from '2', '3', '4' . . . by reference to 'The playground was divided into . . . parts').

2.1   (i) '*Wortarten*': MS 140, 16f., introduces ostensive definition into the language-game, and notes that it can be disambiguated by the supplement 'This *colour* is called "red"' or 'This *shape* is called "ellipse"'. The words 'colour' and 'shape' here determine the way of applying (*Art der Anwendung*) a word, and so too what one can call 'part of speech' (*Wortart*). One could distinguish within customary grammar between 'shape-words', 'colour-words', 'sound-words', 'stuff-words', etc., but not, in the same sense, between 'metal-words', 'poison-words', 'wild animal-words'. It makes sense to say 'iron is a metal', 'phosphor is a poison', etc., but not 'red is a colour', 'a circle is a shape', etc. [For, according to W.'s conception, the former pair are empirical propositions the negation of which makes sense. But the latter pair are grammatical propositions, expressions of rules for the use of their constituent terms, and their negations are nonsense.]

IV. Descriptions and the uses of sentences
  1. Flying in the face of the facts
  2. Sentences as descriptions of facts: surface-grammatical paraphrase
  3. Sentences as descriptions: depth-grammatical analysis and descriptive contents
  4. Sentences as instruments
  5. Assertions, questions, commands make contact in language

---

SECTION 18

1   W. now moves from investigating types of word to types of sentences, from word-meaning to sentence-meaning. This investigation is not *explicitly* linked with the Augustinian conception, but it is arguably implicitly linked with Augustine's picture of sentences as combinations of names, and the consequent idea that the meanings of names are the objects they stand for.

Why might one be troubled by the fact that the language-games (2) and (8) consist only of orders? The sole reason W. has in mind here is that this seems to show that the languages are incomplete. Language-game (2), which was designed to fit Augustine's description (§1), consists only of orders, and we were told to conceive of it as a complete language. Here the question is opened — and immediately closed. Was our language incomplete before the introduction of the symbolism of chemistry or of the calculus? That a language *can* be extended does not show it to be incomplete prior to its extension. If the possibility of extending a language proved that it was incomplete, there would be no such thing as a language that was not incomplete, and hence the phrase 'incomplete language' would be meaningless.

1.1   'the symbolism of chemistry and the notation of the infinitesimal calculus': Clearly, their invention extended our language. It allowed us to frame such questions as 'What is the valency of the CH_3 group?' or 'What is the derivative of arc sin x?' But this no more shows that our language contained gaps than the fact that it is possible to extend a rook-less form of chess to the usual variety shows that the more primitive game contains gaps. In so far as we are prone to view the unextended language (or game) in its relationship to the extended one, we may be inclined to think that it contains gaps. If the extension is radical (i.e. there is disruption of the previous internal relations), then there are possibilities not permitted in the previous form, but then the disruption of internal relations shows that the language (or game) is simply *different*. And if the extension is conservative, then there is nothing but a further articulation of a pre-existing framework; i.e. antecedent permissions and prohibitions are preserved intact.

2   BT 209 compares the relation of a language consisting only of orders to our actual language with the relation of a primitive arithmetic (e.g. the number system '1', '2', '3', '4', '5', 'many') to our arithmetic (of the natural numbers). Just as that arithmetic is not essentially incomplete, neither is this primitive form of language. The completeness of such a primitive number system is an important point (BT 570f.; PLP 78f.; cf. MS 108 (Vol. IV), 152): there are no gaps in such a system waiting to be filled by extending it to include all the natural numbers. Similarly, the natural numbers do not contain gaps to be filled by the rationals, nor the rationals gaps to be filled by the reals, etc. Rather, there are, as it were, no gaps until they are already filled.[11] W.'s view here contrasts with Frege's (cf. BT 570).

3   The contention that a language could consist only of orders is a radical one relative to twentieth-century philosophical accounts of meaning that assign a pivotal role to the concept of truth and the notion of truth-conditions (or

---

[11]   See F. Waismann, *Introduction to Mathematical Thinking* (Hafner, London, 1951), pp. 45–7, 61.

assertion-conditions). For the notion of truth (*a fortiori* assertion-conditions) attaches paradigmatically to the declarative sentence (or, more accurately, to what is said by using it). If the meaning of a word is conceived as its contribution to the truth-conditions (or assertion-conditions) of the sentences in which it occurs, then primacy must be attached to the declarative sentence, and the meaning of imperative sentences must be accounted for in terms derivative from the meaning of declaratives (see 'Descriptions and the uses of sentences'[12]).

SECTION 19

1   §19(a) continues the argument of §18. The imaginary language-games (2) and (8) consisted only of orders. But, W. claims, that is no objection. It is easy to imagine a language consisting only of orders and reports in battle; or only of sentence-questions and yes/no answers; etc. Imagining such languages requires imagining different forms of life — different ways of living, different human relationships, actions, reactions and interactions. A language-game, such as giving orders and obeying them, is part of a form of life (§23).

W. is arguably too hasty here. Is it really possible to imagine a society, and a form of life, sufficiently well organized to engage in battle and to give orders and reports in battle — *and to have no other uses for words*? How would this language be taught to children? How are we to envisage a use for orders or reports in battle, but no use for the same forms of words outside a battle?

§19(b) opens a new argument, that continues through the sequel. Is the call 'Slab!' in §2 a word or a sentence? Why is the question raised? One reason might be linked to Augustine's picture of language: words are names, and sentences are combinations of names. 'Slab' *is* the name of a building-stone, but 'Slab!' is *not* a combination of names. But W. nowhere mentions this as the motive for this new line of investigation. BrB 77f. introduces this question explicitly as an objection: namely, that 'Slab!' in language-game (2) does not have the same meaning as in our language. And if that amounts only to pointing out that the word, in our language, has other uses than this, then that is correct. But the point of investigating the objection is to show that a question about what an expression means and whether it means the same as another expression is not determined by the state of mind of the speaker, i.e. by his meaning, (mis)conceived as a state of mind, or by what 'is present in his mind' when he utters the sign. To be sure, this too links up with one strand in Augustine's description and conception (see Exg. §1) — according to which

---

[12]   For comprehensive critical discussion of the idea that every sentence, no matter what its discourse type (assertoric, interrogative or imperative) contains, on analysis, a truth-value-bearing sentence-radical, see G. P. Baker and P. M. S. Hacker, *Language, Sense, and Nonsense* (Blackwell, Oxford, 1984), chs 2–3.

what a name means is what the speaker means by it. So, if 'Slab!' is uttered
as a call for a slab, then, according to the Augustinian conception, what makes
it into the order that the hearer bring the speaker a slab is that the speaker
means this by his utterance, i.e. that by 'Slab!' he means 'Bring me a slab!'

W.'s response to the opening question is that 'Slab!' can be deemed to be
a word and also be deemed to be a (degenerate) sentence. It is equivalent to
our elliptical sentence 'Slab!' (since it has the same function in language-game
(2) as 'Bring me a slab!' would have in the corresponding fragment of our language). The interlocutor objects to the equivalence on the grounds that our
elliptical sentence is an abbreviated form of 'Bring me a slab!', and there is no
such possibility of expression in language-game (2). W. counters: why should
one not think of 'Bring me a slab!' as an expansion of 'Slab!'? This forces the
interlocutor to bring up the pivotal issue: if one shouts 'Slab!', one really *means*
'Bring me a slab!' — it is how the speaker means (*meint*) his words that determines what they mean (*bedeuten*).

This conception is the target of the rapid sequence of five questions. It is
the first question that provides the implicit key to the matter: viz. how do
you do it, how do you mean this, when you say 'Slab'? For it seems as if
meaning something is a mental act, activity or state — and this is a misconception that W. later assails. Here the 'liberating word' is W.'s question in response
to the interlocutor's final move. For the interlocutor insists that the reason he
takes 'Slab!' in our language to be an abbreviation of the imperative sentence
'Bring me a slab!' is that when he utters 'Slab!', what he wants is *that the assistant should bring him a slab*. The specification of the speaker's purpose is an
indirect report of an imperative sentence. So surely it follows that 'Slab!' is an
elliptical (abbreviated) sentence — and hence that 'Slab!' in language-game (2)
cannot have the same meaning as our utterance 'Slab!', since there is no such
sentence to abbreviate in that language-game? W.'s response is to query what
'wanting this' is supposed to consist in. Does it consist in *thinking* a different
sentence from the sentence one utters while one utters it? (The conception of
speaking with understanding as speaking accompanied by an inner process of
thinking is criticized in PI §§316–62; for discussion of W.'s criticisms of the
'dual-process' conception, see Volume 3, 'Thinking: the soul of language'.)

1.1   (i) 'Lebensform'/'a form of life': this expression occurs in PI §§19, 23,
        241, pp. 174 (148), 226 (192). There are few other occurrences (see 2.1 below),
        and the *Nachlass* adds nothing further. A form of life is a way of living, a
        pattern of activities, actions, interactions and feelings which are inextricably
        interwoven with, and partly constituted by, uses of language. It rests upon very
        general pervasive facts of nature. It includes shared natural and linguistic responses,
        broad agreement in definitions and judgements, and corresponding behaviour.
        The term is sometimes used so that it converges on the idea of a culture; else-
        where it converges on a more biological notion (see Volume 2, 'Agreement
        in definitions, judgements and forms of life', sect. 3).

(ii)   'a degenerate sentence': i.e. a limiting case, as a straight line is a limiting case of a hyperbola or a point a degenerate conic section.

2   BT 201–5 (cf. PLP 285–8) discusses the notion of an elliptical sentence (and the distinction between meaning it as one word or as three). W. introduces a language-game in which the expressions 'Light' and 'Dark' are taught in connection with turning an electric light on and off, and are then used to say that there is light in the room, or to express the wish that there be light in the room. One could say that 'Light' and 'Dark' are meant here as sentences. But what makes an utterance a statement or a wish is not an accompanying process of meaning. The discussion then shifts focus in order to criticize the *Tractatus* conception of a proposition's 'agreeing with reality' (irrespective of whether it is true or false) in virtue of isomorphism — and to repudiate the requirement of logical multiplicity on the atomic proposition. For that notion of isomorphism (the 'harmony between language and reality') demanded a logical multiplicity missing from a one-word sentence. However, agreement with reality does not consist in the proposition and reality having identical multiplicity, but in the explanation (in language) that 'This is (is called) "Light"' (turning the light on when uttering 'This'). What seemed in the *Tractatus* to be an ineffable ('metalogical') relationship of agreement between language and reality is now seen to be an intra-linguistic grammatical relationship. More generally, 'agreement' (*Übereinstimmen*) is an everyday expression with diverse, but unproblematic, uses.

2.1   'Form of life': W. also employed the phrase 'Form des Lebens' (MS 115 (Vol. XI), 239), and once chose as an alternative 'Lebensgepflogenheiten' (customs of life) (MS 137, 59(a)). BrB 134 observes that to imagine a language is to imagine a culture. See also PO 396, C §358.

SECTION 20

1   §19(b) suggested that the sentence 'Bring me a slab!' might be considered a lengthening of 'Slab!' If so, one might retort (§20(a)), someone who says 'Bring me a slab!' must be able to mean this whole sentence as *one* word corresponding to 'Slab!' The rest of §20(a) consists of W.'s handling of a series of questions that grow out of this objection. The point is to establish that the contrast between a person's meaning 'Bring me a slab!' as four words and his meaning it as one word need not consist in anything present in his mind when he utters the sentence. Instead, what is required is his mastery of a language in which this sentence can be used in contrast with other sentences consisting partly or wholly of the same words. Our sentence 'Slab!' is elliptical, not because it abbreviates a 'mental utterance' of 'Bring me a slab!', but because our language contains the possibility of contrasting the sentences 'Bring me a

slab!', 'Take away a slab!', 'Bring him a slab!', etc., each of which might, in certain circumstances, be shortened to 'Slab!'

§20(b) canvasses an objection: if 'Slab!' in §2 is synonymous with our sentence 'Slab!', and hence too with our sentence 'Bring me a slab!', then it must be possible to specify what the sense is that each of these sentences has, which will show these two sentences to have the same sense. W.'s reply is that the identity of sense of the two sentences consists in the identity of their *use*.

1.1   (i) 'he could mean this expression as one long word': here 'mean' amounts to 'intend', unlike 'By "p" I meant "r" ' or 'By "p" I meant that r'. It is unclear in what sense, if any, one can *intend* four words to be or be understood as one (long) word.

(ii) 'Freilich, du *beherrschst* diese Sprache'/'ist dieses Beherrschen': W. amended Rhees's translation to read 'know this language'/'is this knowing' (TS 226$_R$ §24).

(iii) 'geht ihnen die Kopula im Sinn ab, oder *denken* sie sich die Kopula dazu': W. translated 'don't they get the full meaning, as they leave out the copula? or do they *think* it to themselves without pronouncing it?' (TS 226$_R$ §25).

2.1   (i) 'Not because it leaves out something that we think': BrB 78 puts matters thus: 'all that is really relevant is that these contrasts should exist in the system of language he is using, and that they need not in any sense be present in his mind when he utters the sentence'. And it draws the moral: our original question about the meaning of 'Slab!' appeared initially to be about the speaker's putative state of mind of meaning his words, but the idea of meaning we arrive at in the end is not that of a state of mind.

(ii) 'In Russian . . .': MS 110 (Vol. VI), 188, notes that the Russians say 'He good' rather than 'He is good' — but nothing is lost, and they don't add the verb in thought.

SECTION 21

1   W. now turns to language-games admitting contrasting uses of sentences. If language-game (8) is extended to include reports on the numbers, colours and shapes of building-stones, what would distinguish the report or assertion 'Five slabs' from the order 'Five slabs!'?

The answer canvassed is that the difference lies in the tone of voice and facial expression (for, after all, the words are the same). But such differences are not *necessary* — the difference may lie only in what is done with the words. W. does not further clarify this, although it calls out for further elucidation. The implication is that the difference between the report and the order in this primitive language-game is evident from the context, the antecedent and subsequent behaviour of the speakers. It is unclear, however, what W.'s commitments are with respect to our developed language.

The parenthesis canvasses a possibility: we might use 'assertion' and 'order' merely to indicate grammatical forms (i.e. declarative and imperative sentences) and intonations, just as we speak of rhetorical *questions*, which are in effect assertions. Furthermore, a language is imaginable in which all assertions had the form and intonation contour of rhetorical questions, or all orders were couched in the form of the question 'Would you like to . . .?' But this does not mean that all that speakers of this language ever do with words is ask questions.

One might grant this, yet insist, for all that, that our sentential forms indicate the *standard* discourse function: interrogatives to invite an answer to a question, declaratives to say how things are, and imperatives to express a desire. That is compatible with deviations of the kind W. notes. The use of the negative interrogative as a rhetorical question, i.e. implicit assertion, is not arbitrary. 'Isn't the weather glorious today?' is not a request for information, the answer being too obvious. Nor is it simply an interrogative form that is used assertorically; rather, it utilizes the interrogative form to indicate the speaker's judgement and to invite corresponding assent. Similarly, one could use the form of words 'Would you like to . . . ?' (Or 'Would you mind . . . ?') as a standard form for ordering. But it is no coincidence that it is a *polite* form of ordering or requesting, that it *formally* offers the addressee an opportunity to divulge his wishes — unlike the more peremptory imperative form of ordering. The connection between sentential form and standard function is not undermined by these kinds of case.[13] Nevertheless, W.'s emphasis on function as opposed to form (on not classifying clouds by their shape, as it were) is of the greatest importance.

1.1   'Verwendung': W. changed this in translation to 'what is done with the words "five slabs"'.

2   (i)   BT 201ff. (cf. Exg. §19), in describing the language-game in which 'Light' can be used either to express a desire for light or to report that there is light in a particular room, raises the question whether the difference consists in what is meant in the two cases. Does meaning something consist in particular mental processes that accompany the utterance, or in a pattern of behaviour in which the utterance is embedded? If I say 'Light' and somebody asks what I meant, I might reply, 'I meant you to turn on the light'. But my having meant this does not consist in my having had a particular picture in mind when I said 'Light', or in my having said to myself another sentence such as 'Turn on the light'. That would give a narrow, distorted account of the variety of cases in which it is correct to say 'I meant . . .'. For meaning something is neither an act nor an activity of the mind.

[13]   See B. Rundle, *Wittgenstein and Contemporary Philosophy of Language* (Blackwell, Oxford, 1990), ch. 5.

Section 22

1   Together with the following boxed remark (p. 11n.), this criticizes Frege's
account of assertion. He held that a declarative sentence used to make an assertion, the same sentence occurring in a conditional, and the corresponding
sentence-question have a common content — a thought. This is what is asserted
in an assertion, occurs unasserted in a conditional and is queried in a question.
    Background: Frege's analysis, despite various changes, was guided by three
fundamental ideas.
    (i)   A declarative sentence expresses (has as its sense) a thought. A thought
is objective, exists independently of being apprehended, and is the bearer of
truth-values. It is what is grasped when an utterance of a declarative sentence
is understood and what is believed when various people believe the same thing.
As objects, thoughts can be named — the expression 'the thought that *p*' names
a particular thought which is its meaning (*Bedeutung*) (SM 37 (166)). But such
a name does not itself express a thought. Only a sentence has a thought as its
sense (T 61 (354)).
    (ii)   It is possible to entertain a thought without judging it to be true — as
when we raise a question (N 145 (374f.)) or entertain a hypothesis — and to
express a thought without asserting it — as when we express a mere supposition (FC 21 (149)). A judgement is the acknowledgement of the truth of a
thought. An assertion is the externalization of an inner act of judging to be
true (NS 150, 214 (PW 138f., 198)). It is a defect of natural language that it
fails clearly to mark assertoric uses of expressions. For the very same declarative sentence can occur on its own as an assertion, and also within the scope
of a negation (e.g. 'It is not the case that . . .') or as the antecedent of a
conditional *without being asserted*. There is no distinct symbol to signal that
a sentence is being used to make an assertion, whose absence would then
signal that it is being used merely to express a thought (NS 201 (PW 185)).
    (iii)   In natural language, Frege held, the assertoric force is carried by the
assertoric form of the sentence, is bound up with its indicative mood (NS 214
(PW 198)),[14] and especially well marked in the predicate (T 62f. (355f.);
SM 34 (163f.); N 152 (382f.)). Since Frege's function-theoretic concept-script
was constructed to replace the subject/predicate form of natural language (and
to exclude the defects and limitations of traditional subject/predicate logic),
he believed he had to provide an alternative and indeed improved way of
symbolizing assertoric force in his notation.
    Frege's assertion-sign: An assertion in Frege's symbolism is expressed by
prefixing the assertion-sign '⊢' to an expression for the content of a possible
assertion. The articulation of the symbolism conforms to Frege's analysis of
assertion. The expression for the assertion that 2 plus 3 is 5 (i.e. '⊢ $2 + 3 = 5$')

---

[14]   Mood, strictly speaking, is a feature of the verb, not of the sentence. The indicative mood is
common to declarative and interrogative sentences.

subdivides into the assertion-sign '⊢' and the rest ('− 2 + 3 = 5', i.e. the 'horizontal' and '2 + 3 = 5'). Prefixing the horizontal to the expression '2 + 3 = 5' converts the expression of a thought (viz. the thought that 2 + 3 = 5) that supposedly is *also* the name of a truth-value into an unasserted sentence the closest equivalent of which in natural language is '2 + 3 = 5 is the True'. Adding the assertion-sign converts this expression of a thought into an assertion. The assertion-sign itself has neither sense nor meaning (*Bedeutung*), rather it 'contains the act of assertion' (BLA i §5). It signals the performance of the interior act of judging to be true the thought whose expression it precedes.

Frege's 'horizontal' or 'content-stroke': the horizontal is always used to precede the content of an assertion. '− ξ' stands for a function whose value is always a truth-value. If its argument-expression designates the True, its value is the True; otherwise, its value is the False. So the horizontal in effect amounts to the formal predicate 'is the True'. But the resultant expression '−p' cannot by itself be used to make an assertion. It still merely designates a truth-value. '⊢ p', on the other hand, 'does not designate anything; it asserts something' (FC 22n. (149n.)).

W.'s criticisms: §22(a) criticizes Frege's claim that every assertion *contains* an assumption, the assumption being 'the thing asserted'. If this were so, then analysis of the sentence used to make an assertion should yield a part which expresses the assumption and another part which effects the act of assertion. We can indeed effect such a transformation by rewriting every statement in the form 'It is asserted that *p*' (or 'It is the case that *p*'). 'It is asserted' expresses the act of asserting, 'that *p*' expresses the assumption. One might link this to Frege's notation thus:

$$\text{It is asserted} \qquad \text{that } p$$
$$\vdash \qquad\qquad -p$$

The noun clause 'that *p*' which, in this transformation, is (or signifies) 'the thing asserted' is appropriately thought of as a sentence-radical (b.r.f. §22 (p. 11n.)), i.e. something which may be part of a sentence used to make an assertion ('It is the case that *p*') or part of a sentence used to ask a question ('Is it the case that *p*?'), but which cannot *by itself* be so used.

It now seems puzzling that W.'s riposte is that this noun clause is not a sentence, not something that can be used to make a move in the language-game. For surely the purpose of explicitly segregating an expression of the assumption was precisely to produce an expression which cannot by itself be used to make a move in the language-game? W.'s point is that whatever form of words is chosen as an expression of the assumption *must also remain a sentence*, for it is, according to Frege, the expression of a thought (hence not a noun clause). The two statements '*p*' and 'If *p* then *q*' contain the same sentence '*p*', once asserted and once unasserted. Hence we cannot replace the antecedent of the conditional by a noun clause, precisely because a noun clause is not a sentence. Any attempt to represent Frege's claim that every assertion contains an assumption by transformations permissible in language is thus subject to contradictory demands. For the linguistic expression of the contained assumption must both be, and not be, a sentence. The fact is that what we conceive as a declarative sentence is something that *can be* used to make an assertion, but *need not* be so used.

If we relinquish the noun clause as an expression of the assumption and adopt the transformation 'It is asserted: such-and-such is the case' as a form appropriate for making assertions, it is obvious that the prefix 'It is asserted' is superfluous. For the form 'Such-and-such is the case', being a sentence, is already fully fit for making assertions. If a token-sentence '*p*' is not used to make an assertion (but e.g. occurs as the antecedent of a conditional), prefixing 'It is asserted' to it will not make it so used; if it is used to make an assertion, such a prefix will make no difference.

Frege would object. First, 'that *p*' is not an expression of the thought expressed by '—*p*'. On the contrary, it names (i.e. has as its meaning (*Bedeutung*)) that thought. Equally, 'It is asserted' at best describes the act performed by prefixing '⊢' to '—*p*'. Consequently, there is no correct translation of '⊢ *p*' into natural language, and no expression synonymous with either of its two constituents '⊢' and '—*p*'. 'It is asserted that *p*' is but a rough approximation. More accurately, it is a *report* in *oratio obliqua* of what is effected by '⊢ *p*' (BLA i §5). Secondly, this untranslatability merely reveals the defectiveness of ordinary language.

This defence against W.'s criticism assumes that Frege's notation for assertion is intelligible. Frege's explanation of the horizontal presupposes an understanding of what constitutes a sentence, but distorts the concept of a sentence. His characterization of expressions of thoughts as names of truth-values and his stipulation that '—*p*' cannot be used by itself to make an assertion both reflect and support a misrepresentation of sentences. The incoherence in Frege's conception of a sentence can be highlighted by bringing together two aspects of the grammar of 'sentence'. First, *only* a sentence is the expression of a thought. Secondly, any sentence (expressing a thought) can be used by itself to make an assertion. Frege's explanation of the horizontal is inconsistent with at least one of these. If '*p*' is a sentence with a truth-value, then '—*p*' is the expression of a thought; hence, it must *be* a sentence; consequently, it must be capable of being used by itself to make an assertion. Conversely, if '—*p*' cannot be used to make an assertion, it cannot be a sentence; therefore, if it does express a thought, the thesis that only sentences express thoughts must be false. Finally, dropping the stipulation that '—*p*' cannot be used to make an assertion would render both the horizontal and the assertion-sign superfluous, since '—*p*' would just be an idiosyncratic way of writing '*p*' and could be used without the prefix '⊢' to make an assertion. The criticism of §22(a) applies no less to Frege's own notation than to any putative translation of it into natural language.

Not surprisingly, Frege's correlative expression of the assertion-sign is equally defective. His claims that '⊢' contains the act of assertion and that '⊢ p' asserts something are confused. A sign *is not itself* a use; it must *be used*. The inscription '⊢ p' does not *contain* the act of assertion, and it can only be said to assert something if it is used to assert something. If one writes '⊢ 5 > 4' on a blackboard as an example of a proposition of *Begriffsschrift*, one has not thereby asserted that 5 is greater than 4.

§22(b) reduces the idea that every assertion really contains a that-clause conveying its content to absurdity. Since every asserted sentence '*p*' can be rewritten in the form 'Is it the case that *p*? Yes', we could with equal cogency conclude that every asserted sentence contains a question. Indeed, we could mimic the schema

$$\begin{array}{ll} \text{It is asserted} & \text{that } p \\ \vdash & \textit{assumption (Annahme)} \end{array}$$

with the parallel schema

$$\begin{array}{ll} \text{Is it the case that } p? & \text{Yes.} \\ \textit{question} & \vdash \end{array}$$

§22(c) notes that we can introduce the symbol '⊢' into a sentence as a punctuation mark, parallel to a question-mark, to indicate the use of the sentence to make an assertion rather than to ask a question. This sign would correspond to familiar marks of discourse function (e.g. punctuation marks, intonation contours, word-order and moods of verbs). There is a mistake only if one further thinks, as Frege did, that asserting (or perhaps, better, judging) consists of two actions: entertaining a thought and assigning it a truth-value (which pair of actions must be reflected in a perspicuous symbolism for assertion). According to Frege's account, the act of assertion is the externalization of the interior act of judgement. The symbol '—p', considered merely as the expression of a thought, corresponds to the act of entertaining the thought that *p*, and '⊢' corresponds to assigning a truth-value, i.e. judging it to be true. W.'s response is compact. Frege supposes that in performing these acts, we follow the propositional sign, i.e. the unasserted proposition, as we sing from a musical score, and then, in addition, we may perform the act of judging it to be true and perhaps exteriorize this act in an assertion. One might indeed compare *reading* a sentence to singing from a musical score. But one cannot compare reading a sentence and *meaning* it (i.e. reading it aloud as an expression of what one takes to be so) to singing from a score *plus* an interior act.

§22(d) notes that Frege's assertion-sign is in effect a form of punctuation marking the beginning of a sentence and distinguishing a whole period from a subordinate clause within it. This is not a criticism of Frege (MS 109 (Vol. VI), 199; MS 115 (Vol. XI), 87). Nor is the idea original with W. — Russell noted this too (PM 8). The comparison with punctuation is illuminating: we could describe '⊢' as having the same use as the full stop at the end of a preceding sentence or the capital letter at the beginning of the sentence (MS 109 (Vol. VI), 199). (A parallel with the punctuation '⊢ . . . .' for declarative sentences would be the pattern of punctuation for questions in Spanish: '¿ . . . ?'.) In general, declarative sentences are punctuated with full stops and are typically used to assert, while interrogative sentences are punctuated with question-marks and are typically used to question. Comparing '⊢' with punctuation marks, how-ever, gives only a partial account of its grammar. It leaves open many questions: e.g. whether the translation into Frege's concept-script of a declarative sentence used by a fictional character in *The Brothers Karamazov* to make an assertion should be prefixed with '⊢' (MS 113 (Vol. IX), 48v–49r).

1.1   (i)   'Annahme': W. signified dissatisfaction with Rhees's translation 'sup-posal' and restored Frege's German term in TS 226$_R$ §27 (for discussion of Frege's use of 'Annahme', see exegesis of the boxed remark following §22 (previously *Randbemerkung* on p. 11)).

        (ii) 'to distinguish an assertion from a fiction or supposition': it is doubtful whether there could be a 'fiction-operator' or whether the assertion–sign could be dropped from fiction; and suppositions are expressed by incomplete sentences.

2   (i)   MS 113 (Vol. IX), 48r–49r (cf. BT 206–9) compares assertion/assump-tion with chess move/illustrating a chess move in a discussion. One cannot utter a sentence '*p*' as an assumption or supposition without a sequel, i.e. 'Assuming that p, then . . .' and 'Suppose it were the case that *p*' are incomplete sentences.

        W. further observes that Frege conceived of the 'assumption' as what the assertion that *p* and the question whether *p* have in common. But instead of 'Is it the case that *p*?', one can say 'I would like to know whether *p*' — and how is this question to be handled?

        On p. 50r W. queries whether the Fregean assumption that *p* would not have to be identical with the assumption that not-*p*, just as the question 'Is it the case that *p*?' is the same as 'Isn't it the case that *p*?' It is senseless to say (as Frege was committed to saying) that a question is either true or false, or to attach a negation sign to it, or to say that it agrees or disagrees with reality.

        Then follows a draft of §22(c), in which performing the putative acts of entertaining and asserting conceived as following the propositional sign is com-pared with playing the piano from a score. One can compare reading loudly or quietly from a written text with playing the piano from a score, but not what we call thinking [i.e. expressing what we think by an utterance]. If there were, for example, an assertion-sign in the written text, then one would read it with an assertion-*sign* (e.g. in one's tone or emphasis), but not as if the assertion-sign were present in the sentence, and the meaning or thinking the sentence were in thought. (Cf. MS 113, 86f.: the signs in a sentence are not signals of a psychical 'mental' activity of meaning.)

(ii)   RFM 116 observes:

The great majority of sentences that we speak, write and read are assertoric sentences (*Behauptungssätze*) . . . these sentences are true or false. Or . . . the game of truth-functions is played with them. For assertion is not something that gets added to the proposition, but an essential feature of the game we play with it. Comparable, say, to the characteristic of chess by which there is winning and losing in it . . .

Asserting something does not contain two separable acts: entertaining a proposition and asserting it. If such a decomposition were possible, then there would be only an external relation between propositions and assertions; propositions could be characterized independently of assertions, and it would just happen that we assert only propositions (and not e.g. WH-questions). The analogy with chess is meant to stress that the connection is internal. Just as we cannot characterize such a game without specifying what counts as winning in it, so we cannot characterize propositions (what are true and false, what we play the game of truth-functions with) independently of assertion. An assertion no more consists in an assumption and the asserting of it than a command consists in a proposal and the commanding of it.

(iii)   MS 116 (Vol. XII), 321, notes that it is possible to utter an assertoric sentence (e.g. 'It is raining') without making an assertion, e.g. in reading a poem. Whether or not the utterance is an assertion depends on the 'circumstances (the spatial and temporal setting)' in which it is spoken (not on whether the speaker performs certain mental acts accompanying its utterance).

2.1   (i)   'Ungefähr wie wir nach Noten singen': W. frequently employs the analogy of singing from sheet music to illustrate what he means by 'accompaniment' in arguments demonstrating that meaning something by an utterance is not a psychic accompaniment of saying something (BB 35, 42; PG 130).

Imagine people who *sing* all sentences (assertions, questions, etc.) when they *mean* them, and are not only practising their pronunciation, or such-like.

Of the sung sentence they say 'it is alive', of the unsung one, 'it is dead'.

If these men philosophized about the concept of meaning something, they would be inclined to say: 'meaning something' means 'singing (it)'. (MS 116 (Vol. XII), 316)

(ii)   'It distinguishes the whole period . . .': MS 115, 86f. (and hence MS 142, §23) continues thus: 'This is important. For our philosophical difficulties concerning the nature of "negation" and "thinking" in a sense are due to the fact that we don't realize that an assertion "⊢ not p" or "⊢ I believe p", and the assertion "⊢ p" have "p" in common, but not "⊢ p" ' (W.'s corrected translation, TS 226$_R$ §29; see Z §684).

3   Though he derived the idea and the symbolism from Frege, Russell's explanation of the assertion-sign differed somewhat from Frege's:

The sign '⊢' . . . means that what follows is asserted. It is required for distinguishing a complete proposition, which we assert, from any subordinate propositions contained in it but not asserted. In ordinary written language a sentence contained between full stops denotes an asserted proposition . . . The sign '⊢' prefixed to a proposition serves this same purpose in our symbolism. (PM 8)

Russell thus introduces '⊢' as a punctuation mark, and he notes its importance by using it to explain what it is to make an inference by *modus ponens* (PM 8). Later he correlated his use of the assertion-sign with an analysis of assertion identical with that criticized in PI §22(a)–(b):

Any proposition may be either asserted or merely considered. . . . In language, we indicate when a proposition is merely considered by '*if* so-and-so' or '*that* so-and-so' or merely by inverted commas. In symbols, if p is a proposition, p by itself will stand for the unasserted proposition, while the asserted proposition will be designated by '⊢.p.'. The sign '⊢' . . . may be read 'it is true that' (although philosophically this is not exactly what it means). (PM 92)

This contains echoes of Frege's account; it puts forward that-clauses as the proper expression for the content of assertions; and it intimates the reasoning underlying the claim that a proposition (i.e. an unasserted proposition) is an incomplete symbol, completed only by the *act* of judgement (PM 44).

Boxed Remark Following §22 (p. 11n.)

1   This remark, immediately derived from B i §432, was inserted into TS 227(a) and (b) as a handwritten slip in another hand, on which there is a note 'Insertion at the end of §22'. None of the earlier versions of this remark contains the last sentence. It was presumably added by W. when he inserted the slip into the (now lost) top copy of the typescript, elaborating Frege's notion of *Annahme*.

The earlier versions of this remark (MS 113 (Vol. IX), 29r; MS 115 (Vol. XI), 58f. (and the derived TSS versions)) and the correlative introduction of the term 'Satzradikal' occur in a different argumentative context: namely, the discussion of what a rule is and how the formulation of a rule differs from a factual proposition (cf. PLP 144). In each case, the discussion of proposition-radicals is separate from the discussion of the distinction between using sentences to make assertions, ask questions, formulate suppositions, etc. The point of the argument is to deny that the formulation of a rule (e.g. the chess rule: 'Each queen stands on its own colour (in the initial position)') is, as it stands, an assertion of fact. But this sentence forms a nucleus for constructing sentences that are factual propositions: e.g. 'In chess each queen stands on its own colour' or 'The rule that each queen stands on its own colour was not observed in Norway until 1459'. It is this that W. meant to highlight by the analogy with the picture of the boxer. In isolation a picture *says* nothing; it makes no assertion. But it can be used to make a variety of assertions when combined with other signs. A rule-formulation is similar: it has no use by itself as an assertion, but may be a part of sentences that do have such a use. This parallel between the picture of the boxer and the rule-formulation is captured in the simile of a radical in chemistry. A sentence-radical cannot be used by itself to make an assertion, but can be part of sentences used to make assertions.

The final sentence gives this old remark a new application: namely, to elucidate one aspect of Frege's conception of the 'assumption' (the thought, the content of an assertion). It is crucial to the rationale of his concept-script that the proper expression of a thought (e.g. '— 2 + 3 = 5') *cannot* be used by itself to make an assertion (see Exg. §22). Consequently, it is an essential part of Frege's conception of assertion that the correct expression of a thought be a sentence-radical, not a sentence. The purpose of this boxed remark is merely to emphasize this point, since it is what is criticized in §22(a).

It would be mistaken to associate this afterthought about Frege's *Annahme* with approval of philosophical attempts to construe sentences as decomposable into a mood-operator (or force-indicator) and content-phrase. The analysis of sentence-meaning by means of mood-operators ('⊢', '!', '?') and 'sentence-radicals' takes as its model Frege's isolation of the unasserted thought as the common content of an assertion and its corresponding sentence-question. But this is precisely what W. repudiated in §22.

That by itself a picture says nothing, though it can be used together with other signs to make assertions, has a parallel in illustrations of stories (cf. PI §663). What the illustration is an illustration of is determined by the story, not vice versa.

1.1   (i) '(chemisch gesprochen) ein Satzradikal nennen': what W. understood by 'Radikal' ('radical') in chemistry is what is now expressed by the term 'Gruppe' ('group'). These are certain combinations of elements that recur as constituents of more complex compounds although they have no independent existence, e.g. the ethyl group C_2H_5 and the hydroxyl group OH combine together to form ethyl alcohol $C_2H_5(OH)$. So 'a sentence-radical' must be a combination of elements recurring as a constituent of sentences though not itself a sentence. This fits rule-formulations. They are not characterizable as 'true' or 'false', they do not express propositions, and cannot be used to make assertions. This would not be true of typical declarative sentences (descriptions). They do express propositions and may be used to make assertions when uttered in isolation. Therefore, the thesis that the content of every assertion is expressed by a proposition-radical requires that the expression of its content be something other than a declarative sentence, e.g. a sentence-question or a that-clause. This is the thesis discredited in §22(a)–(b).

(ii) 'Annahme': In published writings, Frege only once (FC 21f. (149f.)) used the term 'Annahme' in connection with what he initially called 'the content of judgement' and later 'the thought'. However, W. does stick close to Frege's account. His explanation of *Annahme* as what is common to an assertion and the corresponding sentence-question conforms exactly to Frege's explanation of the thought (BT 207), and W. there adds a bracket after 'Annahme': viz. '(so wie er das Wort gebraucht)' ('(as he uses the word)'). This suggests that Frege sometimes used 'Annahme' as a technical term in the exposition of his conception. So too does W.'s insertion of the German term in correcting Rhees's translation (TS 226$_R$ §27). The most plausible conjecture is that Frege used this term *in conversation* with W.

Note that W.'s observation does not assert that Frege holds there to be an assumption in common to the sentences 'You should stand thus-and-so', 'You should not stand thus-and-so', and 'B did stand thus-and-so at place C and time D', even though each of these utterances might correspond to one use of the picture of the boxer. There is only an *analogy* between the picture and the expression of Frege's assumption.

2.1   'Annahme': W. gives two other criticisms of Frege's thesis that every assertion contains an assumption.

(i)   If we represent the sentence-question corresponding to '⊢ p' by the symbol '? p', then the assumption that p is what '? p' and '⊢ p' have in common (BT 207). But the question '? p' is commonly identical with the question '? ∼ p'.[15] Consequently, the assumption that p must be identical with the assumption that not-p (BT 208; PLP 302, cf. 405f.) — which is absurd. It also conflicts with Frege's thesis that the assertion and denial that p are the performance of the same act (assertion) on *different* 'contents of judgement' (the assumptions that p and that not-p respectively) (N 152ff. (382ff.)).

(ii)   It is, of course, possible to express suppositions and to argue from them,[16] but Frege's distinction between assumption and assertion misconstrues this. An actual assumption is typically expressed by a sentence of the form 'Suppose that p were the case'. But such a sentence is incomplete. Someone who makes a supposition must go on to do something with it, to draw consequences from it (BT 208; see Exg. §22, 2(i)). Making a supposition is not something that can be done in isolation from making inferences: *a fortiori, not something derivable from an assertion by subtracting the act of assertion*, as implied by Frege (FC 21f. (149f.)). Moreover, if 'Suppose that p is the case' is the typical form for expressing a supposition, it is obvious that there is no *supposition* contained in the analysis of an asserted sentence and common to the assertion that p and the supposition that p; nor does a conditional contain a supposition in its antecedent.

---

[15]   This argument is problematic. It is discussed in an early unpublished work by Frege (NS 8, PW 7f.).

[16]   A complication: Frege sometimes argues that it is only possible to make inferences from thoughts acknowledged to be true (e.g. N 145 (375)). Hence he treats an argument from an assumption as the assertion of a hypothetical. This complication is ignored here.

SECTION 23

1   §23(a) opens with the query of how many kinds of sentence there are, and
considers the answer: assertion, question and command. This answer is unsatisfactory, since these are not kinds of sentence, but kinds of use of sentences
that more or less correspond to the standard discourse functions of declarative, interrogative and imperative sentences. W. too rejects the answer, but
not for this reason. His response is that there are *countless* kinds — but he switches
from 'kinds of sentences' to 'kinds of uses of sentences'. One may object that
these are distinct questions. Furthermore, both are insufficiently determined,
since we need to be told what is to count as a kind of sentence, and also what
is to count as a kind of use of a sentence.

W.'s answer is rendered even less clear by his response 'countless different
kinds of use of what we call "signs", "words", "sentences"', which rolls together
kinds of use of words and of sentences, and so masks the differences between
different ways of classifying words and their uses and sentences and their uses.
Why 'countless'? Presumably because the classification (of uses of sentences?)
will depend on our purposes — we can classify according to different sorts of
similarity and difference (cf. PLP 97, 298). The claim is rendered more unclear
by W.'s attempt to explain the variety he discerns by reference to the notion
of the ever-changing diversity of *language-games*. For the question of how many
language-games there are is not the same as the two questions 'How many
kinds of sentence are there?' and 'How many kinds of use of sentences are there?'

§23(c) (the source of which differs from (a) and (b))[17] lists a number of
language-games. It is unclear what principle of classification (if any) is
employed. It is not obvious, e.g., that requesting and thanking, which are
speech-acts, are on the same level as forming and testing a hypothesis or as
acting on-stage, which are not.

We are then invited to compare this list with what logicians and the *Tractatus*
say about the structure of language. The *Tractatus* was oblivious to uses of
language other than assertoric, and mistakenly held that all assertoric uses
of language depicted states of affairs and asserted their existence.

1.1   (i) 'how many kinds of sentence are there?': Assertion, question and command are not classifications of kinds of sentences. These categories are the
internal accusatives of the use of a sentence to assert, query or command. But
one might classify sentences into syntactic kinds: namely, declarative, interrogative and imperative — these being syntactic kinds with standard discourse
functions (not happily captured by 'assertion, question and command'). But,
of course, one can classify sentences into kinds in accord with many different

---

[17] For §23(c)–(d) see MS 152, 47, and BT 209r; cf. MS 115 (Vol. XI), 87f. The various paragraphs were brought together in MS 142, §24, where there are two drafts.

principles of classification other than syntactic type (e.g. mathematical as opposed to non-mathematical, ethical as opposed to non-ethical, empirical, etc.).

(ii)   'assertion, question and command': It is true that the declarative sentence is *also* used for purposes other than assertion, the interrogative for purposes other than questioning, and the imperative for purposes other than ordering. It does not follow that there is not a systematic relation between syntactic type of sentence and standard discourse function (see 'Descriptions and the uses of sentences', sect. 4).

(iii)   'oder eine Lebensform': W. corrected this to 'part of a way of living of human beings' (TS 226$_R$ §30).

(iv)   'what logicians have said': for discussion of Frege and Russell, see 'The Augustinian conception of language', sects 4–5. To be sure, the author of the *Tractatus* was committed to the primacy of description and assertion.

2.1   'the variety of language-games': the list was carefully worked over (see n. 17), but no clear principle of classification is evident.

SECTION 24

1   Failure to note the diversity of language-games is alleged to incline one to assimilate questions to statements and descriptions. Philosophers have indeed taken the assertoric function as primary relative to other discourse functions. It is not obvious that this resulted merely from failure to attend to the multiplicity of language-games. It often had more theory-laden roots. The standard temptation in the late twentieth century was to assign primacy to the notions of truth and truth-conditions in a general theory of meaning. This idea had its roots in Frege and Russell (see 'Descriptions and the uses of sentences', sects 1 and 3).

One might hold that more careful attention to the multiplicity of language-games would make one less tempted to hold that questions are forms of statements or of descriptions. That, however, is unlikely, unless one has already broken the hold of the temptation — which requires an account of why philosophers and logicians are so tempted in the first place.

A question, which is standardly asked by using the interrogative sentence-form, is not a statement of ignorance, or a statement that the speaker wishes to be informed, let alone a description of a mental state. But if, like Frege, one is inclined to conceive of every sentence as containing a sense-conveying, truth-value-bearing sentence-radical, one may think that the role of the force-indicator 'Is it the case' is to indicate the speaker's attitude towards the descriptive content — an attitude of ignorance regarding its truth, or of wanting to know whether it is true, or of uncertainty regarding its truth-value.

W. follows his three rhetorical questions with a fourth, evidently intended to reduce the temptation to absurdity: 'Is the cry "Help!" also a description of a mental state?' Questions are no more statements than pleas are descriptions, although one may make clear how one holds things to be by a rhetorical question.

§24(b) points out that 'description' does not signify a uniform use of sentences (cf. PI §291 and Exg.). So even where a sentence can be said to describe, it may nevertheless be doing very different things that belong to distinct language-games (describing a scene, the impression of a scene, how one imagines a scene, how one wants a scene to be painted or built, the scene in a dream, etc.). The assumption that the role of the assertion is descriptive and the assumption of the logical uniformity of description run deep, and characterized the *Tractatus*.

§24(c) makes the point that the possibility of transforming every question into the form of an assertion does not prove that questions are disguised assertions. It no more shows that there is no distinction between these uses of sentences than the possibility of explaining every word by stating what it signifies shows that there are no distinctions between how words function. It is either false or vacuous that all sentences are descriptions, just as it is either false or vacuous that all words are names (cf. Exg. §10). (This is akin to the dilemma facing the solipsist.)

1.1   '. . . will become clearer in another place': This promise is not redeemed (although solipsism is mentioned in §§402–3).

2.1   (i) 'What is a question?': PLP ch. XX discusses the logic of questions (it is unknown how much of this was W.'s work).

(ii) 'called "description"': MS 116 (Vol. XII), 216, notes that even what are called 'descriptions of a house' may have different applications: e.g. the description of the location and appearance of the house of an actual person, the description of a house in a story, and the description of a house which somebody is to imagine (also an architect's plan).

(iii) 'the cry "Help"': BT 202 and MS 115 (Vol. XI), 83, elaborate: if a drowning man cries 'Help!', is he stating the fact that he needs help? That without help he will drown?

(iv) '(solipsism)': from the 1938 Preface, we know that this was to have been discussed in the book, as it had been in PR ch. VI, BT §§101ff., and BB 57ff. TS 239, §29, has '(idealism)' here, which was changed to '(solipsism)' only in TS 227.

SECTION 25

1   Augustine, according to W., conceived of language as a means for expressing thoughts (see Exg. §1), and of thinking as antecedent to, and in principle independent of, mastery of a language (PI §32). It is in accord with this

misconception that the fact that beasts do not speak is often explained by lack of mental capacity, i.e. an inability to think. This embodies two mistakes: (i) asserting, questioning, etc. are conceived to be consequences of performing a mental act (otherwise the question of mental powers would not arise (§25 is thus linked with §22(c)). (ii) The primary criteria for denying that animals can think other than in the most rudimentary manner is precisely that they do not speak, so the putative explanation that they do not speak *because* they do not think is vacuous. Language is *misrepresented* as a means humans discovered to be useful for communicating thoughts.

Animals do not use language. We do. Using language is engaging in linguistic activities, e.g. giving orders, asking questions, telling stories, chatting, that are features of our natural history. No such language-games are played by animals.

1.1   (i)   '. . . they simply do not talk . . . they do not use language': This rephrasal emphasizes the integration of speaking with action. MS 115 (Vol. XI), 90, interspersed here: 'they do not play any language-games'.

(ii)   'if we disregard the most primitive forms': e.g. animal cries of warning (often selective for different kinds of predator), of threat, anger, sexual arousal, etc. To what extent these may, after all, *not* approximate primitive forms of language is touched on in PI §493, see Exg.

2   (i)   Z §§518 ff. (= MS 136, 128) notes the fact that some concepts are applicable only to beings that possess a language (cf. PI §§250, 650, p. 174/148).

(ii)   PLP 134f. notes that the application of the concept of command becomes increasingly indeterminate the more the organisms addressed differ from human beings.

Section 26

1   This extracts from §25 an important consequence for the Augustinian conception. Understanding an utterance requires grasping its use and hence mastery of a pattern of speech and action. Other things being equal, understanding a word involves knowing how it is used in making moves in a language-game. Therefore, grasping the technique of using sentences is fundamental for understanding the meanings of words. The Augustinian conception inverts this. According to it, one comes to know what a word means simply by learning what it stands for. Understanding a sentence is presumed to involve nothing more than knowing what each of its components names (and their mode of combination). This presupposes that the use of sentences flows from correlating its words with things. But, as has been shown, not even one-word sentences consisting of a name of an object ('Slab', 'Slab!', 'Slab?') fit this conception.

Naming something is a *preparation* for using a word (more generally, establishing the grammar of an expression is a preparation for applying it (cf.

PLP 13f.)). What is basic to learning language is learning to say things, to query, call, agree, deny, beg, order, etc. (see 'Contextual dicta and contextual principles' sect. 4).

Section 27(a)

1   (a) continues §26. According to the Augustinian conception, naming is a preparation for talking about, *referring to*, things. W. makes three responses: (i) The possibility of referring to things does not flow from the mere act of naming. We do talk about things; but this is merely one of many speech-acts that must be learnt. Naming is neither a preparation for this alone; nor is learning a name sufficient for being able to talk about something (a baby learns the name 'Mama', and learns to call its mother, long before it can *talk about* its mother). (ii) There is no *one thing* called 'talking about'. Compare talking about how things are, how they seem to be, how they seem to one to be, how they were, how they will be, how they should be, how they might have been, how they would be if . . . , etc. In each case very different kinds of language-games are involved. (iii) The range of speech activities is manifold. This is true even of one-word exclamations. The differences in use patently do not flow from what the words are correlated with, and the exclamations do not refer to objects.

§27(a) and (b) are separate remarks in MS 142 and TS 220. (b) opens the discussion of names and ostensive definition.

2   What immediately follows PI §27(a) in BT 209v and MS 115 (Vol. XI), 91f., is PI §257. This emphasizes that the act of naming a sensation makes sense only against a background knowledge of the grammar of sensation-words, i.e. mastery of their uses in the language-game.

Chapter 2

Illusions of naming: ostensive definition, logically proper names, simples and samples, and analysis (§§27(b)−64)

INTRODUCTION

§§1–27(a) introduced the Augustinian conception of meaning. §§27(b)−64 examine in detail aspects of the concepts of names and naming that lead philosophers, and had led Wittgenstein, into illusions. At the heart of these illusions is the idea that language has foundations in simple names that connect language to simple objects in reality. The mechanism envisaged to make this connection is ostensive definition, which can readily seem to forge an unambiguous and unmistakable link with the objects in the world that, according to the Augustinian conception, are the meanings of the simple names. Philosophizing within the field of force of the Augustinian conception has led philosophers to the idea that if names are to fulfil their role as the foundations of language, then many expressions that are naturally thought of as names are only apparently such. Therefore we must distinguish between real and apparent names. Logical analysis, conceived on analogy with chemical analysis, will, it was thought, reveal the real names, i.e. the logically proper names, and dissolve the apparent ones. One underlying motivation for this illusion was the idea that the sense of a sentence must be independent of the facts. That idea led to the further notion that the real names, which are the constituents of fully analysed sentences, must have as their meanings simple objects that are indestructible, beyond existence and inexistence. These constitute the substance of the world (TLP 2.021) — the *logical* atoms, as it were, of which it is constituted. All change is to be conceived in terms of the combinatorial rearrangement of these simple elements of reality, and all destruction in terms of the decomposition of complexes of elements into their simple constituents. In this way, logico–linguistic investigation appeared to be sublime (see Exg. §89). For it seemed to lead directly to insights into the essential nature of the world, into the logico–metaphysical forms of all things.

§§27(b)−64 divide readily into four parts. Part A runs from §27(b) to §36. It is concerned with ostensive definition. The salient points are as follows. (i) It is mistaken to suppose that only logically simple expressions are ostensively definable. (ii) Ostensive definition can be misinterpreted. (iii) Ostensive definition does not provide the 'foundations of language'; nor does it 'connect language to reality'. (iv) An ostensive definition, like any other definition, is a rule for the use of a word — but it is only one rule among others that determine the type of expression. (v) Understanding an ostensive definition presupposes a tacit grasp of the logico-grammatical type of expression defined (colour-word, shape-word, etc.). (vi) The characteristic mental acts (of focusing attention) or experiences accompanying the ostension are not what *meaning* the colour, the shape, etc., consists in. (vii) Hence understanding the ostensive definition is neither a matter of knowing nor of recapitulating the accompanying acts or experiences of the person giving the ostensive definition.

The structure of Part A:

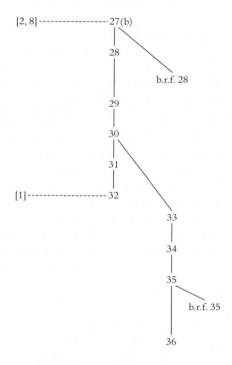

Part B consists of §§37–45. It focuses upon the illusory 'real names'. Taken to extremes, the misconceptions here may even lead one (and did lead Russell) to claim that the only real names are 'this' and 'that', i.e. expressions that are not actually names at all (§38). According to the Augustinian conception of meaning (and according to the *Tractatus*), the meaning of a name is the object it stands for. Ostensive definitions are conceived as correlating a name with an object (in an extended sense of the term), and the object with which it correlates the definiendum is (wrongly) thought to be its meaning. So it may

seem that if that object were destroyed, then the name would become meaningless. This idea generates pressure to restrict real names to so-called logically
proper names, that stand for what cannot fail to exist, i.e. the simple elements
of which reality ultimately consists (§39). Other, apparent names, like
'Nothung', the name of Siegfried's sword, which was broken into pieces, will
disappear on analysis. The error of conflating the meaning of a name with
its bearer is examined (§§40−3), and the connection between the concepts of
meaning and of use is again emphasized (§43) and brought to bear upon the
concepts of a name, its meaning and its bearer. §45 stresses that although the
demonstrative 'this' cannot be without a bearer, it is no name.

The structure of Part B:

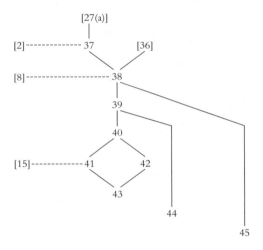

Part C extends from §46 to §59. It examines the idea of simples, conceived
as the objective correlates of logically proper names. §46 uses a quotation from
Plato as an archetype of the thought that simples can only be named (cf. §39),
and identifies Russell's 'individuals' and *Tractatus* objects as exemplifications of
this conception. §§47−8 note that what counts as simple or complex is relative
to context-dependent standards of simplicity and complexity. §48 introduces
an artificial language-game of describing an array of coloured squares, which
provides a model for Plato's account of simple elements (as language-game (2)
provided a model for Augustine's picture of language). §§49−50 use this
language-game to demystify the two characteristic claims made in the *Theaetetus*:
(i) that simples can only be named, but not defined (described); and (ii) that
simples are beyond existence and inexistence. The illusion of necessarily existent elements is produced by a distorted insight into the role of samples. What
looks as if it had to exist is part of, and an instrument of, our language. §§51−4

discuss what the 'correspondence' between name and element in the language-game of §48 consists in (§52 is an aside). This correspondence is of philosophical interest only if it is normative, not mechanical; but what counts as a rule correlating names with elements and how such rules enter into the applications of language are various and complex. §§55–6 are linked both to §39 (the discussion of 'Nothung'), which gave reasons why names must signify indestructible simples, and §46, which cited Plato's conception of elements that are beyond existence and inexistence. These two remarks examine the idea that what corresponds to a name must be indestructible. The motivating thought behind this conception was that sense or meaning must not be at the mercy of the facts. §§57–8 pick up the theme of §50, further probing the thought that the meaning of the name of an 'element' (e.g. 'red') is independent of the existence of anything (e.g. of any red thing). §58 subjects the claim that names cannot occur in the combination 'X exists' to critical scrutiny, referring back to the Platonic conception (§46) that elements exist 'an und für sich' ('in their own right'), remaining the same through all change. §59 closes this discussion, specifying the picture from which the illusions are derived. It also links Part C to the concluding remarks on analysis.

The structure of Part C:

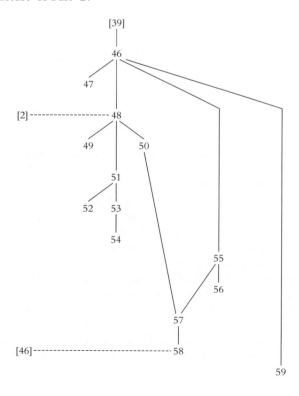

Part D embraces §§60–4. Its theme is analysis. The deep implications of analysis, its alleged insights into the depth structure of language and thought, and its putative power to lay bare the logical structure of the world are brushed aside as illusory.

The structure of Part D:

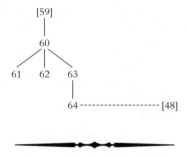

Sources

PI§	MS 152	MS 142§/ TS 220§	TS 226$_R$§	TS 239§	Other
27(b)		27(a)	35(a)	33(a)	
28		27(b)	35(b)	33(b)	
b.r.f. 28					114 Um., 138, 197f.; B i §522
29		28	36	34	
30		29(a)–(b)	37(a)–(b)	35(a)–(b)	
31	50	29(c)–(g)	37(c)–(g)	35(c)–(g)	
32		30	38	36	
33	51–4	31	39	37	
34		31[1]	40	38	
35		32	41(a)–(c)	39	
b.r.f. 35					
(a), (b)					116, 33; B i §36
(c)					116, 310; B i §223
36		33	41(d)–(e)	40	
37		34	43(a)[2]	41	
38	54[3]	35	43(b)–45[4]	42–3	115, 175[3]
39		37	46	44	115, 174f.
40		38	47	45	
41		39	48	46	
42		41	50	48	
43		40	49	47	
44		42	51	49	
45		42[5]	52	50	
46		43	53	51	
47		44–46	54–6	52–3	219, 14[6]
48	54–5	47	57	54	
49		48	58	55	
50		49	59	56	
51	57	50(a)–(b)	60(a)–(b)	57(a)–(b)	
52	57	50(c)–(d)	60(c)–(d)	57(c)–(d)	
53	57–8	51	60(e)–(f)	58	
54	59	52	62[7]	59	
55	60–1 & 69–70	53	63	60	
56	61–2	54	64	61	
57	62–3	55	65	62	
58	63 & 70	56	66	63	
59	63–4	57	67	64	
60	65–6 & 72	58	68	65	

PI§	MS 152	MS 142§/ TS 220§	TS 226$_R$§	TS 239§	Other
61	73	59	69	66	
62	73	60	70	67	
63	73[8]	61(a)–(b)	71(a)	68(a)	
64	66[9]	61(c)–(d)[10]	71(b)–(c)	68(b)–(c)	

[1]   W.'s enumeration slips here. From §31 to §42, his numbering is one short.

[2]   There is no §42.

[3]   PI §38(c) only.

[4]   There is no §44.

[5]   Another error in W.'s enumeration occurred here; consequently his assigned number is hence-forth two short of a correct enumeration.

[6]   PI §47(a) and (b) only.

[7]   There is no §61.

[8]   First sentence only.

[9]   Only a mnemonic sketch.

[10]   In TS 220 it is paragraphs (b)–(c).

Ostensive definition and its ramifications
1. Connecting language and reality
2. The range and limits of ostensive explanations
3. The normativity of ostensive definition
4. Samples
5. Misunderstandings resolved
6. Samples and simples

EXEGESIS §§27(b)–64

1   This opens the investigation of ostensive definition, which, being conceived to connect language to reality (words to their meanings), is central to the Augustinian conception of language. In MS 142, this section is the opening paragraph of §28 — amalgamation with §27(a) occurring only in the Intermediate Draft (ZF).

Three points are made. (a) Ostensive explanation is a correlate of requests for explanations (viz. asking what something is called). (b) The practise of asking for names and answering such requests is itself a language-game (absent in §2 and §8, but raised in §9), which is essentially a preparation for other language-games. (c) Correlative to asking for names, and answering, is the practise of stipulating names for things.

Again it is striking how readily W. slides from talking of names in general to proper names. The parenthesis is important because of features of proper names as opposed to names of colours, materials, smells, etc. The example of giving names to dolls points to the special significance we attach to personal names. Numbers, despite their impeccable individuative powers, lack the aura of proper names; giving prisoners numbers is degrading and dehumanizing; but even proper names of objects and places are significant to us ('2602, 32nd Street' belongs to a different culture from 'Sunny Corner, Rosenithon'). Once a doll has a name, one can not merely talk about it, one can *address* it by name and talk to it. Equally important is the reminder of the vocative use of names. This familiar use strikes one as *remarkable* only when one is thinking along well-worn philosophical tracks, viewing proper names almost exclusively as instruments for singular (unique) reference (cf. 'Proper names', sections 1 and 6).

1.1   'we are brought up': W. crossed out 'brought up', replacing it with 'taught' (TS 226$_R$ §35).

2   (i)   PG 62f. examines in greater detail ostensive teaching that is antecedent to definition inasmuch as the learner cannot yet raise (or answer) questions about meaning. Ostension does not have the same role here as in more developed language-games. First, it is part of the child's training, not a response to a question about meaning. Secondly, the child cannot as yet give an ostensive explanation. But, of course, *that* the child's use *is* correct is manifest in the way his use relates to our usage *and to our explanations*.

(ii)   PLP 198 elaborates the parenthesis of §27(b). (i) Reflect on what particular material objects we name (the Koh-hi-noor, but not any old diamond;
the Canterbury Quad, but not the front quad, etc.) and the reasons which
underlie our name-conferring customs. (ii) Is it true that names (proper
names)[1] have a meaning only in the context of a sentence? They are used vocat-
ively, and one can imagine a language in which that was the *only* way to use
them (e.g. all singular reference being by means of descriptions). They are used
to send messages to people: the messenger (postman) must find the person whose
name is on the envelope. Names are used on place-cards at dinners to mark
where one is supposed to sit. Once could enumerate dozens of further roles,
actual and imaginable.

Section 28

1   With §28, W. begins his elucidation of ostensive definition. The idea (i)
that ostensive definition lays the foundations of language must be swept aside.
That view was associated with the ideas that (ii) only indefinables (empiricists'
simple ideas) are explained ostensively; and (iii) ostensive definition is unambiguous and final (mental ostension, so to speak, always hits the bull's-eye;
for if, in establishing a connection between 'A' and a mental representation,
I *mean* by 'A' just that mental item, it seems that I cannot miss it). The subsequent discussion, challenging all three points, is intended to dethrone ostensive definition, not to deprive it of its citizenship. W. is not arguing that it is
defective relative to other explanations of meaning, but rather that it is on a
par with them.
     W.'s first move here (against (ii)) is to insist upon the wide competence of
ostensive explanation. Of the kinds of term he specifies, the most striking is
that of numerals. Frege's response to the assertion that 'two' can be defined
perfectly exactly by pointing at two nuts can be imagined. But reflect that instead
of saying 'There are two men in the next room', one can say 'There are that
☞ •• many men in the next room', pointing at a pair of nuts.
     One might object that one cannot define a number-word ostensively,
because the addressee won't know *what* one is defining. W. concedes that the
hearer may suppose that one was naming the group of nuts. But any explanation, *a fortiori* ostensive definition, can be misinterpreted (so (iii), as well as (ii),
is undermined (cf. LWL 23)). The possibility of misinterpretation imposes no
restriction on the scope of ostensive definitions.
     A Platonist who conceives of numbers as abstract objects may object that
one cannot *point* at a number. To this one may reply that in so far as there is
such a thing as pointing at a number, then one can so point. The only sense

---

[1]   Although Wittgenstein denied that the bearer of a proper name is its meaning, he did hold
that proper names have a meaning. For critical discussion, see 'Proper names', sect. 7.

there is to 'pointing at a number' is pointing at a group of objects that has a number (just as pointing at a colour consists in pointing at an object that has a colour).

1.1   'one can ostensively define a person's name': tailored to the idea that personal names have a meaning; better: one can ostensively explain who N. is.

2   PLP 104ff. discusses the range of ostensive definition. It emphasizes not only misinterpretability, but also the haziness of the borderline between what is and what is not ostensive definition (see 'Ostensive definition and its ramifications', sect. 2).

Boxed Remark Following §28 (p. 11n.)

1   This note is cut from B i. §522, itself derived from MS 114 (Vol. X) Um., 138 and 197f. TS 227 (SF) has the handwritten instruction (not in W.'s hand, but presumably copied from a note of his) to insert this at the end of §28.

Why would pointing at something green, and saying 'That is not red', not be an ostensive explanation of 'red'? Not because it is misinterpretable, since that is generally true of explanations of meaning. Even if it did generate an understanding of 'red', it would not be an ostensive explanation (any more than if hitting a person on the head while shouting 'red' brought about correct use, the blow would constitute an explanation). It plays a different part in the calculus — in the system of grammatical rules — than that played by an ostensive explanation. An ostensive explanation provides a standard of correct use. Instead of 'red', one can substitute the deictic gesture, the utterance of 'this' and the red sample pointed at in an ostensive explanation. Giving a correct ostensive explanation constitutes a criterion of a person's understanding the word thus explained. In all these respects, pointing at a green sample and saying 'This is not red' falls short of being an explanation of the word 'red'. First, in isolation, it does not constitute a standard of correctness for applying 'red'. Secondly, the partly concrete symbol constituted by the green sample, the ostensive gesture, and the utterance is *not* substitutable for 'red'. Thirdly, pointing at a green sample and saying 'That is not red' is not a criterion for a person's understanding 'red' any more than pointing at N.N. and saying 'This is not Julius Caesar' is a criterion for knowing who Julius Caesar is.

Is pointing thus at a green sample an ostensive explanation of 'not-red'? This too is wrong, for we do not treat 'not-red' as a simple unitary predicate and do not accept unitary samples of 'not-red'; e.g. blue, like green, is not red, but not because it is the same colour (i.e. not-red) as green. Indeed, we explain the meaning of 'red' in 'This is not red' by pointing to something that *is* red (cf. PI §429).

What then is the role of 'That is not red' in the rules of colour grammar? As a grammatical proposition it may supplement an explanation of 'red' by contributing to determination of the boundaries of the concept.

1.1   (i)   'are we still to call this an "explanation"': 'explanation' has less determinate boundaries than 'definition', but not anything goes.

(ii)   The final sentence is typical of W.'s repudiation of causal theories of meaning.

2   W.'s directions for stringing together these remarks in MS 114 (Vol. X) Um., 138 and 197f., puts b.r.f. §28 (p. 14n.) in the context of PG 135ff. and the discussion of intentionality (cp. PI §§443, 446).

SECTION 29

1   The categorial specification might seem logically necessary and sufficient for preventing misinterpretation of ostensive definition. The fact that every ostensive definition not adorned by a category specification can be misinterpreted (§28) seems to show that it must be supplemented to be complete, while the presence of such supplementation apparently rules out the possibility of misinterpretation. W. criticizes both moves.

The claim that a category specification is necessary is doubly misleading. (i) The ostensive definition without category specification is not incomplete; e.g. the definition 'This ☞ is red' is not less adequate than the explanation 'This ☞ colour is red' in providing a norm for applications of 'red' in standard contexts. (ii) It is clearly not necessary that we possess this categorial concept (e.g. colour) prior to understanding how to use expressions belonging to the category (e.g. 'red'); hence we need not understand the 'full' explanation in order to understand the initial one (e.g. 'This ☞ is red').

The sufficiency claim is equally misguided. (i) No explanation is proof against misinterpretation; in particular, the categorial term might not be understood or might be misunderstood, and hence might need explaining. (ii) Categorization, even by categorial terms (formal concepts) like 'colour', is purpose-relative; correct understanding of a category term may vary with our purposes (see 1.1(i)). (W. uses neither of the expressions 'category' and 'formal concept'.)

Categorial specification is required in practice only where misunderstanding is likely (and nothing can *guarantee* success). What form is appropriate for an explanation depends on the circumstances and the learner. The possibility of misunderstanding disqualifies ostensive definitions for the role of anchors for language even when supplemented by categorial specifications.

1.1   (i)   'is there only *one* way of taking the word "colour"': sometimes 'colour' = 'chromatic colour'; sometimes black, white and grey count as colours too.

(ii)   'the last definition': one *can* go on explaining the words used in an earlier explanation of a word indefinitely, just as one can go on building further houses. But one *does not*; sooner or later one stops (as the explanations get farther and farther removed from the original explanandum). This finality is distinct from the finality of justification emphasized in PI §217: 'If I have exhausted the justifications I have reached bedrock and my spade is turned.'

(iii) 'ob er sie ohne dieses Wort anders auffasst, als ich es wünsche': W. preferred 'whether he misunderstands my definition if I leave out the word' (TS 226$_R$ §36).

2   (i)   PR 52f. argues that 'Blue is a colour' merely specifies a value of the categorial variable and gives no information about blue. This conception is closer to the *Tractatus* idea of formal concepts than to the *Investigations* (cf. TLP 2.0131, 2.025–2.0251, 4.122, 4.124, 4.126–4.1274; also PT 2.0252). W. insists that expressions such as 'number', 'colour', 'shape', *need not* occur in the 'chapters' of the book of philosophical grammar. In the *Tractatus*, they *could not* so occur. In the *Investigations*, these expressions are deprived of their nimbus; they are not super-concepts, and they too may need explaining.

(ii)   PG 60f. suggests that an ostensive definition of the form 'That is called "N"' is ambiguous. Categorial specification 'That C is called "N"', however, is wholly unambiguous. Here in PI, by contrast, W. studiously avoids talk of ambiguity. Certainly 'That is N' (or 'called "N"') can be misunderstood. Certainly the misunderstanding might be eradicated by 'That C is N'. But equally, that too might be misunderstood.

PG 61 notes that categorial specification determines the *kind of use* of the word, and hence *the part of speech*.

(iii) BB 83 produces reasons for refusing to classify '1' with other numerals. W. invites us to reflect on our reasons for and against classifying '0' as a numeral, and black and white as colours.

(iv)   PLP 98ff. discusses the nature of categorial specification, with particular reference to 'colour'. Waismann stresses[2] that the sentence ' "Red" is a colour-word' does not mean the same as, is not a translation of, 'Red is a colour'. A person who has been told to paint the wall some colour might say, 'I had to paint the wall any colour, and red is a colour,' but could not intelligibly say, 'I had to paint the wall any colour, and "red" is a colour-word.'

(v)   PLP 106 discusses the stratification of concepts. Understanding may begin with words like 'round', 'square', 'triangular', etc., then ascend to higher-order expressions such as 'shape', and finally to logical categories such as 'property'. With some families of concepts the particular order of learning the stratification is arbitrary, e.g. we may learn 'fir', 'pine', 'oak', first, and only later 'tree'; on the other hand, we may well learn these words in the converse

---

[2]   Perhaps with Carnap in mind (see *The Logical Syntax of Language* (Routledge and Kegan Paul, London, 1937), §74).

order. But with other families of concepts this is not so: e.g. we could not learn the word 'number' prior to learning the numerals '1', '2', '3'. . . .

SECTION 30

1   So the category term is not necessary when it is clear what 'kind of role' (TS 226$_R$ §37, W.'s modification) the word is to play in the language. In the context of the hearer's grasping that role, the unadorned ostensive definition 'That is called "sepia"' is a perfectly satisfactory explanation of the use of the word. But one must remember the manifold problems attached to the expressions 'to know' and 'to be clear'.

The latter observation might be meant to draw our attention to general misconceptions about knowledge, e.g. that to know something (including knowing what a word means) is not to be in a certain mental state, but to be able to do certain things (PI §150 and boxed remarks following §149 (p. 59n.) notes (a) and (b), see also the exegesis of these two notes). More probably (cf. Exg. §31), W. may be drawing our attention to the fact that there is a degree of indeterminacy about what exactly is to *count* as knowing or being clear about the overall role of the explanandum. So, for example, knowing that 'sepia' is a colour-word does not settle where sepia ends and other shades of brown begin — something about which one may still be unclear. While one cannot grasp the concept of colour and not know any colour-names, one may well know what the word 'tree' means without knowing any names of trees, and vice versa. Nor is it clear how far 'knowing the overall role of a word in the language' is to go. Knowing that 'sepia' is a colour-word does not obviously include knowing or understanding that one's mental image of a sepia object cannot itself be said to be sepia.

1.1   (i) 'explains the use — the meaning — of the word': to explain the use *is* to explain the meaning.

(ii) 'before one can ask what something is called': This reiterates the point that *explanation* is correlative with requests for, doubts about, and misunderstandings of what an expression means. Explanation presupposes antecedent training (cf. §§6, 27(b)). What does one have to know already? See §31.

2   PG 61 remarks that to understand an ostensive definition one must already know where the words (e.g. 'red', 'ellipse') are being put (namely, among colourwords and shape-words respectively).

SECTION 31

1   This provides an analogical answer to the concluding question of §30. In §31(a), the learner already knows all the rules, knows that there is a piece called

'the king' and how it moves, but does not know which figure is the king. In §31(b), he can play the game in accordance with the rules, which he has picked up from careful observation of games of chess. But he is ignorant of chess nomenclature and has never formulated the rules of the game in chess terminology. However, if we point at the king and ask 'How does *this* piece move?', he can show us. Unlike the learner in (a), he would not mistake the figure of the king for that of the queen. But, in another sense, he does not even know that there *is* a king and queen in the game. In §31(c) the learner knows none of the rules, but is familiar with board games and the idea of a piece. Being told that this piece is called 'the king' provides a peg on which to hang the subsequently explained rules.

What conclusions are we meant to draw from this? That what one has to know is much more fluid than initially suggested in §30 — that, as there observed, all sorts of problems attach to the words 'to know' or 'to be clear'. What counts as 'knowing such-and-such a rule' requires careful scrutiny from case to case.

§31(d) draws together the discussion of ostensive definition that began at §27(b): ostensive definition and the practices surrounding it (asking for the name of a thing, teaching and explaining the name of a thing, etc.) presuppose that the learner already knows how to do things with words. So, contrary to the Augustinian conception, ostensive definition, far from determining the foundations of language, presupposes (a significant) knowledge of language. This provides the transition to the next remark, which draws this conclusion explicitly.

2   For the idea that the meaning of a word is its place in grammar, see BT 30–3. That (overstatement) is modified here.

2.1   'except for this last point': PG 61 observes that the expression 'colour', in 'That ☞ colour is called "red"', 'settles the grammar of the word "red" up to this last point': namely, that it is the name of a colour (not of a shape or kind of material, etc.). But, W. adds, the question as to which shades are all called 'red' can still arise.

SECTION 32

1   This develops §31: someone who has already mastered a language, and is confronted by an ostensive definition of a word in another (related) language, will indeed have the place in grammar (§29) of the foreign word already prepared (so is akin to the learner in §31(a)). What he already knows (cf. §30(b)) is the difference between, e.g., a colour-word, a shape-word, the name of a stuff. So he can guess (sometimes rightly, sometimes wrongly) that the colour (or shape, or stuff, etc.) is being pointed at (and that the word being explained is a colour-word), and hence the interpretation of the ostensive explanation.

§31(b) brings this to bear upon Augustine's description of initial language-learning. Augustine, W. avers, describes the child learning his first language as if he already spoke a language and was learning a second one. So ostensive definition presupposes mastery of a language (cf. §33), and cannot fulfil the role of constituting the foundations of language. Or, to put it differently, Augustine supposes that the child can already *think* (construing 'thinking' as 'talking to oneself'), but not yet speak our public language. Why so? — because he is supposed to be able to *guess* that the adults are speaking of the colour as opposed to the shape, or of the number as opposed to the texture, etc. (see §33). So the child must already possess a language (of thought) in order to be able to learn a language from adults.

It is noteworthy that the *Tractatus* presupposed a 'language of thought', with psychical constituents that have 'the same sort of relation to reality as words' (CL 68). The unintelligibility of this conception is assailed later (cf. PI §§316–62, *passim*; see Volume 3, 'Thinking: the soul of language', sects 1 and 3).

1.1   'how to interpret these explanations': this point is elaborated below in §34. How one interprets is shown by what one goes on to do.

SECTION 33

1   W. now considers an objection to §§30f.: It is not true that in order to understand the ostensive definition one must already have mastered (a significant part of) a language, i.e. know 'the rules of the game up to this last specification': namely, *the name* of *this* ☞ colour or of *this* ☞ shape. Surely all that is required to understand an ostensive definition is to guess what is *pointed at, meant* or *attended to*: namely, the shape, the colour, the number, etc.

In response W. asks us to reflect on what counts as pointing to the colour rather than to the shape or the number. The natural reply is that one *means* something different in each case. But *to mean* the colour as opposed to the shape, etc., is not an act one performs (see PI §§661–91 and Exg.). One may say that when one means *this* rather than *that*, one concentrates one's attention on it. But how is that done? The question implicitly suggests that only someone who possesses the concept of colour or shape *can* intentionally concentrate his attention on the one rather than the other.[3] By implication, the hearer, to whom the ostensive definition is being given, can only guess that the speaker is concentrating his attention on the colour rather than the shape if he too possesses the relevant concepts. If so, then the objection collapses.

---

[3]   Were this not his suggestion, then his queries would not be replies to the objection under consideration.

(b) pursues the elusive idea of concentrating one's attention on the colour as opposed to the shape. One may grant that different actions (mental and physical) may be involved. Nevertheless, there is no uniformity in the various actions that may be involved in looking at the colour. There is no one thing one does which necessarily accompanies or is involved in looking at or attending to a given feature. So it is not *in virtue* of any such action that someone is rightly said to be attending to one. The matter is pursued further in §34.

1.1   'but in the circumstances that we call "playing a game of chess" ': making a move in chess does *not* consist in the circumstances, nor in pushing a piece from here to there, but in moving a piece *in such-and-such circumstances*.

2   PG 63 argues that one points in a different *sense* to a body, a shape or a colour: 'a possible definition would be: "to point to a colour" means, to point to the body which has the colour'. Analogously, a man who marries money does not marry it in the same sense in which he marries the woman who has it. This argument ramifies in two directions. First, one can point at a colour, shape or length only in so far as one has some grasp of these concepts. What one points at is determined neither by one's gesture, nor by one's 'mental gesture', but by the role of the sample (as a sample of colour, shape or length) in the context — what is appropriately *done* with it. Secondly, the example illustrates the error of identifying the meaning of a name ostensively defined with what is pointed at. If we think that when we define 'blue' we 'point at the colour', we forget that to point at the colour is to point at the object which is blue, and that object (e.g. a book) is obviously not the meaning of 'blue' (and neither is its colour).

Cf. Z §11 (MS 116 (Vol. XII), 31), which compares hearing a piano, its sound, a piece of music, a player, his fluency; what does it mean that one hears in different senses?

SECTION 34

1   Even if there were (contrary to §33(b)) a uniform set of actions (and experiences) accompanying the teacher's attention to shape, they are not the grounds for the hearer to take the definition to be an explanation of a shape-word, even if he knows what the teacher's actions (and experiences) are and recapitulates them himself.

What does understanding the ostensive explanation 'That is a circle' consist in? If we say that it consists in having the same experiences as those accompanying the teacher's attending to the shape, then understanding becomes divorced from correct use. For as long as the learner had the same experiences (and his eyes followed the outline) when he heard the explanation, it does not matter how he subsequently uses the word. So the hearer might nevertheless interpret 'This is a circle' quite differently from the teacher's intended meaning.

W. in effect offers us a choice: *either* the learner has the same experience as the teacher, but his subsequent use is irrelevant to his understanding, *or* hearing the explanation and having the same experiences is not a criterion for grasping the meaning. W.'s answer is obvious: neither intending an explanation thus-and-so nor interpreting it consist in processes which accompany giving or understanding explanations. Intending the ostensive definition 'That ☞ ● is called "a circle"' to be the definition of a shape (namely, a circular one) is to intend the hearer to understand it as such and to go on to apply the word to *circles*. If one interprets the definition as thus intended, then one can go on to apply the word appropriately (and to justify applications by reference to such an explanation).

Section 35

1   §35(a), recapitulating §33, concedes that there *may* be characteristic experiences (W. here assimilates mental acts and experiences) of pointing to a shape. Nevertheless, first, there is no *invariable* 'shape-pointing experience' that always accompanies meaning the shape, any more than there is a unique 'colour-pointing experience'. Secondly, even if there were, its occurrence would not entail that the person who had it meant that shape. Why should not the shape-pointing experience occasionally accompany pointing at the colour? Whether we are entitled to assert that someone pointed at the shape depends upon the circumstances of pointing, in particular what happens before or after (this is parallel to the last sentence of §33). So, the learner may have asked 'I know that *that* ☞ ■ is called 'square', but what is *that* ☞ ● called?' Or, after the ostensive definition has been given, the learner may misapply the word 'circle' and the teacher may correct him by saying, 'No; it is called a circle when it is like *this* (inscribing a circle in the air with his finger)'.

(b) intimates a point discussed in PG 63. The contrast between pointing to the table and pointing to the chair is between pointing at two different objects of the same general type (pieces of furniture, material objects). But to point to a colour rather than to a shape involves a contrast of category. In the first case we change the direction of our gesture. In the second we need not, just because to point to the colour (shape) *is* to point to the object which has it, and the same material object may exemplify both colour and shape in question. This difference is evident in the way we learn the use of the words 'to point to . . .' in the various cases.

1.1   (i)   'do you also know of an experience characteristic of pointing to a piece in a game *as a piece in a game*?': It is evident from the foregoing that the 'experiences' of pointing to the shape or attending to the colour are meant to include

activities — following the outline with finger or eye, attending to the colour
by blotting out the outline with one's raised hand, etc. In this sense, there are
no 'characteristic experiences and *ways of pointing*' or attending to a chess piece
qua chess piece.

(ii) '(Recognizing, wishing, remembering, etc.)': here too there are typical
experiences, but they are neither necessary nor sufficient.

2   BB 80 illuminates one source of the temptation to think that meaning the
colour (as opposed to the shape) is a mental process. If asked 'What did you
point at?', one can normally answer and be certain one's answer is correct.

Boxed Remarks Following §35 (p. 18n.)

1   It is unclear where these cuttings belong. Since §33 introduced the objection that all that is necessary to understand an ostensive definition is to know
what is pointed at, attended to or *meant*, it is possible that these remarks belong
to §35 as clarifications of what it is to mean something. That would make
clearer the rationale for §36, inasmuch as we *are* inclined to conceive of meaning something as a mental activity.

(a) and (b) come from B i §36. This is taken from MS 116 (Vol. XII), 33,
where they are followed by a discussion of asking for word-meanings, as in
'What colour is called "chrome yellow"?', 'What is C‴?', 'What does the word
"*nefas*" mean?' (cf. Exg. §145), and the different ways of answering. This context does not illuminate the intended location here. (c) comes from B i §223
(= MS 116, 310).

'That is blue' can be used as an assertion about an object or as an explanation of the meaning of the word 'blue'. How can this be? The word 'is' is
not ambiguous between 'is' and 'is called'. 'Blue' is the name of a colour, not
the name of a name of a colour. So if 'That is blue' is meant as an explanation, this is not accounted for by the fact that one meant by 'is' 'is called',
and by 'blue' ' "blue" '. Rather, by uttering the sentence 'That is blue', one
meant 'That is called "blue" '; i.e. if asked to explain what one meant, one
would give that paraphrase and reject the paraphrase 'The X (book, sofa, car-
pet, etc.) is blue'. So the ambiguity resides in the use of the sentence, and its
meaning is specified, by the speaker's explanation of what he meant.

Paragraph (b) is accordingly clear. For a person may say 'That is blue', meaning that the X is blue, i.e. ascribing a colour to an object, but be misunderstood by the hearer to be giving an ostensive definition of 'blue'.

The marginal note: 'Here lurks a superstition of great consequence' may be
an allusion to TLP 3.263 and the subsequent criticism in PR 54. In TLP, W.
conceived of simple names as indefinable. Their meanings, however, are explained by elucidations, i.e. *propositions* that contain the indefinable. Hence these
propositions can be understood only if the meanings of those signs are already

known. This is needlessly paradoxical (cp. *Principia* ★1). W.'s point was that the meanings of indefinables can be picked up only from their use in assertions; i.e. their explanation is always extracted from a piece of information. In PR 54 this is repudiated. 'This is A' may be a proposition (assertion) or a definition but not both simultaneously. If it is a proposition, it can be understood only if the meaning of 'A' is known (gathered). But if it is an explanation of what the word 'A' means, it is not an assertion that this object has the property of being A. This is further amplified here. It is *possible* to get an explanation out of what was intended as information. This is not to revert to the *Tractatus*, but merely to avoid dogmatism.[4] However, this does not demonstrate the possibility of eliminating explanations from language. What, then, is the 'crucial superstition'? Perhaps that language is 'connected to reality' by means of sentences such as 'This is A'. That, at any rate, is not a *mistake* (for then it would be false, but make sense). It is a superstition.

(c) is connected with its antecedents via the idea of being able to mean by 'is', first, 'is' (*ist*), and then 'is called' (*heisst*). Meaning is not a spiritual activity; nor are we, as it were, free to mean what we wish by whatever sign we use. Meaning something by an utterance requires that the symbol employed be either predetermined as a signal (as in a code) or else possess the appropriate articulations. Whether I *can* mean so-and-so by uttering such-and-such depends on the general use of the sentence uttered and its relation to those sentences which would, in the language, express what I meant. *Pace* Humpty-Dumpty, it is not just a question of 'who is master'! Unlike 'to imagine' ('Whenever I say "bububu" I imagine that I am going for a walk'), 'to mean', thus used, involves meaning something by an utterance. And what one *can* mean by an utterance depends on its general use (cf. PI §§508f.). What one means must be something representable by the sentence uttered. (Of course, one can fail to express clearly what one means. But that is not at issue here.)

2   Vol. VIII, 154, contains a parallel remark:

'This book has the colour that is called "red".'
'The colour, which this book has, is called "red".'
Put thus, the two sentences sound very much alike; we could clearly even give one of them the sense of the other. But in one case we are fixing the use of the word, hence *enunciating* a grammatical rule, in the other case we are *making* a statement, which can be confirmed or confuted in experience.

---

[4]   Nevertheless, *one* aspect of the TLP doctrine remains firm: namely, that any explanation of a language presupposes a linguistic mastery. 'I cannot use language to get outside language' (PR 54). This point is never relinquished.

SECTION 36

1   This concludes the initial discussion of ostensive definition (the discussion
of samples is resumed in §50; private ostensive definition is examined in §§258ff.).
It characterizes the errors examined in §§33–5 in terms of a general philosophical syndrome. Faced with seemingly unanswerable philosophical problems (they *are* unanswerable — and need unravelling, not answering (MS 158,
33v)), we typically resort to mystification. Since nothing physical corresponds
to pointing to the shape as opposed to the colour, we assume that what differentiates them is a mental accompaniment — a mental act or activity of meaning that pins the word 'circle' to the shape and the word 'red' to the colour.

2   Z §§12f. (= MS 130, 16; MS 116 (Vol. XII), 277) remarks, àpropos 'pointing
in different senses to this body, its shape, colour, etc.', that here 'meaning gets
imagined as a kind of mental pointing, indicating'. We have the impression
that thinking of a person is like nailing him with a thought. B i §224 (= MS
116, 310f.) raises a similar issue. If I think of N or speak about him, how does
what I say connect with N? Using N's name hardly suffices, since many people
may be called 'N'. But if so, some other connection must obtain between my
utterance and N, otherwise I would not have been speaking about him at all.
Certainly; but not a connection of the kind we readily imagine, i.e. not via
a psychic mechanism. 'I mean' is not comparable to 'I aim at . . .'.

SECTION 37

1   Ostensive definition is the envisaged mechanism for assigning a meaning to
a simple name, and so connecting language to reality. But what exactly is it
for a name to *signify* or *stand for* an object? What *is* a name? What is 'the name-
relation'?[5] §37 begins a new set of remarks, running until §45, focused upon
the pressures that induce philosophers (including the author of the *Tractatus*)
to sublimate our ordinary concept of a name, and even to take as the paradigm
of a name something that is not a name at all (namely, the demonstrative 'this').
    §15 implied that there are many more or less similar relations described by
the verb 'to signify', the most straightforward of which consists in marking
the named object with its name. This implication is made explicit here: there
are many possible relations between names and what is named even in
language-games as simple as that of §2. There is no single relation 'to signify'
or 'to stand for'; hence one cannot invoke a 'name-relation' to expose the
essence of names.

⁵   See Carnap's discussion of 'the method of the name-relation' in his *Meaning and Necessity* (University
of Chicago Press, Chicago, 1947), ch. III.

This negative conclusion undermines one pillar of the Augustinian conception of meaning. That presupposes that there is a uniform relation between names and what is named. Every (genuine) name stands for something, and what it stands for is its meaning; the difference in the *use* of colour-names and shape-names, for example, flows directly from the natures of the objects pointed at and named. Of course, with Fregean or Russellian sophistication, one might argue that precisely because the entities named are of different logical types, therefore there is no *one* name-relation, but as many distinct (but analogous) name-relations as there are logical types named. This avails little; indeed, it is merely a more sophisticated variant of the Augustinian conception. It is true that there is all the difference in the world between colour-names, shape-names, names of numbers and of textures, etc., but the differences do not reside in different *relations* between the name and the nominatum.

2   BB 172f. stresses that the quest for 'the name-relation' is not satisfied by answers such as 'The name is written on the object' or 'When his name is called, he comes', etc. This dissatisfaction is correct, but its correctness is masked by looking 'deeper' for some other non-trivial or non-physical relation, e.g. a mental or spiritual one. For this is to persist in looking in the wrong direction. 'A primitive philosophy condenses the whole usage of the name into the idea of a relation, which thereby becomes a mysterious relation.' Rather, we must forget about mysteries and simply examine the uses of names, their various roles in language, for the answer to our puzzlement lies here. 'It is clear that there is no one relation of name to object, but as many as there are uses of sounds or scribbles which we call names.'

PLP 199: 'What a noble role the "relation between the name and the object named" plays in the eyes of certain philosophers.'

3   Cf. Russell:

When we ask what constitutes meaning, we are not asking what is the meaning of this or that particular word. The word 'Napoleon' means a certain individual; but we are asking, not who is the individual meant, but what is the relation of the word to the individual which makes the one mean the other . . . When we are clear both as to what the word is in its physical aspects, and as to what sort of thing it can mean, we are in a better position to discover the relation of the two which *is* meaning. (AM 191)

Russell argues that this relation is causal.

Section 38

1   The demonstrative use of 'this', according to some philosophical accounts operating within the ambit of the Augustinian conception of meaning, e.g.

Russell's (PLAt 179), exemplifies — indeed, uniquely exemplifies — the 'name-relation'. W. elaborates reasons for not assimilating demonstratives to names (cf. 'Indexicals', pp. 111f.).

1.1   (i)   W. does not distinguish here between proper names and common nouns. This is justified here since the *Tractatus* had held that ordinary proper names are not really names at all, and that *logically* proper names name properties and relations as well as individuals (cf. LWL 120). Russell's position is somewhat equivocal (see 'Logically proper names', sect. 1). §38(b) stresses that very different expressions are called 'names' (e.g. names of people, places, animals, objects, colours, tastes, directions, moves in a game, numbers, proofs, etc.), but demonstratives are *not*. (There is perhaps an implicit suggestion that *name* is a family-resemblance concept.) But §38(c) arguably needs the distinction between proper names and common nouns. For the claim that it is characteristic of a name that it can be defined ostensively is *not* obviously true of personal names — a point W. seems to have overlooked. For names of persons are not *defined* at all, and, indeed, in an important sense have no meaning (cf. 'Proper names', sect. 7). One can ostensively *explain* who John Smith, to whom reference was just made, *is* — but such an explanation is not a definition of the name 'John Smith' (which, indeed, has a multitude of bearers, but is not *polysemic*).

        (ii)   'to sublimate', as if ordinary so-called names were adulterated, and needed purification. The simile is a chemical one, and has nothing to do with subliming. So the *real* name is the end-product of analysis. For discussion of W.'s conception of the misguided tendency (of which he accuses his younger self) to sublimate expressions, see Exg. §§89, 94, and 'Turning the inquiry round: the recantation of a metaphysician', sect. 4.

        (iii)   'the philosopher tries to bring out *the* relation . . .': see NB 53; cf. LPE 269 'When I stare at a coloured object and say "This is red", I seem to know exactly to what I give the name "red". As it were, to that which I am drinking in. It is as though there was a magic power in the words "*This is* . . ."' (cf. also LPE 285–8).

        (iv)   'wenn die Sprache *feiert*': W. accepted 'when language idles' (TS 226$_R$ §45), which fits the mechanical analogy (levers, cogwheels) better. When is language idling in this respect? Precisely when one stares at N and repeats the word 'N' or even 'this' to it (addressing it), trying to fathom 'the name-relation', instead of using these words in a language-game.

        (v)   'as it were a baptism': Of course, it isn't. But we think that by uttering a name with intense concentration we shall discover what relation actually obtains between name and object. In baptism, uttering a name in the conventional ceremonial setting confers a name, and the philosopher misguidedly thinks that he can discover this 'relation' by dissecting the *act* of baptism (like trying to find out what a goal really is by repeatedly kicking a ball into a net outside the context of a game).

2.1   'occupy the same position in a sentence': MS 115, 175, is ancestral to §38(c). Having elaborated the three mistakes that lead to the misconceived idea of a logically proper name (see Exg. §39, 2), W. remarks (I paraphrase): There is nothing more dissimilar than a demonstrative pronoun and a proper name — *if* one observes the practice of the language-game, and not just the place of the words in our sentences. We do say '*He* is big' and 'Hans is big'; but don't forget that the first sentence is senseless without the demonstrative gesture and the person pointed at. What can perhaps be compared with a name is not 'he' but the word together with the gesture and the person. One could say that it is characteristic of a name that it can be inserted in a sentence such as 'This is . . .' (e.g. 'This is A'); but it is nonsense to say 'This is this' or 'This is now'.

Indexicals

Logically proper names
    1. Russell
    2. The *Tractatus*
    3. The criticisms of the *Investigations*: assailing the motivation
    4. The criticisms of the *Investigations*: real proper names and simple names

SECTION 39

1   This links together three themes: (i) the idea of 'analysis', (ii) the 'logically proper name', (iii) the 'simple object'. These are here connected by means of the principle (adopted by Russell and the *Tractatus*) that a sentence has a sense only if, on analysis, every expression in it has a meaning. 'Nothung [Siegfried's sword] has a sharp blade' has sense even if Nothung is destroyed. Hence 'Nothung' is not a logically proper name and must disappear when the sentence is analysed. An analysed (elementary) sentence will contain only names the reference of which is guaranteed, and their referents must be simple, otherwise they could decompose, i.e. cease to exist, and their names would cease to stand for anything, and hence lack meaning (see 'Logically proper names').
    The logical atomist's argument exhibits the 'tendency to sublimate the logic of our language' (§38). We have a preconception of what a name *ought* to be and do (e.g. that it ought to have the general form of '*this*' — i.e. the general form of a simple object that is part of the substance of reality (cf. NB 61), that it ought to 'connect language to reality' (NB 53), that it must have a meaning, that the object it stands for *is* its meaning, that its meaning is a

necessary existent (exists 'in and of itself')). When we find that ordinary names do not fulfil these requirements, we conclude not that the requirements are misconceived, but that ordinary names are logically improper — they are not the *real* names, which will come to light only on analysis. We do not *look* to see how names really function — we think we already know how they *must* function if they are to do what we suppose they must do.

1.1   'Nothung': W. substituted 'Excalibur' (Arthur's sword) for the first occurrence of 'Nothung' in TS 226$_R$ §46. Since Nothung, unlike Excalibur, was broken to pieces and reassembled, it is nevertheless a better example for W.'s purposes here.

2   MS 115, 174f. (EPB), which W. wrote from August to November 1936 in Norway, and had with him when he wrote MS 142, is the source of this remark, from 'The sword "Nothung" consists of parts . . .' to the end. The context there is a discussion of indexicals such as 'now', conceived as the name of a moment, 'here', as the name of a place, 'this', as the name of an object, and 'I', as the name of a person. The grounds for such an idea are widely ramifying, W. observes. It is akin to pointing at part of one's brain and saying 'This is the real *person*' ('eigentliche *Mensch*')'. The answer is 'No, that is not the person'; i.e. that is not what one calls 'the person'. But I can understand, W. continues, that under certain circumstances one should want to say such a thing. We want the word 'person' to mean something simple, primitive, non-composite. Not something with unclear boundaries, or a 'more or less'. If one does not want to call a person's proper name or one like 'Nothung' 'a name' in the 'strict, logical' sense ['"strengen, logischen" Sinn']⁶ that is because a *name* ought to signify something *simple*. [Then follows: 'The sword "Nothung" consists of parts . . .'.]

After the end of PI §39, MS 115, 175, continues: This reasoning hangs on various mistakes: (a) the idea that an object must 'correspond' to a word in order that it have a meaning, confusing the meaning of a name with its bearer; (b) a mistaken conception (*ein falscher Begriff*) of philosophical or logical analysis of a proposition, as if it were analogous to chemical or physical analysis; (c) a mistaken conception (*eine falsche Auffassung*) of 'logical exactitude', ignorance of the concept of 'a family'.

2.1   'as no object would then correspond to the name it would have no meaning': cf. PR 72: 'What I once called "objects", simples, were simply what I could refer to without running the risk of their possible non-existence.'

---

⁶   Strikingly, Russell, having dismissed ordinary proper names as concealed descriptions, wrote: 'That makes it difficult to get any instance of a name at all in the proper strict logical sense of the word' (PLAt 179).

SECTION 40

1   §40 attacks only *one* premiss in the argument of §39: i.e. that a name has no meaning if there exists nothing for which it stands. The attack does not involve a direct thrust at the *Tractatus*, since there the bearers of names are sempiternal (as required by the argument of §39); so it is senseless to think of them as ceasing to exist. Those sublimated names and the correlative metaphysics were expressly designed to ensure that every genuine name on analysis stands for an object that cannot cease to exist (see Exg. §39, 2.1).

One point of §40 is to show that the worry which led to the erection of that logico–metaphysical edifice is groundless. The argument was that a *real* name has a meaning only if there exists an object for which it stands. For the object for which it stands *is* its meaning. So, if no such object exists, the name has no meaning. But if the name has no meaning, then any sentence in which it occurs is rendered nonsensical. But this is absurd. *The meaning of a name is not its bearer.* A name, W. insists, may have a meaning even though its bearer no longer exists. So the demise of its bearer does not render nonsensical the sentence in which it occurs. So the supposition that 'Nothung' cannot be a real name was groundless, and the postulation of sempiternal simples needless.

It is clear that the bearer of a proper name is not its meaning (whether we should speak of proper names as having a meaning is discussed in 'Proper names', sect. 7). But is the bearer the reference of the name? A proper name does not lose (cease to *have*) its reference when its bearer dies. Two lines of argument are open. Either ' "N" has a bearer' is timelessly true or false, with the consequence that 'the bearer of "N" ' cannot be substituted for 'N' in the *extensional* context 'N has died'; i.e. N's death does not deprive 'N' of its bearer. This has a needlessly paradoxical appearance. Alternatively, that 'N' has a reference is timelessly true or false, but not the statement that 'N' has a bearer (referent); i.e. that the bearer of 'N' exists. While bearer = referent, to have a reference is not to have a bearer *now*. Rather, 'N' has a reference if it is used to refer to a past, present or future particular. That that particular (the bearer or referent of 'N') no longer exists or does not yet exist (as when an author names his next book before writing it) is irrelevant to whether 'N' has a reference.

1.1   (i)   'sprachwidrig': W. accepted 'ungrammatically' (TS 226$_R$ §47).

(ii)   'das dem Wort "entspricht" ': W. altered a similar translation to 'which the word "stands for" ' (ibid.).

(iii)   'Herr N.N.': 'N.N.' is used in German as a dummy proper name akin to 'A. N. Other' in English.

(iv)   'stirbt': W. deleted 'dies' and wrote 'is dead' (ibid.).

2   The thoughts that the meaning of a word is its place in grammar and that the meaning of a word cannot be said to be its bearer were linked, as is evident from the lengthy discussion in BT 31f.

SECTION 41

1   The meaning/bearer distinction is applied to the simple language-game of
§8 (as supplemented in §15, which added tools and their names to it). Its point
is to show that the questions of whether a name has a meaning and whether
it has a bearer are independent. Whether 'N' loses its meaning after the destruction of its bearer *may be* settled by the practice of its use. The hearer may
simply be clueless what to respond, and one *might* (but need not) say that the
name has become meaningless. (But it may become meaningless despite the
bearer's continued existence, since, for whatever reason, a different name might
replace it, and the old name go out of use altogether.) Alternatively, the name
may continue to be used after the destruction of its bearer, and there may be
an appropriate response to its use (B has to shake his head). In this case, we
should not say that it is meaningless. It is also possible that it is a convention
of the language-game that once the bearer has ceased to exist, the name is
abolished — no longer *to be* used (Z §715).

1.1   Line 1 states that §15 is concerned with proper names; that was not
evident in the text (cf. Exg. §15).

SECTION 42

1   §41 examined the consequences for the meaningfulness of the name 'N', in
the simple language-game (8), of the destruction of its bearer. §42 now examines
the question of whether a name which never had a bearer, i.e. was never applied
to a tool, can be said to have a meaning. For a logical atomist (or his descendant)
might contend that a name has a meaning only if it has or has had a bearer.
This claim could be generalized: that it is impossible to name future or merely
possible individuals. That would be dogmatic. Why is it not possible to name
a future individual? Does *logic* prevent it? Is the meaning of 'name' such as to
preclude it? Cannot one name an unborn or even unconceived child? Cannot
an author name his next, as yet unwritten, book? Or a dancer announce the
name of the new dance she is about to perform spontaneously for the first time?
    Might a sign for a tool, a name, *never* have a bearer and yet have a mean-
ing? W. indicates the kind of ground that warrants ascribing a meaning to such
a sign 'X' in language-game (8). All that is required is that this name of a tool
that lacks a bearer be used appropriately. This can easily be imagined: e.g. as
a joke, asking for 'X' whenever the work in hand is ruined (this would be
analogous — but only analogous — to us asking for Cure-all).

SECTION 43

1   Contrary to what has sometimes been supposed, this section is not a declara-
tion of adherence to a theory of meaning, but the application to the case in

hand of the observation that there is a grammatical nexus between 'the use of a word' and 'the meaning of a word'. The association of meaning and use was emphasized from the opening pages of the book (e.g. §§1, 7, 9f., 20).

In §§30f., meaning was equated *en passant* with use, and ostensive definition was said to explain the use when the overall role of the word in the language is clear. Here the explanation of 'meaning of a word' in terms of use is (a) first qualified, and (b) then applied to the case of an ostensive explanation of the meaning of a name.

(a) The qualification does not show that it is wrong to equate the expressions 'the use of a word' and 'the meaning of a word' — for a large class of cases. A grammatical explanation is not a theory but a norm, and it is not shown to be *false* by a range of exceptions. What the exceptions show is that the scope of the norm is restricted in certain ways. (More involved cases are just more involved cases; the identification of meaning and use for a large class of cases is a pole of a grammatical description, not the ground floor of a theory (cf. RPP I §633).)

(b) From the fact that we often ostensively explain the meaning of a name, we cannot conclude that its meaning is its bearer. For explaining the meaning of a name by a deictic gesture and the utterance 'This is . . .' is not pointing at its meaning. It is giving a rule for its correct use.

Given that the context of §43 is a discussion of proper names, one might object that we do not ordinarily talk of proper names as having meanings at all. In so far as we do, to explain what 'N.N.' *means* is not to explain who N.N. *is*. Conversely, to explain who N.N. *is* is not to *define* the proper name 'N.N.' (cf. 'Proper names', sect. 7).

One might also note that the notion of the use of a proper name is unclear too. Is the use of a personal name individuated by its bearer? Does 'John Smith' have as many different uses as bearers, or does it have only one use? Is the use of 'John Smith' different from that of 'Jack Jones'? Is the use of a name to refer to its bearer different from its use to call its bearer, introduce its bearer, address its bearer? Do all personal names have the same uses? — after all, they are all used to refer to, call, introduce, address, etc. their bearers. (The answers to these questions are decisions, not discoveries. In each case, it is a context-dependent decision. It should be guided by the purpose or purposes at stake.)

One might also be puzzled about the relationship between W.'s dictum that the meaning of a word is its use in the language and his other dicta, which variously associate meaning with (i) what is understood when we understand an expression, (ii) the role of an expression in the calculus, (iii) its place in grammar, (iv) an explanation of meaning (see 'Meaning and use', sect. 3).

1.1   (i)   'For a *large* class of cases — though not for all': what exceptions are envisaged? One possibility would be that proper names when ostensively defined are an exception. That would be mistaken. It would be curious to introduce the principle into a discussion of proper names if such names were typically exceptions to it. For the thrust of the preceding argument is that whether or not 'N' (§41) or 'X' (§42) has a meaning *turns on its use*, not on whether it has a bearer.

Another possibility is to look for exceptions, not to this account of the meaning of a word, but to this explanation of the meaning of 'meaning'. For W. confusingly switches from the question of the meaning of the word 'meaning' to the meaning of the phrase 'the meaning of a word'. Focusing on the former, we may note that meaning may be ascribed to gestures, facial expressions, natural phenomena (e.g. 'Those clouds mean rain'), signals (e.g. traffic lights), colour patterns (BB 17), events and rituals. So the dictum that the meaning of a word is its use in the language is only a partial explanation of the meanings of 'meaning', restricted to word-meaning. But this too would be a mistaken interpretation of the text of §43.

An alternative, more plausible possibility is to look for exceptions to this explanation of 'the meaning of a word' (cf. AWL 48 (see 2.1 below)). For the phrases 'the meaning of a word' and 'the use of a word' are not everywhere interchangeable. W. speaks of *experiencing the meaning of a word*, but one would surely not call that 'experiencing the use of a word'. He speaks of *meaning blindness*, but one could not speak of this phenomenon as 'use blindness'. This interpretation is reinforced by PLP 175f., where Waismann notes that 'the meaning of a word is the way it is used' is not quite correct, for there are cases where it seems forced.[7] To remedy this defect, he continues, we need a detailed account of the grammar of 'meaning' as it appears in various linguistic contexts: i.e. an account of what it is to understand the meaning of a word, to explain the meaning of a word, for two words to have the same meaning, etc. W. emphasized that not every use is a meaning, and not every difference in use is tantamount to a difference in meaning (see 'Meaning and use', sect. 4, and Exg. §§549–70).

(ii)   'This word can be explained in this way': it should be noted that W. here uses the term 'erklären' and not 'definieren'. The notion of explaining is broader than that of defining and also more flexible. It would, however, be quite absurd to view this dictum as any kind of *theory of meaning*.

(iii)   'And the *meaning* of a name . . .': 'But', rather than 'and', would have been clearer. For although the meaning of a word is said to be its use, *nevertheless*, we sometimes explain the meaning of a word by pointing to its bearer (which is not the meaning).

(iv)   'pointing to its *bearer*': note that in the case of ostensive definition of, e.g., colour-words, one points at a *sample*, but the sample *cannot* be said to be the bearer. We explain who N.N. is by pointing to N.N., the bearer of the name. We explain what black is by pointing to a sample of black (a piece of paper or cloth, etc.), but what 'black' means is '*that* ☞ ■ colour', and the black patch of paper is not the *bearer* of the colour-name 'black'. Nor can one

---

[7]   His example: namely, 'the meaning [of this word] has dawned on me', is poorly chosen.

say that the colour black is the meaning of the word 'black' (otherwise one could say that some meanings are darker than grey).

2   The Intermediate Draft (ZF §43) added another paragraph:

Vielleicht wäre es richtiger zu sagen: Eine Bedeutung eines Wortes ist eine Art seines Gebrauch in der Sprache. Hier ist die Frage offen gelassen, was wir einen einheitlichen Gebrauch, und was etwa zwei Arten des Gebrauchs nennen werden. Ich glaube es wird sich zeigen, dass sich dafür keine scharf geschnittenen Regeln angeben lassen.

(Perhaps it would be more correct to say: a meaning of a word is a way of using it in the language. Here the question is left open what we would call a single use and what two kinds of use. I believe that it will be manifest that there is no clear-cut rule for this.)

Though deleted, this theme is examined in PI §§547–70.

2.1   (i)   'For a *large* class of cases — though not for *all*':

I have suggested substituting for 'meaning of a word', 'use of a word', because *use of a word* comprises a large part of what is meant by 'the meaning of a word'. The use of a word is what is defined by the rules, just as the use of the king of chess is defined by the rules. . . .
I also suggest examining the correlate expression 'explanation of meaning'. . . . it is less difficult to describe what we call 'explanation of meaning' than to explain 'meaning'. The meaning of a word is explained by describing its use.
It is a queer thing that, considering language as a game, the use of a word is internal to the game whereas its meaning seems to point to something outside the game. What seems to be indicated is that 'meaning' and 'use' are not equatable. But this is misleading. (AWL 48)

   (ii)   'the meaning of a word is its use': BB 65 remarks that 'The meaning of a phrase for us is characterized by the use we make of it. . . . We ask "*What do you mean?*", i.e., "How do you use this expression?"', and BB 69 adds: 'We are inclined to forget that it is the particular use of a word only which gives the word its meaning. Let us think of our old example for the use of words. Someone is sent to the grocer with a slip of paper with the words "five apples" written on it. The use of the word in *practice* is its meaning.' Is the meaning (for a large class of cases) *identical* with the use? — see 'Meaning and use', sect. 4.

SECTION 44

1   This and §45 link the discussion with §39 and §38f., respectively, showing 'why it should occur to one' to make 'this' into a name (this is made explicit in the original draft of the next remark).

Proper names can be used in the absence of their bearers, and there are obvious reasons for having this convention. Nevertheless, we can imagine expressions we should not hesitate to call 'proper names', which could be used only in the presence of their bearers. These would be replaceable by 'this ☞' (pointing at the bearer).

1.1   'when Nothung is already shattered': Nothung, Siegfried's sword in Wagner's *Der Ring des Nibelungen* was shattered and later reforged.

2   (i)   MS 142, §42, contains additional material (I paraphrase): suppose we are watching a cinema screen on which three coloured spots move about slowly changing their shapes. Suppose we ostensively name them 'P', 'Q', and 'R'; then we describe their changes as they move around the screen. In this language-game the names are used as synonyms for 'this ☞ ◆' (pointing at a coloured spot). If one of the three spots disappears, we cannot say 'P has disappeared' any more than we can say 'This ☞ has disappeared'. But we might say 'The letter "P" is out'. In this language a name does lose its meaning when its bearer ceases to exist (assuming that we do not speak about past events or use some other mode of expression for the spots). So here a name cannot cease to have a bearer. But this is not an asset of the language-game. For a name can have a use, a meaning, without having a bearer (e.g., W. avers, 'Odysseus' has meaning).

(ii)   Z §715 (MS 133, 12r–v) discusses a language-game in which a name ceases to have a use on the demise of its bearer. Here the names, as it were, have the object on a string; if the object is destroyed, the string is useless.

(iii)   PLP 196ff. stresses the family-resemblance character of the concept of a name.

SECTION 45

1   The atomist's conviction that the only real names (from a logical point of view) are 'this' and 'that' (PLAt 179) is motivated by the misguided insistence that a real name cannot fail to have a bearer. The demonstrative use of 'this' is indeed such that it is only used correctly when something is pointed at and referred to by 'this' (but 'this' has other uses too; cf. 'Indexicals'). So, of course, 'this', thus used, cannot lack a bearer. But that does not make 'this' into a name, since a name is not typically used with, but only explained by, ostensive gestures.

1.1   'whether *this* is simple or complex': for further reasons, the *Tractatus* demanded that the bearers of its 'simple names' be simple.

2   MS 142, §42, prefixes to this remark: 'But this language-game with coloured spots can, I think, show us a reason why one might wish to say that a demonstrative pronoun is a name: for . . .' (TS 226$_R$ §52).

SECTION 46

1   The quotation from *Theaetetus* 201e–202b opens the discussion of simples,
providing an archetype exemplified in logical atomism. The simples are the
objective correlates of logically proper names (what that means is explored in
§51 and §53). In §48, W. constructs a simplified language-game as a model
for this conception, in order to shed light on the confusions embedded in it,
and to illuminate our own practices of naming and describing. Note that here
the essence of names is to stand for the elements that are their meanings, and
the essence of a sentence is to be a combination of names that constitutes a
description.

       Not all of what is asserted of the primary elements in the *Theaetetus* is true
of Russell's individuals or of *Tractatus* objects (hence W. has dropped crucial
parts of Plato's text). In particular, Plato denies that primary elements can have
even external properties or relations. By contrast, combination with another
object is an external property of a *Tractatus* object. Plato denies that one can
add even a 'this' or 'that' to the name of an element, whereas 'This is A' was
apparently an example of an elementary proposition that is also an elucidation
(cf. PR §6).

1.1   (i) 'Russell's individuals': For detailed discussion, see 'Logically proper
names', sect. 1. Sometimes Russell used the expression 'particulars' instead
(TK 55f.; PLAt 177). They were defined as terms of relations (the relata, not
their names) in atomic facts that are objects of acquaintance. What particulars
there actually are in the world, he declared, is an empirical question.

       (ii) 'my "objects"': *Tractatus* objects are simple (TLP 2.02), have both
internal and external properties (TLP 2.01231), are the substance of the world
(TLP 2.021), and are the meanings of the simple names (TLP 3.203). They
can only be named (TLP 3.221); their names are primitive and indefinable
(TLP 3.26) and concatenate in a proposition (TLP 4.22) to form a description
of how things are (TLP 4.023, 4.26, 4.5).

2   BB 31: the objects (individuals, elements) of the *Tractatus* were conceived
of as necessary existents; if they did not exist, we could not even imagine them.
What can be imagined, though it may not exist, must be a possible combination of such necessary existents.

       AWL 11: Russell and W. had expected to find the first elements or 'indi-
viduals' by logical analysis. Russell thought that subject/predicate propositions
and two-term relations would be the result of a final analysis. This wrongly
took logical analysis to be akin to chemical analysis, and conceived of atomic
propositions as something to be discovered.

3   There is an unmentioned aspect of Plato's primary elements which W. held to
resemble his own early conception. This is that the Forms are self-predicable,

with the corollary that only a Form perfectly instantiates a property, that any other object exhibits a property only by partaking of the correlated Form, by containing part of the Form as an ingredient adulterated with other properties. In *The Big Typescript* 434 (cf. GB 135), W. connected his erroneous conception of object and complex in the *Tractatus* with this Platonic theme, expressed in such phrases as 'As dead as death', or 'Nothing is so dead as death itself; nothing is so beautiful as beauty itself'.

SECTION 47

1   There is no such thing as absolute simplicity or complexity. 'Simple' and 'complex' are attributive adjectives; hence 'Is A simple or complex?' makes sense only if it is to be understood as 'Is A a simple or complex X?' The answer depends not only on what an X is, but also on what standards of simplicity or complexity are set up for Xs. Similarly, what counts as an element (constituent) depends on our choices and interests in laying down what is to be called 'a component part'.

The analogy with the boy wondering whether 'to sleep' means something active or passive holds because he has crossed language-games, by disregarding the fact that he has been playing a game of classifying verbs according to whether they are in the active or passive *voice*. Now he turns to a verb in the infinitive, and raises the quite different question of whether the verb means something active or passive. Obviously, 'He is sleeping' is in the active *voice*. 'To sleep' is the infinitive form of the verb. And to sleep is not to engage in an *activity*.

1.1   (i)   'what are the simple constituents . . .': not a physicist's but a metaphysicist's question.

(ii)   'that would be an answer to the *grammatical* question': W. distinguishes the question 'What are here *called* "simple constituent parts"?' (i.e. What, in this context, does 'simple constituent part' mean?) from 'What are the simple constituent parts?' (i.e. 'Specify the various simple constituent parts').

(iii)   'the correct answer is: "That depends on what you understand by 'composite'!"': that this is a rejection of the question would be even more obvious if it were replaced by a direct question: 'What do you mean by "composite"?' This would exemplify the philosophical method of answering a question with a question (RFM 147), while the original question exemplifies the philosopher's sin of giving words a metaphysical employment outside their natural context (PI §116) and then wondering what they mean (like a child scribbling, and then asking his parent what he has drawn (RFM 483)). Outside its proper context (in which criteria of simplicity and complexity are laid down) the question 'Is X composite, and what are its parts?' has no use, no sense.

2   (i)   PR 252f. is a remote ancestor. W. asserts that (a) a larger geometrical
shape is not composed of smaller geometrical structures; (b) 5 is not composed
of 3 and 2 any more than 2 is composed of 5 and −3; (c) whether a chess-
board is complex or not depends (in part) on what we count as complexity,
for if we disregard the squares, we can see it as a unity (a large rectangle).
There are, however, other points of disagreement between these remarks and
the *Investigations*.

(ii)   TS 219, 14 (dated 1932/3 by von Wright) contains variants of PI
§47(a)–(b). Following (b), W. notes that the whole picture of logical 'analysis'
is misleading, for an analysis is a search for simpler constituents, and logical
analysis, except in very special cases, is not concerned with that.

Section 48

1   The method of §2 (see Exg.) was to invent an imaginary language-game
for which the description given by Augustine would be apt (since it is a primitive and incorrect picture of the way *our* language functions). Here W. invents
a language-game for which Plato's conception of simple elements is apt. For
here the words are names of coloured squares, and the sentence describes the
arrangement of the coloured squares. It would be natural to call the coloured
squares 'the simples' (if we were asked, for example, what here might count
as simple and what as complex). *But* it is easy to imagine other conventions,
other stipulations regarding what is to be deemed simple and what complex.
For, *pace* Plato (and the *Tractatus*), *simple* and *complex* are attributive adjectives,
and there is no such thing as absolute simplicity or complexity.

That there is no such thing as absolute simplicity has an important corollary: the possibility of imagining a context in which something (e.g. a
monochrome square) would not count as a simple does not show that it cannot correctly be taken as simple in another (or a more restricted) context.

1.2   (i)   'for which this account is really valid': misleading, since W. goes on to
show that it is not valid. Perhaps what he meant is that it is apt; nevertheless,
the kinds of conclusions Plato drew cannot, for all the aptness of the language-
game, be derived from it. Similarly, language-game (2) is apt to illustrate
Augustine's description of how he learnt to speak and hence too the primitive picture of language there presupposed, but not to validate the Augustinian
conception of the essence of language even for that restricted case.

(ii)   'Does it matter which we say . . .': Given that the principle of counting for letters is the same as that for elements, it does not matter whether types
or tokens are in question — as long as we avoid misunderstandings.

2.1   (i)   'a sentence is a series of these words': MS 152, 55, queries whether every
sentence is a complex of names. W. asserts that one can *compare* a sentence to

a complex of names. In some cases the comparison is a good one. But in others it is more and more infelicitous, until in the end it is more misleading than illuminating.

(ii)   'I wouldn't know what else . . . call "the simples" ': Z §338 (= MS. 133, 16v–18v) stresses that we can give various senses to 'This chair is complex', i.e. stipulate various possible criteria of complexity for chairs. Not so with 'Red is complex', for 'We are not familiar with any technique to which this sentence might be alluding'. And this itself leads us astray. We see that no criteria of complexity naturally apply to colours, and we confuse the *absence* of any criteria of complexity with the *presence* of criteria of simplicity. The truth is that the simple/complex dichotomy has, for us, no natural application to colour.

(iii)   'But under other circumstances . . .': In MS 152, 55, W. observes that if he thinks of the figure as a mosaic, then he is inclined to call each square an element. But if he thinks of it as a four-coloured stamp printed on paper, then he might be otherwise inclined.

SECTION 49

1   The language-game of §48 is a model for the conception of primary elements in the *Theaetetus*. According to that conception, elements cannot be explained (described) (§46). (That simples can only be named, not described, was also a salient thesis of the *Tractatus* (TLP 3.221). This claim did not mean that simples could not have external properties, but rather that they could not be described by their internal properties; i.e. that names of simples were indefinable.) But what does it mean to say of the elements of §48 that they cannot be explained (i.e. described), but only named? W. offers one possible account: in a limiting case in which the complex to be described consists of only *one* square, its description is just the appropriate name. So 'R' may sometimes be a word, sometimes a sentence; or, better, the sign 'R' may be used to name an element or to describe its occurrence. The difference does not lie in any mental 'act of meaning' concurrent with its utterance (that way lie 'philosophical superstitions'), but in the context of utterance. If 'R' is uttered in the course of memorizing words, or in explaining the meaning of the signs of §48, etc., then it is not a description. But when 'R' occurs by itself in the *application* of the signs of the language-game, then it is a one-word assertion; i.e. it describes a limiting case of the complex.

That one *sometimes* merely names an element by uttering 'R' is no reason for thinking that elements *can* only be named, not described. For naming is not on the same level as describing. Not only are the two roles not in competition (like whispering and shouting), but naming is a *preparation* for describing. Stipulating a meaning for a sign is to give the sign a range of possible roles, including describing. *Nothing* has been done by giving a thing a name except in so far as this *prepares* the sign for possible moves in a language-game.

1.1   (i)   'leads to all kinds of philosophical superstition': e.g. that what makes it a proposition rather than a word is that its utterance is accompanied by a mental act of meaning by the sign the state of affairs consisting of the obtaining of a single coloured square ('the intention is the method of projection').

(ii)   'memorizing the words and their meanings': W. preferred 'and what they mean', thus removing any nuance of reification (ibid.).

(iii)   'This was what Frege meant too': It is doubtful whether this is what Frege meant, and certain that it is not all he meant (see 'Contextual dicta and contextual principles', sects 1–2).

2   (i)   PG 208f. (TS 214(c)) discusses the thesis that an object cannot be described. Here 'described' must mean 'defined', for of course it is not denied that the object can be ' "described from the outside", that properties can be ascribed to it and so on'. Rather, what is claimed is that 'no account can be given' of the indefinables (or, more accurately, the undefined expressions) of a calculus (or language). W. criticizes this thesis in two respects. (a) What a so-called indefinable such as 'red' means can be explained ostensively. (b) Indefinables can have internal properties and relations, expressed in grammatical propositions. That blue is on the bluish side of blue-red and red on the reddish side is a proposition of grammar, which is akin to a definition.

(ii)   PLP 13f. emphasizes the difference between the grammar and the application of language, comparing it to the difference between deciding on the metre as the unit of length and carrying out measurements of objects. Waismann uses this distinction in clarifying the nature of naming (PLP 199) and the difference between a word (name) and a (one-word) sentence (describing) (PLP 318–20). Naming is the preparation of a word for use; it belongs not to the application of language, but to setting up or clarifying part of grammar. Consequently, the contrast between a word functioning as a word (naming) and a word functioning as a sentence (describing) is the difference between learning a language and the application (*Anwendung*) of a language. Even if an entry in a dictionary (e.g. 'ambulo') could function as a sentence, it does not so function there since it is not applied. A similar distinction can be made for systems of signals (e.g. railway signals), between the occurrence of the signals in a chart explaining their use and their subsequent use to control the movements of trains.

(iii)   Asserting that naming and describing stand on different levels exemplifies W.'s practice of emphasizing 'a distinction between determination of a sense and employment of a sense' (RFM 168).

Contextual dicta and contextual principles
1. The problems of a principle
2. Frege
3. The *Tractatus*
4. After the *Tractatus*
5. Compositional theories of meaning
6. Computational theories of understanding

The standard metre
1. The rudiments of measurement
2. The standard metre and canonical samples
3. Fixing the reference or explaining the meaning?
4. Defusing paradoxes

Section 50

1   This explores the significance of the *Theaetetus* claim (§46) that neither existence nor non-existence can be attributed to 'elements'. If 'existence' and 'non-existence' are understood in terms of the obtaining and non-obtaining of connections between elements (as in the *Tractatus* or Descartes), then trivially no sense has been assigned to speaking of the existence or non-existence of an element, as opposed to that of a connected complex of elements. The same point holds for 'destruction' (cf. §§55ff.), if it is explained in terms of separation of elements (cp. Descartes's proof of the immortality of the soul in his 'synopsis' of the *Meditations*). But it is easy to misconstrue this.

It seems that we *cannot* ascribe existence or non-existence to an element. Why not? If 'X' names an element, it is self-defeating to deny that X exists, because if X did not exist, one could not name it. So one could not say that X does not exist. Correlatively, to say of an element that it does exist is empty. For if 'X' names an element, then, it seems, X must exist. (Should we conclude that elements are *necessary* existents, even though we cannot *say* that they exist (cf. TLP)?)

W. invokes an analogy with the standard metre, i.e. the platinum–iridium bar (see 'The standard metre'). To say that an object is a metre long is to say that it is the length of the standard metre bar — that if suitably juxtaposed with it, their ends would coincide. Of course, this does not explain what it would mean to ascribe the length one metre to the standard metre bar itself.

We cannot juxtapose the standard metre with itself. So we cannot say either that it coincides in length thus with itself or that it fails to coincide.[8]

(b) diagnoses the matter. The standard metre bar functions as a (canonical) sample of the length of one metre. So it cannot function as a standard of measurement for itself. Hence it cannot be said either to be or not to be one metre long. This does not mean that the metre bar has a *special property*. Rather, it has a *special role* in the practice of metric measurement. It *sets the standard* for what it is to be a metre in length, but it is not *an example* of what it is to be one metre long. For to give an example of something that is a metre long presupposes the concept of being a metre long; i.e. it presupposes the standard of measurement.

(c) reverts to the atomist illusion of necessary but ineffable existence. Whatever looks as if it *had* to exist is a sample or paradigm in our language, something that belongs to the means of representation. This is applied to the language-game of §48; its elements (the simples) are the coloured squares correlated with the names 'R', 'B', 'G', 'W', i.e. the samples used to explain these names. The illusion that these elements are necessary existents is a misstatement of the fact that if there were no coloured squares, coloured squares would not serve the purpose of samples for explaining the words 'R', 'B', 'G', 'W'. An apparent metaphysical truth about the elements of which reality consists is thus deflated into a grammatical platitude: only what exists can be used as a sample. That is a truism about how certain words are explained.

1.1   (i)   'the standard metre': Is the standard metre the length of the metre bar in Paris,[9] or is it the metre bar itself? Suppose I explain the term 'metre' by pointing to the metre bar in the Louvre and saying, 'That is a metre'. This might be described as ostensively defining the word 'metre' by reference to the standard metre. But there seems a double reference; for what I point at is the metre bar (a piece of metal), but what I say is that the *length* of this *bar* is called 'one metre' or perhaps that *this length* is one metre. Since the standard metre is *ex hypothesi* the canonical sample for defining the term 'metre', this apparent ambiguity in the notion of a sample might give rise to two interpretations of the expression 'standard metre'.

If 'standard metre' is taken to mean *the length* of the metal bar in Paris (under certain standard conditions), then there are arguments against the intelligibility of either ascribing or denying to it the property of being a metre long. For the length of the metre bar is a property of objects, viz. the property of

---

[8]   Of course, it would be absurd to conclude that the standard metre is *necessarily* one metre long, but that this cannot be *said* — although this would be parallel to the thought that the elements are necessary existents, but indescribably so.

[9]   The metre bar is now kept in the International Bureau of Weights and Measures at Sèvres, not as previously in Paris (at the Louvre). This point will be ignored henceforth. Note that the phrase 'Imperial Standard Yard' means the *unit of length* defined by means of the Imperial Standard Bar, according to the Weights and Measures Act 1856.

being a metre long, and therefore to assert or deny this property of itself is nonsense.[10]

If, on the other hand, 'the standard metre' means the metre *bar* in the Louvre, then there is not *this* impropriety in ascribing it a length. W. clearly uses 'the standard metre' to refer to the *metre bar*. For it is the metre bar that is uniquely to be found in Paris, not its length, which may be instantiated in many different places. It is the metre bar that functions as a paradigm with which comparison can be made (e.g. in settling disputes about standard samples used in making metric measurements). It is the canonical sample *of* a certain length. So, for a quite different reason from the length one metre, the standard metre bar too cannot be said to have that length (cf. BT 241).

(ii) 'something with which comparison is made': Note that not every sample is used as an object of comparison for judging the applicability of the term it helps to define. This role is characteristic of standard samples, but not of optional ones (cf. 'Ostensive definition and its ramifications', sect. 5); for example, explicit comparison with a sample is not normally involved in describing something as red. Nor is it the case that what functions sometimes as a sample always does so; for example, what serves on one occasion as a sample of red can on another occasion be described as red. W.'s point is merely that objects, when being used as samples, have a normative role; they belong to the means of measurement, not to what is measured. There is a distinctive direction of fit involved in comparison with something being used as a sample; for example, in holding a metre stick against a table, we measure the table, not the metre stick, as long as we are using it as a (standard) sample of one metre. W.'s own translation emphasized this point: 'the role of a standard with which something's compared' (TS 226$_R$ §59).

2.1   'this gives this object a role . . . it is now a *means* of representation': MS 111 (Vol. VII), 112, points out that if one calls green an object, one must recognize that it is part of the symbolism. To be sure, W. continues, this overturns the whole *Tractatus* concept of an object. But that is as it should be. Red, left, etc., are not objects, rather the red patch, the table, etc.

SECTION 51

1   The words of §48 'correspond' to colours, but what does the correspondence consist in ('what does "the name-relation" consist in?')? The description of

---

[10]   Though nonsense, it is the root of a philosophical illusion. A property is itself treated as an individual, but as an individual exhibiting that property in its pure form. 'Here the image which we use in thinking of reality is that beauty, death, etc., are the pure (concentrated) substances' (BT 433f.). By contrast, when properties are predicated of ordinary individuals, they appear as ingredients, as constituents of something compounded (complex) (BB 17). This illusion ensnared both Plato and W.

§48 merely set up this connection, but did not say what it was. The first response is that 'R', 'W', etc., would be taught by pointing at paradigms. This is correct. But this is to say something about the 'preparation' for the language-game. We want an explanation of what correspondence consists in *in the practice of the language*; i.e. we want to know how the teaching relates to the practice of using the signs. In particular, we must reveal the normative component of teaching that provides a standard of correct use.

Two suggestions are made. (i) 'R' corresponds to a red square if and only if the speaker always says 'R' when there is a red square. But this is a mere regularity, not a normative regularity. Surely 'R' may correspond to R even if someone occasionally mistakenly says 'R' instead of 'B'. Indeed; but then what is the criterion for their making a *mistake*? (ii) 'R' stands for a red square if and only if those who use 'R' always have an image of a red square when they do so. This is equally defective; the imaging of an object is neither necessary nor sufficient for understanding its name, and mental association gives no public criterion for understanding.

What is the general point of this remark? First, there is no unique 'name-relation' or correspondence-relation such that if we understand what it consists in we will grasp once and for all how language manages to represent. Secondly, correspondence may involve many different things (connecting words with paradigms, pinning labels on things, etc.), but does not consist in any of them. We must clarify what aspect of the practice of using signs we wish to call 'correspondence', and then examine different cases and scrutinize the different possibilities.

1.1   (i)   'corresponded to the colours of the squares': strictly speaking, he had said that they corresponded to the coloured squares.

(ii)   'Praxis der Sprache': 'practice of the language'; this is sanctioned by TS 226$_R$ §60, and gives a consistent rendering of 'Praxis' (cf. §197).

(iii)   'a red square always comes before their minds': cf. PI §396, 'It is no more essential to the understanding of a sentence that one should imagine anything in connection with it than that one should make a sketch from it.'

2   PG 97 stresses that the correlation between names and things, no matter whether effected by ostension, labelling, a chart, etc., is part of the symbolism; i.e. is normative, not mechanical. It is not a name-relation that gives a name its use, but explanations of its meaning, e.g. by pointing at a sample. It is misguided to see such explanations as setting up 'the name-relation'.

Section 52

1   A not very helpful metaphor to illuminate the pernicious effect of philosophical preconceptions. §51 concluded that to see more clearly what the

correspondence of names and coloured squares consists in, we must (as in count-less other cases) focus on the details of what goes on. But evidently there is great resistance to this. Why? The metaphor is meant to illuminate this. We think investigation of details unnecessary when we are convinced that certain possibilities are excluded a priori. So if we think, for example, that the cor-respondence between name and nominatum *cannot* consist in a variety of possibilities (cf. §53), some of which (e.g. teaching the use of a name in such-and-such a way) are antecedent to, and others (e.g. justifying the applica-tion of a name in such-and-such a way *ex post actu*) are subsequent to, the application of the name, then we will not bother to investigate such matters. And that was, indeed, the path followed by the author of the *Tractatus*, who evidently thought that the correspondence *must* consist in a concurrent mental (occult (MS 152, 54)) process of meaning, e.g. R by 'R'.

1.1   'Was es aber ist, . . . müssen wir erst verstehen lernen': 'But what it is that . . . we have yet to come to understand' (cf. TS 226$_R$ §60). The explanation is most vividly set forth in PI §§89–108.

2.1   MS 152, 57, elaborates the metaphor somewhat differently.

3   Cf. PI §340 and also Schopenhauer:

> What is most opposed to the discovery of truth is not the false appearance that proceeds from things and leads to error, or even directly a weakness of the intellect. On the contrary, it is the preconceived opinion, the prejudice, which, as a spurious *a priori*, is opposed to truth. It is then like a contrary wind that drives the ship back from the direction in which the land lies, so that rudder and sail now work to no purpose.[11]

SECTION 53

1   The two suggestions canvassed in §51 were defective. Nevertheless, the language-game of §48 provides various grounds that could license saying that a sign is a name of a coloured square. W. mentions two here in §53(a), con-cerned with teaching that embodies grammatical rules: namely ostensive definition ('. . . were taught the use of the signs in such-and-such a way') and correlation in a chart (table) that is used in teaching and also functions as a court of appeal. Note that, unlike the rejected pair of suggestions, both of these involve normative considerations, providing criteria of correctness and hence too criteria for what is to count as a mistake. In §51 the method of

---

[11] A. Schopenhauer, *Parerga and Paralipomena*, tr. E. F. J. Payne (Clarendon Press, Oxford, 1974), vol. 2, §17.

introduction of an expression was taken for granted, and the question was what does correspondence consist in. Here the answer is given, not in terms of 'a correspondence-relation', but in terms of the various roles a rule might have in the practice of using an expression. The existence of such practices of explanation and justification does warrant claiming that these signs are names of coloured squares, even though the practices need not be exhibited in every case of an application of a given name.

§53(b) examines a third case, in which one might say that the rule 'enters into' the actual practice of the language, taking over, as it were, the role of memory and association. Here the chart *is* used whenever the name is applied. The parenthesis acknowledges that this is the abnormal case for ordinary colour ascriptions.

1.1   (i)   'Gebrauch': W. translated this as 'practice' (TS 226$_R$ §61), bringing it into line with 'Praxis der Sprache' in §51 (cf. MS 152, 58).

(ii)   'This chart . . . the role of memory and association': when it comes to fine shades of colour, for example, we may well find, if asked to purchase peach-blossom pink cloth, that we cannot remember which colour peach-blossom pink is, i.e. which colour is called 'peach-blossom pink' (or what 'peach-blossom pink' means). We might then use the colour-chart as an *aide-mémoire* in respect of the meaning of this colour-name. If one cannot remember the colour, one can carry the chart around with one and consult it when necessary.

Clearly every process of imagining (conjuring up a mental image) alleged to be involved in understanding a colour-name, e.g. 'red', can be replaced by looking at public patches of red on a colour-chart. This manoeuvre is used by W. to dispel the illusion that the life of signs resides in the mind (BB 4, 89).

(iii)   'a rule . . . may have very different roles in the language-game': see 'Rules and grammar' in Volume 2.

2.1   'This chart . . . the role of memory . . .': PI §265 exploits this comparison in attacking the supposition that a table which exists *only* in a speaker's imagination might constitute a rule for the use of a sign in a private language.

SECTION 54

1   Developing the final point of §53, W. illustrates, by reference to games, various roles that rules may fulfil in language. The first two here correspond to those discussed in §53. Further, he hints at the answer to the question of what distinguishes a mere regularity from a normative regularity. A counter-instance falsifies a statement of an exceptionless regularity. The behavioural criteria for a mistake (the normative reactive, corrective behaviour) confirm the existence of a rule and distinguish rule-following behaviour from behaviour constituting a regularity.

1.1   'correcting a slip of the tongue': note that the behaviour of self-correction
        is no less a criterion of rule-governed behaviour than correction by others.

2   PLP 129–35 discusses the role of rules in games and the distinction between
        a rule-governed regularity and a mere regularity.

Section 55

1   §39 first raised the matter of the apparent requirement of the indestructibility
        of the bearer of a 'real' name. It seemed, for example, that 'Nothung' could
        not be a real name, since Nothung can be spoken of even after it has been
        broken into pieces. The reasoning explicitly presupposed that a name has a
        meaning only if there exists an object corresponding to it, since the object
        corresponding to it is conceived to *be* its meaning (on the Augustinian model).
        §46 linked the objects of the *Tractatus* and Russell's 'individuals' with the Platonic
        conception of primary elements. §50(a) noted that if destruction is construed
        as decomposition of a complex into its elements, then it is senseless to speak
        of the destruction of an element. §55(a) now probes deeper. Not only might
        one argue that 'Nothung' is not a real name since one can say that Nothung
        has been destroyed, one might further claim that it must be possible to describe
        a state of affairs in which *everything* destructible is destroyed. Such a descrip-
        tion will make sense only if its constituent names have meanings. If their
        having meaning is conceived of as their corresponding to something, then what
        they correspond to must, it seems, be indestructible.
        §55(b) is a riposte. Granted that if the description of the state of affairs in
        which everything destructible is destroyed is to be possible, then what gives
        its words their meaning cannot be destroyed. But that is not what we natur-
        ally think of as the object corresponding to a name. One may say that the
        man N.N. corresponds to the name 'N.N.'. But he is not the meaning of his
        own name; and he does not give his name its meaning (assuming, as W. does,
        that proper names have a meaning). Moreover, the name 'N.N.' retains its
        meaning even after N.N. dies (§40). Differently, one may also say that a paradigm
        or sample used in connection with a simple predicate (e.g. 'red') corresponds
        to the predicate. Here what corresponds to a word does contribute to deter-
        mination of its meaning, since such a paradigm is sometimes used with the
        word and plays a role in explaining its meaning. But the sample, which belongs
        to the means of representation (cf. §50), is not the meaning of the name.
        To be sure, samples are no more immune from destruction than any other
        objects. Does this mean that the premiss (that it must be possible to describe
        a state of affairs in which everything destructible is destroyed) that led to the
        false conclusion (that what names signify must be indestructible) is itself false?
        Not so. But it does not follow from the fact that it must be possible to describe
        the state of affairs in which everything destructible is destroyed that it must

be possible *in that state of affairs* to describe how things are. That is a separate and patently misguided claim.

Samples can be destroyed. If there were nothing that could function as a sample for explaining a word that is actually explained only by reference to samples, then this word could not be explained as it now is and hence it would (in due course) cease to have the meaning it now has.[12] Our language does not have to contain the samples that it does, but if it did not do so, it would be a different language (cf. PG 143).

2   MS 152, 60, notes that the idea of the indestructibility of the simple conceives of destruction as decomposition and of the indestructible simples as kinds of atoms. W. observes that what we think of as having to exist is what belongs to language, and notes '[Neurath?]'.

SECTION 56

1   This starts from an objection to the final sentence of §55 and develops a fresh argument for the indestructibility of simples. Is a paradigm really a substitute for something indestructible? For, to be sure, samples are *not* indestructible (see Exg. §55, 1). Is it not enough for a word like 'red' to have a meaning that we bear in mind the colour it stands for, i.e. that we can call up a mental image of red? If so, then what corresponds to 'red' is the possibility of calling up an image of red (i.e. remembering what red is). And what we thus call up is, in a sense, indestructible, since it is *always* possible for us to call it up.

W.'s reply does not attack the presupposition of the reasoning: namely, that public samples can be replaced by mental (private) ones and that understanding sometimes consists in associating an image with a word. Instead, he queries whether the indestructibility of simples can be established even granted these premises. Red is proved to be indestructible only if one can always remember what *red* is, i.e. only if one can always call up an image of *red*. But even if one can always form some image if one asks oneself what 'red' means, how does one know that it is the *correct* image (i.e. whether it is red that one is calling to mind)? There must be a distinction between producing a mental image of red and one of green, and also between thinking one is producing the right mental image and producing the right mental image. For the objector cannot claim that 'red' means 'whatever image occurs to one when one hears or speaks the word "red"' (PG 70; PI §239).

There are criteria for correctness of memory images. If a patch of colour may change (e.g. become darker), so too the mental image of a given colour

---

[12]   If all red things were destroyed, and the possibility of making more blocked, then the word 'red' would gradually fall into desuetude, as it could not be taught to the next generation or explained to anyone who does not already know what it means.

or shade of colour that occurs to one on a given occasion may differ from that which occurs to one on a later occasion. 'As I remembered, peach-blossom pink was not as pink as this', we may say, as we check our memory against a colour-chart. The objector, however, cannot avail himself of public samples without surrendering his supposition that the meaning of 'red' is independent of such samples. But then, on his account, we are at the mercy of memory. So his proposal fails to establish his thesis that red is indestructible. And it is also at odds with our practice. For we do not regard the deliverances of memory as the verdict of the highest court of appeal. Public samples are destructible. So are we at their mercy? Or at the mercy of the chemical reactions that we rely on to produce colour samples? We can typically replace samples if they are damaged or destroyed (e.g. the Imperial Standard Bar was destroyed in a fire and replaced). Something is a sample only if we decide to use it as a sample. So there is an important sense in which we are not at the mercy of samples at all (see 'The standard metre', sect. 3), although, of course, our linguistic practices are dependent upon background regularities of nature (and of our nature).

1.1   'zur Sprache gehört': W. preferred 'is used in the language' (TS 226$_R$ §64).

2   PG 95 states the lack of finality of memory more explicitly and perspicuously than does PI §56:

> If the use of the word 'red' depends on the picture that my memory automatically reproduces at the sound of this word, then I am as much at the mercy of this reproduction as if I had decided to settle the meaning by looking up a chart in such a way that I would surrender unconditionally to whatever I found there.
> If the sample I am to work with appears darker than I remember it being yesterday, I need not agree with the memory and in fact I do not always do so. And I might very well speak of a darkening of my memory.

Section 57

1   This introduces a second objection to the suggestion at the end of §55 that what was valid in the role demanded of simples is actually satisfied by samples. All red *things* can be destroyed, but *red itself* cannot be destroyed. *That* is why the meaning of 'red' is independent of the existence of red things, *a fortiori* independent of the existence of samples (which are destructible) used to explain 'red'. (This argument is the inverse of that in §55(a). That argument inferred metaphysical truths from the apparent requirement of logic, whereas this draws conclusions about logic from putative metaphysical truths.)

W. concedes that we cannot say that the colour red is torn up or pounded to bits. But these are only particular modes of destruction of red things. We do say of a sunset sky, for example, 'The red is vanishing'. So why should 'all the red there is' not vanish? Seeking refuge in our capacity to produce mental images of red or the capacity to produce a chemical reaction yielding a red flame is futile. Might we not tomorrow be unable to produce the required chemical reaction? Or might it not yield anomalous results? But 'red' does not mean 'whatever colour the flame has when X reacts with Y in such-and-such conditions'. Similarly, it is perfectly possible that we might no longer remember what colour is named by 'red'. Then we can no longer engage in the language-game with it. This loss of ability is comparable to the loss of a defining paradigm. So, our linguistic practice is dependent on the availability or reproducibility of defining samples (although not, typically, of any particular object functioning as a sample), and on the persistence of our mnemonic and recognitional abilities. The metaphysical underpinning of our linguistic practices is unavailable (because unintelligible); but also unnecessary. For our abilities generally persist, and the samples we need are available.

1.1   '(as opposed to the pigment)': pigment can't be torn up either, but can be destroyed.

2   BB 31: a complex, e.g. my watch, exists if it has not been destroyed. But what could be meant by 'destroying redness'? — destroying everything that is red? But that would not prevent us imagining red things! This is correct; the ability to use 'red' would not be destroyed by painting all red things green. The interlocutor then queries, 'Surely, red objects must have existed and you must have seen them if you are able to imagine them?', and W. responds by suggesting that our initial (and perhaps only) 'acquaintance' with red might be having an image of red. (This position is rejected in LPE, PI and Z.)

Section 58

1   Beginning from a further argument for the indestructibility of simples, §58 draws together the elements of the preceding remarks and diagnoses the roots of the misleading metaphysical picture of the *Theaetetus* (quoted in §46) and hence too of logical atomism.

The interlocutor now says that the term 'name' should be restricted to what cannot occur in the argument-place of 'ξ exists'. His reasoning depends on the thought that a (genuine) name has meaning simply in virtue of being correlated with something (*vide* the Augustinian conception of meaning). If it made sense to say 'X exists', then it would also make sense to say 'X does not exist'. But if red did not exist, nothing would correspond to 'red', and therefore the sentence 'Red does not exist' would be meaningless. (This recapitulates the argument of §50(b).) Consequently, the defender of this conception will want to confine 'name' to expressions which do not make sense in the combination 'X exists'. And this (third) move (the others being in §55 and §57) seems to guarantee the indestructibility or sempiternality of the simple objects that are the meanings of names. This restriction is part of Russell's characterization of logically proper names and of the conception of names in the *Tractatus* (cf. 'Logically proper names', sects 1f.).

W.'s response in §58(a) takes the sting out of the interlocutor's metaphysical thrust. The argument is that one cannot say 'red exists', since one cannot assert its negation 'red does not exist', because if red didn't exist, one could not speak of it in order to say that it does not exist. But all that 'red exists' really amounts to is that the word 'red' has a meaning. So 'red exists' is not an attempt to state an ineffable truth about red, but an innocuous proposition about the word 'red'. Consequently, the metaphysical thesis that red necessarily exists and is indestructible boils down to the trivial claim that the word 'red' has a meaning.

(b) elaborates the contrasting view: it seems that in saying that 'Red exists' makes no sense we are enunciating metaphysical truths about the essential nature of red: namely, that it exists 'in and of itself' (cf. the *Theaetetus* quotation in PI §46), that it is a necessary existent, that it stands outside time or that it is indestructible (TLP; see 2(iii) below).

(c) diagnoses the source of the idea that logic forces us beyond the bounds of sense into metaphysics. Anyone in the grip of this conception wants to take as equivalent the pair of statements 'Red exists' and ' "Red" has meaning', and also the pair 'Red does not exist' and ' "Red" has no meaning'. For it is the existence of red (and nothing else) that makes 'red' a name (i.e. gives it a meaning). But there is an obstacle to taking them as equivalent. Although the sentence ' "Red" has no meaning' seems unproblematic (it is simply a contingently false statement about an English word), the 'equivalent' sentence 'Red does not exist' seems to contradict itself. For, if it were true, 'red' would lack a meaning, and then so too would the sentence 'Red does not exist'. At this juncture, we erroneously conclude that 'red' is a real name, standing for a necessary existent of which we cannot say that it exists or does not exist. The apparent contradiction in this picture stems from two incompatible thrusts: the metaphysical and the linguistic. In fact, sentences of the form 'Red exists' do have a role, but it is neither to make metaphysical statements nor to make metalinguistic ones. It is merely to note that there are things thus coloured.

1.1   (i)   'Und so kann man': this is not the derivation of a conclusion, but an example. So better less emphasis than 'thus'; perhaps: 'And so one cannot say'.

(ii)   'a metaphysical statement': note that W. takes the statement that red exists 'in and of itself', i.e. that it is a necessary existent, to be metaphysical. In general, he construes metaphysical statements to be modal propositions concerning what must or cannot or may be thus or otherwise. They are at best confused formulations of grammatical propositions (i.e. rules for the use of words in the form of descriptions), sometimes confused recommendations to adopt a new form of representation, but most commonly nonsense — transgressions of the bounds of sense. For further discussion, see Exg. §116 and Volume 2, 'Grammar and necessity', and *Wittgenstein's Place in Twentieth-Century Analytic Philosophy*, ch. 5, sect. 4.

2   (i)   PG 137: '"the colour brown exists" means nothing at all; except that it exists here or there as the colouring of an object, and that is not necessary in order for me to be able to imagine a brown stag.'

(ii)   RFM 64: 'Red is' has no use. But if it were to be given one, it would be appropriate to use it as an introductory formula to statements about red objects — a formula to be pronounced when looking at a red sample, i.e. 'reminding oneself' that 'red' has meaning. What is misleading about this pseudo-sentence is that one is tempted to pronounce it when looking attentively at a sample, i.e. in a situation similar to one in which one observes the existence of an object, e.g. an insect. And so one thinks that one is plumbing meta-physical truths about the necessary existence of universals.

(iii)   The *Tractatus* asserted that simple objects are the sempiternal substance of the world (TLP 2.021), the unalterable and subsistent (TLP 2.0271). One cannot, W. then thought, say of an object that it exists (this would not be a well-formed proposition). Nor could it, so to speak, have a sense, since its 'negation' would not describe a possibility (so saying that an object exists would not be bipolar either). But that simple objects subsist is shown by any pro-position that describes a state of affairs.

SECTION 59

1   This final atomist move links the preceding discussion of simples with the brief examination of analysis in §§60–4. A name, on the atomists' account, signifies an unchanging, indestructible *element* of reality. Change is the re-arrangement of constant elements, which are the 'substance of the world'. But *experience does not show us* these elements. Rather, this metaphysical picture is a multiply motivated, but misguided, projection of the mundane fact of the constitution of spatial complexes of smaller (simpler) constituents. Such com-plexes (e.g. a chair) are commonly destroyed by being disassembled, but their constituent parts typically remain unchanged. (The picture is supported by the permissibility of talking of 'combinations of colours and shapes', which, W. asserts, is the root of the misleading expression 'a fact is a complex of objects' (MS 111 (Vol. VII), 19).)

1.1   (i)   Lines 3–4: W. preferred 'While we were saying the sentence it was already before our minds. We expressed an entirely definite idea' (TS 226$_R$ §67).

(iii)   'experience does not show us these elements': this is true of the objects of the *Tractatus*. They were *demanded* by the picture W. wanted to use (for

his own later detailed diagnosis, see 'Turning the examination around: the recantation of a metaphysician'). Analysis, he assumed, would sooner or later
uncover the real objects (RLF 171). This conception was later criticized as
'dogmatism' (WWK 182f.)

2.1   MS 152, 64, runs differently. After line 6, W. continues thus (I paraphrase):
Destruction, one wants to say, is in some sense the separation of elements.
That means that destruction can somehow be compared with this picture. But
that means only that this picture somehow, well or badly, fits. Imagine my
saying that every pair of shoes somehow fits me.

SECTION 60

1   According to logical atomism, analysis would reveal the hidden logical form
of propositions, and render explicit the hidden sense of sentences. More importantly, it would reveal the essence of the world. The philosophical significance
of the theory of descriptions did not lie in the fairly trivial method of grammatical paraphrase of definite descriptions, but in its sublime (metaphysical)
implications (central to the *Tractatus*) and its apparent epistemological consequences (crucial for Russell's philosophy). These lent the theory its depth. Once
they were seen to be illusory, W. had no further interest in the workings of
the singular definite article in English or German.
     The preceding discussion has undermined the doctrines that lent analysis its
depth. Implicitly it has also made clear the radical separation of meaning and
understanding involved in logical atomism. For to the extent that analysis revealed
the hidden sense of sentences, either (i) what we understand in understanding sentences in advance of analysis falls short of their meanings (which is absurd)
or (ii) what we explain in our ordinary explanations falls short of the correct
explanations of what we mean, and our understanding is, in advance of
analysis, transcendent. According to (ii) correct use is compatible with total
inability to give a correct explanation of meaning; the latter is a programme
for future 'scientific' philosophy, which no one has yet executed (cf. RLF 171).
So if we do understand what our sentences mean, what we understand is not
something we can say in advance of an adequate analysis (or, according to
others, in advance of a 'theory'). This conception informed late twentieth-
century endeavours to construct a 'theory of meaning' for a language.
     §§60–4 treat of the residue of analysis, what is left of it once purified of
logical atomism. §60 argues that the so-called analysed form of a sentence does
not reveal the hidden sense of the analysandum. (The whole idea of a hidden
sense is now rejected as incoherent.) Furthermore, the analysed form of a sentence does *not* make explicit what a speaker who uses the unanalysed sentence
really means or had in mind, or was thinking of. By implication, therefore, it
is quite wrong to suppose, as the author of the *Tractatus* had, that analysis is

an *elucidation* of the sense of the analysandum (TLP 4.112). Moreover, the analysed sentence does not mirror a hidden, mental, articulated process in the language of thought (cf. CL 68) that, for example, accompanies the order 'Bring me the broom'.

The second half of §60 contrasts two versions of a language-game in an argument parallel to §19(b). The unanalysed sentence is no more elliptical for the analysed one than the analysed one is a lengthening of the unanalysed one.

2.1   The style of analysis of 'The broom is in the corner' dates back to NB 4: '$\Phi(aRb) = Df. \Phi(a). \Phi(b). aRb$'.

3   Examples of the conception of analysis under attack:

> . . . definitions which describe the real nature of the object or notion denoted by a word . . . are only possible when the object or notion in question is something complex. You can give a definition of a horse, because a horse has many different properties and qualities, all of which you can enumerate. But when you have enumerated them all, when you have reduced a horse to his simplest terms, then you can no longer define those terms. They are simply something which you think of or perceive . . . [W]hen we define horse . . . we may mean that a certain object, which we all of us know, is composed in a certain manner: that it has four legs, a head, a heart, a liver, etc., etc., all of them arranged in definite relations to one another . . . We might think just as clearly and correctly about a horse, if we thought of all its parts and their arrangement instead of thinking of the whole.[13]

Also:

> The only kind of unity to which I can attach any precise sense — apart from the unity of the absolutely simple — is that of a whole composed of parts . . . [I]f the parts express the whole or the other parts, they must be complex, and therefore themselves contain parts; if the parts have been analysed as far as possible, they must be simple terms, incapable of expressing anything except themselves . . . All complexity is conceptual in the sense that it is due to a whole capable of logical analysis, but is real in the sense that it has no dependence upon the mind, but only upon the nature of the object. Where the mind can distinguish elements, there must be different elements to distinguish; though, alas! there are often different elements which the mind does not distinguish. (PrM 466)

The thought that we have to wait on analysis to tell us what we mean by our words seemed to W. 'a hellish idea' (WWK 129f.).

Section 61

1   We might agree that a particular order in (a) says the same as one in (b); i.e. they 'achieve the same' in the respective language-games. But this does

---

[13]   G. E. Moore, *Principia Ethica* (Cambridge University Press, Cambridge, 1960), pp. 7f.

not establish a general agreement over the sameness of sense of sentences. For sameness of sense turns on sameness of functions in the different language-games and on the similarities and differences between the language-games.

This point is exemplified in the differences between Frege and Russell in their accounts of singular definite descriptions. We may agree that a sentence containing a Russellian expansion *says* much the same, achieves the same, in a given context, as a corresponding 'unanalysed' sentence. Nevertheless, we may deny that in general any two such sentences are synonymous. So too, we may agree that the two imperatives in (a) and (b) achieve the same, but deny that the 'unanalysed' one 'contains' a description of the components of the complex.

The final sentence raises the question of the criteria for sameness and difference of sense or meaning, which is pursued in the next three sections and then resumed in §§547–70.

Section 62

1   The criteria for whether a person does *the same* in executing an order in (a) and (b) is not determined in advance of our fixing criteria of sameness of action, and that depends, *inter alia*, on our interests. Even where we agree on such criteria (e.g. sameness of *point*), the determination of what, e.g., counts as part of the point is both unclear and context-dependent (so may vary in different language-games). And the unclarity and context-dependency spill over into an indeterminacy regarding concept-identity and sameness of sense or meaning.

1.1   'between essential and inessential': In general, there is no sharp distinction between what is essential and what inessential independently of context and purpose. In particular, our concepts of concept-identity and synonymy are dependent upon distinguishing between what is essential and what is inessential, and that distinction depends on context and on our classificatory purposes. (For W.'s examination of the issue see §§547–70 and Exg.)

2.1   The Intermediate Draft (ZF §62) links this remark with the last paragraph of ZF §43 (quoted in Exg. §43, 2), which was subsequently deleted. This paragraph observed that there is no sharp boundary between what counts as one use and what counts as two different kinds of use. This too manifests W.'s conviction that the distinction between sameness and difference of meaning is fluid and purpose-relative.

Section 63

1   Russell's Theory of Descriptions (the paradigm of analysis) did indeed seduce philosophers into thinking that the analysed form of a sentence containing a

singular definite description is more fundamental than its unanalysed form. (For the idea that only analysis shows us what our words and phrases really mean, see Exg. §60, 3.) The illusion is discussed again in §91.

1.1   'an aspect of the matter is lost on you . . .': illustrated by the example in §64.

SECTION 64

1   This elaborates the final sentence of §63. Not only is it false that the 'analysed' sentence is more fundamental, but analysis may disguise an aspect of the matter, as exemplified in the imagined variant of language-game (48). The *Gestalt* of a complex configuration is 'more than the sum of its parts'.

2   RFM 425ff. examines language-games with names for colour-complexes.

Chapter 3

Family resemblance, determinacy of sense, and the quest for essence (§§65–88)

INTRODUCTION

§65 opens with the remark: 'Here we come up against the great question that lies behind all these considerations.' That great question — 'What is the essence of language?' — had been at the heart of the *Tractatus*. But the discussion thus far has demolished the struts upon which the *Tractatus* answer had rested. §§1–27(a) have argued that it is misguided to construe the essence of words to be naming, at best vacuous to hold that words stand for things, and incoherent to suppose that the meanings of words are objects in reality with which they are correlated. Furthermore, it is mistaken to suppose that sentences must be complex (e.g. composed of names of functions and of arguments), or, indeed, that a language must consist of propositions (assertoric sentences in use) at all. §§27(b)–64 have argued that the supposition of a meaning-endowing connection between language and reality, linking simple names to indestructible simple objects in the world, is a misconception; that the very idea of sempiternal simple objects was confused, conflating samples with simples and elements of the means of representation with elements of what is represented; and, finally, that the whole conception of philosophical analysis, conceived as disclosing simultaneously the logical structure of language and the metaphysical structure of the world was awry. If these criticisms hold, then the philosophy of the *Tractatus* collapses (as do many other philosophies). In particular, the thought that language essentially consists in the totality of propositions generated out of elementary propositions by means of truth-functional operations (or, more specifically, by means of the N-operator) must be abandoned. But W. has offered no alternative answer to the great question of the essence of language. He has introduced the notion of a language-game, and emphasized the multiplicity and diversity of language-games, but he has nowhere explained what the essence of a language-game is or what the essence of language, conceived as a motley of language-games, is.

W., as will become clear, is indeed trying to understand the nature of language (PI §92; cf. Exg.). But not in the sense he had originally had in mind.

For he is not trying to disclose the common properties or *essence* of everything correctly deemed to be a use of language. The concept of language is not defined by specification of necessary and sufficient conditions in virtue of which something qualifies as language or a part of language. It is not sharply circumscribed at all. For language is a motley of language-games, none of which is essential. And new language-games are constantly being assimilated into our linguistic practices. The concept of language, and the concept of a proposition too, are *family-resemblance* concepts.

§§65–88 are concerned with introducing the notion of family resemblance, with dismissing the Fregean and *Tractatus* exclusion both of vagueness and the very possibility of vagueness (Frege's demand for determinacy of sense), and with combating the dogma, going back to Socrates and Plato, that there must be something common to everything that falls under a given concept. According to that conception, philosophical investigation is a quest for the *essences* of all things. And the logical (or philosophico-logical) investigation of names, concept-words, and propositions is an investigation into the essence of language (which mirrors the essence of the world). What that conception led to, and why, W. explains in §§89–108. First, however, he turns to undermine the idea that a concept must apply to the things that fall under it in virtue of their possession of common properties. §§65–88 can be split into two parts. The first introduces the concept of family resemblance, and confronts various objections to it and to the intelligibility of vague concepts. The second traces the roots of the Platonic dogma of common essences to misconceptions about meaning something by, and about understanding, a word.

Part A consists of §§65–74. First, the notion of family resemblance is introduced, clarified and applied (§§65–7(b)) to *game* and *number*. Three objections are then rebutted. (i) An apparent family-resemblance concept does have a common property: namely, a disjunctive one (§67c). (ii) It is a logical sum of sub-concepts each of which is definable by specification of characteristic marks and so has sharp boundaries after all (§68). (iii) A concept, which is explained merely by listing a few paradigmatic examples, is useless. The third objection has two versions. The first, associated with Plato (MS 142, §67), is that a person who cannot define a concept-word by giving its characteristic marks does not really know what he is talking about when he uses it in a sentence. W. counters that not being able to *define* an expression one uses does not imply that one cannot *explain* perfectly adequately what one meant (§70). (b.r.f. §70 (p. 33n.) is an aside: meaning something is not the same as something's coming before one's mind.) The second version, associated with Frege, is that any concept must have a *definite* boundary; it must determine (together with the facts) what does and what does not fall under it. A concept without a sharp boundary is not really a concept at all. So there can be no vague concepts at all — indeed, even the very possibility of vagueness should be excluded (which is what Frege's requirement of determinacy of sense amounts to).

W. counters that explaining a concept-word by means of a series of paradigmatic examples is a perfectly decent and intelligible form of explanation,
just as telling someone to stand 'roughly here' is a perfectly decent instruction. For some purposes, what is not sharply determined may be exactly what is
wanted (§71). §§72–4 pick up the theme of 'seeing something in common'
mooted in §71, and clarify the concept. First, there is no one thing called
'seeing something in common', and §72 differentiates three different kinds of
case. §73 examines and rejects the classical empiricist idea that the point of
explanations by samples and examples alike is to engender in the mind of the
learner a general idea (or 'an abstract general idea') of what is common to all
cases of things that fall under the concept thus explained. W. rehearses objections that run parallel to Berkeley's objections to Locke. §74 repudiates the
idea that an explanatory sample is *used* as a representative (and so fulfils its
function) only if it is *seen* in a certain way.

The intended conclusion of §§65–74 is that we should take explanations
by examples at face value. We do give such explanations for many words,
and they successfully introduce and guide the application of legitimate
concept-words. Hence the demand that every explanation of a complex
concept-word take the form of a definition in terms of characteristic marks
is unjustified. Explanations that are not definitions, including explanations of
family-resemblance concepts by means of a series of paradigmatic examples,
constitute rules for the use of words no less than do definitions.

The structure of Part A:

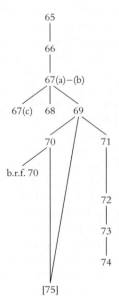

Part B consists of §§75–88. It continues the previous discussion by exploring an attempt to rehabilitate the idea that there *must* be something in common to everything that falls under a given concept-word. The fundamental idea that is to be examined (and rejected) is that our understanding of what an expression such as 'a game' (i.e. a family-resemblance concept) means may transcend our ability to say what it means (§75, linked to §70). Our use of it might be thought to manifest possession of knowledge of common properties, while our inability to specify them in a definition would merely show that this knowledge is tacit. But, it might be argued, one would recognize an appropriate definition were it formulated. But, W. counters, if a definition were formulated, it would *not* correctly express the concept in question. For it would give sharp boundaries to a concept whose lack of sharp boundaries is an intrinsic feature of what we understand by that concept-word; the resultant degree of distortion, in certain cases (e.g. in ethics and aesthetics), might be very great (§§76–7).

Two parallel suggestions are similarly criticized. First, the meaning of a proper name cannot be identified with a definite description or cluster of descriptions; rather, it has no *fixed* meaning, but a fluctuating one. But it is no less useful for all that (§79). Secondly, ordinary concept-words, like 'chair', do not meet the demands of determinacy of sense — and do not need to, since those demands are not coherent. It does not detract from the adequacy of the rules for the use of a concept-word that they do not determine whether it applies or not in every conceivable aberrant circumstance (§80).

§81 warns against conceiving of our languages, which do not everywhere have fixed rules, as approximations to ideal languages that logicians dream of (and invent). Such calculi are not more perfect than natural language. And logic is not a logic for such an ideal language. If it were, then it might indeed be said to be a logic for a vacuum. But to clarify this, we must first elucidate the concepts of understanding, meaning something, and thinking (reasoning). For this will make clear what can lead one to suppose, as W. had supposed in the *Tractatus*, that to utter a sentence and mean or understand it, is to operate a calculus according to definite rules. The following remarks explore further the misconceived idea that the rules we follow in our linguistic activities must be fixed and rigid (§81), determining for every possible case whether a concept-word does or does not apply (§80).

§82 examines what we call 'the rule by which someone proceeds'. Evidently, it need not be a clear and definite rule. By implication, it is 'completely expressed in the explanations that I could give' (§75), and, as has been shown, in the case of a proper name, such explanations may fluctuate between different rules (§79). Indeed, it must be possible to describe an action as not following a rule, or as switching from one rule to another as one goes along, or as making up the rules as one goes along, otherwise the expression 'following a rule' is vacuous (§83). Moreover, the idea of an activity that is *everywhere* bounded by rules, whose rules exclude not merely all actual doubts but also all *possible* doubts is incoherent (§84). Rather, a rule is comparable to a signpost. There are various ways of *interpreting* it (but normally, we do not *interpret* it at all (cf. PI §198(c), §201(b))). And sometimes there may be doubts about how to follow it, and sometimes there may not. Of course, there *can* be rules for applying rules. But, first, there need not always be, and if there are not, that does not necessarily betoken incompleteness in the rules (§86). And secondly, the mere *possibility* of doubt does not terminate — not even when explanations reach the apparent (empiricist) bedrock of 'simple indefinables'. An explanation requires a further rule to guide its application only to prevent an *actual* misunderstanding that would arise but for the further rule. In short, a signpost is in order if it fulfils its purpose — and so is an explanation of what a word means. §88 concludes the discussion by pointing out that inexactness (or vagueness) does not amount to uselessness (cf. §69). It may sometimes be exactly what is needed. Moreover, exactness is not an absolute notion but a purpose-relative one. So there is no single ideal of exactness. Hence too, the fact that an explanation of what a word means may be 'inexact' and may not specify a 'fixed' meaning or necessary and sufficient conditions of application does not imply that it may not be a successful explanation, let alone that it is not a complete and correct one.

It should be stressed that many of these themes will be raised again in the long debate concerning following rules (§§185–242). There the ramifications of the current discussion and its bearing on much more general issues will be made clear.

The structure of Part B:

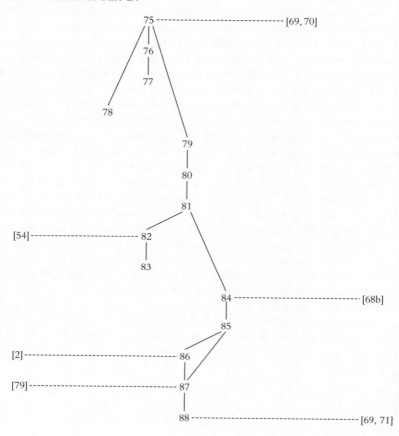

Sources

PI§	MS 152	MS 142§/ TS 220§	TS 226$_R$ §	TS 239§	BT	Other
65	66–7	62	72	69		
66	67–8, 73–4	63	73	70		
67	74	64	74	71		
68	75–6	65	75	72		
69	76	66	76	73		115, 41
70		67	77	74	248–9	115, 42
b.r.f. 70						114 Um., 194; B i §545
71	76f.[1]	68	78	75		302, 14
72		69	79	76		
73		70	80	77		
74		71	81	78		
75		72	82	79		115, 40
76		73	83	80		115, 40–1
77		74	84	81		
78		75	85	82	248	115, 41
79	77–8	76	86	83	251–7	112, 93r–95r; 115, 43–5
80	79	77	87	84		
81		78	88	85	252–3	112, 94v; 115, 45–6
82		79	89	86	253	115, 46–7
83		80	90	87	254	115, 47
84	78, 80	81	91	88		
85	80–1	82	92	89		
86		83	93	90		
87	84–5[2]	84	94	91		
88	152, 86–7	85	95–6	92		

[1]　Beginning of (b) only.
[2]　Second half of (a) only.

Family resemblance
1. Background: definition, logical constituents and analysis
2. Family resemblance: precursors and anticipations
3. Family resemblance: a minimalist interpretation
4. Sapping the defences of orthodoxy
5. Problems about family-resemblance concepts
6. Psychological concepts
7. Formal concepts

EXEGESIS §§65–88

SECTION 65

1   The great question apparently thus far avoided is: 'What is essential to a language?' This lay at the heart of the *Tractatus*. But here W. has talked about language-games in all their diversity, without confronting the question of what makes them all language-games, and hence what the essence of language is. In the *Tractatus* the answer to the latter question had been given by reference to the idea of the general propositional form, i.e. the essence of the proposition. For language was there conceived to consist of the totality of propositions that can be generated from the elementary propositions by the operation of joint negation. (Differences between languages were disregarded as irrelevant, since all languages were conceived to have the same essence.) Now he has demolished the whole idea of analysis, of simple names that are the constituents of elementary propositions and that reach right up to reality, and of simple objects constituting the substance of the world — but has not proposed a new answer to the really deep question.

W. concedes that instead of pointing out ((TS 226$_R$ §72)) common properties of everything we call 'language', he is actually saying that all these phenomena, all these language-games, have no one thing in common that makes us call them all 'language'. So why *do* we call them thus? Because of the multiple kinds of affinities between them.

1.1   (i) 'the *general form of propositions*': the discussion is resumed first at §§92–115, which explore the roots of the temptation to search for this phantasm, and then again at §§134–6, which anatomize the *Tractatus* answer.

(ii) 'weswegen wir . . . verwenden'; 'dieser Verwandtschaft, oder dieser Verwandtschaften wegen': W.'s interest is not the *cause* of our using the word 'language' when we do, but the *reason* or *justification* (AWL 33, 45). The question is normative, not causal.

2   (i)   The claim that 'proposition' and 'language' each stand for a family of phenomena is supported by much earlier writing (see BT 60–74; PG 112–27; PLP 93f., 280–303, 364–76). The general drift of W.'s argument is that language is a motley of language-games, none of which is necessary for something to be a language. Does a language have to consist of propositions? No, we can imagine a language consisting only of orders (PI §§18f.). Does a language have to contain logical operators? No, a rudimentary language such as language-game (2) does not (cf. VoW 69, n. 101 (F 89)). And so on.

SECTION 66

1   The concept of a game is examined to refute the preconception that a concept-word (such as 'language' (§65)) is correctly applied to each of a set of objects only if these share some common property in virtue of which they fall under this concept. We see, W. contends, that there is nothing common to all the activities called games. They are connected only by a complicated network of similarities.

Two difficulties crop up immediately.

(i)   Is the presence or absence of a common property something open to simple observation? This worry might have been forestalled by a lower-key exposition. The question is whether we now *know* of any properties common to all the things called games, not whether we can, with sufficient ingenuity, concoct some (as in §67(c)), or discover any.

(ii)   Does W. prove that there is *nothing* common to all games? that we can *never* discover a common property? By running through various kinds of games, he marshals inductive support for this negative existential statement. But might it not be refuted by a more penetrating analysis of games (see 'Family resemblance', sect. 3)? His claim seems precarious, but also unnecessarily strong. He need defend only the claim that there are no properties common to all games *on account of which* we call them 'games'; i.e. that justifications and criticisms of applications of 'game' do not mention any such common properties, but mention only select similarities to *agreed paradigmatic examples*. Or perhaps only the still weaker observation that the practice of explaining 'game' does not include singling out properties severally necessary and jointly sufficient for an activity to be a game. No discoveries could overthrow these statements, since they can be established by careful *reflection* on what is explicit in our practice of using and explaining the word 'game'.

1.1   (i)   'die Vorgänge, die wir "Spiele" nennen': the activities characterized as *Spiele* in German are perhaps a wider set than those called 'games' in English. *Spiel* is used as an internal accusative of *spielen*, so any activity which can be characterized as playing, like throwing a ball in the air or ring-a-ring o'roses, is called *ein Spiel*. This does not significantly affect W.'s point.

(ii)   'Kampfspiele': W. translated 'athletic contests' (TS 226$_R$ §73), but these are not called 'games' in the same sense at all, for the Olympic Games or Commonwealth Games are no more *played* (even though they now include some games) than were gladiatorial games.

(iii)   'Reigenspiele': W. translated 'singing and dancing games' (ibid.).

(iv)   'Ähnlichkeiten im Grossen und Kleinen': not 'over-all similarities' and 'similarities of detail', as Anscombe translated this phrase. (How would over-all similarities among games be distinct from properties common to all games?) The expressions 'im Grossen' and 'im Kleinen' (also 'in the large' and 'in the small') are used in mathematics, and W.'s expressions may be meant to be compared with this technical usage (as indicated by his correction to Rhees's original translation: 'similarities in large respects and in small').

The mathematical distinction can be clarified by considering a series of simple two-dimensional manifolds. Take three strips of paper (preferably a good deal longer than they are wide). Tape or paste the narrow ends of the first strip together to form a cylinder. Do the same with the second, but twist one end 180° before joining it to the other; this makes a Möbius strip. And the same with the third, but twist one end through 360° before joining it to the other; we could call this a twisted cylinder. Topologists say that these three structures are alike 'in the small'. By this they mean that any small enough piece (say a square) cut out of one of these structures has exactly the same structure as a small piece cut out of any other one. Each such fragment is isomorphic with a small piece of the plane. (This is why all three structures are classified as two-dimensional manifolds, along with the surface of spheres and tori, of prisms and cubes, etc.) The differences between the structures (and also some other similarities) are said to be differences (similarities) 'in the large'. The Möbius strip, e.g., is (misleadingly) said to have only one side; it is possible to get from any point on it to any other point along a path that does not cross the edge. And it is (equally misleadingly) said to have only one edge, whereas the cylinder and the twisted cylinder are each said to have two sides and two edges. (Why this is misleading is discussed in Volume 2, 'Grammar and necessity', sect. 8(iv).) Similarly, each structure behaves quite differently if cut all the way around along its middle, parallel to its edge (edges). These similarities and differences are said to be 'in the large' because they cannot be described except by reference to the whole manifold. (The whole has properties not shared by any of its sufficiently small parts.)

This distinction has an intuitive application to many of the concepts W. considers. Why is war not a game? It certainly shares many characteristics of games. It is highly competitive; it involves skill, but leaves room for chance; there are rules (conventions) of war; it has winners and losers; and it is very absorbing and exciting. What makes the crucial difference is the status of the whole activity in the context of the way people live: the global role of making war in human affairs. Similarly, why is the 'dancing' of bees not a language? The answer seems to turn not on detailed features of what they do, but rather on considerations of how their dancing is co-ordinated with the whole pattern of their behaviour. This brings out how games and languages are linked by similarities in the large as well as similarities in the small.

2   Several parallel texts (e.g. M 104; PG 74–6; PLP 180ff.; AWL 32; BB 86f.) avoid the difficulties generated by §66. Instead of the exhortation to look and see whether there are any common properties, there is a description of the error to be avoided. When we notice that what we would naively take as the hallmark of games is not present in every case, instead of concluding that

there is no common property, we postulate one, supposing it to be something awaiting discovery. In such a case, essence is conceived to be hidden (cf. PG 74). This line of thought betrays a prejudice about the rationale for applying concept-words, and it also exhibits the error of proceeding from descriptions to explanation (hypothesis) in philosophy. Instead of the claim that there is nothing common to games, W. suggests that even if some common feature were discovered, it need not define 'game'. Indeed, it might have no part whatsoever in the explanation of the word.

3   W. occasionally refers to Jean Nicod's 'Geometry in the Sensible World'[1] (e.g. MS 105 (Vol. I), 43; PR 252f.; MS 115 (Vol. XI), 81; cf. Exg. §130), which contains a discussion of resemblance among sense-data that may be one of the germs of ideas elaborated in W.'s account of family resemblance. Three parallels are noteworthy.

(i)   Nicod distinguishes global resemblance from partial similarities (then subdivides the latter into local and qualitative similarities) (pp. 78ff.). The contrast between 'global' and 'local' similarities is at home in discussion of topological spaces and is there equivalent to the contrast between similarities 'in the large' and similarities 'in the small'.

(ii)   Nicod notes that two things may be partially similar in one respect but dissimilar in another. As a consequence, it may happen that '*two overlapping structures or networks of similarities cross each other* and arrange the same data in two different ways' (p. 84).

(iii) He remarks that a particular relation of partial resemblance may form the nucleus of a set of relations forming a family around it; e.g. that the relations of inclusion, encroachment and separation form a family around the relation of 'local resemblance' (p. 85).

SECTION 67

1   §67(a)–(b) complete the exposition of family resemblance. They introduce two important analogies: with the resemblances among members of a family and with the construction of a thread out of many overlapping fibres. (Note that the unknown genetic explanation of resemblances among members of a family is irrelevant — indeed, runs contrary to the point of the analogy, which is to show us that there need be no common properties among the extension of a concept *in virtue of which* we deem them all to fall under the concept.)

§67(b) applies the notion of family resemblance to the concept of a number. It is not in virtue of common properties that natural numbers, signed integers, rationals, reals, complex numbers, etc. are all deemed numbers. This is a cornerstone of W.'s philosophy of mathematics, but plays no role in the

[1]   In J. Nicod, *Foundations of Geometry and Induction*, tr. P. P. Wiener (Kegan Paul, Trench, Trubner, London, 1930).

Investigations (although, when this remark was written, it was perhaps meant to prepare the ground for the envisaged mathematical sequel (TS 221)).

§67(c) introduces the first of a series of arguments in defence of the orthodox demand for definitions of concept-words in terms of characteristic marks. The objector suggests that the various things that fall under such a concept *do* have a common property: namely, the disjunction of the various overlapping similarities. W.'s retort is contemptuous: that is just playing with words. Why? The expression 'to have something in common' is an ordinary one. It makes perfectly good sense to say that all those ☞ books have blue bindings in common, or that they share the common property of being by Dickens; equally, it makes sense to say that a yellow ellipse and a London bus have nothing in common. The intelligibility of such statements presupposes that it is possible to specify sets of objects that have nothing in common; otherwise to say of any set of objects that its members have something in common would be vacuous. W.'s riposte is simply that this presupposition would be undermined if we accepted the disjunction of all the overlapping properties as itself something *common* to all the objects falling under such a concept. For then *any* set of objects, no matter how heterogeneous, would necessarily have something in common. This would make any application of 'having something in common' (*gemeinsam*) an idle ceremony. The argument is analogically illustrated by W.'s final remark. It would be absurd to say that the continuous overlapping of the fibres is something running through the whole thread, because this would make unintelligible the contrast between there being and there not being something running through the whole thread.

1.1   'hier spielst du nur mit einem Wort': with *a* word, i.e. with 'gemeinsam'.

SECTION 68

1   This explores a second line of defence for orthodoxy. The objector concedes that the disjunction of all the respects of resemblance among different kinds of numbers is not itself something common to all numbers. But he need not defend that position. It suffices for his case that a concept-word such as number (the candidate for a family-resemblance concept in §68) be defined as a logical sum of well-defined sub-concepts.

However, unless the 'etc.' in the objector's definition of 'number' (line 3) is the 'etc.' of laziness, he has not defined 'number' as a logical sum of sub-concepts. We are being asked to *assume* that 'number' is defined by a closed list of sub-concepts. W.'s objection is that this explanation would give the concept of number a range of application laid down once for all. The list of sub-concepts would exhaustively determine the kinds of thing that are to be counted as numbers, making the concept analogous to the concept of primary colour. This, W. contends, is not how we use 'number'. Its extension is open, not circumscribed. Mathematicians have from time to time introduced new kinds of entities (e.g. quaternions) which were subsumed under the concept of number though distinct from any previously recognized sub-concept. We do not treat such additions to the extension of 'number' as altering its meaning.

Note that the openness of a family-resemblance concept must be distinguished from vagueness, even though many family-resemblance concepts are also vague. But a concept may be a family-resemblance concept without being vague, as indeed is the concept of number here discussed. For each of the sub-concepts of cardinals, rationals, reals, etc. is sharply defined — so there are no borderline cases, even though the general concept is not closed by a frontier. The concept of a game, by contrast, might be held to be both open and vague.

The objector counters with the suggestion that the notion of an essentially open concept is incoherent. If the application of 'number' is not everywhere bounded by rules, how can there be a determinate practice of using this word or a distinction between correct and incorrect uses of it? The reply exploits the game analogy. Tennis is not *everywhere* regulated by rules, but that does not imply that it is *nowhere* regulated by rules. And, as we shall see (PI §§84–8), the very idea of being *everywhere* bound by rules (determinacy of sense, as conceived by Frege and the young Wittgenstein) is of questionable intelligibility.

1.1   'in the same way the concept of a game . . .': What are the corresponding sub-concepts? Perhaps W. meant board games, field games, word games and so forth.

2   It is assumed here that the sub-concepts such as *cardinal number*, unlike the concept of number, do have extensions closed by a frontier. PG 113f. draws this contrast explicitly. The concept of cardinal number, whose extension is determined by the formal series $[1, \xi, \xi + 1]$, is 'a rigorously circumscribed concept'. By contrast, we are free to decide just what constructions to count as numbers in virtue of their degree of similarity to cardinal numbers, rationals, irrationals, etc. It 'depends on us' whether we draw the boundary here or there. Each of the concepts number and cardinal number, he concludes, is 'a concept in a different sense of the word'. (This conclusion is implicitly repudiated in the *Investigations*; otherwise one might indeed object that a blurred concept is not really a concept at all.)

SECTION 69

1   This opens with the challenge to clarify how we *do* explain what a game is. We give an explanation by examples, perhaps with a similarity-rider. This accords with the observation (§68) that we so use the word that its extension is not closed by a boundary (cf. BT 68f., quoted Exg. §76, 2).

An objection is intimated: since such a concept lacks boundaries, is it not useless? This is rejected here (then reconsidered in §71): such a concept is no more useless than the unit of measure 'one pace' was before it was given the definition '1 pace = 75 cm'. The *vagueness* of the concept of a pace did not derogate from its usefulness for the purposes for which it was used. The supplementary objection that such a unit of measurement was not exact until so defined is met by a demand for an explanation of what 'exact' means (further explored in §88). The implicit assumption that usefulness is proportional to exactness is what needs to be questioned. The measure '1 pace' was not less useful for not being exact,[2] and neither are family-resemblance concepts that lack sharply circumscribed boundaries.

§69 also hints at a further objection to W.'s account of 'game': namely, that what we understand by 'game' transcends what we explain in explaining what the word means, that we know more about what a game is than is embodied in our explanations (this issue is the topic of §§75–80). §69 suggests W.'s answer (sketched in §75) that our knowledge of what a game is, is completely expressed in the explanations we can give of 'game'. In particular, there *are* no boundaries to our concept of a game precisely because we draw none in explaining what a game is by citing examples.

SECTION 70

1   This continues the argument of §69. There it was assumed that we do know what a game is, even though the concept of a game has no closed boundary. W.'s interlocutor in §70(a) challenges this assumption: the fact that the concept has no closed boundary proves that we do not know what we mean by 'game'. W.'s initial reply is a rhetorical counter-question: is it claimed that somebody who says 'The ground was covered with plants' does not know what he is talking about unless he can give a *definition* of 'plant'? That would, of course, be quite absurd. It would imply that no one understands what they say until they can *define* the words they use (and this is, in effect, the characteristic Socratic/Platonic view). It would also mean that we all need to wait on the philosopher or linguist to find out what we mean by our words! This, as W. remarked, is 'a hellish idea' (WWK 129f.).

§70(b) clarifies matters. If I can give an explanation of what I mean by using the description 'The ground was covered with plants', then I *do* know what I am talking about. And I might give such an explanation (*Erklärung*) independently of giving a definition (*Definition*) of 'plant', e.g. by drawing a picture and saying, 'The ground looked roughly like this'.

---

[2]   'I asked him for a bread knife and he gives me a razor blade because it's sharper!' cf. MS 120 (Vol. XVI), 142v.

The rest of §70(b) treats an objection to this explanation of the description: namely, that it is an inexact explanation because it contains the word 'roughly' (*ungefähr*) (cf. BT 249v., quoted at Exg. §88, 2. 1). But this is easily circumvented, for one could draw a picture and say, 'The ground looked exactly like this'. To this the interlocutor retorts: so just *these* blades of grass and *these* leaves were arranged just like this? That, W. answers, is *not* what this explanation means. The explanation explains not what was on the ground but how the ground looked, and that could be described exactly by the drawing without giving an exact description of what was on the ground.

Note that W. distinguishes here between 'definition' (*Definition*) and 'explanation' (*Erklärung*). Definition (here construed narrowly as specification of characteristic marks) is a species of the genus *explanation*. Explanations, as has been shown, may take other forms, e.g. ostensive explanations (for present purposes not to be called 'definitions'), explanations by examples, explanations by exhaustive enumeration. The word 'game' has been explained (by examples) in §69; the objection is that we do not understand it because we are not able to define it. W. challenges that inference. It is explanation, not definition, that is the 'correlate' of understanding (BT 11). Explaining what a word means by correctly defining it is *a* criterion of understanding it, of knowing what it means; but failure to define it is not a criterion for not knowing what it means.

The further objection to the interlocutor that a precise definition of a concept that has no closed boundary introduces a new concept and would therefore *not* explain what one meant at all is deferred until §76.

2   (i)   MS 142, §67, confirms this interpretation of PI §70; for it contains an additional paragraph inserted between §70(a) and (b):

(Socrates (in   )[3]: 'You know it and you can speak Greek, so you must be able to say it'. — No. 'To know it' does not here mean to be able to say it. *This* is not our criterion of knowledge here.)

Socrates made the inference that W. challenges in §70(a). He inferred from the fact that someone could not give a definition of 'justice', 'piety', 'courage', etc. that this person was ignorant of what justice, piety, courage, etc. were. W. contradicts this claim: to know what justice is (to know what the word 'justice' means) is not equivalent to being able to define 'justice'. We can see from their *explanations* (e.g. by examples) that some of Socrates' interlocutors do manifest understanding of the terms that they are being challenged to define (cf. BB 20, PG 120f.). Socrates distorts the concept of understanding by refusing to acknowledge giving any explanations apart from definition as a criterion of understanding. (Note that 'able to say' ('sagen können') here in MS 142, §67, must be read as equivalent to 'able to *define*'.)

---

[3]   W. did not fill in the reference. Perhaps it is Plato, *Charmides* 159a.

BT 248ff. also confirms this interpretation by linking PI §70 with §75, where the contrast between definition and explanation is prominent:

What does it mean to know what a plant is?
What does it mean to know it and not be able to say it?
'You know it and you can speak Greek, so you must be able to say it.'
Uselessness of a definition, say of the definition of the concept 'plant'. (BT 248)

Note, particularly, that it is a *definition*, not an explanation, of 'plant', that is characterized as useless. Its dispensability is what PI §70 demonstrates: namely, that the criteria for understanding 'plant' include giving *explanations* of 'plant' and of sentences in which it occurs.

(ii)   BT 248 criticizes the idea that understanding a sentence incorporating the term 'plant' presupposes the ability to define 'plant': 'Somebody who told us that we don't know what we are talking about until we have given a definition of a plant we would rightly take to be mad. Surely we would not be able to make ourselves any better understood in ordinary circumstances had we such a definition.' For further discussion of these passages, see Exg. §78, 2(ii).

Boxed Remark Following §70 (p. 33n.)

1   This slip was cut from B i §545, derived from MS. 114 (Vol. X) Um., 194, and inserted in TS 227b, p. 60, which begins with the last three sentences of PI §69 and ends with §71(a). Its original context is printed as PG 117–20, in which it occurs on p. 119.

Its immediate context (PG §75) is a repudiation of the idea that the meaning of a word is something that comes before our mind when we hear a word. Certainly what comes before our minds, W. concedes, is characteristic of the meaning; but only in this sense — that it is an example, an application of the word. This *coming to mind* does not consist in an image being present whenever one hears or speaks the word, but in the fact that when asked what the word means, applications of the word occur to one. This (boxed) remark then follows.

This suggests that this remark is related primarily to §70, though thematically to its environs. The connection with §70 is specifically to 'Eine Erklärung dessen, was ich meine . . .' ('An explanation of what I meant' (W.'s translation)). For it blocks off the suggestion that an explanation of *what I meant* consists in describing something that *I had before my mind*, e.g. an image. That the parent did not mean me to teach the children a gambling game does not consist in the antecedent occurrence of images in his mind, but is shown by what he subsequently says (the past tense of 'I meant' here is deceptive (see Volume 4, 'The mythology of meaning something', sect. 5, and Exg. §§187, 664)). So too, in explaining what I meant by 'The ground was covered with plants' by means of a drawing, it would be wholly mistaken to suppose that the drawing was a representation of a mental image that crossed my mind when I uttered the sentence.

SECTION 71

1   §71(a) accepts the description of the concept of a game as having 'blurred edges' (in §70 as being 'without boundaries' (*unbegrenzt*)). This invites the Fregean challenge: is a blurred concept a concept at all? W. counters with the question 'Is an indistinct photograph a picture of a person at all?' The intention is to ridicule the suggestion as dogmatic. (Clearer, perhaps in BT 248v: 'What if someone were to say: "a blurred picture is no picture at all"?!')[4] For certain purposes, a blurred picture may be exactly what one wants; so too, for many purposes, concepts without sharp boundaries are exactly what we want ('by dusk' may be far more appropriate than 'by 19: 24').

§71(b) criticizes Frege's demand for 'completeness of definition'. Frege wrote as follows:

A definition of a concept (of a possible predicate) must be complete; it must unambiguously determine, as regards any object, whether or not it falls under the concept . . . Thus there must not be any object as regards which the definition leaves in doubt whether it falls under the concept; though for us men, with our defective knowledge, the question may not always be decidable. We may express this metaphorically as follows: the concept must have a sharp boundary. . . . To a concept without sharp boundaries there would correspond an area that had not a sharp boundary-line all round, but in places just vaguely faded away into the background. This would not really be an area at all; and likewise a concept that is not sharply defined is wrongly termed a concept. Such quasi-conceptual constructions cannot be recognised as concepts by logic; it is impossible to lay down precise laws for them. The law of excluded middle is just another form of the requirement that the concept should have a sharp boundary. . . . has the question 'Are we still Christians?' really got a sense, if it is indeterminate whom the predicate 'Christian' can truly be asserted of, and who must be refused it? (BLA ii §56, trs. P. T. Geach and M. Black.)

W. does not distinguish here between the demand for a definition in terms of characteristic marks, which will 'close the extension of a concept by a boundary' (§68) and the requirement for completeness of definition (or determinacy of sense) that unambiguously determines for any object whether it falls under the definiendum or not. But only the former demand is assailed here. The latter is subjected to criticism in §80 and §§84–7.

---

[4]   Frege claims that rules of the use of concept-words *must* specify necessary and sufficient conditions for their application. W. queries what the nature of dogma is here — is it not the assertion of necessary truths about all possible rules? (BT 250), i.e. that rules for the use of concept-words *must* conform to such demands.

W. denies that a roughly indicated region is no region. So too, a concept that is not defined by specification of characteristic marks *is* a concept for all that, and may be more useful for certain purposes than one that is sharply circumscribed. We do not explain what a game is by giving a sharp definition, but rather by giving a series of examples. The examples are not meant to intimate something that we cannot express: namely, something common to all games in virtue of which we call them all 'games'. The examples are not, in this sense, an *indirect* means of explaining what a game is. They constitute a perfectly decent explanation. They are the expression of a rule for the use of the word. But, to be sure, they have to be taken as paradigms, and *used* as standards for the correct application of the word thus explained. And that, indeed, is our practice.

1.1   (i)   'Frege compares a concept to a region (*Bezirk*)': W. fails to lay out the function-theoretic rationale for Frege's demand for determinacy of sense (a function, Frege held, is adequately specified only if its value for every possible argument can be given) without which it seems gratuitous. This omission is presumably warranted, since that rationale did not rest on observation of the ways in which we use words and explain what they mean, or on a clear conception of what it is for words to have a meaning. It was a theory-motivated imposition of a form of representation (namely, the representation of (first-level) concepts as functions from objects to truth-values) masquerading as a discovery about the essential nature of concepts.

       (ii)   'But is it senseless to say: "Stay roughly there!"?': This is a further rhetorical reply to the interlocutor's suggestion in §70 that if the concept is uncircumscribed, then one does not know what one means by an utterance in which it is incorporated. So W. was wrong to write in 1915: 'It seems clear that what we MEAN must always be "*sharp*"' (NB 68). What we mean when we say 'Stay roughly there' is exactly what we say — *roughly* there.

       (iii)   'jede allgemeine Erklärung': 'every general explanation' — it is important to preserve W.'s distinction between '*Definition*' and '*Erklärung*'. No form of explanation (not even definition) guarantees understanding. Any explanation can be misunderstood (cf. §§26, 86f.).

2.1   (i)   'Frege compares . . . cannot be called a region at all': MS 152, 77, adds: 'Does a boundary stone not have a width, and where is its exact middle, etc. etc.!', and on p. 87 W. notes, *en passant*, 'Frege on "Are we still Christians".'

       (ii)   'And this is just how one might explain . . . what a game is': The place of a word in grammar is its meaning (PG 59). Explanations of words like 'game' or 'rule' explain their grammatical place 'in rather the way in which the place of a meeting is specified by saying that it will take place *beside* such and such a tree' (PG 118). That is to say, the examples are paradigms proximity to which warrants calling an activity 'a game'.

       (iii)   'in default of a better': They are not something second-best: 'Examples are decent signs, not rubbish or hocus-pocus' (PG 273; cf. AWL 96).

Section 72

1   The italicized opening phrase, in early drafts (MS 142, TS 220, TS 226$_R$, TS 239), was evidently meant to pick up the same phrase, originally also italicized, in §71(b). The idea of 'seeing what is in common' has, of course, also featured in the argument of §§66f. It stands in need of clarification, inasmuch as it is important to realize that there is no one thing called 'seeing something in common'. The idea implicitly being assailed is that we apply a concept-word 'F' to an object as a consequence of seeing that the object possesses a certain feature or features common to all things that are F. Colour-words seem, at first blush, to be the strongest and simplest kind of case to vindicate this idea.

Three examples are displayed.

In the first, seeing what is in common is indeed a pre-condition for understanding the explanation of the colour-word 'ochre'. The person can examine the pictures, and point, say, to the boat in one, the straw hat in another, and the cane chair in a third and say, 'This is the only colour common to all three pictures, so "ochre" is *this* ☞ colour'. Here it is given that a colour is the common feature; the person can look for the shared colour; and when he spots it, he concludes that 'ochre' is *this* ☞ colour. Having found what is common to the pictures, he knows what 'ochre' means and can now, for example, bring an ochre object on demand (cf. BB 131).

In the second, to see what the shapes have in common *is* to see that they are all the same colour. There is no intermediary step of looking to see *what colour* is common to all cases, and *then* concluding that this colour is ochre.

In the third, the range of application of 'blue' is characterized by showing shades of blue. We naturally say things such as 'What is common to these shades is that they are all blue'. But in fact one cannot (non-trivially) say what is common to dark blue and light blue. The answer to the question 'What do these colours I am pointing at have in common?' here ought to be 'I don't know what game you are playing' (BB 134). (Perhaps the answer is that they are the colours of the two most ancient British universities.) Of course, one can answer that they are both shades of blue, that they are both called 'blue' — but not on the grounds of first noting something in common. 'To say that we use the word "blue" to mean "what all these shades of colour have in common" by itself says nothing more than that we use the word "blue" in all these cases' (BB 135).

What this teaches us is not only that 'seeing what is common' subsumes many different kinds of cases, but further that the idea that the ability to apply a word rests on first apprehending what is common to all the cases to which it applies is misconceived. Indeed, in many cases, we might say that someone has 'seen what is common' to all cases *because* he applies the same word to them all (rather than vice versa).

Having thus shaken the grip of the idea that the foundation of the mastery of the use of a concept-word consists in the ability to see what is common to all cases to which it applies, the thought that *all* concept-words, including 'game', 'proposition', 'number', etc., apply to members of their extension in virtue of common properties is correspondingly weakened.

2   BB 130–5 makes W.'s target perfectly explicit. It is the idea that seeing what is in common is a pre-condition for applying the same word to things — comparable to the thought that one *must* understand an order before one can obey it, or know where one's pain is before one can point to it, or know a tune before one can sing it (BB 130). This is a recurrent theme in W.'s reflections, for it is one of the sources of the idea that knowing or understanding are mental states from which manifestations of knowledge and understanding flow.

Section 73

1   This explores a further (classical empiricist) misconception about 'seeing what is in common'. We explain concept-words in various ways, often ostensively. We explain colour predicates by pointing to samples. This is comparable to giving a person a colour-chart. We may explain a sortal noun such as 'leaf' by pointing at various examples of leaves. It may seem as if the point of the samples or examples is to engender in the mind of the learner an 'abstract general idea' — a mental sample or picture. If we show someone a variety of leaves, explaining that *this* and *this* and *this* are all called 'leaf', the point is not that he should have *a variety* of mental images stored in his memory, but that he should abstract from the experiences of seeing these leaves *a single* general mental picture of a leaf — akin to a Galtonian composite photograph[5] (BB 18) — which incorporates *what is common to all leaves*. When he has such a 'general picture' in his mind, an empiricist may argue, then he understands the word defined — then he has grasped *what is common* to all instances falling under the concept in question.

W.'s counter-argument parallels Berkeley's familiar criticism of abstract general ideas.[6] What shape will the picture-leaf in the mind have if it is to exhibit only 'what is common to all leaves'? What shade is the 'sample in the mind' which supposedly represents what is common to all shades of green? Of course, samples are not 'in the mind'. And what gives a sample the generality it has is not its intrinsic properties, but the way in which it is used — the method of projection, as it were.

1.1   'a schematic leaf': it is not wholly clear whether this is meant to be a leaf or a picture of a leaf. But it is clear that the difference between a picture of

[5]   Francis Galton, *Inquiries into Human Faculty and its Development* (Macmillan, London, 1883), sect. 3 and Appendix A.
[6]   An idea is general, Berkeley claimed, in virtue of its 'being made to represent or stand for all other particular ideas of the *same sort*' (*Principles of Human Knowledge*, Introduction).

a particular leaf and a picture understood as a schema of a leaf lies in *how these pictures are used*. A schematic picture is not a special picture with extraordinary properties, but an ordinary picture used in a special way.

2   (i)   AWL 78 suggests two factors that make us believe that there must be such a general idea in our minds. First, we note that we may be shown a variety of plants, say violets, roses, etc., without having an idea of *plant* in general. So we think that something more is necessary: namely, forming a general idea of *plant* in one's mind. Secondly, we misconstrue understanding as a mental process, and think that understanding the word 'plant' involves some mental occurrence: e.g. that a mental image of *plant* comes to mind when one hears the word. However, understanding a word is not a state or process, but an ability to use it correctly — and an ability is not an accompaniment of its exercise. Nothing *need* go on in one's mind when one hears or uses a word with understanding, and if any images do flash across one's mind, they are neither necessary nor sufficient for understanding the word.

(ii)   BB 18 connects the empiricist conception that grasping a general concept-word 'F' consists in possessing an abstract general idea of F with the Augustinian conception, i.e. that the meaning of a word is a thing correlated with the word – in this case, a mental image. If one thinks thus, one is looking at words as if they were all proper names, and confusing the bearer of a name with its meaning (as if the meaning of 'leaf' were the general idea of *leaf* one is supposed to possess, and the word 'leaf' were the name of this idea).

(iii)   PG 272f. adds two further points: (a) There is typically no general picture before my mind when I utter or hear such words as 'egg' or 'plant'. Rather, 'I make the application as it were spontaneously'. (b) The *multiplicity* of examples used in explaining such words is not merely a mechanical device for getting somebody to see what he could in principle see in a single example. It is an essential aspect of the rules.

Section 74

1   §73 asserted that what makes a sample general, i.e. a 'schema' of what it defines, is the way it is used. One might, however, think that this does not suffice to endow the sample with the requisite generality. It may seem that a pre-condition for using the individual leaf as a sample of leaves in general is *a particular way of seeing it*. W. moves to block this.

First, he asserts that to regard a beech leaf as a *general* sample of a leaf is *not* to see it differently from the way one sees it if one regards it simply as a sample of a beech leaf. One *might* see it differently, he concedes; but even if one did, all that the psychologistic claim would amount to is the *empirical* observation that someone who sees an object in a certain way, will also be prone to use it in such-and-such a way, i.e. as a general sample of a leaf. It would still be the *use* of the sample that gives it its generality, not the accompanying experience.

There is such a thing as seeing an object in one way or another. Indeed, there are even cases in which, if one sees a sample in a certain way, one will be prone to use it in a certain way, and if one sees it differently, one will be inclined to use it differently. For example, someone who sees a drawing of a cube as a plane figure consisting of a square and two rhombi will follow the order 'Bring me something like this!' differently from someone who sees it three-dimensionally. But what makes a schema into a schema is not how it is seen.

1.1   'Blatt' (lines 2 and 6): W. substituted 'drawing' for 'leaf' (TS 226$_R$ §81).

2   PG 270–6 (MS 111 (Vol. VII), 90ff.) criticizes the ideas (a) that a person who grasps an explanation of 'plant' by examples does not see these examples in the same way when he 'sees the concept in them', i.e. *sees the common element*, as when he sees them merely as representatives of a particular shape or colour, and (b) that his understanding of 'plant' consists in his experience of seeing each example as an example illustrating the concept 'plant'. W. cites three arguments against this conception, which, he confesses, he once held.

(i)   The idea of 'seeing something in' something (or seeing something in a particular way) is taken from cases where we see different aspects of a figure, e.g. different 'phrasings' of '||| . . .', and this cannot be transferred to understanding the examples used in explaining 'plant'.

(ii)   W. queries whether a person who uses the sign as a sign for the concept of number sees these three strokes differently from someone who uses '|||' to denote the number three. If he saw in them the concept of number in the first case, then he would have to see them in the same way that he saw '|||| . . .', for that too is a sign for this concept. Would that mean that he could not distinguish between and '||| . . .' and '|||| . . .'?

(iii)   On this conception, too, the multiplicity of examples used in explaining 'leaf' or 'number' would be no more than a mechanical device, for the learner could in principle see the explained concept in a single example. But the multiplicity of examples is an essential part of these explanations.

W.'s general diagnosis of this misconception is that it treats a particular experience (seeing the examples in a particular way) as belonging to the essence of grasping the meaning of a word, whereas what matters is the system of rules governing these examples. It is the geometry, not the psychology, of the mechanism relating the examples to the use of the explained word that concerns philosophy.

Section 75

1   This is linked to §70, which queried whether one does not know what one is talking about until one gives a definition. That suggestion was there

rejected, for although one could not give a *definition*, one could give an *explanation* of what one meant. Now the question is examined afresh.

We all know what a game is, but (as Augustine found with respect to time), when we are asked, we cannot give a *definition*. So, does our knowledge outstrip our ability to explain? Is our knowledge 'equivalent' to an unformulated definition? Is it a form of *tacit knowledge*, manifest as such in our recognition of a properly formulated definition if given one — as Plato held. This conception too is rejected. For isn't my knowledge of what a game is *completely* expressed by the explanations I could give? Explanation by examples is not defective. It fulfils its role perfectly adequately, both in constituting a criterion of understanding and in providing an adequate explanation that functions as a guide to, and standard of, correct use in our practices.

Note the contrast between §75 and §70 in the treatment of the distinction between knowing and being able to say. In §70 the interlocutor wished to conclude that being unable to define 'game' entails absence of understanding, and that was a mistake. The presupposition of §75 is that understanding and the ability to define 'game' are distinct. Here W.'s adversary wishes to conclude that a person's understanding transcends what he is able to say in answer to 'What is a game?' But it does not follow from the fact that he cannot define 'game' that he cannot explain what a game is.

1.1   'Wie man nach Analogie dieser auf alle möglichen Arten andere Spiele konstruiren kann': W. corrected Rhees's translation to read: 'how you can construct other games analogous to these in all sorts of ways' (TS 226$_R$ §82).

2   MS 115 (Vol. XI), 40f. (cf. BT 250f.) opens with the same two sentences, but then continues:

(Socrates: "You know it and you can speak Greek, so you must be able to say it.") Does this knowledge have the multiplicity of a proposition which has not been formulated? So that if it were uttered, I should recognise it as an expression of my knowledge? — Isn't it rather that any exact definition would have to be rejected as the expression of our understanding? That is, wouldn't we have to say of it that it determines a concept related to ours, but not really ours itself?

The concluding two sentences then correspond to the last two sentences of PI §76.

2.1   'Isn't my knowledge completely expressed': VoW 487 (F 94) makes it clear how misleading is Augustine's reaction to his inability to *define* time:

But if I know how I am to use the word 'time', if I understand it in the most diverse contexts, then I know precisely 'what time is', and no formulation can make this clearer to me. And should I have to explain the meaning of this word to somebody, I would teach him to use the word in typical cases, i.e. in cases such as 'I have no time', 'this is not the time for that', 'too much time has passed since then', etc. In short, I would lay out before him the whole complicated grammar of this word, I would, as it were travel down all the lines that language has prepared for the use of this word — and that would convey to him an understanding of the word 'time'.

SECTION 76

1   This continues the criticism of the idea that knowledge of what a game is, is equivalent to an unformulated definition. But, W. objects, we would refuse to acknowledge any definition as a correct explanation just because it would draw a sharp boundary where there is none (§68). No definition will correspond exactly to what we understand by 'game', because absence of a sharp boundary is an intrinsic feature of our concept.

The claim that a sharply bounded concept and the concept of a game could not be the same, but at best akin, raises the general issue of the criteria of concept-identity. W. does not discuss this. No doubt he would think this unnecessary here, for we might well agree with his judgement in this instance without thereby coming to any general agreement about concept-identity (cf. PI §61).

2   BT 68f. (cf. 254) enlarges on the idea that lack of a sharp boundary is an intrinsic feature of the concept of a game:

So I call 'a game' whatever belongs to this list, as well as anything that has a certain degree of similarity (that I have not further specified) to these games. Moreover, I reserve the right to decide in each fresh case whether or not I count something as a game.

This is not the avowal of a personal idiosyncrasy, but an aspect of the practice of using the word 'game'.

SECTION 77

1   This continues the simile of §76, arguing that there are degrees of kinship among concepts. In certain cases a sharp definition may approximate the concept in use that is not sharply bounded. But in extreme cases, e.g. certain concepts in aesthetics and ethics, the indeterminacy is too great for any fruitful approximation. Investigation of such concepts can usefully begin by reflecting on how the concepts are learnt, in what contexts, and what the rudimentary moves in the language-games with them are, and this will show that they must (sic) have a family of meanings (see 1.1 below).

1.1   (i)   ' "good" for instance': it is unclear whether W. is thinking of goodness in general, or only of ethical goodness. The last sentence of §77(a) speaks
of 'concepts in aesthetics or ethics', which may suggest the narrower interpretation, but the investigation of how one learnt to use the word 'good' would
start with the use of 'good' in interjections and exclamations, not with
'morally good' or the use of 'good' in moral contexts (LA 1f.; see 2.1(ii) below).
How useful such scrutiny is may be doubted, for it sheds very little light upon
the complex relationships between the goodness of artefacts (instrumental
goodness), of skills (technical goodness), of what is useful, advantageous and
favourable (these being forms of utilitarian goodness), of that which is good
for or does good *to* a being (the beneficial, another sub-category of utilitarian
goodness), of the goodness of organs, faculties and health (medical goodness),
the goodness of pleasure and of what gives pleasure (hedonic goodness), of
welfare (the good of man), of happiness (the summum bonum), and of intentions, motives, actions and character (moral goodness).[7]

        (ii)   'then it will be easier for you to see . . . must have a family of mean-
ings': It is not clear why examining the rudimentary uses of 'beautiful' as interjections of admiration of, or pleasure in, appearances will show one this. Nor
is it obvious that the rudimentary uses of 'good' to express approval (of food,
say (LA 1; see 2.1(ii) below) will show that 'good' has a family of meanings
or is an instance of a family-resemblance concept.

        (iii)   'a family of meanings': this, and its other variants from MS 142, §74,
through to TS 227 are the only occurrences of the phrase in W.'s writings.
It is not clear whether, according to W., a word that has a family of meanings differs from a family-resemblance word. Prima facie one might think that
'a family of meanings' involves a variety of different but systematically related
meanings, whereas a family-resemblance concept has a unitary meaning span-
ning *phenomena* that are related by way of family resemblances.[8]

2.1   (i)   'concepts in aesthetics or ethics': The debate about whether 'good' is
ambiguous goes back to Aristotle. Interestingly, Dugald Stewart's anticipation
of W.'s conception of family-resemblance concepts (see 'Family resemblance',
sect. 1) was a criticism of Diderot's essentialism in his article on beauty in
the *Encylopédie*. Stewart objected to the 'prejudice, which has descended to

---

[7]   The classification and the terminology are derived from G. H. von Wright's masterly study of
axiology, *The Varieties of Goodness* (Routledge and Kegan Paul, London, 1963).

[8]   W. does speak of words being used in such a manner that there is a 'fluctuation between
various related meanings' (cf. BT 255; MS 115 (Vol. XI), 47f.; PLP 70), but this is in connection with the use of a proper name (see Exg. §79), hence arguably a different kind of case. For
even if we accept, for the sake of argument, that 'Moses' has related meanings, given, on different occasions, by different definite descriptions (e.g. the brother of Aaron, the man who led the
Israelites out of Egypt, the man to whom God gave the Ten Commandments), these 'meanings'
are not related *by similarities* at all. Furthermore, W. certainly did not take proper names to be
family-resemblance concepts.

modern times from the scholastic ages; — that when a word admits of a variety of significations, these different significations must all be *species* of the same genus; and must consequently include some essential idea common to every individual to which the generic term can be applied'. Stewart extended his criticism to similar attempts to account for the 'different significations' of 'good'.[9]

There is no reason to suppose that W. ever saw Stewart's discussion. But he may well have seen that of Ogden and Richards (he certainly looked at, and disapproved of, their book *The Meaning of Meaning* (CL 104)). They held that 'good' is probably a collection of homonyms with no common characteristic, and that words such as 'beautiful' have to serve 'functions for which a hundred would not be too many'.[10] So, on their view, these are mere homonyms. W. did not think *that*.[11] But it is striking that when the idea of family resemblance dawned on him, he too was prone to hyperbole, at least in his lectures, observing that we use the word 'beautiful' 'in a hundred different games' (M 104). In that lecture he introduced his discussion of beauty in the context of an account of family resemblance. So at that point he seems to have thought that *beauty*, like *a game*, is a family-resemblance concept.

(ii) 'concepts in aesthetics': The concept of beauty (*Schönheit*) is discussed in MS 157a., 25–9, but the analysis is perfunctory (see also AWL 34–8; LA 1–3). W. speaks of a 'family of cases' to which 'beautiful' applies, but that is more an objection to an essentialist account than an argument that the concept of beauty is a family-resemblance concept. He in effect shows only that 'good' and 'beautiful' are attributive adjectives.

(iii) 'How did we *learn* the meaning of this word?': LA 1 remarks that examining how we were taught a word both destroys misconceptions and gives us a primitive language in which the word is used. The latter gives one a rough approximation of the kind of language-game that is going to be played. So 'beautiful', 'fine', etc. are learnt roughly as interjections. 'Good' is generally first applied by a child to food. It is taught in conjunction with exaggerated gestures and facial expressions, and with distinctive tones of voice that are expressions of approval.

This may well be true, but does not get us much beyond the crude thought that these words have a use as expressions of approval and commendation. So it is, at best, a very modest beginning.

---

[9]   Dugald Stewart, *Philosophical Essays* (Edinburgh and London, 1810), pp. 214f. I am grateful to Jonathan Witztum for pointing this out to me and for other pertinent observations here.

[10]   C. K. Ogden and I. A. Richards, *The Meaning of Meaning* (1923) (ARK paperbacks, London, 1985), p. 130.

[11]   But he seems at least to have toyed with the idea of homonymity in the case of 'beauty' in 1933. Discussing cases of applying the word to the expression of eyes and to the shape of a nose, he remarked: 'So perhaps we might say: if there were a language with two words so that there were no reference to anything common to such cases, I should have no trouble about using one of these two special words for my case and my meaning would not be impoverished' (CV 24).

(iv) '("good" for instance)': PG 77 says that 'good' in an ethical sense 'is a combination of a very large number of interrelated games, each of them as it were a facet of the use. What makes a single concept here is precisely the connection, the relationship, between these facets.' This does not seem to imply that moral goodness possesses a *family of meanings*, at least if that phrase intimates a multiplicity of different but related meanings. It is unclear what W. has in mind by the 'large number of interrelated games'. But one might say that von Wright's account of moral goodness as a *derivative* form (or variety) of goodness shows that the concept of moral goodness lies at the intersection of a large number of interrelated language-games with the word 'good'.

AWL 33 holds that 'good' is a family-resemblance concept:

In view of the way we have learned the word 'good' it would be astonishing if it had a general meaning covering all of its applications. I am not saying it has four or five different meanings. It is used in different contexts because there is a transition between similar things called 'good', a transition which continues, it may be, to things which bear no similarity to earlier members of the series. We *cannot* say 'If we want to find out the meaning of "good" let's find what all cases of good have in common'. They may not have anything in common. The reason for using the word 'good' is that there is a continuous transition from one group of things called good to another.

But this is unconvincing. For it is supposed to be characteristic of family-resemblance concepts that new members of the family accrue or can accrue without any change in the concept (the concept of game has not changed by the addition of the category of computer games, and did not change in the past by the introduction of card games). But it is unclear whether there can be any new forms of goodness. We have, over the centuries, seen the acceptance of many new forms of *art*, but not of goodness. We may dispute whether photography or so-called conceptual art are really forms of art. But we cannot dispute whether the pleasant, the skilful, the useful or the healthy are forms of goodness.[12]

That goodness is not a family-resemblance concept in *this* sense does not mean that W. was not right in his more minimal claim that things are not all called 'good' in virtue of possessing common characteristics. (Of course, this too is contentious. It has been claimed that what unites all instances of goodness is that a good X is an X that has what is wanted of an X. But a good intention is hardly to be characterized as an intention that has what is wanted of an intention, any more than a good man can be said to have what is wanted of a man.)

---

[12] von Wright, *Varieties of Goodness*, pp. 16f.

Section 78

1   The location of this remark and its brevity make its interpretation, and its
point here, contentious. It may seem that W. is inviting us to assimilate knowing what a game (or a plant) is to knowing how a clarinet sounds, and is presenting the latter as a case of knowing and being unable to say. Or it may
seem that knowing how the word 'game' is used is unlike knowing the height
of Mont Blanc (namely, knowing and being able to say that it is 4,807 metres
high), and is a case of *knowing how* (a 'practical ability') that is to be contrasted
with *knowing that* (theoretical knowledge, exemplified in such cases — perhaps
after centuries of intellectual effort, as Frege said of knowing what a number
is — by giving a definition). This would imply that W. is now arguing that
users of the word by and large *cannot* explain what a game is or say what the
word 'game' means. But that conflicts with §75: namely, that my knowledge
of what a game is is completely expressed in the explanations I could give,
and is *not* equivalent to an unformulated definition of 'game'.

The sources of the remark (see 2 below) show that these interpretations are
not what W. intended. So, of course, does the argument of §§69–77. The
truncation of the remark (relative to its ancestors) and its location is, perhaps,
injudicious.

It is best taken as no more than a clarification of the Socratic thought that
someone might know something but be unable to say what he knows. This
thought may seem surprising, when one has in mind cases like the first example. For there it has no application. By contrast, it seems that one may know
how a clarinet sounds but *not* be able to say how it sounds. What then of
knowing how the word 'game' is used? It is certainly not like the case of the
sound of a clarinet, for the word 'game' is not explained by reference to a
sample. Nor is it like the case of knowing the height of Mont Blanc. For we
explain how the word 'game' is used, but not how high Mont Blanc is, by
giving *a variety of examples.*

1.1   'How a clarinet sounds': It is misleading of W. to cite this as a case of knowing but being unable to say. For although the idea is an empiricist commonplace, it is one that W. was eager to combat (see 2.1 below). Is it really the
case that I know what 'black' is, what the word 'black' means, but cannot say
it? After all, if asked, I would say 'Black is *this* ☞ ■ colour'. So too, I can
explain what a clarinet sounds like by imitating it, or by relating it to the sound
of other woodwinds, or by putting on a recording of a clarinet concerto and
saying '*That* is what a clarinet sounds like' as the instrument makes its entry.
To quibble over whether that is really *saying* seems pointless pedantry. What
is important is to recognize different kinds of explanations, and there is no
question but that we *can* explain what a clarinet sounds like, just as we can
explain what black is or what the word 'black' means. But it seems probable
that all that W. meant was that we do not recognize anything as a *definition*

here (assuming, with logicians and the prevailing tradition, that ostensive definitions are not really *definitions*).

2   (i)   MS 115 (Vol. XI), 40–2 (cf. BT 248), sheds light on the purpose of PI §78. W. opens with the query 'What does it mean to know what a plant is?' (cf. PI §§70, 75). In particular, what does it mean: to know and not to be able to say it? — and W. quotes Socrates: 'You know and can speak Greek, so you must be able to say it.' It is *not* as if this 'knowing' has the multiplicity of an unexpressed definition that I would acknowledge as the expression of my knowledge, were it formulated (cf. PI §75). Isn't it rather that no exact definition would match what we understand by 'plant'? — [this is then followed by a variant of the last two sentences of PI §76]. Then follows:

Compare:

1.   'Knowing what a plant is'
2.   'Knowing how one uses the word "plant"'
3.   'Knowing what 25 × 25 is' // 'how tall the spire of St Stephen's is'
4.   'Knowing how a clarinet sounds'

~~In the third case, at any rate, it would be odd to say that one knows it but cannot say~~ it. If we wonder how somebody can know something and not be able to say it, are we not being misled by an apparent analogy with a case like No. 3? 'I know what a plant is: // what plants are: // I can show you plants // some //, draw some, describe some.' For what do we call 'An answer to the question: "What is a plant?"' Well, perhaps: 'Look: that, that, and that are plants.' We would perhaps also call a botanical verbal definition an "answer"; but it would be a different one, and not equivalent to the first. (MS 115, 41)

The passage then continues along the lines of PI §70(b)

(ii)   Note that BT 248, from which MS 115, 40–2, is derived, remarks on the irrelevance of a strict definition of 'plant', for example. But isn't a definition a prerequisite of exactness? After all, when we say the ground is covered with plants, we don't mean bacillae. Yes, to be sure, we would be thinking of green plants of a certain order of magnitude. Someone who told us that we don't know what we are talking about until we have given a definition of 'plant', we should rightly think mad. In ordinary cases we would not make ourselves better understood by means of such a definition. Indeed, it would seem, in a sense, to be worse, since in this case it is actually the undefined [expression] that seems to belong to our language. A correct explanation in such a case could be given by means of a painted picture together with the words 'The ground looked like this'.

In the sequel, W. makes two important points: (a) That one cannot apply the notion of a calculus to such a language. He goes on to compare a language like ours, which has such expressions, to tennis, which likewise is not everywhere regulated by rules (cf. §68). Nothing is specified in the rules of tennis as to whether, if someone throws the ball so high that it never comes

down, or hits it so hard that it circles the earth, the ball is 'in' or 'out'. But
we can lay down rules for such cases when they arise; as things are, it is quite
unnecessary. (b) That we can, nevertheless, give grammatical rules for the use
of the word 'plant', and we can answer questions like 'Does it follow from
this state of affairs, that there is a plant over there?' But there will be borderline cases that we can think of, to which there is no answer other than to
point out that no such cases have hitherto arisen, and that there is no need to
worry about them now.

2.1   'how a clarinet sounds': MS 162(b) discusses describing shades of colour,
aromas, the atmosphere of a piece of music, facial expressions, memory
experiences, etc. Much of this critically examines the idea that descriptions
leave out certain features which are essentially indescribable (e.g. atmosphere
(PI b.r.f. §165 (p. 66n.)), the aroma of coffee (PI §610; for discussion, see Exg.)).

   If I say: a particular shade of colour is indescribable, then of course I have a particular
mode of description in mind. I say, e.g., not as a simple ornament with simple colours
is *describable*.
   I think of a particular method of description and say 'it doesn't fit'.
   Then we think of descriptions which come nearest to the desired description . . .
   We feel that all these methods of description come close to the one we are talking
about; but they do not get there. (MS 162(b), 31r–32r)

The idea that indescribability is not absolute, but relative to a particular
norm of description, is elaborated. Discussing describing the aroma of coffee
(cf. PI §610(a)), W. wrote: 'A particular ideal [norm] of description is fixed
in our mind. Perhaps that of a composition of an aroma from a precise set of
aroma-elements.' Philosophers divorce the notion of description from particular language-games of describing (*Beschreibungsspiele*) and thereby create the
illusion that there is a single form of description and an absolute notion of
indescribability.

   We call 'describing the aroma' a particular use of language. E.g. 'The aroma of this
coffee is similar to that but it smells more darkly roasted.' If one believes that there is,
irrespective of such descriptions, also something else, which would be in a more distinguished sense the description of the aroma: then one is chasing a philosophical chimera.
(MS 162(b), 59)

So we *can* describe the aroma of coffee ('This smells delicious', 'It smells freshly
roasted', 'It has a burnt smell', etc.). These are perfectly decent descriptions,
and they seem defective only when juxtaposed with what is called 'description' in *other* language-games than the description of perceptual qualities.
   Given this criticism of the philosophical employment of the notion of
indescribability, it is misleading of §78 to suggest that the sound of a clarinet is
indescribable — that one knows but cannot say what it sounds like. One *can*

explain, in various ways, what it sounds like, but there is no such thing as *defining* its sound, on one paradigm of *defining*.

> Proper names
>   1. Stage-setting
>   2. Frege and Russell: simple abbreviation theories
>   3. Cluster theories of proper names
>   4. Some general principles
>   5. Some critical consequences
>   6. The significance of proper names
>   7. Proper names and meaning

SECTION 79

1   The preamble 'Consider this example' suggests that W.'s aim is to illustrate, by reference to proper names, some point made in the immediately preceding remarks. If so, §79 should be interpreted in relation to that specific purpose. It is certainly not a comprehensive presentation of W.'s views on proper names; other important points on that subject are made in §§40–4, and in other writings (see 'Proper names').

What antecedent remarks are meant to be further illuminated by consideration of proper names? The obvious candidates are the suggestions that my mastery of the use of an expression is 'completely expressed in the explanations that I could give' (§75), that a sharp boundary delimiting the use of certain kinds of expressions would distort them (§§76f.), and that some expressions have a family of meanings (§77). The subordination of the discussion of 'Moses' to this purpose is patent from the sources (see 2 below). It is one of a number of related moves leading up to the denial, in §81, that in speaking a language we are operating a calculus according to rigid rules.

§79(a) introduces as an example the sentence 'Moses did not exist'. This may mean various things, and we do ask, in such a case, 'What do you mean? Do you wish to say that . . . or . . . etc.?' Possible answers are suggested. Then, W. remarks, it would accord with this variety of answers to follow Russell's practice of saying that the name 'Moses' can be *defined* by means of various descriptions. For that would assign different senses to the sentence 'Moses did not exist' (and to every other proposition about Moses) according to which *definition* is given to the name 'Moses'.

(b) raises an objection to Russell's idea that the meaning of a proper name is given by a description or descriptions used to define it. One uses a proper name like 'Moses' *without* determining which description or descriptions are substitutable for the name. One has, as it were, a whole range of props to lean on, and if one is removed (i.e. if one description is proved to be false), one may lean on another. More generally, one may have a whole range of beliefs about N, all or any of which one might cite when asked what one understands by 'N' (and one might cite different descriptions on different occasions). So, one's definition of 'N' might seem to be a conjunction of all the descriptions one uses or might use to explain 'N' on different occasions. But, W. objects, this would make the sentence 'N is dead' false if a single one of these descriptions, a wholly incidental one, were not satisfied by N. This is misconceived. For if I had explained the name 'N' thus, I might well be ready to withdraw this incidental description. In short, *no* definition of a name 'N' captures what I mean by 'N'. (This conclusion is parallel to §76.)

(c) summarizes (b) in the statement: 'I use the name "N" without a *fixed* meaning'. And it adds that this does not make 'N' useless. (This is parallel to the conclusion of §77(b): using 'N' without a fixed meaning might be phrased as using 'N' with a family of meanings between members of which it fluctuates.)

(d) dismisses the objection that (b) should be summarized in the statement that I am using a word whose meaning I do not know and so am talking nonsense. (This objection restates for proper names the Socratic position discussed in §70.) W.'s reply is ironic.

(e) draws an analogy between the fluctuation in science between taking a phenomenon as an inductively established concomitant of F and using it as a characteristic mark of the concept of F, on the one hand (cf. PI §354, Z §438), and the fluctuation between different meanings, given by definite descriptions, of proper names.

The upshot of the investigation is negative: no sharp definition of a name 'N' encapsulates what I understand by 'N' because I do not use 'N' strictly in conformity with a single definition. 'N' has a family of meanings among which I fluctuate freely. The positive points of §79 are few and humdrum. (i) Sentences of the form 'N did not exist' may have various meanings. (ii) What I understand or mean by 'N' may be explained by descriptions specifying who N is. (iii) Definitions of 'N' by descriptions may vary from occasion to occasion, and they may be revised in the light of further information. (iv) The variability and revisability of possible definitions of 'N' does not detract from the usefulness of the name 'N'.

The discussion is flawed by W.'s accepting the ideas that proper names can rightly be said to have a meaning or family of meanings (even if it is not 'fixed'), and that in explaining whom I meant by 'N' by giving a description or array of descriptions, I am giving the (fluctuating) meaning of 'N' (for discussion, see 'Proper names'). Nevertheless, there is an important insight implicit in W.'s remarks: namely, that there are multiple criteria for knowing who N is.

The attribution to W. of a cluster theory of proper names has no textual warrant.

1.1   (i)   'Nach Russell können wir sagen': It is doubtful whether the text of §79 expresses any commitment to Russell's analysis of names. The phrase 'nach

Russell können wir sagen' is neutral, and W. himself gave an antiseptic paraphrase of it in translation: 'in Russell's terminology' (TS 226$_R$ §86). The 4th edition of the *Investigations* has the equally neutral 'According to Russell, we may say . . .'. This simply introduces a (correct) statement of Russell's view. What W. does is to cite Russell's view that the sentence 'Moses did not exist' (or any other sentence about Moses) may have various senses, according to what definition of the name 'Moses' is accepted as specifying its meaning.

(ii) 'eindeutig bestimmten Gebrauch': fixed and determined for all possible cases. This phrase is to be contrasted with 'used without a *fixed* meaning' (§79(c)).

(iii) 'ohne *feste* Bedeutung': W. preferred 'without a *rigid* meaning' (TS 226$_R$ §86).

2   The origin of §79(a)–(d) is early. It first appears in MS 112 (Vol. VIII), 93r–95r, and then recurs with only minor modifications in BT 251ff., MS 115 (Vol. XI), 43ff., MS 152, 77f., and thence in MS 142, §76 (cf. also VoW 213–17 and PLP 69ff.). The immediate argumentative context is stable throughout these various drafts. In each version the remark introduces a discussion of the mistake of thinking of understanding or meaning something as operating a calculus of rules and refers to the *Tractatus*'s subscribing implicitly to this dogma (i.e. the substance of PI §81).

(i)   MS 112, 93v (cf. BT 252) comes much closer to approving of Russell's abbreviated description account than PI:

Ich will doch wohl das sagen, was Russell dadurch ausdrückt, dass der Name Moses durch verschiedene Beschreibungen definiert sein kann. . . . & dass je nachdem wir die eine oder andere Definition annehmen der Satz 'Moses hat existiert' einen andern Sinn bekommt & ebenso jeder andere Satz, der von Moses behandelt.

(I wish to say just what Russell expresses by saying that the name 'Moses' can be defined by different descriptions. . . . And according as we assume one or another definition, the sentence 'Moses existed' takes on a different sense — and so too does every other sentence about Moses.)

Nevertheless, W. parted company with Russell in much the same way as in PI §79. He concluded that we use 'N' without a fixed meaning, or that we are ready to change the rules of the game as we go along. Interestingly, he then noted: 'That is reminiscent of what I once wrote about the use of concept-words, e.g. of the word "leaf" or "plant".'

(ii)   In his dictations to Waismann (VoW 213–17 (F 3), cf. PLP 69–71), W. discusses the same topic under the heading 'Vagueness' (this again confirms that this discussion is not an investigation into proper names, but rather uses the example of proper names to make a general point about language and linguistic meaning). Here he opens with a less favourable reference to Russell:

Russell says the name Moses stands for a description — but for which one? Is a definition of the name Moses anywhere to be found? On being questioned, would we be in a position to state one right away? . . .

If one now asks a person: 'What do you really mean by the word Moses?', then he will not only be in no position to give a definition, but he will also, if we present him with different definitions, be unable to choose between them. He would be *irresolute* about his use of this word. (VoW 213)

. . . if we call the sense or meaning of the word Moses what comes in answer to the question about what it means, then we can, with some justification, call the meaning of the word Moses a *fluctuating* one. We can only say: no rules are laid down here. *But this too is a result.* (VoW 215)

SECTION 80

1   Our concepts are not everywhere circumscribed by rules (cf. §§68–70). But what would it be to have rules ready for all possible eventualities (cf. §84)? The case of the disappearing chair leaves us bereft of words — we do not know what to say.[13] We do not have any rules to budget for such cases. But the idea that our mastery of the use of the word 'chair' consists in knowledge of a rule that settles the truth-value of 'There is a chair' *in every conceivable circumstance* is confused. We have rules for the use of the word 'chair' wherever we need them (and if a new need crops up, we can devise a new rule to budget for it, modifying our concept of a chair accordingly). Our concept of a chair is none the worse for not being determined by rules that cover the imagined kind of case, precisely because it does not arise. 'The signpost is in order — if, under normal circumstances, it fulfils its purpose' (§87).

The idea under attack corresponds to Frege's conception of determinacy of sense. On his view, a concept-word must be completely defined; i.e. its definition 'must unambiguously determine, as regards any object, whether or not it falls under the concept . . . Thus there must not be any object as regards which the definition leaves in doubt whether it falls under the concept' (BLA ii §56). But, if this implies that the rules for the use of concept-words must budget for all possible circumstances and every imaginable doubt, this is doubly misconceived. First, as argued, it is mistaken to suppose that vague concepts are not really concepts or are not really of any use. Secondly, this conception of determinacy of sense conflates vagueness (the existence of disagreements over borderline cases) with the possibility of vagueness. But it is neither necessary nor possible to guard against the mere possibility of vagueness. No determinate

---

[13]   Comparable to J. L. Austin's exploding goldfinch, 'Other Minds', repr. in his *Philosophical Papers* (Clarendon Press, Oxford, 1961), p. 56.

totality is signified by 'all possible circumstances'. We can imagine bizarre circumstances in which we would not know whether or not to call something 'a chair'. But, *pace* Frege, this does not make our common use of the word 'chair' in the slightest bit doubtful, and it certainly does not imply that the word lacks a meaning.

2   MS 152, 78, follows its discussion of the proper name 'Moses' with a preliminary draft of PI §84: i.e. with the query 'What does a game that is everywhere bounded by rules look like?' This is then followed by a draft of PI §80.

The incoherence of the idea of a set of rules covering *all* eventualities is developed in MS 115 (Vol. XI), 50–3, from which Z §440 is derived.

Section 81

1   Many words of our language are not everywhere bounded by rules (§§68, 71, 75–7). In some cases, such as proper names, W. claims, we use expressions without a 'fixed' or 'rigid' (*feste*) meaning at all (§79). The rules for the use of our words do not budget for every conceivable eventuality — and are none the worse, for all that (§80). But there is a powerful philosophical temptation to deny that this can be so. W., when he wrote the *Tractatus*, succumbed to it, thinking that the vagueness and indeterminacy exhibited by natural language is only a surface-grammatical phenomenon that disappears on analysis. All that is necessary is that one mean something by what one says (for 'It seems clear that what we MEAN must always be "*sharp*" ' (NB 68)); (see 1.1(v) and 2.1(iv) below). Analysis will reveal that every apparent indeterminacy is determinately indeterminate, consisting of a disjunction of individually determinate possibilities. Logic, he thought, *demanded* that every language satisfy the requirement of determinacy of sense. And logic seemed to be the *essence* of language (cf. PI §97), since all the propositions of language, he held, are generated by logical operations on elementary propositions. Elementary propositions divide logical space *sharply* into two. They consist of simple names, the meanings of which are simple objects in reality — this being how the demand for determinacy of sense was satisfied.

A different temptation, and a different reaction to the fact that the words of natural languages are not everywhere circumscribed by rules, is to view natural languages as being defective to the extent that they do not meet this requirement. In philosophy, especially since the mathematicization of logic in the late nineteenth and early twentieth century, we often compare the use of words in natural language with the calculi of logic, which have rigid rules. It is then tempting to say that natural language *approximates* such calculi — that the calculi of logic are ideal languages,[14] by comparison with which natural languages are deficient. It is against this temptation that W. now warns.

If we think thus, we shall misconceive the nature and role of logic (see Exg. §108, and 'Turning the inquiry round: the recantation of a metaphysician', sects 5f.). For to claim that natural language only approximates such an ideal language may mislead us into thinking that our reflections on logic are concerned with what would be true of an ideal language, which either does not exist at all or exists only in the form of conceptual notations. So this logic is not the logic of *our* language and thought, but the logic for an ideal language that none of us speaks, that is not involved in the bustle of life, that is not used in the expression and manifestations of the human soul — and, in that sense a logic for a vacuum (for empty space bereft of air (cf. PI §107; a similar metaphor is invoked in §130).

Logic does not treat of language or thought in the sense in which a natural science treats of a natural phenomenon.[15] It is neither a description of, nor a theory about, phenomena; nor does it *analyse* phenomena as chemistry does. We *construct* 'ideal languages' — as Frege and Russell did — but it is misconceived to suppose that they are better or more complete than everyday language, as if the sentences of *Begriffsschrift* or of *Principia* are correct sentences, by contrast with those with which we are familiar. So what is logic? W. does not say here (but see Exg. §108). It is not the depth grammar of natural languages; nor is it the surface grammar of non-natural (so-called ideal) languages. It is a form for presenting arguments, and a formal standard for judging their validity. It is *partly constitutive* of what we call 'thinking' and 'reasoning'.

§81(b) adds a caveat: this can be fully understood only when one has attained clarity about understanding — an ability, not a state (see 'Understanding and ability'), meaning something by a word or utterance — not a mental act or activity (see Volume 4, 'The mythology of meaning something'), and thinking (reasoning) — not a mental process, but a transition from one proposition to another according to a rule (see Volume 2, 'Grammar and necessity', sect. 5). For only then will it become clear what can mislead one, and misled W. when he was writing the *Tractatus*, into thinking that when one utters a sentence and means or understands it, one is operating a calculus according to definite rules.

---

[14] Frege and Russell both thought of their calculi as logically perfect languages. *Begriffsschrift* was, as its title announced, 'A Formula Language of Pure Thought', which avoids the 'softness', 'instability' and 'ambiguity' of natural languages ('On the Scientific Justification of a Conceptual Notation', in CN 86). Russell held that the language of *Principia* needs only to have a vocabulary added to it to make it 'a logically perfect language' (PLAt 176).

[15] Frege held that 'The task we assign logic is only that of saying what holds with utmost generality for all thinking, whatever its subject matter . . . Consequently logic is *the science of the most general laws of truth*' ('Logic', PW 128, emphasis added).

1.1   (i)   'Ramsey once emphasized . . . it was doubtless closely related . . .': In view of MS 112 (Vol. VIII), 94v (see 2.1(i) below), it is not obviously 'doubtless' at all, and in view of the history of the term 'normative science' (see 3 below), it seems rather doubtful.

(ii)   'für den luftleeren Raum': W. deleted Rhees's 'for empty space', replacing it by 'for a vacuum', which he then deleted and substituted 'not taking into account friction and air resistance' (TS 226$_R$ §88).

(iii)   'als wären diese Sprachen besser, vollkommener': 'as if these languages were better, more complete' — since they leave no gaps or indeterminacies.

(iv)   'and *means* . . . it': according to the *Tractatus*, thinking the sense of the sentence is the method of projection (TLP 3.11), and 'thinking the sense of the sentence' is *meaning*, by the sentence uttered, the state of affairs it depicts (its sense). That in turn involved meaning, by the constituent names, the objects in reality that are their meanings. Since those names are not present in the surface grammar of the spoken sentence, the mind must, unbeknownst to the speaker (TLP 4.002), be operating a complex calculus of rules that will carry him from the fully analysed proposition in thought to the proposition uttered. (Understanding the utterance of another will then be the reciprocal operation.)

If one does not have an adequate conception of what meaning something by a word is, it may appear that when one uses a word such as 'game' or 'plant', then one means by it an array of characteristic marks of the concept (i.e. properties of whatever falls under it), even though one cannot say what they are. (Who would have thought that attributions of qualities to objects contain rational and irrational numbers (RLF 165)?) So too, if one does not have an adequate grasp of what understanding an expression is, it may seem as if one might understand an expression, have an implicit knowledge of the relevant rules of the calculus of language to which it belongs, even though one is unaware of them and cannot say what they are. *Analysis*, one may think, will bring to light what was implicit in our use of language all along. This is the philosophical fantasy that W. is now keen to extirpate.

2   BT §58 (248–62) contains much of the material of PI §§65–88. Part of the section heading is 'Die Logik normativ'.

2.1   (i)   'Ramsey once emphasized . . . a "normative science"': MS. 112 (Vol. VIII), 94v, contains an early version. It occurs in the context of a draft of PI §79(b)–(c). After 'without a fixed meaning', W. continues:

or that we are willing to change the rules of the game as required (make the rules as we go along). That reminds me of what I once earlier wrote about the use of concept-words, e.g. 'leaf', or 'plant'. And here I recollect that Ramsey once said that logic is a "normative science". If one means by this that it sets up an ideal, which reality only approximates, then it must be said that this 'ideal' interests us only as an instrument for an approximative description of reality.

Note that 'reality' here is the reality *of our language*. (Cf. BT 253; MS. 115 (Vol. XI), 45.)

(ii) 'logic was a "normative science"': BT 68v notes: 'In saying that logic does not know how to deal with fuzzy concepts, Frege is speaking the truth in so far as it is precisely the sharpness of concepts that belongs to the method of logic. This is what the expression "logic is normative" can signify.' He continued: 'It is in the nature of logic to draw boundaries, but in the language we speak such boundaries are not drawn. That does not mean that logic misrepresents language or [represents] an ideal language. It portrays the blurred colours of reality by means of an ink-drawing, that is its task.'

BT 252v adds: '"Logic is a normative science" should really mean that it sets up ideals which we should try to emulate. But this is not how it is. Logic sets up exact calculi.'

(iii) 'mich verleitet hat': MS 142, §78, adds in parentheses 'Log. Phil. Abh.'.

(iv) 'and *means*': MS 109 (Vol. V), 281, observes that one would like to say that merely meaning something by what one says ensures that one is following a rule, and queries whether one can say that if one means something, one has chosen one's words according to a rule (see Exg. §102, 2.1). A corollary of this misconception is the idea that not following a rule in using words to say something is to string words together aimlessly, i.e. not to mean anything by them (cf. BT 254).

3   'normative Wissenschaft': this terminology has been traced[16] to the school of Schleiermacher, and to Wundt. The conception of laws of logic as normative laws dictating how we *ought* to think if we wish to attain truth in our inferences was widespread in the nineteenth century. It posed a difficulty for psychologicians who conceived of the laws of logic as *also* constituting descriptions of how we are constrained to think in virtue of the constitution of our minds. Frege saw this as a point in favour of a Platonist conception of logic as being, like ethics, a normative science ('Logic', PW 128; BLA i pp. xv–xvi). W. thought that both conceptions misconstrued the nature of logic (see Volume 2, 'Grammar and necessity', sect. 5).

SECTION 82

1   This confronts the conception of meaning or understanding an expression as operating a calculus of fixed rules, and begins to dissolve it. The point here

---

[16] By C. S. Peirce, *Collected Papers* (Harvard University Press, Cambridge, Mass., 1960), Vol. 1, p. 314, and Vol. 2, p. 5n. I. A. Richards noted (*Scrutiny* I, 408 (1933)) that Ramsay liked to quote Peirce's remark 'Logic is the Ethics of thinking, in the sense in which Ethics is the bringing to bear of self-control for the purposes of realizing our desires'.

established is that given what we understand by the expression 'The rule by which he proceeds' there are expressions in language which are applied in the absence of any *fixed* rule stating conditions for their correct application. The example which is held to show this is that of a proper name 'N' (§79(b)).[17] First, the name is not applied by invoking any such rule. Secondly, although the speaker offers explanations of 'N', he is willing to withdraw and alter his explanations of 'N' in certain circumstances. He uses the name 'without a *fixed* meaning' (cf. §79(c)).

How do we determine *the* rule by which a person proceeds? W. suggests various possibilities (already raised in §54): (i) the hypothesis that fits his observed use of the expression in question (see 2 below); (ii) the rule he overtly consults when using the expression; (iii) the rule he cites when asked.

This sketch of what we might call 'the rule by which he proceeds' suffices to undermine the idea (§81(b)) that meaning something and understanding always involve 'operating a calculus according to definite rules'. When he says 'N is dead', he consults no rule. Explanations that he is prepared to withdraw or alter cannot be *the definite* rule that he *always* follows. This leaves the burden of the claim that he is following a definite rule on the supposition that observation of his behaviour will always disclose that it conforms to some fixed rule that we can formulate. But why may it not happen that observation brings no such rule to light?

It might be objected that all that we need to justify describing him as following a particular rule is a hypothesis that fits his use of the expression, and that we cannot fail to find such a hypothesis because *any* (finite) set of observations can always be subsumed under some general explanatory hypothesis. This would prove too much. For then no use of a word by a speaker could fail to accord with a rule (cf. §201). But then to assert that meaning or understanding something consists in using words according to *definite* rules is to say nothing whatsoever.

1.1   (i)   'does not clearly reveal any rule': The topic is still the use of the proper-name 'N'. For reasons already explained the choice of this part of speech to illustrate the point is unfortunate.

(ii)   'Was soll der Ausdruck ". . ." hier noch besagen': W. preferred 'What use is there left for the expression' (TS 226$_R$ §89).

2   BT 253 links §82 to §81(b) by way of TLP 5.5563:

---

[17]   Note that to do the work that W. wants it to do, 'N' must be someone else's name, not one's own — perhaps, indeed, only the name of someone with whom one is not acquainted. There are many facts about oneself and one's close acquaintances that one could reject only at the price of madness (as W. noted in *On Certainty*).

Was it not a mistake of mine (for so it now seems to me) to assume that someone who uses language is always playing *a specific game*? For was that not the point of my remark that everything about a proposition — no matter how casually it is uttered — is 'in order'. But didn't I want to say: everything must be in order, if someone utters a sentence and applies it? But there is neither something in order nor something out of order about this — it would be in order if one could say: even this man is playing a game according to a specific, rigid set of rules.

A precursor of §82 immediately follows. This concludes with the remark that one can only determine which rule he is following by reference to his answer to the question 'Who is N?'

SECTION 83

1   The game analogy is exploited to cast doubt on the idea that whenever we use words we must be operating a calculus according to definite rules. We can imagine an activity with a ball which moved from one rule-governed game to another, without finishing any, interspersed with unregulated 'playing about' with the ball. Someone (a dogmatic philosopher perhaps) might conceive of this motley as constituting a unitary game in which the players are everywhere following definite rules. With sufficient ingenuity, he might indeed come up with a hypothetical set of rules by reference to which their behaviour can be described as rule-governed (cf. §82, line 2). But it is not rule-governed for all that, since they are not *following* a definite set of rules at all. For *following* a rule is intentional, and the players, as is evident from W.'s example, are not playing with the ball with the intention of conforming to such a definite system of rules (see Volume 2, 'Following rules, mastery of techniques and practices' for discussion of this conception of following rules, which is at odds with much late twentieth-century linguistic theory).

§83(b) offers a game analogy for the flexibility and fluctuating character of rules discussed in §79.

2   BT 254 makes explicit the purpose of the analogy in §83 by continuing immediately with a discussion of the use of the proper name 'N' in the sentence 'N is dead' (PI §79(b)):

But — somebody will object — whoever uttered the sentence 'N is dead' did not string words together aimlessly (and indeed that is what his 'having meant something by his words' amounts to). — But one could well say: he uttered the sentence aimlessly, and this is manifested in the above-mentioned uncertainty [cf. §79(b)]. Certainly he got the sentence from somewhere and, if you like, he is also playing a game according to very primitive rules; for it is certainly true that I got *an answer* to the question 'Who is N?', or a series of answers that were not altogether irregular. — We could say: Let us investigate language in respect of its rules. If here and there it has no rules, then that is the result of our investigation.

The difficulty in philosophy is to recognize that this result is the end of the matter.

Section 84

1   §84 opens with an implicit back-reference to §68(b) (explicit in MS 142, §81): the application of a word is not everywhere bounded by rules. This introduces a discussion (§§84–7) of what it would be for a set of rules to determine the application of a word in every possible circumstance (as Frege demanded of the definition of a concept-word).

This can be interpreted in two ways by exploiting the game analogy. First, a game can be described as not everywhere bounded by rules if not every aspect of playing it, or not every activity involved in playing it, is explicitly regulated by the rules. This form of unboundedness seems anodyne, and if lack of regulation here or there impedes the playing of the game, a new rule can be introduced. Secondly, a game could be said to be not everywhere bounded by rules if all possible doubt about how to apply its rules is not closed off, i.e. if there can be cases about which the rules leave doubts. This is the interpretation discussed in §84. For any game there are countless imaginable possibilities each of which raises doubts about how to apply its rules (cf. MS 142, §114 = Z §440). We can, of course, think up further rules to guide the application of the rules in any imaginary problem case. But then further doubts about the application of *these* rules can be imagined. Therefore, there is no such thing as a game 'everywhere bounded by rules' in *this* sense.

It detracts nothing from a game that it is possible for us to imagine doubts about how to apply its rules. (By parity of reasoning, it detracts nothing from a concept-word that we can imagine circumstances in which it is possible to doubt whether it applies to an object, not through factual ignorance, but because there are no rules for the imagined case.) Imaginable doubts about how to apply a rule in imaginary circumstances do not demonstrate that it is not certain how to apply it in actual cases. What would be damaging for a game is not the possibility of doubting how to apply its rules in imaginary circumstances, but the existence of real doubt about how to apply them in important or frequently recurring situations. For in this case the game would disintegrate into arguments or quarrels. Actual doubts are important and can be treated one by one, perhaps by extending the rules of a game. Possible doubts are inexhaustible and harmless.

(Frege's demand for determinacy of sense is quoted in Exg. §71.)

1.1   (i) 'sie sei nicht überall von Regeln begrenzt': 'not everywhere bounded by rules'. This is an allusion to §68.

(ii) 'what does a game look like . . .': There is no such thing, and we have no clear conception. But, as W. notes in §100, we are inclined to say that a perfect game would satisfy this demand — for we are bedazzled by a misconception of the ideal in our language (cf. Exg. §100).

2   (i)   MS 142, §114 (= Z §440) uses the game analogy to discuss the equivalent question of what it would be to have a *complete* set of rules for the application of a word. It is always possible to construct doubtful cases not clearly decided by the manual of rules for a game. In chess, e.g., the rule that black and white make moves alternately would be problematic in its application if players did not ordinarily agree in their memories of who had made the last move. If such possibilities were taken to show that the rules of a game are not complete, then there would be no such thing as a complete set of rules for a game.

      (ii)   MS 115 (Vol. XI), 51f., explores a different response to the possibility of doubt about how to apply the rules of chess. After describing the case as just mentioned (2(i)), it continues with two questions: 'But does the possibility of such a doubt make chess into a game that is not altogether ideal? and what conception have we of this ideal?' In trying to answer this last question, we are driven into a paradox. 'It seems as if everything that we call "ideal" is merely an approximation to the ideal in contrast with the ideal ideal.' We have no conception of what is ideal here (cf. PLP 149f.), and we find it impossible to construct one that satisfies us (cf. §88 (e)).

SECTION 85

1   The comparison of a rule with a signpost (continued in §87(c)) introduces an illuminating and fruitful concretization of rules, which will later be invoked to shed light upon the nature of following rules and the relationship between a rule and the practice of applying it (§198).

1.1   (i)   'Eine Regel steht da, . . .' / 'Aber wo steht': the pun is lost in translation.
      (ii)   'der Wegweiser lässt doch einen Zweifel offen': in TS 227(b), the typescript has 'keinen Zweifel', which was printed in the first three editions. In TS 227(a), the 'k' is deleted by hand, to read 'einen Zweifel', i.e. 'So I can say, the signpost does after all leave room for doubt'. This makes better sense in context. The mere signpost, without the practice of following it, leaves ample room for doubt — for many possible conventions could determine how it is to be used and what counts as following it. In practice, signposts sometimes leave room for doubt and sometimes don't. But that is now an empirical statement.

SECTION 86

1   §85 compared a rule to a signpost, and the concrete example of a signpost served to emphasize that a rule may or may not leave room for doubt, but if

it does not, that is not because it has made provision for all possible doubts, but rather because no doubts actually arise in practice. §86 applies the argument to an extension of language-game (2), and takes it a step further. The chart envisaged contains signs and pictures of building-stones. A issues his orders by displaying a sign; B looks up the sign in his chart, looks at the picture opposite, and fetches the building-stone pictured. B will have been trained to look up signs in the chart, and will have learnt to pass horizontally from sign to picture. This way of reading the chart could itself have been given in the form of a schema of parallel horizontal arrows. Such a schema would in effect be a rule for following the rule (and might be said to be an *interpretation* of the rule). But the training was not incomplete for lack of such a rule to guide the pupil in following the rule to bring a building-stone that corresponds to the picture opposite the sign which the building master (A) displays. Nor was the rule incomplete for lack of an interpretation (a further rule guiding one in the application of the rule).

To be sure, the rule might have been different. For example, when A shows the sign 'a', B might have to bring a building-stone the picture of which is opposite the sign 'b' in the chart, etc. This rule too could be explained by giving a rule for applying it in the form of a different schema. But it too is not incomplete without the further interpretation. Moreover, one could imagine that the schema itself is explained (interpreted) by yet another schema, determining yet another rule. So one *can* go on adding rules for interpreting rules, for interpreting rules, etc. But one does not have to. And the statement of a rule is complete if there are *in fact* no misunderstandings about what counts as complying with it. This conclusion is duly drawn in §87.

Note that the theme of following a rule, and of giving interpretations of rule formulations, will be explored *in extenso* in §§185ff. Here the conclusion pertinent to the issue of the completeness of a rule (given that one can always add a rule for the application of a rule) is that the rule is complete and that the statement of a rule is in order if no misunderstandings about the application of the rule arise. In §201 the conclusion pertinent to the question of what counts as understanding a rule (given that interpretations can always be given to determine the application of a rule) is that there is a way of understanding a rule which is not an interpretation.

SECTION 87

1   This articulates the tacit conclusion of §86. No explanation can avert every possible doubt about how to apply the defined expression. According to §79, proper names are *sometimes* used with a fluctuating meaning. Let us disregard this, and suppose that one stipulates that by 'Moses' one means . . . , and one specifies necessary and sufficient conditions for the application of the name. But this *still* does not remove all possible doubt. For the application of the

constituent words of the explanans may be called into doubt. Nor would the possibility of doubt come to an end when one got down to 'indefinables' like 'red', 'dark' and 'sweet', which the empiricists envisaged as the termini of explanations (names of simple ideas given in experience). *No* explanation can ensure that all possibility of doubt is excluded.

Does this mean that there is no final (or 'ultimate' (TS 226$_R$ §94)) explanation? The final explanation is the last we give in the normal practices of explanation, the explanation that standardly suffices to guide the recipient in correctly applying the explanans. It is not the last we *would* give to people defective in understanding, or if called upon to resolve questions of application in special and abnormal circumstances. (The last house in the road leading out of town is not the last that *could* be built.)

Does this mean that no explanation is complete? To call an explanation incomplete is to criticize it for failing adequately to serve its purpose. The purpose of an explanation is to convey an understanding of the explanandum, and it fulfils this purpose provided it guides speakers correctly in applying the expression in standard contexts. If, in the practice of using the word, the explanation constitutes a standard of correctness in normal contexts and does not lead to misunderstandings, then it is complete. The need for additional explanations, for a further rule to guide the application of a rule, arises only when it is necessary to avert a misunderstanding that would otherwise occur.

§87(b) repudiates the demand for determinacy of sense as misconstrued by Frege, for example ('there must not be any object as regards which the definition leaves us in doubt whether it falls under the concept' (BLA ii §56) — so we must lay down a rule excluding Julius Caesar from the class of numbers). It is not necessary for a secure understanding that all possible doubts be settled in advance. We do know what a chair is, even though we would not know what to say if one sprang in and out of existence (PI §80). §87(b) also repudiates Cartesian methodological doubt ('first doubt everything that *can* be doubted, and then remove all these doubts') — the unintelligibility of which is a theme of *On Certainty*.

§87(c) reverts to the signpost example of §85, for there it is easy to see matters clearly. It is possible to misinterpret a signpost. But if no one does, if it successfully guides people in normal circumstances, then it is in order.

Section 88

1   This rounds off the argument of §§65–87, reverting pointedly to §71. So the order 'Stay roughly here' is implicitly functioning as an analogue for explanations by example. They can be called 'inexact' (cf. §69), but that does not imply that they may not work perfectly well. Indeed, more exact specifications may be defective for the purposes at hand. The concept of exactness needs to be clarified.

§88(b) makes it clear that more exactness may drag in its wake more uncertainty, not less, and how striving for a greater degree of exactness can be wholly pointless in some contexts. §88(c) shows the purpose-relativity of the concepts of exactness/inexactness, and emphasizes that exactness is a matter of degree. Relative to a fixed purpose, some ways of determining time may be characterized as *more* or *less* exact than certain others.

§88(d)–(e) draws the conclusion. First, 'exact' and 'inexact' (and so too 'accurate'/'inaccurate', 'perfect'/'imperfect', 'complete'/'incomplete' and 'ideal'/'non-ideal') are terms of praise and blame. What is inexact typically attains a given goal less well than what is more exact. Consequently, applications of such terms presuppose purposes in the context. Secondly, and consequently, there is no *single* absolute, purpose-independent ideal of exactness. What is an exact specification of a time for a guest to arrive for a meal ('Come at 1.00' (as opposed to 'Come around lunchtime')) is inexact for navigating by time differences between radio signals.

These two points have implications for explanations of meaning. An explanation like 'Chess, cricket, patience, backgammon and similar things are games' may be called inexact (cf. §69), but that does not mean that it is unusable. Moreover, unless it is shown how such an explanation is defective in comparison with others in securing mutual understanding, this application of 'inexact' will not carry the customary pejorative connotation of 'inexact', any more than does the instruction on a cricket field, 'Stand roughly here'.

These points about 'exact' 'inexact' and related terms shed further light on W.'s repudiation of the idea that using language is operating a calculus according to strict rules (§81). The sequel, §§89–108, explores what leads philosophers (and what led W.) to become bedazzled by an 'ideal' of exactness, of determinacy of sense, of crystalline purity — in short, by a misconception of logic, its role and nature (see §§100–8 and Exg.). And this in turn led to a misconception of the nature of philosophy itself.

1.1   (i)   'Stay roughly here': a back-reference to §71.

(ii)   'may not any other one fail too': in particular, cannot *more accurate* ones be defective in a given context (in a field game, telling a player to stand roughly here is perfectly in order; telling him to stand 25.625 metres north of the entrance to the pavilion and 37.782 metres west of the gate would be pointless).

(iii)   'have a different though related meaning': what one has to do to set an atomic clock to the *exact time* differs from what one has to do to set one's alarm clock, but it is *not* obvious that this warrants saying that the phrase has a different meaning in the two applications

2   In earlier writing, W. had treated inexactness (and vagueness) in a very different way. It stood for an intrinsic property of certain objects and certain experiences. It was used to distinguish the geometry of the visual field from

Euclidean (or even non-Euclidean) geometry (PR 263, 269; WWK 55ff.; PLP 49). It was an essential feature of memory images and also of some visual experiences (PLP 208–12). W. had even argued that the 'inexact' words of everyday language were often better suited to express the blurredness (*Verschwommenheit*) of experience than the symbols of an 'exact' language would be; that they can often describe *exactly* what we experience (PLP 210f.; cf. PR 260). This defence of the thesis that ordinary language is 'in order as it is' is no more intelligible than the very different one given in the *Tractatus*.

2.1   'Why shouldn't we call it "inexact"?': the justification for calling the order 'inexact' is that it contains the word 'roughly' — cf. BT 249v: 'What is an "exact" definition in contrast with an inexact one? Well, perhaps a definition in which the word "roughly", "approximately", or a similar one, does not occur.' To be sure, this is a purely formal criterion, which is not general, and needs supplementation by a functional one.

Chapter 4

Philosophy (§§89–133)

INTRODUCTION

§§65–88 examined the reasons why the quest for the essence of the proposition and of language was chimerical — rooted in preconceptions and dogmatism. One source of the dogmatism was a misconception about the nature of logic and the relationship between logic and natural language. The transition from that discussion to §§89–133 is perfectly natural. The Fregean conception of logic as a description of the laws of truth and as accordingly determining the normative laws of thinking took logical investigation to be a sublime quest after the laws governing the relations of *all* thoughts, no matter what their subject matter. Logical investigations, e.g. into number, were held to reveal the essences of things. Logic, thus conceived, seemed to be an ideal to which natural language ought to approximate, and on which an ideal language such as *Begriffsschrift* purported to converge. (It is, in effect, a logic for a vacuum (§81).) The *Tractatus* conception of logic as transcendental, as a condition of the possibility of thought and linguistic representation, similarly took logical investigation to be an investigation into the essence of the world. Analysis would disclose the essence of all things. On that conception, logic is not an ideal, but is the deeply buried structure of any possible language, which can be disclosed by analysis. But, as has now been made clear, this conception of analysis was awry. So what is the nature of logical investigation? In what sense is it, as it seemed to be, something sublime (§89)? And, above all, what is logic? If it is not part of the depth grammar of any possible language, what is its role and what is its relation to natural language? W. turns first to the misunderstandings that underlay the *Tractatus* conception of logico-philosophical investigation, to the misguided idealization of the concepts of name, proposition and language, and to the confusions concerning the role of logic (§§89–108(a)). This, in turn, leads to a constructive discussion of philosophical methodology (§§108(b)–133).

This sequence of remarks (§§89–133) is the sole sustained discussion of the nature of philosophy in the book. The manuscript sources date primarily from 1930–1 and 1937. Only two remarks, §117 and §125, have a later source. It is noteworthy that the general conception of philosophy that informs Wittgenstein's later work emerged already in 1930–1. The 1937 reflections, by contrast, are backward-looking, reflecting on what misunderstandings informed the *Tractatus* conception of logic and logico-philosophical investigations. These dominate §§89–108, and provide the transition from §§65–88 to the methodological reflections on philosophy. The main *polished* sources of the remarks are *The Big Typescript*, chapter 12, and the Early Draft, TS 220, §§86–116. The latter (and its MSS antecedents) is illuminating source material. It contains almost all the remarks in the final version, but it is more than twice the length and very differently arranged. The most striking feature of the Early Draft version is the extent to which the remarks are explicitly directed against positions adopted in the *Tractatus*. For many of the sibylline pronouncements of §§89–133 were originally embedded in detailed discussions of those misconceptions. The pruning of the Early Draft has increased its obscurity by removing much of the original context and targets.

In content the chapter divides, very roughly, into two: (i) remarks about the nature of philosophical illusion and its sources, implicitly focused upon the errors of the *Tractatus*; and (ii) methodological remarks, indicating ways of combating such illusions and stating the nature and limits of philosophy.

In structure the chapter splits into two parts. Part A runs from §89 to §108(a) and is largely concerned with the diagnosing the illusions consequent on conceiving of logico-philosophical inquiry as a sublime investigation into the essence of the world, its *a priori* structure that determines what is possible. This part splits up into two groups: (α) §§89–97; (β) §§98–108(a).

Group α opens with §89, querying the nature of the apparent sublimity of logic. §§90–2 explore afresh the misconceived ideals of analysis and of exactness (cf. §§60–4, 88). These misconceptions support the supposition that the essence of language, of the proposition, is buried beneath surface grammar and is accessible only by analysis. §§93–6 examine some of the roots of the idea that the essence of the proposition is hidden and mysterious — since it seems as if the proposition *does* something extraordinary. It represents how things are, and also, *mirabile dictu*, how things are *not*. The essence of thinking seems equally remarkable — for the intentionality of thinking appears wonderful and mysterious too. We can not only think what *is* the case, we can think what is *not* the case. The concepts of proposition, language, thinking, world, seem to stand in line, one behind the other — all sharing a common form (as was supposed in the *Tractatus*). §97 is transitional, linking group (α) to group (β) and also to Part B (§§108(b)–133). It pinpoints the source of the problems in a misconception of logic as presenting the a priori order of language and the world. Conceiving things thus, we are prone misguidedly to treat the concepts of word, proposition, language, world, etc. as super-concepts — structural metalogical concepts presupposed by all thought. But they are ordinary concepts with humdrum uses.

The structure of Part A, group α:

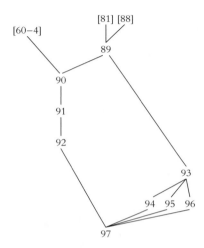

Group β of Part A runs from §98 to §108(a). §§98–103 examine one aspect of the *Tractatus* misinterpretation of the correct idea that ordinary language is in good logical order: namely, the thought that sense *must* be determinate, and therefore all apparent vagueness will disappear on analysis. Here W. goes over ground just covered in §§65–88, but with a different purpose: namely, to explain the misunderstanding of the role of the ideal in language. Because we misconceive the role of logic, we project on to language demands (ideals) set by our misconception. When we cannot find these ideals on the surface of language, we think that they must be present in the depth grammar — to be revealed by analysis. §104 offers a diagnosis: we predicate of the proposition what actually lies in our method of presenting propositions, so what looks like an essential property of what we are describing (determinacy of sense, pictoriality, the general propositional form) is, as it were, inscribed on the glasses through which we observe it: namely, a particular form for presenting propositions. §§105–7 show how the ordinary notions of word and proposition are then sublimated to satisfy misguided requirements of a preconceived idea. §108(a) concludes the discussion and provides the starting point for the sequel.

The structure of Part A, group β:

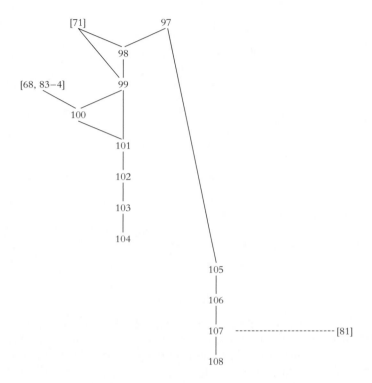

Part B (§§b.r.f. 108–133) divides into two groups: (α) §§b.r.f. 108–121, (β) §§122–33, the second (largely methodological) group being linked with §109.

Group α examines the consequences of the need to return to the examination of ordinary language in order to resolve the problems of philosophy. §108 is the key section of the group, linking it to the antecedent discussion and indicating the need to 'turn the whole inquiry round' in order to grasp correctly the role and rigour of logic. It is linked with §97 through the repudiation of construing 'proposition' and 'language' as 'super-concepts', and with §89 via rejection of the 'crystalline purity' of logic. §109 is a methodological remark that is linked to both §§110–21 and to §§122–33. The argument that follows §109 has three 'branches'. §§110–15 again dwell upon the captivating illusions of philosophical depth, the 'compulsion' of such preconceived pictures as the general propositional form, and the projection of forms of representation on to what is presented. Of these remarks, §§112–15 should perhaps have been placed earlier in the discussion, since they belong more properly to the criticism of the conception of philosophy repudiated in §§89–108. §116 criticizes the philosophical sublimation of words (e.g. 'knowledge', 'being'), emphasizing that what W. does is to bring words back from their meta-physical to their everyday use. §117 is an addendum to §116, blocking the metaphysician's suggestion that since one knows what a certain word ordin-arily means, one must also know what it means in a metaphysical context. Since philosophy destroys the grandiose claims of metaphysics, whence does it derive its importance (§§118–19)? From the elimination of nonsense, and clarification of philosophical questions. §§120–1 stress the ordinariness of the language which philosophy describes, as well as the ordinariness of the lan-guage with which it describes it.

The structure of Part B, group (α):

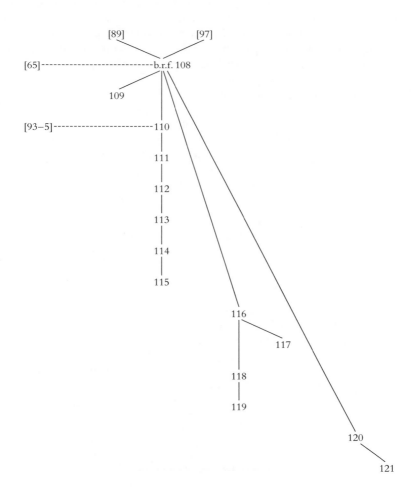

Group β consists largely of various linked claims about the nature and limits of philosophy. §109 was the first substantial elaboration of the new conception of philosophy. This theme is now continued. The group has two 'branches': §§122–9 and §§130–33. §122 is concerned with the pivotal notion of an overview; §123 is an addendum to it. §124 adds a corollary: since it is the task of philosophy to provide an overview of a segment of grammar that is the cause of trouble, philosophy obviously may not *interfere* with the existing grammar it tries to survey. Its task is to describe that grammar in such a manner that the problems dissolve. §125 is an addendum to §124(d), elaborating the consequences of this conception for the philosophy of mathematics. §§126–9 elaborate further consequences. The philosophical task is not explanatory in the sense in which the sciences explain. Since it moves within the domain of the grammar of our language, nothing is hidden (for if it were, it could have no normative role). It reminds us of how we use words, but propounds no *theses* — for what it reminds us of are not theses. The final remarks (§§130–3) emphasize that W.'s invented language-games are no more than objects for comparison, not preparations for a future regimentation of language or requirements to which language must correspond.

The structure of Part B, group β:

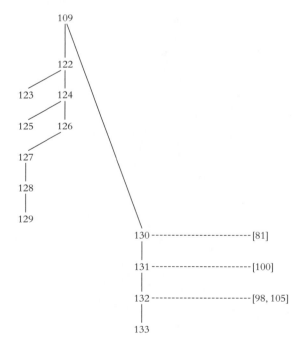

Sources

The following list of sources traces §§89–133 from MS 142 to the Early Draft of TS 220 and its English translation by Rhees with W.'s handwritten amendments in TS 226$_R$ and its reworking in TS 239. It also gives the further MS sources and BT correlations underlying these. The double references to section number and page number of MS 142 are because pp. 78–91 of MS 142 were redrafted on pp. 91–102 (and these remarks subsequently numbered §§86–110). So the section reference is to the second draft, the page reference to the first. Paragraphs within remarks have not been separately correlated, although all their sources (in so far as I could find them) are listed.

PI§	MS 142	TS 220§	TS 226$_R$§	TS 239§	157a	157b	BT	Others
89	§86; p. 79	86	97	93	47v–r			
90	§§87–8; p. 80	87	98	94	47r	7v		
91	§89; pp. 80–1	88	99	95		7v–8r		
92	§90; p. 81	88	100	96	47v	8r		
93	§§91–2; p. 81	89	102	97	61r–62v			
94	§93; p. 82	89	104	98	63r			
95	§94; p. 82	89	105	99	49r, 50v			
96	§94; pp. 82–3	89	106	100	48v, 49r, 50v, 69r–v			
97	§§95–6; p. 83	90	107	101	50v, 51r–v;			152, 91 & 93
98	§97; p. 84	91	109	102	64r–65v			
99	§98; pp. 84–5	91	109	103		4v		
100	§101; pp. 85–6	91	111	105	66r	11v–12r		
101	§102	92	112	106	55v	11v–13r		
102	§104; p. 86	92	112	108		5v–6r, 13r		
103	§102; pp. 87–8	92	112	107	57r–v	3r, 9v;		183, 163
104	§126	110		122				
b.r.f. 104								124, 133; 127, 14; 129, 177
105	§107; p. 88	94	114	110	53r–v			152, 89–91 & 95
106	§107; pp. 88–9	94	115	111				115, 49; 146, 94
107	§108; p. 89	95	116	112	69v	11r		152, 84
108	§109; p. 90	95		113	68r	2v–3r		

PI§	MS 142	TS 220§	TS 226ᵣ§	TS 239§	157a	157b	BT	Others
b.r.f. 108							71r	107, 240; 110, 221f.; 114 Um., 108f.
109	§110; p. 90	96		114				152, 94
110	§110	96		115	54v			
111	§§111–12	97		116			412	110, 176
112	§113	98		118				
113	§126	110		121				
114	§125	110		113				
115	§124	109		123				
116	§§127–8	110–11		126		14v, 16v–17r	412	110, 34; 136, 94b
117				125				127, 73–5, & 79
118	§129	111		127		17r	411	112, 115v; 153, ii, 2v, 3r
119	§129	111		128			425	108, 247
120	§130; p. 103	112		129			72	152, 92; 110, 230f.; 114 Um., 109f.
121	§130	112		130			67	111, 110; 114 Um., 104; 156b, 23r
122	§115	100		131–2			417	108, 31; 110, 257
123				133			421	153b, 27r; 112, 24r
124	§116	101		134			417f.	110, 189f., & 222; 114 Um., 109
125								130, 12 & 14
126	§§117–18	102–3		136			418–19	108, 160; 110, 90 & 217
127	§119	104		137			415, 419	153b, 36r; 112, 118v
128	§119	104		137			419	110, 259
129	§120	105		138			419	110, 259; 112, 117v
130	§133	115				17r–v		
131	§122	107		144		15v–16r		
132	§131	113		146			257v	153b, 34r; 115, 52
133	§§132–4	114–16		147–8			431–2	152, 88; 112, 47v; 115, 50 & 53;
b.r.f. 133								116, 186; 120, 85r

Turning the inquiry round: the recantation of a metaphysician
1. Reorienting the investigation
2. The sublime vision
3. Diagnosis: projecting the mode of representation on to what is represented
4. Idealizing the prototype
5. Misunderstanding the role of the ideal
6. Turning the inquiry round

EXEGESIS §§89–133

SECTION 89

1   §89(a) signifies a thematic shift, albeit still closely connected with the previous remarks. (In this respect, the opening line resembles that of §65.) The
foregoing considerations bring us to the question of whether logic is, in some
way, sublime (cf. TS 226$_R$ §97). Why so?
    The previous 'chapter' (§§65–88) was concerned with undermining the con-
ception of logico-philosophical investigation as a quest for definitions in terms
of characteristic marks; these analytic definitions had been conceived of as disclosing the common properties of all things that fall under the concepts thus
defined. So such logical investigation would not only uncover the essence of
language, it would also bring to light the essences of things. §§65–88 have
shown that there is nothing awry with concepts that lack characteristic marks,
and are not sharply bounded. Indeed, W. now claims that crucial concepts,
such as *proposition, language, number*, are family-resemblance concepts, and that
there are no common properties shared by everything that can be deemed
language, or a proposition, or a number. Equally, there is nothing awry with
explaining such concept-words by means of a series of paradigmatic examples.
Such concepts are not defective, and such explanations do not betoken a defective understanding. But the demand for sharp definitions and for determinacy
of sense had seemed to be imposed by logic itself. And logic had seemed to
constitute the depth grammar of any possible language and to reflect the structure of the world. Since the requirements of sharp definition and determinacy
of sense have now been rejected, the question of the status of logical investigation and of logic itself needs to be addressed.
    Does the question in §89(a) concern the *subject* of logic or its *subject matter*?
Is the 'depth' and 'universal significance' in §89(b) the depth and significance
of logical investigation, or of the propositions of logic that, according to the
Tractatus, constitute the scaffolding of the world (TLP 6.124), the logical
syntax of language that shares its forms with the world, and the laws of logic
that, according to Frege, are the laws of thought? The connection of this sequence
of remarks with the antecedent investigations of essentialism strongly suggests
the former. This is confirmed by MS 142, p. 79:

Es schien doch, als komme der logischen Betrachtung eine eigentümliche Tiefe zu. Als
nähme sie einen höheren Flug. Und zwar, irgendwie, weil sie das Wesen der Dinge zu
erforschen trachtet. // sie will den Dingen auf den Grund sehen, & soll sich nicht um
die zufälligen — erfahrungsmässigen Tatsachen // das Geschehen // kümmern.

(There seemed to pertain to logical investigation a peculiar depth. As if it took a higher flight. Namely, somehow or other, because it tries to explore the essence of things // it wants to see the foundations of things, and shouldn't concern itself with the accidental, experiential facts // what happens.)

'Logic' is being used, as it was often used by Russell and the young W., to signify philosophical investigations. What is sublime about logic, on this conception, is that it aims to reveal the essence of the world, of experience, of thought (MS 157a, 51v). But, of course, *logic itself*, i.e., what philosophical investigation investigates, had appeared to be 'sublime', and this illusion too must be dissolved (cf. §108 and Exg.).

The first half of §89(b) gives reasons for the thought that logic is sublime. It appears to have a universal significance in that it gives the *foundation* of all sciences (TS 226$_R$ §97). Logical investigation is not concerned with mere facts, contingent events and causal connections. It is rooted in an *urge* to penetrate appearances in order to disclose the *essence* of everything empirical. It explores the *nature* of all things. (This, properly understood, is not absurd (cf. §92), though it is misconceived to suppose that logic gives the foundations of all sciences. But in the *Tractatus* it had not been properly understood.)

The second half of §89(b) stresses an aspect of the essentialist quest. It does not call for the discovery of new *facts*. For the essence of things is necessarily present in all that we know. It is not hidden, in the manner in which empirical facts about the constitution of things are hidden and can be disclosed only by experimentation and theory. Our quest is for the understanding of something that we already, *in some sense*, know — something that is evident. (Again, these two claims, properly understood, are perfectly correct. But it was an error of the *Tractatus* to suppose that logical analysis will disclose what we seek — the logical syntax of language that was thought to lie beneath the surface of language (cf. §92) and to be, at least in this sense, hidden.)

§89(c) clarifies the sense in which we do not understand. It is the sense in which Augustine did not know what time is when he was asked.[1] It could not be said of an empirical, scientific question that we know the answer when no one asks us, but no longer when we are asked. Yet that is how it is in philosophy. To be sure, as the problems are understood by the essentialist, sublime, tradition, the resolution of the problems is not conceived to be a matter of describing, and perspicuously representing, the use of words. According to the Platonic conception, to which W. here alludes, it is a matter of recollection. And so indeed it is — but, of course, what has to be recollected, and arranged, is the way in which we use the words that are the source of our difficulties.

---

[1] Augustine, *Confessions*, Bk. XI, §14, tr. R. S. Pine-Coffin (Penguin, London, 1961): 'What, then is time? I know well enough what it is, provided that nobody asks me; but if I am asked what it is and try to explain, I am baffled.'

1.1   (i) 'sublime': cf. §§38, 94. The apparent sublimity of logic consists in its
seeming to penetrate to the essence of language, thought and world — something more profound than the contingent facts of nature investigated by the
empirical sciences. This conception informed the *Tractatus*. A corollary was
the sublimation of the concepts of word, name, proposition, inference (cf.
PI §38) — conceiving of what we ordinarily call 'words' or 'propositions' as
impure or crude, and in no way the *real* words or propositions (MS 157a,
52; MS 183, 164) — which will be disclosed only by depth analysis.

W.'s use of 'Sublimierung' and its cognates treads a fine line between subliming and sublimating, i.e. between the 'higher' (most important or profound)
and the 'purified' (unadulterated, refined). The idea that the study of logic is
sublime concerns the former sense (e.g. MS 157a, 51v). But the suggestion
that in logical investigations conducted in accordance with this 'sublime'
conception, one is prone to idealize the concepts of name and proposition
involves the idea of *sublimating* the 'impure', 'crude' or 'raw' names and propositions of ordinary language (MS 152, 82; MS 157a, 53r–v; PI §94).

(ii)   'has to be *called to mind*': This deliberately echoes Plato's *Meno* and *Phaedo*,
and is linked to §127.

2   BB 26f. discusses the Augustinian puzzle about time. It is not, W. argues,
a request for a definition — although the question 'What is time?' makes it
look so. Nor is it a quest for causes or reasons, but rather an expression of
typical philosophical puzzlement which, W. intimates, illustrates Hertz's point:

> . . . the answer we want is not really an answer to this question. It is not by finding
> out more and fresh relations and connections that it can be answered; but by remov-
> ing the contradictions existing between those already known, and thus perhaps by reduc-
> ing their number. When these painful contradictions are removed, the question as to
> the nature of force will not have been answered; but our minds, no longer vexed, will
> cease to ask illegitimate questions.[2]

The apparent contradiction in Augustine's case (i.e. how can one measure time
if the past has already gone, the future has not yet arrived, and the present
is an extensionless point?) stems from the different methods of application of
'measurement' in respect of length, on the one hand, and time, on the other
(cf. PLP 40f.). Augustine needed to remind himself of how we use 'time' and
'to measure time'. Once the grammar is displayed and properly arranged, the
problems will evaporate (see VoW 487, quoted in Exg. §75, 2.1).

2.1   §89(b) echoes W.'s first philosophy: i.e. logic is an investigation into the a
priori order of the world (NB 53), the nature of the world (NB 79); logical

---

[2]   H. Hertz, *The Principles of Mechanics*, tr. D. E. Jones and J. T. Walley (Macmillan, London,
1899), pp. 7f.

propositions show the logical properties of the Universe, every real proposition mirrors some logical property of the universe (NB 108; TLP 6.12, 6.13).

Section 90

1

Labouring under the illusion of being engaged in a sublime super-science, it seems to us (as it had to the author of the *Tractatus*) as if we had to *see through* phenomena to explore their hidden nature. But the investigation is not one into phenomena, but into the '*possibilities*' of phenomena. However, philosophy is not a sublime super-science of metaphysical possibilities, as W. had once supposed. It is, one might grant, an investigation into the possibilities of phenomena — but not by discovering their 'ultimate constituents' and 'combinatorial possibilities' (cf. RLF). Rather, we proceed by examining the grammar of the language and reminding ourselves of what makes sense. For what is (logically) possible just *is* what makes sense. This examination is to be conducted not by depth analysis (§§91–2), but by calling to mind the familiar kinds of statements we make, and grouping them in a surveyable arrangement.

§90(b) grants that some of the misunderstandings that philosophy must clear away can be removed by substituting one expression for another, as in Russell's Theory of Descriptions. There, worries about reference failure and truth-value gaps, arising from analogies between proper names and singular definite descriptions, are eliminated by replacing 'The φer . . .' with 'There is one and only one . . .'. This procedure might be called 'analysis', since it *sometimes* looks like taking something apart. (Note the link with PI §§60–4.) But, by implication, this is *not* the conception of analysis that informed logical atomism, even though it was inspired by this paradigm. For such analysis is a *grammatical* investigation — not, as Russell and the young W. had supposed, an investigation into the nature of things.

1.1 (i) 'durchschauen': W. has 'see through', and translates 'richtet sich nicht auf' as 'not one into' (TS 226$_R$ §98). *Durchschauen* should be contrasted with *übersehen*; the former is chimerical, the latter is the proper concern of philosophy.

(ii) 'yet our investigation is directed not towards *phenomena*': that empiricist conception (e.g. Hume or Russell) was already rejected in the *Tractatus*.

(iii) '*possibilities*': in scare-quotes presumably because one might indeed say that the philosopher's concerns are with the possibilities of phenomena, as long as these are not conceived in the manner of the *Tractatus*. Rather, what is logically possible is what makes sense, and hence the investigation is one into the kind of statements we make about phenomena.

(iv) 'We call to mind': see §89(b).

(v)   The kinds of non-philosophical statements Augustine recalls to mind
are that we say 'a long time' or 'a short time' only of time past or to come;
that a hundred years ago we call 'a long time past', that a hundred years hence
we call 'a long time to come', etc. (Having 'reminded himself' of the way
temporal expressions are used, Augustine unfortunately fails to arrange the
grammatical data in such a way that the problems dissolve, and instead produces a philosophical 'theory' (see *Confessions*, XI, §20).)

(vi)   'our problem': what problem? — the problem of the essence of
things, which seemed to require seeing through phenomena to the underlying logical structure of the world.

(vii)   The misleading analogies of language in Augustine's case are the analogies between measuring time and measuring length (PLP 40–3).

2   MS 157a, 47r, illuminates an aspect of the transformation of W.'s conception:

Dieses *Verständnis* schienen wir durch eine besondere Art des *Einblicks* gewinnen zu
müssen aber es wurde uns klar dass wir mit diesem Einblick nicht die Tatsachen // die
Erscheinungen // durchschauen wollten // versuchten // sondern unsere Sprache von
diesen Tatsachen // nicht die Erscheinungen sondern die Sprache in der wir von ihnen
reden durchschauen wollten.

(It seemed that we must achieve this *understanding*[3] through a special kind of insight,
but it became clear to us that we did not want // were not trying // to see through
the facts // phenomena // with this insight, but our language about these facts // wanted
to see through, not the phenomena, but the language in which we talk about
them.)

2.1   (i)   'sheds light on our problem': MS 142, §87 (cf. p. 80) has 'Unsere
Betrachtung ist daher also eine grammatische. — Wenn sie aber zum Ziele
führt, so geschieht dies dadurch, dass sie Missverständnisse wegräumt.
Missverständnisse, nämlich, welche den Gebrauch der Worte in unserer
Sprache betreffen . . .' ('Our investigation is therefore a grammatical one. —
But if it leads to the goal, this occurs because it clears away misunderstandings, namely those concerning the use of words in our language . . .') It is
evident here that the goal is the understanding of what is in plain view discussed in §89b.

(ii)   'analysis': PG 211 (MS 116, 80–2) confesses:

Formerly, I myself spoke of a 'complete analysis', and I used to believe that philosophy had to give a definitive dissection of propositions so as to set out clearly all their
connections and to remove all possibilities of misunderstanding. I spoke as if there was
a calculus in which such a dissection would be possible. I vaguely had in mind something like the definition that Russell had given for the definite article, and I used to

---

[3]   The understanding of the essence of facts (as clarified by MS 157a, 46v).

think that in a similar way one would be able to use visual impressions etc. to define the concept of a sphere, and thus exhibit once and for all the connections between concepts and lay bare the source of all misunderstandings, etc.

BT 417 observes that a proposition is completely logically analysed when its grammar is laid out completely clearly. This stands in contrast with the atomist conception of analysis into depth grammar that mirrors the forms of the facts.

SECTION 91

1   This, originally continuous with §90(b) (MS 157b, 7v), continues the theme of analysis, recapitulating §63. The fact that certain misunderstandings can be removed by substituting analysans for analysandum, as in the Theory of Descriptions, induces the illusion of a single *final* analysis of our forms of language (cf. PI §§60–4). Both Russell and the *Tractatus* succumbed to this illusion (by contrast with Frege, who embraced the conception of analysis, but held there to be alternative analyses in accordance with alternative forms of functional decomposition).

§91(b) links up with §88. The atomists' ideal of analysis was coupled with the illusion that there exists an absolute ideal of exactness, which it was the goal of analysis to achieve. But exactness, like simplicity, is a relative and variable notion (§88). We often eliminate misunderstandings by making more exact statements that eliminate vagueness or ambiguity in what we initially said; but in philosophy this may foster the illusion that there is a state of language ('fully analysed language') that is the real goal of our investigation. So, W. had once thought:

> The idea is to express in an appropriate symbolism what in ordinary language leads to endless misunderstandings. That is to say, where ordinary language disguises logical structure, where it allows the formation of pseudo propositions, where it uses one term in an infinity of different meanings, we must replace it by a symbolism which gives a clear picture of the logical structure, excludes pseudo propositions, and uses its terms unambiguously. (RLF 163)

2.1   '. . . something hidden . . . that had to be brought to light': BB 81 accuses Russell of thinking that analysis would reveal which kind of things are real 'individuals'. In TLP too, analysis was to yield the real 'objects' correlative to the real names, as well as elementary propositions and their forms. If there were 'something hidden' in our ordinary propositions, this would have non-trivial consequences for the account we should then have to give of the concept of understanding. MS 157a, 55v, remarks: 'The role of "logical analysis". How can I understand a proposition *now* if analysis is supposed to show me

what I really understand. // what it is that I understand. // Here there sneaks
in the idea of understanding as a peculiar mental process.' Cf. WWK 129f.,
which criticizes Moore's conception of analysis as disclosing for the first time
what we really mean by our words. Contrary to this misguided conception of
analysis, in matters relevant to philosophy, 'nothing is hidden' (§435), and what
is hidden is of no interest (§126).

SECTION 92

1   The illusions of 'final analysis' and 'complete exactness' are expressed in the
quest for the essence of language, of a proposition, of thought — i.e. 'the
great question that lies behind all these considerations' (§65). When this quest
is pursued under the misconception of the sublimity of logic, then the essence
of language appears to be something hidden beneath the surface of ordinary
language, to be revealed only by depth analysis. The questions 'What is language?', 'What is a proposition?' or 'What is thinking?' seem to demand an
answer in terms of essential common properties that uniquely characterize language, every possible proposition, every form of thought. That answer must
be given independently of experience, since it must antecede experience.
       The quest for the essence or, perhaps better, the nature of language, under-
stood as an investigation into the function and structure of language, is here
endorsed. This is, indeed, what W. is doing, not by analysis but by an overview
of the grammar of 'language', 'proposition', 'thought'.
       Essence, *correctly understood*, is open to view and surveyable by an ordering
of grammatical data. The nature of language is not hidden, accessible only when
one sees through the surface grammar of language and digs the essence out by
analyses which disclose the real (ideal) names and elementary propositions, which
reflect in their forms the essence of the world. The latter conception, which
characterized the *Tractatus*, involves three interwoven errors. First, it assumes
that language, proposition, and thought *have* an essence, i.e. are defined by
essential characteristic marks. Secondly, it assumes that essences (thus understood) can be 'hidden', but are discoverable by logical analysis. Thirdly, it assumes
that the essences of things (that have an essence) are determined by nature
independently of language, and *reflected* in grammar or logical syntax (cf. RFM
64, 73–5; PI §§371–3).
       There is an unavoidable difficulty in translating §92, since W. plays on the
polysemy of 'Wesen', which does service here for both 'essence' and 'nature'.
The quest for the clarification of the nature (*Wesen*) of language is endorsed,
but the search for its hidden essence (also *Wesen*) is rejected, since *language* is
a family-resemblance concept (and there are no hidden essences).

1.1   (i)   'Denn wenn wir auch in unsern Untersuchungen . . .': W. translated 'For
although in our investigations we are trying . . .' (TS 226$_R$ §100), which clarifies
that he too aims to understand the nature or essence of language. The point is

even clearer in MS 157b, 8: 'Denn wenn wir auch, in einem (hausbackenem) Sinn, das Wesen der Sprache, etc., in unseren Untersuchungen kennen lernen . . .' ('For although we too, in a (homely [plain]) sense, get to know the nature of language, etc., in our investigations . . .'). It is evident that this remark is meant to be compatible with the claim that *language* is a family-resemblance concept.

(ii) '*übersichtlich*': W. paraphrased as 'becomes transparent. I mean capable of being seen all at a glance' (TS 226$_R$ §100). Here W., like his translators, had difficulty in translating 'Übersicht' and its cognates.

(iii) 'a process of ordering': grammatical data must not only be *selected*, they must also be properly *ordered* if they are to dissolve problems.

(iv) 'once for all; and independently of any future experience': Is W. *condemning* the idea that the answer to these questions is to be given once and for all independently of future experience? Since he too thinks that philosophy might be a name given to what is possible *before* all new discoveries and inventions (§126(b)), why is he apparently critical of this? Two possibilities may be canvassed.

First, since he now thinks that the concepts of language and proposition are family-resemblance concepts, the answers are subject to future modification, since the family may grow. This interpretation is implausible, since it is incorrect that a family-resemblance concept *changes* with the accretion of a new member (the concept of a game is not changed by the invention of new kinds of games (e.g. computer games)). So W.'s new (grammatical) explanation of the concepts of language and proposition seems likewise to be independent of future experience.

Secondly, according to the sublime approach to logic, we are trying to disclose the hidden essences of all things — the order of *all* possibilities, irrespective of how things *actually* are — and so independently of experience (§89(b)). But how can a priori logical insights into the essence of the world *anticipate* experience? 'How can we make preparations for the reception of something that may happen to exist — in the sense in which Russell and Ramsey always wanted to do this? We get logic ready for the existence of many-placed relations, or for the existence of an infinite number of objects, or the like' (PG 309). Now, it seems, we have two options.

(a) We can follow Carnap, and try to anticipate experience. But that is misguided: 'The attempt to build up a logic to cover all eventualities, e.g. Carnap's construction of a system of relations while leaving it open whether anything fits it so as to give it content, is an important absurdity' (AWL 143). For content is given to the calculus by correlating it not with *reality* but with *our language*. 'Discovering' an *n*-place relation is not like discovering a new metal; it is discovering that a word in our language is used as we used the *n*-place relation term in the calculus. What looks like preparing logic for future eventualities, e.g. for the existence of 27-term relations, is in fact no more than a confused attempt to prepare logic for a grammar (PG 309–14).

(b) We can take the *Tractatus* option: namely, to deny that it is possible to answer a priori the question of whether one may need a sign for a 27-term relation in order to signify something (TLP 5.554–5.555), and so deny that logic can anticipate what belongs to its application (TLP 5.557–5.5571). But then *the application of logic* seems, in a certain sense, to be dependent on experience. W. had indeed been committed to that view: 'we can only arrive at a correct analysis by, what might be called, the logical investigation of the phenomena themselves, *i.e.*, in a certain sense *a posteriori*, and not by conjecturing *a priori* possibilities. . . . An atomic form cannot be foreseen. And it would be surprising if the actual phenomena had nothing to teach us about their structure' (RLF 163f.). So the price of making our sublime *logical* investigations into the essence of language and the world independent of experience is that we await the *discovery* of the forms of facts by the application of logic. And that is absurd.[4]

So, the sublime conception of our investigation impales us on the horns of a dilemma, which can be avoided only by abandoning this conception. Our quest for the nature of things *is* a grammatical investigation, not *faux de mieux* (this being the only way to attain insight into the essence of the world) — but essentially. We are not trying to understand something *mirrored* in language (the essence of the world), or something *hidden* in language (the depth grammar of every possible language) — but something open to view, even though it is something of which it is difficult to remind oneself or to survey. We need to turn the investigation around (PI §108(a)).

2.1   'independently of any future experience': MS 157a, 47v–48r, illuminates:

So schien es, wir müssen das *Wesen* der Sprache kennenlernen. (Das Wesen des Satzes, des Folgerns, der Grammatik) Und in der Antwort auf die Frage nach diesem Wesen, liege das was sich über das 'Wesen der Welt' sagen liesse & die Antwort auf unsere Fragen.

Und es war wesentlich dass sich jene Antwort *ein für allemal*, also unabhängig von zukünftiger Erfahrung geben lassen müsse. Und es durfte also in dieser Antwort nicht heissen Es gibt 13 Arten von . . . Und morgen finden wir also vielleicht eine 14te. Es durfte also überhaupt nicht von *Arten* die Rede sein.

Und so schien es, als müsse unsere Antwort im *höchsten* Grade einfach sein. Ja, auch nicht einmal *ein*fach. In dieser Forderung lag das Sublime; & es konnte natürlich keinen Sinn haben zu sagen: Du musst diese Forderung eben herunterschrauben. Denn die Antwort darauf musste sein: Dann interessiert mich eben das nicht wovon Du sprichst. Der Begriff 'Sprache' ist zwar eine Familie, aber auch wenn er es nicht wäre, so wäre unser jetziger Standpunkt dennoch ein anderer als der der **Log. Phil. Abh.** Wo aber läge *dann* der Unterschied?

---

[4] 'This is all connected with the false concept of logical analysis that Russell, Ramsey and I used to have, according to which we are waiting for an ultimate logical analysis of facts, like a chemical analysis of compounds — an analysis which will enable us really to discover a 7-place relation, like an element that really has the specific weight 7 (PG 311f.).'

(So it seemed as if we had to get to know the *essence* of language. (The essence of the proposition, of inference, of grammar) And in the answer to this question was to be found whatever can be said about the 'essence of the world', and the answer to our questions.

And it was essential that that answer must be capable of being given once and for all, hence independently of future experience. And so this answer could not say There are thirteen kinds of . . . And then perhaps tomorrow we shall find a fourteenth. So there was to be no talk whatever of *kinds*.[5]

And so it seemed as if our answer must be to the *highest* degree simple. Indeed, not even 'onefold'.[6] In this requirement lay the sublime; and it could of course have no sense to say: you must just lower this requirement. For then the answer to this would have to be: Then I am just not interested in what you are talking about. The concept 'language' is, to be sure, a family, but even if it were not, our current point of view would differ from that of the **Tractatus**. But *then* where would be the difference?)

W. does not answer the latter question. For discussion, see 'Turning the examination around: the recantation of a metaphysician', pp. 266–9.

SECTION 93

1   Why should one think that the proposition[7] is something remarkable? One good reason is because of its importance. It is the expression of sense, the means of description, and the bearer of truth. But a misunderstanding of the logic of our language seduces us into thinking that propositions *do* something extraordinary and unique — and that leads us astray.

What specific misunderstanding W. had in mind is not obvious, although illumination comes from the source (see 2 below) and §94. Probably he had in mind such phrases as 'the proposition *expresses* a sense', 'the sense *of* a proposition', ' "*p*" *has the same sense* as "*q*" ' (cf. MS 114 (Vol. X) Um., 12f. (see 2.1 below)).[8] These incline us to think of the sense of a proposition (or sentence-in-use) as an ethereal entity associated with, or 'attached', to it. We construe 'having a sense' on the model of a binary relation, and take 'having the same

---

[5]   Probably an allusion to TLP 5.554–5.5571.

[6]   There is an untranslatable pun on 'einfach', which means 'simple' and (given the terms 'zwei'- or 'drei'-fach' i.e. twofold and threefold), is here used punningly to mean, as it were, 'onefold' ('*einfach*'). What W. means is that the simplicity is of the highest degree, and that there is no conceivable alternative to the answer (not only is it not twofold, it isn't even 'onefold').

[7]   We must bear in mind that the German 'Satz' can do service both for 'sentence' and for 'proposition'. In general, W. uses 'Satz' to signify the proposition, conceived as the sentence-in-use, and 'Satzzeichen' to signify 'sentence' or 'propositional sign'. It is perhaps unfortunate that he did not explicitly distinguish between the sentence, the meaning of a sentence, and what is said by the use of a sentence on a given occasion.

[8]   The corresponding forms of expression concerning thinking would then be 'I have a thought in mind', 'I arrived at the thought that . . .', 'We both had the same thought'. This is pertinent to §95.

sense' to signify a third thing which two propositions have in common, and so akin to 'Mr A and Mrs A have the same bank account (or passport)' rather than akin to 'X and Y have the same weight (colour, price)'. So we assume a 'pure intermediary between the propositional sign and the facts' (cf. §94). We seem to see something *behind* the sentence — something ethereal or metaphysical (MS 157a, 61r) — the Fregean *Gedanke*, for example, or the real (fully analysed) proposition in the medium of thought.

Thinking thus, it seems to us that the proposition *does* something strange and extraordinary. — What? We think it extraordinary that the proposition should be able to *represent* things (cf. §435), to represent both how things are and, indeed, also (§429) how things *are not* (here we have the 'mystery of negation' that so mesmerized the author of the *Tractatus* (NB 30)). *If* we misconstrue the notion of a proposition, then *representing* (*Darstellen*) can look as if it is something altogether remarkable — even though it is in fact quite ordinary. For it may seem, as it did to W., that the proposition represents possible states of affairs in virtue of the propositional sign's being a fact constituted of simple names whose meanings are isomorphic sempiternal objects in reality.

Why should misunderstandings of phrases concerning propositions prevent us from looking to see how propositions really function? Because they delude us into thinking that the real propositions are not the sentences-in-use of ordinary language, but something hidden. The real proposition, it may then seem (and once seemed to W.), *must* have the general form 'Such-and-such is thus-and-so', and *must* be composed of logically simple names combined in accordance with logical syntax. Although it is not evident in surface grammar, every proposition *must* actually be a fact, for only facts *can* represent facts. Every non-elementary proposition *must* be analysable into truth-functionally combined elementary propositions consisting of simple names. Only thus, it seems, can it *do* what it does. And what *we* thus do is impose a particular form of representation, derived from a selected prototype, upon propositions, and then dismiss the propositions of ordinary language — which do not conform to these requirements — as 'impure', mere surface manifestations of the real underlying propositions (cf. §§103–5 and Exg.).

2   MS 157a, 60r, is preceded by the following train of argument (paraphrased): the idea of the essence of the proposition that we wanted to specify was not simply a description of what the word signifies, but was to achieve the ultimate clarity concerning the incomparable. How did one arrive at this Ideal? [*Here follows* PI §103.] Why does one contrast this Ideal with what one sees? — One constructs it out of what one sees. But why does one think that something must correspond to this construction? Why do I say that the proposition *must* be constructed thus-and-so? . . . The role of the wrong conception of analysis. We are held captive by an *error* — but how? Analysis, thinking as a mental activity. We strive, in this error, not after *description*, but after a uniform *representation* through an idea. [*Then* §93(a).] For if he doesn't see it

as altogether ordinary, that means that he sees something behind the proposition. 'It is something very remarkable' — the whole mistake is already here. The ethereal, the metaphysical, is already here. [*Then* §93(b).]

2.1   (i)   'On the other hand . . .': MS 157a, 61v, has: 'On the other hand this, and some other things, e.g. the unity of the word "proposition", seduces us into thinking that there must be something extraordinary, unique, to be found in the way a proposition functions.'

         (ii)   'a misunderstanding of the logic of our language': MS 114 (Vol. X) Um., 12f., notes that the nouns 'sense', 'meaning', 'interpretation' mislead us into thinking that this sense, etc. corresponds to a sign in the way the bearer of a name corresponds to its name. As if one could say: 'The sign has a quite particular meaning (*Bedeutung*), is meant (*ist gemeint*) in a quite particular way, that I, for want of a direct way, must express by means of yet another sign.' The meaning (*Die Meinung* [*sic*]), the intention, would be, as it were, its soul, which I should prefer to show itself, but which regrettably I can point out only indirectly by reference to its body.

SECTION 94

1   The thought that the proposition is a remarkable thing induces us to sublimate our whole account of logic. Why? It depends on what we think propositions must do. If what they must do is itself strange and unique (see Exg. §93, 1), it will become evident that ordinary sentences-in-use could not possibly do those things. So we will be prone to think that the real proposition is a quite different kind of entity from a sentence-in-use. We may think of it as a pure and immaterial 'intermediary' between the propositional sign and the facts — such as the Fregean *Gedanke*, which is the sense of a sentence, a 'mode of presentation', and accordingly has to 'present' a truth-value as the value of a function for an argument (and so has to be composed of the sense of an argument-expression and the sense of a function-name). Or we may 'sublimate' the propositional sign itself and think that the real, purified, propositional sign is hidden in the medium of the mind, where the real form and structure of the analysed proposition must be found — and *this* mediates between the mundane propositional sign and reality. For we become dissatisfied with actual signs, and seek for the real sign in the idea of the sign at the present moment (§105b) — a psychic constituent of a thought (see CL 68). So we progressively lose sight of what logic is and of what role it actually fulfils.

1.1   (i)   'der ganzen Darstellung': W. translated 'of our whole point of view/ treatment/of logic/our subject' (TS 226$_R$ §104).

         (ii)   'eine reines Mittelwesen': W. translated 'a pure (immaterial) entity mediating between'.

(iii)   'that nothing out of the ordinary': W. translated 'none but trivial and well-known things are involved'.

(iv)   'chimeras': e.g. the 'fully analysed' propositions, the logically independent elementary propositions of which all propositions are truth-functions, the real names that are the constituents of elementary propositions, the corresponding thought-constituents, etc.

2.1   (i)   BB 32 observes that 'proposition' and 'sense of a sentence' are misguidedly introduced to designate a hypostasized shadowy intermediary.

(ii)   MS 157a, 63v, adds at the end: 'Die grössere "Reinheit" der nicht auf die Sinne wirkenden Gegenstände, z.B., der Zahlen' ('The greater "purity" of imperceptible objects, e.g. numbers'). W., like others, associates so-called abstract entities with 'purity', and psychic entities with the 'ethereal' or 'pneumatic'.

SECTION 95

1   §93 asserted that the forms of expression we employ in talking about propositions and about thinking prevent us from seeing the way propositions function. Having discussed the sublimating of the notion of a proposition in §94, W. now turns to thinking. For we are equally inclined to misconstrue thinking as unique and extraordinary. Why? Because of misconceptions concerning the intentionality of thought and proposition (§§428–65; see Exg. §§428–9).

The parroting of a sentence is just noise. But uttering a sentence with understanding, meaning something by it, is surely what is involved in expressing a proposition — for then the sentence is 'alive'. And what gives the mere signs 'life' can readily seem to be *meaning* or *thinking* the sentence one uses (or, on the side of the hearer, *understanding* and *interpreting* it). When the propositional sign is informed by a mental act of meaning *by* the sign *the state of affairs it is being used to depict*, then, it seems, we have a proposition. Similarly, 'It is not the sentence [*Satz*] // the propositional sign [*Satzzeichen*] // that is the thought, but rather the understood propositional sign, and in *understanding* we go right up to reality' (MS 157a, 49v–50r). So thinking, i.e. meaning (*meinen*) and understanding (interpreting), conceived as mental activities or processes, lie behind the use of a propositional sign. 'The method of projection', the *Tractatus* asserted, 'is to think the sense of the proposition ("das Denken des Satz-Sinnes")' (TLP 3.11), or, again, 'one could say that *the intention* is the method of projection' (MS 108, 219).[9] The mental activity of *thinking* (meaning or

---

[9]   Cf. MS 145, 49: 'Mit "Intention" meine ich hier was das Zeichen denkt was das Zeichen richtet was ihm die Meinung gibt was das Zeichen seine Funktion erfüllen macht was das Zeichen im Gedanken verwendet. Die Intention scheint zu interpretieren die endgültige Interpretation zu geben.' ('By "intention" I mean here what thinks the sign what guides the sign what makes it mean what makes the sign fulfil its function what applies the sign in thought. The intention seems to interpret to give the final interpretation.')

intending, on the speaker's side, and understanding, on the hearer's) is what gives the proposition its intentionality. For thinking, which is unique, reaches right out to its object. When one thinks that NN will arrive at 4.00, and he arrives, that is the very thing one thought would occur. *What* one thinks is not a proposition — a Fregean *Gedanke* — a 'pure intermediary' (§94) which stands in some relation to what is the case when one's thought is true. Rather, in thinking, when we think truly, we do not stop anywhere short of the fact — of what is the case. But now there is a paradox. What is it that we think when we think *falsely*? For the fact that would make our thought true does not exist (obtain). Yet, we do not think *nothing*. What we think is what is *not* the case. Where is the paradox? What we think when we think truly *seems* to be (identical with) what is the case. What we think when we think falsely is not what is the case. But what we think when we think truly and what we think when we think falsely are the very same thing. How can that be? And if our thought reaches right up to reality when it is true, it must equally reach right up to reality when it is false. How is that possible? (See 1.1(ii) below and, in detail, 'Intentionality' in Volume 4, Part I.)

1.1   (i)   'mit dem, was wir meinen': W. translated 'with what we mean // our meaning //' (TS 226$_R$ §105).

        (ii)   'do not stop anywhere short of the fact': there is no intermediary between the thought and what makes it true. But therein lies a problem, for:

> We may now be inclined to say: 'As the fact which would make our thought true if it existed does not always exist, it is not the fact which we think'. . . . The next step we are inclined to take is to think that as the object of our thought isn't the fact it is a shadow of the fact. There are different names for this shadow, e.g. 'proposition', 'sense of the sentence'. (BB 31f.)

If it were the fact that we think when what we think is true (i.e. if thinking truly were a binary relation between the thinker and a fact), then if what we think is false, we would think nothing at all (since there is no fact). The solution proposed by the *Tractatus* is that what we think is *not* the fact that makes it true, but rather *the sense of the sentence*, i.e. what it represents (NB 8). What it represents is *a possible situation*[10] — it represents how things are *if* it is true (and how things are *not*, if it is false); and it represents the very same possibility no matter whether it is true or false. If the possibility is actualized in reality, then the proposition (the sentence in its projective relation to the world) is true; if it is not, then the proposition is false. So *what* we think is indeed the very same thing irrespective of whether what we think is true or false. Note that the sense of a sentence 'p' might indeed be characterized as 'a shadow

---

[10]   To be sure, in the *Tractatus* neither a possible situation nor a fact are 'objects', and to think that p is not to stand in a relation to p.

of the fact' that *p*, since all that is missing from it, as it were, is *its obtaining*.[11] Furthermore, according to the *Tractatus*, the thought reaches right up to reality, no matter whether it is true or false, for its constituents signify (are correlated with) simple (sempiternal) objects in reality, and it shares its logical form with reality (so what it represents is something that *can* be the case).

Thinking thus, thought seems unique, indeed queer and mysterious (§428). But this is a superstition, produced by grammatical illusions (§110).

(iii) '*das und das — so und so — ist*': an allusion to the *Tractatus* conception of the general propositional form, and hence too to the general form of a fact.

2   MS 157a, 49f., is more explicit:

Oder auch: 'Denken muss etwas Einzigartiges sein.' (Warum?) (Hier liegt der Hund begraben.) Aber wie wenn man sagte: 'Sprechen' oder 'Schreiben muss etwas Einzigartiges sein'? Aber da ist eben der Unterschied dass das Denken, oder auch das *sinnvolle* Sprechen und Schreiben, etwas ganz Besonderes *kann*.

Im Gedanken (also z.B. im sinnvollen gesprochenen oder geschriebene Satz) wird die Wirklichkeit eingefangen sie selbst (*sic*). Der Gedanke ist nicht bloss Bild — er ist Bild und Deutung zugleich.

Denn das Satzzeichen ist nicht der Gedanke sondern das verstandene Satzzeichen. & im *Verstehen* gehen wir bis zur Realität. Wenn wir meinen dass es sich so verhält so halten wir nicht irgendwo vor der Tatsache sondern meinen dass *das & das so & so ist*.

Was hierdurch angedeutet ist ist eine der merkwürdigsten & und folgereichsten Sprachtäuschungen an denen wir beim Philosophieren laborieren.

(Or also: 'Thinking must be something unique.' (Why?) (Here is the rub.) But what if one said: 'Speaking' or 'Writing must be something unique'? But that just is the difference, that thinking, or also *meaningful* speaking or writing, can *do* something quite exceptional.

In thought (hence, e.g., in a meaningful spoken or written sentence) reality itself is captured.[12] The thought is not just a picture — it is picture and interpretation together.

For it isn't the propositional sign but the understood propositional sign that is the thought. And in understanding we go right up to reality. If we mean that things are thus-and-so, we do not stop anywhere short of the fact, but we mean that *such-and-such is thus-and-so*.

What is here indicated is one of the most remarkable and consequential linguistic confusions under which we labour when philosophizing.)

For the continuation, see Exg. §96.

---

[11]   But, as W. subsequently noted, if it is not a fact that *p*, how can the fact that *p* cast a shadow? See Exg. §429.
[12]   Cf. PI §428; Anscombe translated 'is caught in the net'.

2.1　　'Thought must be something unique': cf. PI §110 and §428 (and Exg.).

SECTION 96

1　　This is a portmanteau of *Tractatus* doctrines. Thought, proposition and fact were indeed lined up behind one another as logically isomorphic structures. Thinking (meaning) projects language on to the reality it depicts, and a thought just is a proposition, composed of psychic constituents in the language of thought (CL 68).

The final, parenthetical remark is 'a reminder' to examine the actual use of these apparently 'super-concepts' and so to destroy their illusory grandeur that leads to metaphysical nonsense (see §97(b)).

1.1　　'Other illusions': e.g. that thinking too is a language, and that its psychic constituents have the same kind of relation to reality as words (CL 68); that thought, language and world share the same forms ('each equivalent to each') — indeed that the world *has* a 'form', that it is 'everything that is the case'.

2.1　　(i)　'Thought, language, now appear to us as the unique correlate, picture, of the world': MS 142, pp. 82f. adds here: 'Und unsre Untersuchung das Wesen der Sprache betreffend, als ~~eine Untersuchung über~~ // ein Eindringen in // das Wesen der Welt.' ('And our investigation into the essence of language [appears to us as] ~~an investigation into~~ // penetrating // the essence of the world.') Cf. NB 82: 'Now it is becoming clear why I thought that thinking and language were the same. For thinking is a kind of language. For a thought too is, of course, a logical picture of the proposition, and therefore it just is a kind of proposition.' (Cp. TLP 4.014 (the fairy-tale alluded to is Grimm's 'Golden Children')[13].)

In a dictation to Waismann, W. remarked:

The mistaken method of investigation is really a metaphysical one: One speaks of the nature of the world, progresses from there to the nature of thought, which is supposed to reflect the nature of the world, and the nature of thought is again equivalent to the nature of the proposition or, as the case may be, to the nature of the propositional calculus which thereby also acquires a certain aura. In this way one arrives at the conception that this calculus is somehow privileged, that it mirrors, as it were, the nature of Being.' (VoW 383)

The 'mistaken method' is surely the method of the *Tractatus*, conceived as a sublime investigation into the nature of the world.

(ii)　'These concepts: proposition . . . equivalent to each': MS 157a, 49r, adds: 'Und so war die Frage nach dem Wesen des Satzes — nach der allgemeinen

---

[13]　This reference is due to R. W. Newell.

Satzform — die Frage nach dem Wesen der Welt.' ('And so the question about
the essence of the proposition — about the general propositional form — was
the question about the essence of the world.')

(iii) 'the language-game . . . is missing': MS 157a, 69v–71r, to MS 157b,
1r, explains the errors of the younger W. If one conceives of the words 'world'
and 'language' as super-concepts (PI §97(b)):

> Wozu aber ist dieses Wort 'Welt' & 'Sprache' etc. dann zu *brauchen?* Es fehlt das
> Sprachspiel, das mit ihnen zu spielen ist. Die Kristallreinheit // klarheit // der Logik,
> hatte sich mir ja nicht *ergeben,* sondern ich hatte sie gefordert. . . .
>
> In der Meinung die Ordnung der Dinge zu untersuchen, habe ich eine *Ordnung der*
> *Dinge vorausgesetzt.* Vorausgesetzt war die Idee des *Wesens* (der Welt, des Satzes,
> u.s.w.). (Der Satz, dieses merkwürdige Wesen.)
>
> Die Wörter 'Satz', 'Welt', u. andere, & ihre ausserordentliche Bedeutung d.h.
> Wichtigkeit in unsrer Sprache verführen uns zu der Fiktion einer Anwendung
> dazu, die Existenz transcendenter Wesen anzunehmen mit einer allumfassenden
> Ordnung. . . .
>
> Wenn man also das Wesen des Satzes ausspricht, so muss alles andre folgen. Es kann
> dann nicht anders sein.
>
> Der Satz aber war äquivalent mit der Sprache, die Sprache, aber mit der
> Beschreibung dessen was der Fall ist, mit der Welt.
>
> Ich nahm als gegeben an die Einzigkeit der Bedeutung der Wörter 'Welt' &
> 'Sprache' ohne dass ich einen Begriff von einem *Gebrauch* des Wortes [MS 157b, 1r,
> continues] 'Welt' hatte.
>
> Denk' es würde gefragt: 'Was ist das Wesen eines Tisches?'; so könnte der Eine
> sagen: 'Schauen wir uns an, was wir alles einen Tisch nennen'; der Andre aber ~~würde~~
> ~~sagen:~~ 'Du verstehst doch das Wort Tisch — oder nicht? — dann musst Du auch
> *ohne* auf besondere Beispiele zu schauen, sagen können, was Du unter dem Wort
> verstehst.
>
> Die 'Ordnung der Dinge', die Idee der *Form(en)* der Vorstellung, also des a priori
> ist selber eine grammatische Täuschung.

> (What is this word 'world' & 'language', etc. to be used for, then? The
> language-game that is to be played with it is lacking. The crystalline purity/clarity/ of
> logic was not given, rather I demanded it. . . .
>
> Believing that I was investigating the order of things, I *presupposed an order of things.*
> The idea of the *essence* (of the world, of the proposition, etc.) was presupposed. (The
> proposition, that queer entity.)
>
> The words 'proposition', 'world', and others, and their extraordinary significance,
> i.e. importance, in our language seduces us into the fiction of an application, into assum-
> ing the existence of transcendent entities with an all-encompassing order. . . .
>
> If one states the essence of the proposition, then everything else must follow. Then
> it cannot be otherwise.
>
> But the proposition was equivalent to language, and language to the description of
> what is the case, with the world.
>
> I presupposed as given the singularity of the meaning of the words 'world' & 'lan-
> guage' without having a conception of a *use* of the word 'world'.

Imagine it were asked: 'What is the essence of a table?'; someone might say: 'Let's look and see what all the things are that we call a table'; but another ~~would say~~: 'You do understand the word, don't you? — Then you must be able to say, *without* looking at any special example, what you understand by the word.

The 'order of things', the idea of the *form(s)* of phenomena, hence the a priori itself, is a grammatical illusion.)

Note that the remark that the a priori too is an illusion does not mean that there are no a priori propositions, but only that they are not descriptions of an objective, sempiternal, a priori order of the world (it is the latter that is illusion). Rather they are norms of representation.

SECTION 97

1   'Thinking, language, now appear to us as the unique correlate, picture, of the world' (§96). Labouring under that illusion, we surround thinking with a nimbus. For thinking seemed to share its essence with the world itself. The essence of thinking, W. had held, is logic (for logic determines what *counts* as thinking and reasoning, as well as the logical forms of thoughts); and the essence of logic presented the a priori order of the world — the order of possibilities common to both thought and world. For the propositions of logic seemed to present the scaffolding of the world (TLP 6.124), and to be a mirror image of the world (TLP 6.13). The substance of the world (the totality of objects), according to the *Tractatus*, determines all possibilities available to the world, and the objects of thought (the meanings of the thought-constituents) *are* the sempiternal objects constituting the substance of the world. The combinatorial possibilities of objects (the constituents of situations) are the combinatorial possibilities of their representatives in thought and language. Thought and world have the very same limits, for whatever is thinkable is also possible.

§97(b) begins to dismantle this mythology. The profundity of philosophy is misunderstood if it is thought to be derived from the endeavour to grasp the essence of language by grasping the order that obtains between the concepts of language, experience, world, conceived of as 'privileged' and fundamentally different from all others. Philosophy is, in a humdrum sense, an endeavour to grasp the nature of language (§92), but not by revealing a super-order between super-concepts. The words 'language', 'experience', 'world' are *words*; they have currency in our language, just as humble a currency as 'table', 'lamp' and 'door'. We speak of learning a language; we ask people how many languages they know; we talk of the language of chemistry — but not of language as consisting of the totality of elementary propositions and the propositions that can be produced from them by the N-operation. We speak of traveling all over the world, of the world of physics or opera; we ask where in the world we left something, and wonder about the world of the artist or the 'lost world of the Kalahari' — but we do not speak of the world as being 'everything that is the case'. As will be made clear in subsequent remarks, these misuses of the words 'world' and 'language' are *metaphysical, sublimated* uses of the words.

W.'s concern here is not with the whole range of categorial concepts which the *Tractatus* had conceived to be represented in language by variables and incapable of occurring in unquantified sentences, e.g. *colour* and *number*, which cannot occur in sentences such as 'Red is a colour' and '1 is a number'. His interest is only in those that seemed to characterize the general form of elementary propositions, independently of their specific content. These apparent 'super-concepts' are such as 'experience', 'thinking', 'world', and also 'word', 'proposition', 'inference', 'truth'. For, W. had thought,

> My *whole* task consists in explaining the nature of the proposition.
> That is to say, in giving the nature of all facts, whose picture the proposition *is*.
> In giving the nature of all being. (NB 39)

And in the *Tractatus*:

> To give the essence of a proposition means to give the essence of all description, and thus the essence of the world. (TLP 5.4711)

1.1   (i) 'Thinking is surrounded by a nimbus' (TS 226$_R$ §107) — looked at awry, it seems to achieve remarkable, even almost magical, things.

(ii) 'utterly simple': a reference to TLP 5.4541 (cf. NB 83). The whole of logic flows from the mere idea of the elementary proposition as such.

(iii) 'purest crystal': *crystal* is implicitly contrasted here with *amorphous* (cf. MS 157a, 66v). Logic, being, as it were, pure form (free of all empirical, contingent, contamination), is 'purest crystal' — sharp lattices of necessary possibilities.

(iv) 'incomparable essence': incomparable inasmuch as its essence seemed also to be the essence of the world. Of course, that seemed to be true of thinking as well, but 'thinking is a kind of language', and a thought 'just is a kind of proposition' (NB 82).

2   The primary source, MS 157a, 51v–52v, is more explicit (I paraphrase): The quest for the essence of language, of following, of grammar, also seemed to be a quest for the essence of the world (p. 47v). Indeed, the question about the general propositional form was a question about the essence of the world (p. 49r). Logic must not have anything experiential about it. For what interests us is what can be said in advance of any experience: namely, the essence of what we call 'experience'. And *thinking* and *experience* are equivalent. This much is clear: what the psychologists can say about thinking is of no interest to us. Whatever it is that we're striving for, it isn't psychological knowledge (pp. 50v–51r). If logic is to give the essence of language (of thinking), then it must have a transparency (a crystalline clarity) that we cannot find in the

sciences. Thinking // The concept of thinking // is, for this investigation // surrounded by a nimbus.

We are under the illusion that what is sublime, essential, about our question is that it tries to grasp // the incomparable essence of language // the essence of experience, thinking, the world //. I.e. the order that obtains between the concepts of proposition, word, inference, truth, etc. And this order is a super-order between, as it were, super-concepts. Whereas the words 'world', 'language', 'experience' have a meaning as humdrum as 'door', 'table', 'lamp'. Our problems don't obtain their depth from // their asking after the essence of language // the fact that they are answered by an explanation of the essence of language //, but from the fact they // are linguistic errors.// are disquietudes that arise from the essence, the depths, of our language // linguistic expressions //.

2.1   (i) 'logic presents an order': MS 152, 93, sketches out some of the *Tractatus* commitments W. is now rejecting:

Ich habe mich ja seinerzeit gesträubt gegen die Idee der nicht volkommenen Ordnung in der Logik. 'Jeder Satz hat einen *bestimmten* Sinn'; 'In der Logik kann es nicht Unklarheit geben, denn sonst gäbe es überhaupt nicht Klarheit (& also auch nicht Unklarheit)', 'Ein logisch-unklarer Satz ist // wäre // einer, der keinen bestimmten Sinn hat, also *keinen* Sinn' — Hier spukt immer die Idee des aetherischen Sinnes // Satzsinnes //, dessen was man *meint, des geistigen Prozesses*.

Die Logik schien das Urbild der *Ordnung*. Ich wollte immer (gegen Ramsey) sagen: Die Logik kann doch nicht zur empirischen Wissenschaft werden. Aber wie wir die Sprache // Wörter // gebrauchen, dass ist freilich Empirie // Erfahrung //.

(At that time I baulked at the idea of an incomplete order in logic. 'Every proposition has a *determinate* sense', 'In logic there can be no unclarity, for otherwise there would be no clarity at all (and so no unclarity either)', 'A logically unclear proposition is // would be // one which lacks determinate sense, and so has *no* sense' — Here the idea always creeps in of an ethereal sense // propositional sense // *of that which one means, the mental process.*

Logic seemed the prototype of *order*. I always wanted to say (against Ramsey): logic cannot become an empirical science. But how we use language // words // is surely empirical // experience //.)[14]

See further, Exg. §109.

(ii)   'the a priori order of the world': cf. 'The great problem round which everything I write turns is: Is there an order in the world a priori, and if so what does it consist in?' (NB 53). And, 'There cannot be an orderly or a

---

[14]   He does not address the latter point here. Of course, it is a matter of experience that English contains the sign 'and'. But, given its use, it is no more a matter of experience that 'p and q' is true only if both conjuncts are true than it is a matter of experience that the English conjunction 'and' has three letters.

disorderly world, so that one could say that our world is orderly. In every possible world there is an order even if it is a complicated one, just as in space too there are not orderly and disorderly distributions of points, but every distribution of points is orderly' (NB 83).

(iii) *'utterly simple'*: MS 152, 81: 'Wir haben nun die Tendenz in der Logik eine Art Ideal zu sehen (simplex sigillum veri). Und dies bewirkt es, dass wir z.B. unter einem Wort nicht das Zeichen von Fleisch & Blut // aus Druckerschwärze // verstehen wollen, sondern etwas Sublimiertes. Man könnte sich etwas Ähnliches auch für Schachspiel denken.' ('We have the tendency to see a certain sort of ideal in logic (simplex sigillum veri). And this has the consequence that we don't, e.g., want to understand a word to be the flesh and blood sign // the sign in printer's ink // but something sublimated. One could think of something similar for chess.') For W.'s invocations of Herman Boerhaave's dictum 'simplex sigillum veri' see NB 83, TLP 5.4541. For the thought regarding chess, see Exg. §108.

(iv) 'the purest crystal': MS 157a, 69v, echoes Schiller's response to Goethe's conception of the Primal Plant (cf. 'Surveyability and surveyable representations', pp. 316f.).

Die Kristallreinheit // klarheit // der Logik hatte sich mir ja nicht *ergeben*, sondern ich hatte sie gefordert.
Die Logik musste rein sein: denn was sollte rein sein, wenn nicht sie?
'Die Logik muss einfach sein': das ist eine *Forderung*, nicht ein Ergebnis.

(The crystalline purity // clarity // of logic was not *given* me [in experience], but rather was something I demanded.
Logic had to be pure; for what should be pure if not it?
'Logic must be simple': that is a *requirement*, not a result [of experience].)

(v) 'if the words "language" . . . have a use, it must be as humble a one . . .': MS 152, 91, articulates the temptation to sublimate them into super-concepts: 'Man glaubt, man muss in Bezug auf das Wort "Wort" oder "Regel" exakter sein als in Bezug auf "Lampe" oder "Kohle" // "Uhr" //; denn wie will man sonst das Allgemeinste über jene Dinge aussagen, was man verstehen muss, um über das Wesen der Sprache Klarheit zu erhalten.' ('One believes that in relation to the word "word" or "rule" one must be more exact than in relation to "lamp" or "coal" // "watch" //; otherwise how would one state the greatest generality about those things that one must understand in order to maintain clarity about the essence of language?'.)

SECTION 98

1.1   '. . . our language "is in order as it is"': an allusion to TLP 5.5563 (see 2.1), *contra* Russell and Frege. In the Preface to the *Tractatus* Russell had revealed his incomprehension:

Mr. Wittgenstein is concerned with the conditions for a logically perfect language —
not that any language is logically perfect, or that we believe ourselves capable, here
and now, of constructing a logically perfect language, but that the whole function of
language is to have meaning, and it only fulfils this function in proportion as it approaches
to the ideal language which we postulate. (TLP p. x)

This view W. repudiated, both then and later. What was wrong with the *Tractatus*
conception of the 'good order' of ordinary language was, among other things,
its forcing the requirement of determinacy of sense upon language. This theme
is pursued in §§98–107.

2.1   (i)   Of TLP 5.5563, W. wrote to Ogden: 'By this I meant to say that the
propositions of our ordinary language are not in any way logically less correct
or less exact or *more confused* than propositions written down, say, in Russell's
symbolism or any other "Begriffsschrift". (Only it is easier for us to gather
their logical form when they are expressed in an appropriate symbolism.)[15]
        (ii)   '. . . perfect order even in the vaguest sentence': MS 157a, 64r, observes
ironically:

> 'Auch der (unbestimmteste), verschwommenste Sinn ist *ein bestimmter Sinn.*'
> 'Ich habe doch immer einen bestimmten Gesichtseindruck!' Woher weisst Du dass
> es 'immer' ist? Das ist doch a priori; also heisst es, es hat keinen Sinn hier von
> 'Unbestimmtheit' zu reden und also auch nicht von Bestimmtheit. ('Ein Stab hat doch
> immer eine bestimmte Länge!')

> ('Even the most indeterminate, hazy sense is *a determinate* [particular] *sense.*'
> 'I always have a determinate [quite particular] sense-impression!' — How do you
> know that it 'always' is? That is a priori — so what it means is that it is senseless to
> speak here of 'indeterminacy' and hence too of determinacy. ('A rod always has a deter-
> minate [quite particular] length!')

W.'s point is that this use of 'bestimmt'[16] does not pick out a determinate sense
as opposed to an indeterminate one. All that is said is that every sentence with
a sense has the sense it has — and *that* says nothing at all. This is analogous
to 'A rod has a determinate length', which merely says that there is no such
thing as a rod without a length. However, W. continues, the assertion that
every rod has a determinate [quite particular] length is actually an acknowledgement of a particular form of expression: namely, one that subserves the
form of an ideal of exactness (as it were as a parameter of representation). And
the acknowledgement of a form of expression, if it is expressed // formulated
// as a proposition about the object of investigation is // at any rate has to

---

[15]   *Letters to C. K. Ogden,* ed. G. H. von Wright (Blackwell, Oxford, 1973), p. 50.
[16]   Compare this use of 'bestimmt' ('determinate' or 'quite particular') with the use of 'quite
particular' discussed in BrB 149f., 158–62, 174–7 (translated as 'bestimmte' (EPB 232)). See also
Exg. §609.

be // *a priori*. For its opposite really will be unthinkable, since there corresponds to it a form of thought, a form of expression, that one simply does not think. That is how it is, W. notes, when he says: 'There can be no vagueness *in the sense* of a sentence'. Cf. Z §442.

SECTION 99

1   If the good logical order is conceived to depend on absence of vagueness, then it may seem that even the vaguest-seeming sentence must be in order — it must be determinately indeterminate. A sentence with a sense may leave this or that open, undetermined, but *what* it leaves open must be determinate:

> Every proposition that has a sense has a COMPLETE sense, and it is a picture of reality in such a way that what is not yet said in it simply cannot belong to its sense. . . .
> If a proposition tells us something, then it must be a picture of reality just as it is, and a complete picture at that. — There will, of course, also be something that it does *not* say — but what it does say it says completely and it must be susceptible of SHARP definition.
> So a proposition may indeed be an incomplete picture of a certain fact, but it is ALWAYS a complete picture.[17] (NB 61)

> . . . if possibilities *are left open* in the proposition, *just this* must be *definite*: what is left open. . . . What I do not know I do not know, but the proposition must show me WHAT I know. (NB 63)

Such claims, W. now suggests, are akin to Frege's assertion (BLA ii §56) that an indefinite boundary is not a boundary at all (cf. PI §71). But it is not true that a boundary that is not sharply defined is no better than none. If there is only one hole in an enclosure, then there is only one way out, and we need to keep an eye on one point only.

2   MS 142, §99 and p. 85, and TS 220, §91b (= Z §§441f.) elaborate the argument for determinate indeterminacy: one might claim that the rules of a game may allow a degree of freedom, but must nevertheless be quite definite. That is like claiming that a prisoner is allowed a certain freedom of movement in his cell, but the walls must be perfectly rigid. Yet the walls could be elastic, and still imprison him! — But do they not have to have a determinate degree of elasticity? — What does that amount to? That it *must* be possible to state it? It is not always possible. That, at any rate, it must have a determinate elasticity, whether we know it or not? — That is not a truth about reality, but an avowal of adherence to a form of expression, one that subserves the form of an ideal of exactness, as it were as a parameter of expression. [The

---

[17]   Cf. TLP 5.156.

sequel (= Z §442) is a variant of MS 157a, 64r–65r, paraphrased in Exg. §98, 2.1(ii). It differs in the penultimate sentence, which runs: 'there corresponds to it a form of thought, a form of expression, *that we have excluded*' (emphasis added).]

2.1   (i)   ' "You haven't done anything at all" ': all the early drafts add here: 'And yet he *did* do something.'
         (ii) 'an enclosure with a hole . . .': MS 157b, 4v, has: 'The boundary a sack has — one would like to say — is as good as *none*. But is that true?'

Section 100

1   The switch from discussing determinacy of sense of sentences (in PI §99) to discussing vagueness in the rules of a game (in §100) was originally mediated by a remark (Z §441) which provided an analogy for §99. It began with the thought: 'The rules of a game may well allow a certain freedom, but all the same they must be quite definite rules.' Cutting this (MS 142, §§99f. (= TS 220, §91(c)–(d))) has impaired continuity. The omitted remark made it clear that the interlocutor's 'But still, it isn't a game, if there is some vagueness in the rules' is a response to W.'s insistence on the vacuity of that statement.

      PI §100 is linked with §84 (what would a game look like that *was* everywhere bounded by rules?) and with §68 (there are no rules for how high to throw the ball in tennis, 'yet tennis is a game for all that' (see Exg.)). It continues, analogically, the theme of §99: it seems as if a sentence *must* have a definite sense — and one might similarly be tempted to think that a game *cannot* tolerate any vagueness in its rules. A game which does seems not to be a complete or perfect game. Ordinary games, one might say, are 'impure', and what the interlocutor is interested in is the pure. This is analogous to the *Tractatus* interest in the 'real name' and the 'real proposition', relative to which ordinary names and propositions are impure.

      But if we think thus, W. now responds, we misunderstand the notion of the 'ideal'. The role of the ideal in our mode of expression is not *as an ideal object to which to approximate*. So, for example, actual triangles are not approximations to an Ideal Platonic Triangle; rather, something *counts* as a triangle only if it satisfies such-and-such a specification, and that specification is not a description of an Ideal Triangle, but a norm of description — a rule for the application of the word 'triangle' in sentences (including descriptions). Nor is the ideal contained within the impure variants that we encounter, as was supposed by the claim that 'There must be perfect order even in the vaguest sentence' (§98).

      So, we are bedazzled by the ideal, and *that* prevents us from seeing how the word 'game' is actually applied — i.e. that it *is* correctly applied to all the games to which we apply it, even though they do not have common properties

in virtue of which they are all games, and even though some games have
rules that are, to a degree, vague. By parity of reasoning, this bedazzlement
prevents us from seeing clearly the use of 'word', 'name', 'proposition', etc.
(which, like 'game', are family-resemblance concepts). Why does this misunderstanding so prevent us? The answer unfolds in the next three remarks.

1.1   'Then it has been contaminated, and what I am interested in now is what
it was that was contaminated': here W. presents us with an analogy for the
quest for the logically proper name, the fully analysed proposition, the hidden
logical syntax of language. Such 'sublimation' or 'idealization' is characteristic
not only of philosophical, but also of mathematical, reflection (e.g. Platonist
conceptions of geometry).

2   What, then, is the role of the ideal in language? MS 157a, 66r, provides a
different reply to the interlocutor's opening statement:

> Aber das Ideal ist Deine Ausdrucksform und ein Missverständnis verführt Dich das Ideal
> *falsch anzuwenden.*
> Es ist, als wenn Du sagtest: 'Der Umfang dieses Rades ist wirklich Dπ' (so genau
> ist es gearbeitet).

(But the ideal is your form of expression and a misunderstanding tempts you to *misapply* the ideal.
    It is as if you said: 'The circumference of this wheel really is Dπ' (it has been so
exactly wrought).)

(MS 142, §101, and TS 220, §91, add the final sentence as a parenthetical
conclusion to PI §100.) MS 157a, 68r, continues the theme:

> Man könnte π ein Ideal nennen, denn es spielt in einem Sinne die Rolle eines
> Ideals, aber *dieser* Ausdruck wäre mit *Vorsicht* zu gebrauchen: 'Wir streben bei der
> Konstruktion eines Kreises das Ideal an, dass der Umfang D.π betrage'. . . .
>   (Ich glaube, man kann sagen:) das *a priori* ist eine Darstellungsform.

(One could call π an ideal, for in one sense it does play the role of an ideal, but *this*
expression would have to be used *carefully*: 'We strive, in the construction of a circle,
after the ideal that the circumference should amount to D.π.' . . .
    (I believe one can say:) the *a priori* is a form of representation.)

The ideal constituted by D.π is not an ideal *object* which we strive to approximate, but a form (and norm) of description. The circumference of a circle *is*
D.π, just as the sum of the angles of a triangle *is* 180°.
    MS 157b, 11v–12v, contains many redraftings of the final two sentences
of PI §100 (I paraphrase). The ideal is the form of representation itself.
Misunderstanding the function and grammar of 'ideal', we misapply it. The
ideal itself is no more than, as it were, the glasses we wear, but we misguidedly think that it reveals the nature of reality. You too, W. continues, would

call it a game, only you are dazzled by the ideal and so do not see the actual application of the word 'game'. But how did you ever arrive at this ideal, from which material did you form it? Until you can resolve this, you will not shake yourself free of the fascination of the ideal. The roots of error must be uncovered. (This discussion is embedded in TS 220, §107, in which it belongs to the same remark as (a draft of) PI §131 (see Exg.).)

SECTION 101

1   §101 continues the theme of the 'ideal' raised (and rejected) in §98 and said to be misunderstood in §100. We are held captive by the idea that this ideal exactness, determinacy of sense, *must* be found in reality, i.e. in the reality of our language, in the strict, clear rules of the logical structure of propositions (§102) — even though it is not evident in the propositional signs we use. But we think we see it there, nevertheless. Why we so think is explained in §§102–3.

1.1   (i)   ' "*must*" be found in reality' and 'must be in reality': the ideal of absolute determinacy of sense must actually obtain in existing language — in its depth grammar if not on the surface. So analysis will show that every apparent vagueness is actually determinate — every vague proposition will be shown on analysis to be a disjunction of determinate possibilities. (So 'the spot is in the circle' = 'the spot is either there, or there, or there, or . . .')

       (ii)   'nor do we understand the nature of this "must" ': its nature is clarified by the comparison of the form of representation with spectacles (§103), and by the statement that we predicate of the thing what lies in the method of representation (§104). Cf. MS 157b, 11f.: the ideal lies in your form of expression (*Ausdrucksform*), but you misunderstand its role there.

2.1   (i)   MS 157a, 55v–56r, has a draft of the second and third sentences, followed by a remark on logical analysis (How can I understand a sentence if it is for analysis to show me what I understand?), and then:

Das 'Ideal' muss jetzt schon seine volle Anwendung // Anwendbarkeit // haben. Und ausserhalb dieser ist es *Ideal* nur sofern es eine Form der Darstellung ist.
Woher hast Du dieses Ideal? Was ist sein Urbild? Denn das ist es ja, was ihm Leben gibt.
'Wenn *ein* Satz ein Bild ist, so muss jeder Satz ein Bild sein, denn sie müssen alle wesensgleich sein. Jeder Satz sagt: es verhält sich so & so.' Hier haben wir auch so ein Ideal, das sich in die Erscheinungen hineindrängt.

(The 'ideal' must already have its full application // applicability // in the present. And apart from that, it is an *ideal* only in so far as it is a form of representation.
Where did you get this ideal from? What is its prototype? For it is that which gives it life.

'If *one* proposition is a picture, then every proposition must be a picture, for they must all be essentially the same. Every proposition says: Things are thus & so.' Here too we have such an ideal, which forces itself into the phenomena.)

The passage gets redrafted in MS 157b, 11v and 12r–v.

(ii)   'there can't be any vagueness in logic': cf. MS 157b, 4: 'What does it mean: there can't be any vagueness in logic? Above all there cannot then be any exactness either.'

(iii)   'The idea now absorbs us': MS 157b, 12v, had as an alternative: 'We are held captive by the idea'.

SECTION 102

1   The ideal of crystalline clarity, of determinacy of sense, of strict and clear rules of logical structure was a requirement on language, not something evident in ordinary sentences. Nevertheless, it seemed that these ideals *must* be present, if not in surface grammar, then hidden in the medium of the understanding. Why so? — Because one understands the propositional sign, one *means something* by it.

Notebooks 1914–16 manifests this line of thought again and again: e.g., 'But the sense must be clear, for after all we mean something by the proposition, and as much as we *certainly* mean must surely be clear' (NB 67; cf. 68, 70). The author of these remarks did 'not as yet *see* how it occurs', nor did he 'understand the nature of this "must" '. According to the *Tractatus* conception, *meaning* by the sentence the situation that it represents ('thinking the sense of a sentence') *is* the method of projection (TLP 3.11). The correlation of the simple names with the objects that are their meanings is *psychological* (NB 104). And, as W. later intimated, he not only thought of meaning the sense as a psychological process, he also thought of it as constitutive of the rules for the use of the signs involved (see 2.1 below). These imaginary rules did indeed appear to him as strict and clear, hidden in the medium of the understanding.

1.1   'I mean something by it': meaning something by an expression was indeed conceived to be the method of projection, see MS 108 (Vol. IV), 219.

2   MS 157b, 5r–6r, is helpful. Following the draft of PI §99 (see Exg.), W. wrote (I paraphrase): 'If you understand a proposition — mean it — then you must mean *something*!' [Then a variant of PI §108(a):] Logic seems to have lost its rigour, but actually it now plays a different role. From being a preconception about reality, it has become a form of representation. So where has the crystalline clarity ended up? It has become no more than a form of representation. Understanding is not an ethereal (*pneumatischen*) process. The concept of a family [i.e. the family-resemblance character of the concepts of proposition

and language] strikes two blows against this. It shows that I didn't *have* a general conception of a proposition and of language. I had to recognize such & such as a sign (Sraffa)[18] — and couldn't give its grammar. What is ethereal (*das Pneumatische*) about understanding completely disappears, and with it the aetherealness of sense. **At first the strict rules appear to us as something still in the background, hidden in the nebulous medium of the understanding; and one could say: they *must* be there — or: I see them, so to say, through a dense medium, but I see them.** So they were *concrete*.[19] I used a simile (of method of projection, etc.). But through the grammatical illusion of a unified concept it didn't seem to be a simile. The more obvious this illusion becomes, the clearer it becomes that language is a family, the more evident it is that the apparently concrete was an abstraction, a form, and that when we pretend that they[20] are pervasive, our statements become empty and senseless.

MS 142, p. 88, redrafts and continues (I paraphrase): The tendency to generalize the case seems to have a strict justification in logic: here one seems *completely* justified in inferring: 'If one proposition is a picture, then any proposition must be a picture, for they must all be of the same nature. (Every proposition says: this is how things are.)' For we are under the illusion that what is sublime, what is essential, about our investigation consists in its grasping *one* incomparable, comprehensive essence (cf. Z §444(b)).

MS 142, §105, continues the draft of PI §102 with Z §444(a), characterizing the resultant account (in TLP) as a theory — 'a dynamic theory' of the proposition (analogous to Freud's 'dynamic theory of dreams'[21] (cf. TS 239, §109n.)). What is characteristic of such theories is that they take one special

---

[18]   He is referring to Sraffa's famous gesture, which broke the grip on W.'s mind of the ideas of analysis and hidden logical form (see N. Malcolm, *Ludwig Wittgenstein: A Memoir*, 2nd edn (Oxford University Press, Oxford, 1984), p. 58).

[19]   Four pages later (MS 157b, 10r) W. elaborates the metaphor of the 'concrete': 'We have found // come across // a form of representation that strikes us as obvious. But it is as if we had seen something that lies beneath the surface. But this tendency seems to have a strict justification in logic. One seems here to be fully justified in writing: "If *one* proposition is a picture . . ." — As if what, in the sciences, are only abstractions, were here *concrete*.' In MS 142, p. 86, W. continued the above passage differently. After 'they *must* be there', he wrote: 'Even now I see them "as if from afar" — for I understand the signs, mean something by them. So the ideal, strict construction seemed to me to be something concrete. I used a simile — but through the grammatical illusion — that *one* thing corresponds to the concept-word, what is common to everything that falls under it — it didn't seem like a simile.'

[20]   i.e. the strict rules.

[21]   There is a brief explicit discussion of Freud's 'dynamic theory of dreams' (every dream is a wish-fulfilment) in MS 157a, 56v. W. emphasizes that it is a theory, a hypothesis, a *supposition*. It brings a very specific kind of construal to the phenomenon of the dream. But if one were to ask without more ado: 'What is a dream really?', the right answer would be — 'Have you never dreamt? Don't you know?' The analogy with 'What is a proposition?', the *Tractatus* 'dynamic theory', and the correct way of answering (i.e. making fun of the question and then surveying the grammar) holds.

clearly intuitive ('illustrative' (TS 226$_R$ §113)) case and transform it into a prototype for all possible cases. This analogy is apt, for, according to the *Tractatus*, ordinary language stands to its depth structure (analysed form) as the phenomenal dream to its underlying explanation (revealed by analysis). The *Tractatus* too attributes to the unseen mechanisms of the mind the *explanation* of the *apparently* remarkable and queer things the proposition *does* (PI §93).

2.1   'Hidden in the medium of the understanding': this is clarified by MS 109 (Vol. V), 281, which elaborates a misconception of rules and of the following of rules that may be a reconstruction of W.'s earlier thought (see also Exg. §§81, 95).

> One would like to say: 'One only has to mean something by what one says, then everything essential is given.' And so I consider 'meaning something' and 'following a rule' as synonymous.
> Can I say: If I *mean* something, then I have chosen my words according to a certain rule?
> Or thus? If I mean something, then I have portrayed something, i.e. represented according to a rule.

Thus understood, then, to be sure, the rules are hidden in the medium of the understanding. Presumably these rules carry one from the supposed fully analysed sentences in the language of thought to the mundane propositions of ordinary language that one uses to express what one means.

SECTION 103

1   The 'ideal', *misconstrued*, is evident in the preconception of the strict rules of the logical structure of propositions, in the idea that the sense of *every* sentence *must* be absolutely determinate, in the thought that *every* proposition *must* have the form 'Such-and-such is thus-and-so', in the supposition that the *real* name *must* be simple, in the conception of the sentences and words of ordinary language as merely crude surface manifestations of the *real* propositions and names hidden in the medium of the understanding. Caught thus in the web of illusion, the conception seems irresistible (see PI §§113–15 and Exg.).
    The simile of spectacles is explained in PI §104. It derives from Kleist's metaphor for Kant's transcendental idealism in his letter to Wilhelmine von Zenge, 22 March 1801.[22]

1.1   'Like a pair of glasses': a powerful metaphor for the form of representation that we employ. 'In unsern Gedanken, sitzt unverrückbar fest': 'is unshakably embedded in our thoughts'.

---

[22]   See H. von Kleist, *Geschichte meiner Seele*, ed. Helmut Semdner (Insel, Frankfurt am Main, 1977), pp. 174ff.

(ii) 'Woher dies?': W. preferred 'How does this queer situation arise?' (TS 226$_R$ §112).

2   MS 157a, 57r–v, is explicit (I paraphrase). The idea of essence, if we want to specify the essence of the proposition, did not amount simply to describing what one calls 'a proposition' or what one designates by this word, but was rather supposed to attain an ultimate clarity about the incomparable. How did you come across this ideal? [Then a draft of the first three sentences of §103]. Why doesn't one jettison this form? It is anchored in a variety of connections, and we can think of no other possibility. But it isn't that either. It is as if we didn't recognize a form of expression as a form of expression. Or almost as if we took the colour of the spectacles or a drawing on the spectacles through which we see to be the colour or some other property of the thing we are looking at. 'Every proposition says: this is how things stand' — is such a pair of spectacles.

MS 183, 162f., clarifies the ideality of the 'simple name' (I paraphrase). The ideal name is an ideal, i.e. a form of representation to which we are inclined. We want to represent destruction and change as the separation and rearrangement of elements. One might call this idea, in a certain sense, 'elevated'; it is so inasmuch as we observe the whole world through it. But there is nothing more important than that we should become clear what phenomena, what simple and humdrum cases, are the prototype for this idea. That is: ask yourself, when you are tempted to make general metaphysical statements, 'What cases am I really thinking of?' This question produces resistance in us, for we seem to endanger the ideal with it, although in fact we are doing no more than locating it in its proper place. For it is supposed to be the picture with which we compare reality, with the help of which we represent how reality is. It is not itself a picture of how things are. The 'sublime conception' forces me away from concrete cases, since what I say doesn't fit them. I set out into an ethereal region, talk of *real* signs, of rules that must obtain (even though I can't say where or how) — and have got on to slippery ice [cf. PI §107].

SECTION 104

1   This brings the discussion of 'the ideal' to a head, clarifying what it really was. Interpretation is made difficult by the relocation of the remark here in the final TS. Its original significance is evident (see 2 below). The moot question is whether relocation was intended to preserve significance, perhaps with reduced scope, or whether it implied reinterpretation. This is a matter that calls for judgement, so the source material is paraphrased *in extenso* in 2 below.

The apparently ideal phenomena that *must be found* in reality were in fact no more than projections of the mode of representation (*Darstellungsweise*). These *logically ideal* phenomena were the ideal name, the ideal (fully analysed) proposition, the general propositional form, determinacy of sense. (The corresponding *ontological* phenomena were the simple object, states of affairs (shadows of facts), facts as composed of simple objects in concatenation.) But these 'ideals' are not actually to be found in reality at all, neither in the alleged depth grammar of language (to be brought to the surface by analysis) nor in the medium of the mind (in the supposed 'language' of thought (cf. Exg. §105)). They are, W. now declares, mere projections. We unwittingly project on to what we describe (in this case, propositions, their constituents and role) features of our way of representing what we thus describe, and then project on to reality the ontological conditions to satisfy the requirements of the ideals thus misconceived. What does he have in mind?

W. had claimed that every proposition has the form 'Things are thus-and-so' (*Es verhält sich so-und-so*) — this being part of what he meant by saying that a proposition is a picture. This form had struck him as both intuitively obvious, and as providing an insight into something deeper than mere appearances, something beneath the surface (MS 157b, 10v). But that was not because he had examined every proposition and noticed that they all had this form. It was rather because, for example, one can rewrite a standard proposition 'Fa' in the form 'a has the property of being F', and a relational proposition 'aRb' in the form 'a stands in the R-relation to b'. This was a way of presenting propositions that, for various reasons (see below), appealed to him. But rather than taking this to be a fruitful comparison of propositions to models or pictures of how things stand in reality, a comparison which may go so far but no farther,[23] W. had insisted that *every* genuine proposition *really* has the form 'Things stand thus-and-so'.[24] This form of representation displayed all the referents of names in a sentence as being held together in a net of purely *logical* relations (i.e. having a property, standing in a dual relation, etc.). Thus presented, a sentence appears as a concatenation of names: adjectives are names of properties, relation-words are names of relations, etc.

Further, W. was driven to the idea of an 'ideal name' that must function thus: 'To this name corresponds *that*', and the '*that*' must be absolutely simple (MS 157a, 58v).[25] One motive for this (ibid.) was the attraction of representing all change as the rearrangement, and all destruction as the decomposition,

---

[23] e.g. it is *not* fruitfully applicable to many kinds of propositions, e.g. propositions of ethics, aesthetics and religion, propositions of mathematics, all of which were excluded from the category of propositions in the *Tractatus* — as well as many kinds of empirical propositions, e.g. avowals of experience, counterfactual conditionals, subjunctives and grammatical propositions (that were condemned as metaphysical nonsense in the *Tractatus*).

[24] But, he now observes, if something only *really* is such-and-such, *then that means* that it really *isn't* (MS 157a, 55r). It is noteworthy that nowhere in his later reflections on the general propositional form does he examine the formal apparatus of TLP 6.

[25] As he had written in NB 61: 'What seems to be given us *a priori* is the concept: *This*. — Identical with the concept of the *object*.' And, he added in the next remark, 'Relations and properties, etc., are *objects* too.'

of indestructible elements (see, for example, Plato, Descartes). The requirement for simple names appeared unavoidable, since it seemed essential to ensure
determinacy of sense (TLP 3.23). And determinacy of sense seemed essential
to ensure that logic would apply to all propositions. So where one finds vague
propositions (to which the laws of logic apparently do not apply), that must
be merely surface vagueness. It must mask *determinate* indeterminacy in depth
grammar, in which the superficially vague proposition is analysed into a disjunction of individually determinate possibilities. But what that means is that
we choose a way of presenting propositions under analysis in which vagueness
is presented thus. And that in turn implies that merely to have a sense *is* to have
a determinate sense. So there can be no indeterminate sense at all; and hence,
too, no determinate sense either. For without a contrast to exclude, the concept of determinacy of sense becomes vacuous — a typical metaphysical use
(or misuse) of words. But in fact all we have done is to project upon propositions a feature of the specific form of presenting them that appeals to us.

1.1   (i) 'the possibility of comparison': not simply the comparison of two things
that resemble each other, but the comparison of a ruler and what it measures
(cf. §131), this being a metaphor for the relationship between a form of representation and the thing represented. We do not simply compare propositions to models or pictures, cultures to organisms that mature and then decline
(Spengler), or electricity to the flow of water (the hydrodynamic model) —
we *represent the one in terms of the other*. (Goethe's conception of the primal
plant was similarly a recommendation to represent all organs of the plant as
transformations of leaves — a form of representation that, unlike the hydrodynamic model in electricity theory, did not prove fruitful in botany.)

(ii) 'höchst allgemeinen Sachlage': 'a highly general state of affairs'. We
think we perceive that *every* proposition has the general form 'Such-and-such
is thus-and-so', that *every* proposition has an absolutely determinate sense, that
every real name stands for an object, that *every* proposition consists (on analysis) of a concatenation of names, etc.

2   This enigmatic remark originates in MS 142, §126, in a different but revealing context. It was relocated to its present context only in TS 227a. It initially
occurred (as in TS 239) following drafts of PI §§113–14, which were typed
in reverse order, the draft of §113 having an opening sentence that ran: 'If
I think about the essence of the proposition, of understanding, of private
experience of which only I am conscious: "This is how it is . . ." I say to myself,
repeating the same sentence over and over again.' After the rest of §113, there
followed a draft of PI §104, which opened: 'The expression of this illusion is
the metaphysical use of our words. We predicate of the thing . . .' (continuing as in the final draft). It was followed by a draft of PI §115.

W. first reversed the order of the two preceding remarks, deleting the
opening remark of the draft of §113. So PI §104 now followed PI §114,

becoming a comment on the illusion of the general propositional form. He
then deleted the opening sentence (i.e. 'The expression of this illusion . . .'),
and relocated the remark to its present position after PI §103, where it is a
comment on the 'ideal' that we think *must* be found in reality.

In MS 142, this remark, with the above-cited opening sentence, occurred
at the end of a long and important discussion (MS 142, §§122ff.). The line of
argument is as follows (paraphrased): We can only free ourselves from the
spell of the ideal if we can recognize whence we derived it, what concrete
representation (*welche konkrete Vorstellung*) was its prototype (*Urbild*). It is of
the greatest significance that we *can* always think of an example to which
a logical calculus really applies, [that we can, e.g., give numerous examples
of presenting arguments quite uncontroversially in the form of the predicate
calculus] rather than giving an example and saying, 'This isn't the ideal case
to which the calculus really applies, but we have not yet got that.' [As W.
had done while composing TLP; see RLF.] To say the latter is the mark of
a misconception (cf. MS 111 (Vol. VII), 118).

Following an analogy concerning the application of numbers to countables,
a draft of PI §131 occurs: the model is an object of comparison, a measuring
rod, not a preconception to which reality *must* correspond.[26] For here lies a
certain dogmatism into which our philosophy can easily fall. What is true is
that a unit of measurement is well chosen if many of the lengths that we want
to measure with it are expressed in whole numbers.[27] But dogmatism would
assert that every length *must* be a multiple of our unit of measurement (MS
142, §122).

I once said (in Log. Phil. Abh.), W. continues, that an elementary proposition is a concatenation of names. Objects correspond to names, and the proposition to a complex of objects.[28] If the proposition 'The bottle stands to the
right of the glass' is true, then what corresponds to it is the complex consisting
of the bottle, the glass and the relation to-the-right-of. But this is a misuse of
the words 'object' and 'complex'. A block of houses consists just of the houses,
not of the houses and their mutual positions. And if I say that I see three objects

---

[26]   W. adds here: 'I am thinking of Spengler's approach (*Betrachtungsweise*)' — see Exg. §131.
[27]   That is to say, there should not be too many borderline cases. So, for example, Spengler's
model is only useful if *most* cultures can be illuminatingly described as going through a 'life-cycle'
of childhood, youth, maturity and old age.
[28]   W.'s use of the term 'complex' here is misleading, since in TLP the expression 'complex' was
reserved for the denotation of definite descriptions. Complexes were sharply distinguished from
facts and states of affairs. This does not, however, vitiate the critical points he makes, since facts,
no less than complexes, were (wrongly) said to be composed of objects. In MS 127, 75–9 (dated
March 1943), having copied out TLP 4.22, 3.21f., 3.14, 2.03, 2.0272 and 2.01, W. makes the
same point, using 'configuration' rather than 'complex': 'What a misuse of the words "object and
configuration"! A configuration can be made up of balls that are spatially related in a certain way;
but not of the balls and their spatial relations. And if I say "I see here three objects", I do not
mean: two balls and their mutual position.'

on the table, I don't mean the glass, the bottle and their spatial relation (MS 142, §123).

Looking frantically for a unity of all propositions, I became a prisoner of certain forms of expression and remained enmeshed in the web of language. For if, instead of 'The bottle is blue', we say 'the bottle has the property of being blue', and instead of 'The bottle is on the table', we say, 'The bottle stands to the table in the relation of being on', etc., then it can indeed appear as if every such sentence is a concatenation of names. For all the words with a 'material' meaning appear to be distributed in a net of purely logical relations. One can, perfectly intelligibly, speak of combinations of colours and shapes (e.g. the colours red and blue with the shapes square and circle),[29] just as one can of combinations of different shapes. And this is the root of my confused expression: a fact is a complex of objects.[30] To say that a red circle 'consists of' red and circularity — is a complex with these components — is a misuse of these words, and mistaken. Frege told me this.[31] The fact that this circle is red does not 'consist' of anything. (Frege objected to my expression, in that he said to me: 'The part is surely smaller than the whole.'[32]) And again: all the words in a sentence correspond to objects, since 'Paul' signifies *that*, 'eats' signifies *that*, 'three' signifies *that*, and 'apple' *that*. The *picture* held me captive. I couldn't escape it, since it lay in my language, which seemed to me to repeat it inexorably (MS 142, §124).

'Every proposition says: This is how things stand' — here is such a form that can mislead us. (And that misled me.) In Plato: 'Whoever means something, means something that exists' (*Theaetetus* 189a).[33] This is the kind of proposition one repeats to oneself countless times. One thinks that one is again and again registering nature, and yet one is merely registering the form by means of which we look at it. [= PI §114. This is followed by Z §443 — see Exg. §114.] Again and again we trace the form of expression, and think we have drawn the thing itself. Through an optical illusion, we seem to see — within things — what is drawn on our glasses (MS 142, §125).

---

[29]   One might perhaps talk thus of Matisse cut-outs.

[30]   He did not say this, but rather that a fact (i.e. an obtaining state of affairs (TLP 2)) is put together (*zusammengesetzt*) out of objects (TLP 4.2211), has objects as components (*Bestandteile* (NB 62)), is a combination (*Verbindung*) of objects (TLP 2.01). But the criticism goes through despite the shift of terminology.

[31]   W. added: related to the confusion of colour and pigment, referring again (see Exg. §4) to Frege's BLA ii §150.

[32]   W. is probably referring here (from memory) to Frege's letter of 28 June 1919, in which Frege objected to TLP 1.1 ('The world is the totality of facts, not of things') and its consistency with TLP 2.011 ('It is essential to things that they should be possible constituents of states of affairs'). For, he observed, if a thing can be a constituent of a fact, then since a part of a part is a part of the whole, so a thing *is* a part of the world.

[33]   This is a quick reference to the battery of problems of intentionality tackled in PI §§428–65: e.g. if one thinks something, there must *be* something that one thinks; but then how can one think something that is not the case (i.e. something false)?

[This is followed by a draft of PI §113, and then PI §104:] **Only when this optical illusion is removed, can we simply see language as it is. The expression of this illusion is the metaphysical use of our words. For one predicates of the thing what lies in the mode of representation** [*Darstellungsweise*]. **We take the possibility of comparison, which impresses us, as the perception of a highly general state of affairs** (MS 142, §126).

For, one has never called the position of a thing 'an object'. And does one say of the proposition 'It is raining' that it says 'Things are thus-and-so'? How does one really use this expression? For it is from this use that you learnt it! If you use it contrary to its original use, and think that you are still playing the old game with it, that is as if you were to play draughts with chess pieces and to think that the pieces still retained something of chess (MS 142, §127).

We bring words back from their metaphysical to their everyday use (= PI §116(b)). (The man who says one can't step twice in the same river, says something false; one *can* step twice in the same river. And sometimes an object ceases to exist when I stop looking at it, and sometimes not. And sometimes we *know* what colour another person sees when he looks at this object, and sometimes not. This is what the solution to all philosophical difficulties looks like. Our answers, if correct, must be ordinary and trivial. For these answers make fun of the questions (MS 142, §128, derived from BT 411f.).

Boxed Remark Following §104 (p. 46n)

1   It is not obvious what this remark is doing here. The history of its location illuminates matters.

TS 227b, p. 82, contains the draft of PI §§102–3, typed in reverse order, with a pencilled rearrangement in another hand. The concluding sentences of the draft of PI §102 are deleted in the same hand. They ran as follows: 'The ideal rigorous construction seemed to me something concrete. I used a simile; but through the illusion that what corresponds to a concept-word is // must be // unique ('dem Begriffswort entspräche Eines // müsse Eines entsprechen //'), what is common to all its objects, it didn't seem to me like a simile // it didn't appear to be a simile //.' A pencilled note indicates that §104 is to be inserted from p. 86. Turning to p. 86, we find that the section in question is what is now PI §104. What was originally its first line, viz. 'The expression of this illusion is the metaphysical use of our words' has been deleted in the same hand. Before the sentence 'We predicate of the thing what lies in the method of representing it' is an asterisk, referring to the bottom of the page, where there is an MS note 'Zitat von Faraday "Water . . ."'. This note has been crossed out. The quotation from Faraday was on a separate cutting, inserted between p. 85 and p. 86, numbered 340, derived from B i §340 (= MS 127, 14 = MS 124, 133 = MS 129, 177).

What attracted W. to this remark? The context of its occurrence in MS 129, 177, is suggestive. It comes after the following: 'One could say: we look at what we do when we follow the rule from the perspective of *always* the same. One could say to the person one instructs: "Look, I always do the same: I . . . ." '[34] The point concerns the internal relation between following a particular rule (e.g. the rule for a series) and the determination of act–identity; i.e. if we call this behaviour 'following the rule of the series', we will also call the various actions 'doing the same'. Faraday's insistence that water is always the same despite its transformations expresses his determination to fix the concept of water thus. (It is, one might say, an idea, not an experience; to be sure, it is a scientifically fruitful idea.[35])

It is plausible to conjecture that W. found Faraday's remark attractively illustrative of the projection on to phenomena of the unity of the concept by means of which one chooses to represent it. That water is 'one individual thing', and that 'it never changes' is, after all, a *decision*. (What! — It never changes? Is ice the same as water? Can one walk on water? Is steam liquid and potable?) Since we do not know the order of the deletions on TS 227b, it is possible that W. wanted to insert the quotation from Faraday to illustrate the (subsequently?) deleted passage in §103 (then reallocated to §102). Alternatively, having deleted the concluding sentences of §103, he may have wanted to use the Faraday quotation to illustrate predicating of the thing the unity that lies in the way of representing it.

2   Faraday's remark, in his lecture,[36] occurs in the following context:

Here in this bottle, is a quantity of water — pure distilled water, produced from the combustion of a gas-lamp[37] — in no point different from the water that you distill from the river or ocean or spring, but exactly the same thing. Water is one individual thing — it never changes. We can add to it by careful adjustment, for a little while, or we can take it apart, and get other things from it; but water, as water, remains always the same, either in a solid, liquid or fluid [*sic!* gaseous?] state.

This is comparable to another conception that we know attracted W.'s attention: namely, Goethe's attempt to find a principle of unity which will yield an understanding of plants (cf. 'Surveyability and surveyable representations', pp. 315–20.) and a principle of ordering for them:

---

[34] This remark, in TS 227, was typed in between PI §223(a) and (b), and then deleted.
[35] A comparable thought is expressed in MS 125, 58r–v: 'When white changes to black some people say' "It is essentially still the same". And others, when the colour darkens the slightest bit, say, "it has changed completely".')
[36] M. Faraday, *The Chemical History of a Candle* (Hutchinson, London, 1907), p. 44.
[37] This being the experiment Faraday has just conducted.

However plants may sprout, bloom or bear fruit, it is always just the *same organs* that in manifold ways and many variable forms manifest nature's pattern. The very same organ that unfolds on a stem as a leaf and assumes the greatest variety of forms is contracted into a bud, develops into flower petals, is contracted into the sexual organs, in order to develop finally as the fruit.[38]

Both remarks reveal how the quest for scientific insight is expressed in the endeavor to find a principle of unity in terms of which the diversity of phenomena can be described. Whether water is everywhere one and the same, whether the organs of the plant are all the same (transformation of leaves), whether we will *accept* these forms of representation, turns on the fruitfulness of the paradigm and the hypotheses one can construct by reference to it. Boltzmann sapiently remarked: 'Only half of our experience is ever experience, as Goethe says. The more boldly one goes beyond experience, the more general the overview one can win, the more surprising the facts one can discover but the more easily too one can fall into error.'[39] That ice, water and steam are 'one and the same' has proved a fruitful determination. That the organs of plants are all leaves led Goethe into a cul-de-sac.

SECTION 105

1   §104 diagnosed the source of our misconceptions concerning the ideal sign. §105 describes their consequences. We *demand* crystalline clarity, determinacy of sense, etc., and when we find that ordinary signs (words, sentences) do not *really* satisfy these requirements, we conclude that they are not the *real* signs that logic (i.e. the laws of logic) deals with. W. had once wondered, 'can we deal with a proposition [*Satz*: sentence in use] like "The watch is on the table" without further ado according to the rules of logic? No, here we say, for example, that no date is given in the proposition, that the proposition is only apparently . . . etc., etc. So before we can deal with it, we must, so it seems, transform it in a particular way' (NB 66). The transformation that seemed necessary was not mere decontextualization. To produce a 'real' proposition that the laws of logic deal with, it seemed that we must show that any vagueness is merely superficial (otherwise the laws of logic will not apply). So we must display the real proposition as 'pure and clear-cut', as a truth-function of elementary propositions the sense of which is determinate; and these must consist of simple names, to ensure determinacy of sense; etc.

---

[38]   Goethe, 'Die Metamorphose der Pflanzen', §115, in *Goethes Werke*, Hamburger Ausgabe, Band 13 (Wegner, Hamburg, 1955). W. was well acquainted with Goethe's essay and the corresponding poem.

[39]   L. Boltzmann, 'On the Development of Theoretical Physics in Recent Times', in *Ludwig Boltzmann: Theoretical Physics and Philosophical Problems*, ed. B. McGuinness, tr. P. Foulkes (Reidel, Dordrecht, 1974), p. 96.

But why should we come to think that the real signs are 'ideas' of signs, i.e. mental representations of signs? *One* route is the one W. had followed: '. . . thinking is a kind of language. For a thought too is, of course, a logical picture of the proposition, and therefore is just a kind of proposition' (NB 82). A thought has psychic constituents that have the same sort of relation to reality as words (CL 68). These thought-constituents correspond to the objects of the thought, i.e. the entities in reality that the thought is about (TLP 3.2). That is why *a fully analysed proposition* of natural language is expressed in such a manner that the elements of the propositional sign (the 'simple signs' or 'names') *correspond to the objects of the thought* (the simple objects in reality) that are their meanings (TLP 3.2–3.3.22). We have, as yet, no such analysis (RLF 171), but it seemed evident that the 'real signs', the signs that do satisfy our requirements, exist as thought-constituents that underlie the gross signs of natural language.

Why 'the idea at the present moment'? Among other things, because it seemed that only in the current 'act of meaning' is determinacy of sense secured: 'it seems clear that what we MEAN must always be "*sharp*"' (NB 68; cf. 67).

2   MS 157a elaborated the matter. We are under the illusion that what is deep and essential about our investigation consists in its trying to grasp incomparable linguistic entities. But the depth of our problems doesn't consist in having to explain the essence of language, but in the fact that our problems are disquietudes arising from the depths of our language.

Wir scheinen jene Über-Ordnung in der wirklichen Sprache finden zu *müssen*. So fragen wir uns auch was das *eigentliche* Wort, der eigentliche Satz unserer Sprache sei, denn die geschriebenen & gedruckten Wörter & Sätze besitzen in ihrem Wesen nicht die Klarheit die die sublime Sprache erfordert. So gehen wir auf die Suche nach dem eigentlichen Wort & glauben es etwa in der Vorstellung des Worts zu finden.

Und so kommt es dazu, dass wir Idealbegriffe haben & sagen, sie *müssen* auf die Realität der Sprache anwendbar sein, aber nicht sagen können wie. (MS 157a, 53r)

(It seems that we *must* find this super-order in actual language. So we ask ourselves what the real word, the real proposition of our language is, for the written or printed words and propositions do not have in their nature the clarity which the sublime language demands. So we go in search of the real word, and believe that it may be found, e.g. in the idea of the word.

And so it comes about that we[40] have ideal concepts and say that they *must* be applicable to the reality of language, but cannot say how.)

MS 152, 89f., merits paraphrase: I don't ask 'What is a word (a sentence, a rule)?', W. insisted. I use these words as they are ordinarily used, and give

---

[40] Perhaps the interpolation of 'think that we' would have been appropriate here.

explanations only where they are necessary to ward off misunderstandings. . . .
In order to answer the question 'What is a word?', 'What is a rule?', one actually has to do no more than look to see how these words are used; of what
we say that it is a rule, and what the expression of a rule; in what cases we
say that something occurs in accordance with a rule. But this doesn't appear
to suffice. For we believe that we have to play a game with these expressions
with ideally exact rules. For that alone can eliminate the doubts that the use
of language produces. We are inclined to say that we don't even know what
a word is, what a rule is. . . . If we ask 'What is a word?', 'What is a rule?',
etc., we should, as it were, like to find purer entities than those we ordinarily signify with these expressions. We want to represent the latter as a contamination of the former.

The word (the meaningful word) should really be the *idea* of the word —
not the hypothetical object,[41] i.e. the ink mark, etc. But just look how we *use*
the expression 'the word "table" ', for example. To be sure, the actual grammar of such items is the occasion for numerous confusions and philosophical
worries. But that is not because our language is here flawed, so that we must
first translate it into another. Nor is it because this language is all right for
everyday, but inadequate when we want to probe deeper in philosophy.

W. returns to the issue on p. 95: we ask, 'What are the words (sentences,
propositions) that logic deals with? What is the real sign?' — as if our language were not in order, and we had to put it in order. As if the word 'word',
as used hitherto, didn't have the final word. It is as if one felt the reality of
these expressions, so to speak, through thick gloves, which one has to remove
in order to feel the real shapes. One should think of chess here [cf. PI §108(d)].
Our investigation is again and again led away from everyday things into
deceptive depths. For the problem doesn't appear to us in its true colours:
namely, as a confusion of our forms of expression; rather, it seems as if we
must penetrate great depths to the actual constituents of reality. [Following
this, W. wrote a note for himself: 'the question is, where do I want to go
from here?' And he listed the following themes: the ideal name; the simple;
the role of the calculus in our presentation; the application of the calculus, i.e.
actually not ideally; what is a name? What is a proposition? Elementary propositions, etc., etc., understanding, meaning, reading, following, the simple as
a more sublime concept and the simple as important form of representation,
but with humdrum application. And with respect to what things this form of
representation misleads us. . . .]

SECTION 106

1   The solution to our predicaments is to return to what we ordinarily call
'sentence' (*Satz*), 'word', 'sign', and carefully to describe how these words are

---

[41]   i.e. not the material object, the ink mark, construed as a hypothesis based on sense-data.

used, where this is necessary to ward off philosophical confusions. So we might point out, for example, that 'the sense *of* a sentence (*Satz*)' and ' "S$_1$" and "S$_2$" *have the same* sense' are (*contra* Frege) not so used as to warrant the assumption that the sense of a sentence is a further entity attached to a sentence, and that 'have the same sense' is not used like 'possessing the same passport', but is more akin to 'having the same price'. And so on.

The extreme subtleties are the supposed fine-grained structures of the depth grammar of language. Why do we imagine that we can't describe them? Because it seems as if ordinary language is too crude to describe such subtleties (cf. §120).

The torn spider's web is ordinary language — torn, it seems, because of the apparent lacunae in it. We feel, in philosophy, that our task is to show how these apparent faults are remedied or resolved in the depth grammar. But it is impossible to do so, for there are none.

1.1   'we must stick to matters of everyday thought': so we must engage in 'connective analysis', tracing the manifold conceptual connections between expressions, rather than in 'depth-analysis' that purports to discover hidden structures.

SECTION 107

1   This rounds off the preliminary discussion of the illusory subliming of logic and of its crystalline purity (§97). The supposedly hidden 'ideal language' that seemed to contain the required structures constantly conflicts with actual language. The workings of language must be described as they are, without the preconceptions of a theory which dictates how they must be (see 'Turning the examination around: the recantation of a metaphysician').

1.1   (i) 'in danger of becoming empty': as in the case of the requirement of determinacy of sense, cf. Exg. §98, 2.1(ii).

(ii) 'where there is no friction': The metaphor is reminiscent of Kant's metaphor of the dove (*Critique of Pure Reason*, A5/B9). It also makes contact with §81: comparing our language with artificial calculi may make it appear as if our language approximates such calculi, i.e. as if a language akin to such a calculus would be an ideal, perfect language (Russell). Then it will seem as if our logic is actually the logic for this non-existent, ideal language, i.e. a logic 'not taking into account friction and air-resistance' (W.'s translation (TS 226$_R$ §88)).

2   MS 157a, 70r, after a draft of the second sentence of PI §107 on p. 69v, notes that meaning to investigate the order of things, W. had *presupposed* an order (see Exg. §96, 2.1(iii)).

MS 157b, 11r, after a draft of the first sentence, remarks that the attempt to sustain this requirement becomes increasingly empty. The ideal is one's mode of expression, and one misunderstands its function (its grammar), as one does in the case of certain misfired fallacies.

2.1   'Back to the rough ground': MS 152, 83f., clarifies:

Widerstreit der sublimen Auffassung & der Tatsachen die Natur des Wortes Satzes etc. betreffend. Man will ihn lösen, dass man in die persönliche Vorstellung zu dringen sucht. Da, im augenblicklichen Geschehen müsse man das eigentliche Wort, z.B., finden & da etwa auch das Verstehen etc. Da werde das Sublime gefunden. Aber da scheint unsre Sprache zu versagen. Wir sind aufs Glatteis geraten wo die Reibung fehlt also die Bedingungen in gewissem Sinne ideal sind aber wir eben deshalb auch nicht gehen können. Wir wollen gehen — dann brauchen wir die *Reibung*. Zurück zu *konkreten* Beispielen! // auf den rauen Boden! // zu *wirklichen Beispielen*.

(Conflict between the sublime conception and the facts concerning the nature of the word, the proposition, etc. One wants to dissolve it, in that one tries to penetrate the [workings of the] subjective representation. There, in an instantaneous occurrence, one must find, e.g., the real word, and there too perhaps, the understanding, etc. That is where the sublime is to be found. But there our language seems to fail. We have got on to slippery ice where there is no friction and so in a certain sense the conditions are ideal, but also, because of that, we are unable to walk. We want to walk — so we need *friction*. Back to *concrete* examples! // the rough ground! // to *real examples*.)

This nicely summarizes the mythology of symbolism and of psychological processes of meaning, understanding and interpreting that underpinned the *Tractatus* conception of the proposition and its resolution of the problems of intentionality.

3   Unto a mill the mind compare,
      That grinds whatever grain is there;
      But if no more of it is brought,
      The stones on one another caught
      Mere splinters, dust and sand prepare.[42]

SECTION 108

1   The first sentence of §108(a) acknowledges W.'s misconception in the *Tractatus* of taking 'language' and 'proposition' to be sharply determined (formal) concepts. But they are actually family-resemblance concepts. Does recognition of this fact not undermine the rigour of logic, and so destroy it? What sense of

[42]   Grillparzer, quoted by Boltzmann, 'On a Thesis of Schopenhaner's', in *Luding Boltzmann*, p. 197.

'logic' is in question here? What is it that *appeared* to possess a crystalline purity? It is not the apparently sublime (§89) *study* of logic, but the *subject matter* of such a study:[43] namely, the calculus and laws of logic.

Why should logic *seem* to be losing its rigour (or 'rigidity', as W. said in his lectures (AWL 99))? *If* we conceive of the calculus of logic as constituting the depth grammar of every possible language, then, if we acknowledge that the concepts of language and of a proposition are family-resemblance concepts, it seems that logic itself must possess whatever degree of elasticity is necessary to constitute the depth grammar for everything that falls under these family-resemblance concepts. If vague propositions *are* genuine propositions (*contra* Frege), and if vagueness is not merely a surface phenomenon that disappears on analysis (*contra* the *Tractatus*), must logic not lose its 'rigidity' and crystalline clarity? Must we not introduce a 'logic of vagueness', replete with smudge operators? (Equally important is the realization that the truth-functional connectives and quantifiers are not topic-neutral, and that not all logical relations are explicable in terms of truth-functional composition. So logic does not have the *purity* and *generality* it had appeared to have.)

Why should logic seem to disappear? It was conceived to mirror the logical structure of the world. But if the world has no logical structure? And if the propositions of logic do not show the formal, logical structure of any possible language, if natural languages do not have a depth structure — if 'nothing is hidden' — *then* what remains of logic?

These anxieties, W. insists, are based on misunderstanding. We cannot *bargain away* the rigour of logic. We cannot beat down its demands, plead for elasticity in its rigid rules, beg for a relaxation of its inexorability — insisting, for example, that the law of non-contradiction holds *only by and large*, that the law of excluded middle should be jettisoned, or that *typically* if p and if p then q, then one may infer that q. But we need to abandon the misconceived idea of crystalline purity that seemed to be a reflection of an a priori order of the world. Only then can we see the role that logic actually has, and what the nature of its rigour really is. This preconception of crystalline purity can be removed *by turning the inquiry* (Betrachtung), or *investigation, around*. What does W. mean?

We need to realize that our philosophical investigations are not (as W. had once thought they were (NB 14)) investigations into 'the logical structure of the world'. We are examining the grammar of our language (where it causes

---

[43]   MS 152, 93, equates the complete order in logic with determinacy of sense — and here 'logic' is clearly the propositions of logic, not their study. MS 157a, 69v (a source of §108) says that logic must be a crystal, contain nothing amorphous — a crystal system. This too is a comment on the propositions and laws of logic, not on the investigation into such propositions and laws. §97, which introduced the metaphor of the 'crystalline', was concerned with logic understood as the essence of thinking.

us trouble), not the objective 'foundation or essence of everything empirical' (PI §89). We must turn from the sublime to the mundane, from the essence of the world to the description of the grammar of our language, from *Wesensschau* to the 'quiet weighing of linguistic facts' (Z §447) — and the impressiveness (the apparent sublimity) retreats to the illusions (PI §110). If we turn the examination around thus, we can locate the crystalline clarity of logic in its proper place. W. does not elaborate, but perhaps what he meant was as follows. The rigour of logic has a quite different role from that which it seemed to possess. It is not a mirror-image of 'the a priori order of the world', but a feature of a mode of representation. The rigour of logical inference, for example, determines what we *call* 'thinking'; by reference to it, we fix what *counts as* valid reasoning. We use it as our canon for the evaluation of arguments. The calculus of logic is not the depth grammar of any, let alone of every possible, language. It is not something glimpsed through the untidy surface forms of natural languages, buried beneath them. It is a mode of presentation. We can *re*-present sentences of natural language in the forms of sentences of the predicate calculus. We can recast our arguments in these forms and display their validity (or invalidity). We can perspicuously disambiguate certain kinds of equivocations in ordinary language by means of quantifier shifts in the calculus. And so on.

1.1   (i) 'was wir "Satz" . . . nennen': 'what we call "proposition"' — it is the extension of the concept of a proposition (not of a sentence) that is here said to be a family of structures.

(ii) '(Man könnte sagen: . . .)': '(One might say: the inquiry must be turned round, but on the pivot of our real need.)' This raises two problems.

(a) Why 'turned about' or 'rotated' (*drehen*)? The metaphor is unclear. It is plausible to suppose that W. meant that we must change our way of looking at the problems, so that our investigation will no longer be into something apparently behind our ordinary use of words and sentences (i.e. *from* ordinary language *to* the ideal names and propositions hidden beneath its surface, and from these *to* the essence of the world), but rather into that very use itself. Then we can correctly locate the normative role of logic within the practice of the use of ordinary words and sentences. This 'relocation' of the 'ideal' is the 'turning about' W. has in mind (see 2.1(i) below).

(b) What is our real need? For conceptual clarity, surely, so that we shall not be deceived by the grammar of our language. We *do not* need to understand the essence of everything empirical (PI §89) or to penetrate phenomena to fathom the logical structure of the world (PI §90) — that *urge* (PI §89) was based on illusions and confusions (the *world* does not *have* a logical or logico-metaphysical structure — not because it is sadly logically amorphous and lacking something that it might have had, but because there is no such thing). But we do need to understand the grammar of 'word', 'proposition', 'language', etc. in order to dispel such philosophical illusions.

2   MS 157b, 2v–3r and 5r, illuminates: the rigour of logic seems to come apart. But how can logic lose its rigour? Not by bargaining something out of it; but only by a rearrangement in which the idea of rigour is given a different place: namely, in which the idea of order is acknowledged as part of the mode of representation. . . . It is transformed from a preconception about reality into *a* form of representation. What has happened to the crystalline purity? — It has become a form of representation, nothing else.

Norman Malcolm connected the following remark with §108 (but also §§123 and 309): Wittgenstein said to him that 'A person caught in a philosophical confusion is like a man in a room who wants to get out but doesn't know how. He tries the window but it is too high. He tries the chimney but it is too narrow. And if he would only *turn around*, he would see that the door has been open all the time!'[44] The beginning of the turning around lies in §§1–89. §108(b)–(d) consists of the metaphilosophical reflections on this rotation of the whole point of view

2.1   (i)   'turning our whole inquiry around': MS 157a, 67r, says (I paraphrase) that it is *not* as if we can let ourselves bargain away any of the crystalline purity. But the *preconception* that lies within it can be removed only by our turning our whole examination around, thereby giving this purity another place // locating this purity in another place. // But it is also not as if one could say: 'The preconception is that this ideal *exists* — whereas in fact it is something we must strive to achieve.' For here too is a misconception, and the role of the ideal is still not grasped. (For further discussion, see 'Turning the inquiry around: the recantation of a metaphysician', sect. 5.)

(ii)   'of our real need': MS 157, 68r, has 'around the pivotal point of our actual interests // needs //; that must remain // stand // firm//'.

(iii)   'the spatial and temporal phenomenon of language': MS 110 (Vol. VI), 222, follows this paragraph with the remark that dogmatism in philosophy consists in making statements that are not recognized by every one as grammatical rules of their expression // language //. So this again creates the appearance that in philosophy we must make constructions, new revelations, discover connections.

(iv)   'What is a word really?': PR 61 (cf. BT 71; PG 121) — 'Here, the crudest conception must obviously be the only correct one', and 'This can only be dealt with from the standpoint of normal common sense. (It's extra-ordinary that that in itself constitutes a change in perspective.)'

(v)   'analogous to "What is a piece in chess?"': MS 152, 81f., remarks on the fact that there is a tendency in logic to see a certain kind of ideal, as a consequence of which we sublimate the concept of a word (see Exg. §97, 2.1(iii)). One can imagine something similar for chess, W. continues.

---

[44] Malcolm, *Ludwig Wittgenstein: A memoir*, p. 44.

One would then be inclined to say that apart from the chess king of wood, bone, etc. there is also *the* chess king (so to say the meaning of the material figure). This meaning is the real chess king (whereas the piece of wood is only, as it were, its proxy in the domain of crude sensible phenomena); this chess king is sublime, indestructible and the real object of the game.

One says to oneself that logic surely cannot be about ink marks.

'What interests us in a chess game is not just a few bits of wood.' — Certainly not. And what the tailor makes a suit for is not a few little bits of paper. But the *value* of the banknote is not a kind of ethereal banknote that stands behind the material one. Don't ask what the chess king is, but rather, how do we use the phrase 'chess king'. . . . Logic is not *about* sublime objects.

Philosophy
1. A revolution in philosophy
2. The sources of philosophical problems
3. The goals of philosophy: conceptual geography and intellectual therapy
4. The difficulty of philosophy
5. The methods of philosophy
6. Negative corollaries
7. Misunderstandings
8. Retrospect: the *Tractatus* and the *Investigations*

BOXED REMARK FOLLOWING §108

1   These three paragraphs were late additions to the text.[45] W. now emphasizes that in philosophy of logic we *are* talking about ordinary words and propositions, not about ideal ones laid up in the mind or in a Fregean third realm.
To be sure, we are not interested in the physical shape of written words, any
more than when describing the game of chess we are concerned with the shape
of the pieces. Nor are we interested in the particular language to which the
sentences belong, any more than a description of chess concerns itself with
the difference between wooden, ivory or bone chess pieces. Our concern is
not philological or genetic (as the history of development of chess is irrelevant to its current description). Rather, we are concerned with the uses of
expressions, which are determined by the rules for their employment, and with
our practices of applying these rules (as the description of chess is a description of the powers of the pieces and the permissible, possible transformations
in the game). This may make it look as if we are talking about an ideal entity,
but 'Is the chess king that the rules of chess deal with such an ideal and abstract

---

[45]   They were added only in TS 227 from B i §502 (see BT 71; PG 121).

entity too?' (PG 121). (The analogy between language and chess is discussed in 'The language-game method', pp. 46–8.)

1.1   In the first three editions, these paragraphs were printed as §108(b)–(d).

SECTION 109

1   It had been right to say that philosophy is not a natural science (TLP 4.111). It was indeed irrelevant that someone might insist that as a matter of fact one can think this or that (an allusion to Ramsey, see 1.1(i) below). For one should, as the *Tractatus* had insisted, avoid getting entangled in the psychological study of thought processes (TLP 4.1121).[46]

Further, there can be no theories in philosophy. What does he here understand by the term 'theory' in philosophy, and why does he oppose theorizing? The *Tractatus* had sharply differentiated philosophy from scientific theory (TLP 4.111; NB 44). Its programme for future philosophy limited it to clarification (TLP 4.112, 6.53). The moot question is whether the *Tractatus* itself should be thought of as constructing a metaphysical theory to explain the possibility of representation and the limits of language. Is he implicitly criticizing the *Tractatus*? Or is he merely re-emphasizing a pre-existing exclusion of theory?

He evidently thought of the *Tractatus* as advancing theories — a theory (a 'dynamic theory') of the proposition (MS 142, pp. 86f., and §105), that specified the essence of every possible proposition by characterizing the general propositional form, and a theory of logic (MS 152, 93), that specified the nature of logical necessity and of all logical relations. He also characterized Frege's account of cardinal numbers and of concepts and objects as 'theories' (MS 112 (Vol. VIII), 136r). He spoke of Russell, Ogden and Richard's causal theory of meaning, and of Ramsey's theory of identity (MS 110 (Vol. VI), 114). He thought of theories in philosophy, in particular in metaphysics, as typically purporting to be (i) explanatory, (ii) general (exceptionless), (iii) involving assumptions, suppositions or hypotheses, (iv) committed to explaining how, given the assumptions, things in its domain *must* be, (v) refutable by a single counter-example. Metaphysics, as he conceived it, was a misguided endeavour to emulate, in the domain of philosophical, i.e. conceptual, investigation, where only description is intelligible, the theory-building explanatory procedures of science. It was, he held, characteristic of philosophical theories to take words out of the context of their everyday use and to use them in an 'ultra-physical' (i.e. incorrect) sense (MS 107 (Vol. III), 177). In the *Tractatus* he had

---

[46]   But the *Tractatus* had erred in supposing that the investigation of thinking, meaning and understanding belongs exclusively to psychology. The clarification of these *concepts* is crucial for philosophy. Moreover, the metapsychological presuppositions of the *Tractatus* were anything but innocuous, as W. came to realize.

explained how the world *must* be (it *must* have a sempiternal substance, *must* consist of facts constituted of objects in concatenation, etc.), and how language *must* be (it *must*, on analysis, consist of simple names concatenated into elementary propositions with a common form, etc.) if representation is to be possible. But, he now insists, there can be no theories. The task of philosophy is not to explain anything in the sense in which a theory in science explains natural phenomena, or in the sense in which a putative metaphysical theory purports to explain (cf. Exg. §126). Philosophy should only describe, and what it should describe is the use of words, the grammar of the language — in so far as that is necessary for the resolution of the philosophical problem at hand. (For further discussion, see 'Philosophy', sects 5–6.)

Philosophical problems are not empirical. They are to be solved by description of grammar, by looking into the workings of our language. Nothing new or unfamiliar will be found there, for we are examining our rule-governed use of words — and if anything new were involved, the description would not be a specification of the familiar uses of words. For one cannot be *following* rules with which one is wholly unacquainted. What needs to be done is to assemble, marshall or order what we have long been familiar with, i.e. the rules for the use of some expression or type of expression that is causing us troubles, grammatical propositions constituted by familiar explanations of meaning.

1.1   (i) ' "that, contrary to our preconceived ideas, it is possible, contrary to our preconceived ideas, to think this or that" ': This alludes to Ramsey (see MS 152, 93–5), who, in conversations with W., insisted on the conceivability of extensional infinity, arguing against W., 'Can't we imagine a man living for ever, that is, simply never dying, and isn't that extensional infinity?' (PR 304 (= MS 105, 23), and then PR 165f.) and 'I can surely imagine a row of trees going on without end . . . it makes sense to say it never comes to an end . . .' (Z §272; cf. PR 166f.). W. often insisted, against Ramsey, that it makes no sense to speak of a completely new, hitherto unknown sense-perception that one might one day have. Ramsey used to reply by saying, 'But it *just is* possible to think of such a thing' (MS 116 (Vol. XII), 51). W.'s response is that one must investigate *what* one is thus thinking — the mere insistence that one can think thus is useless — what one must do is examine how the sentence is supposed to be used, what things look like *around it*. That will show its sense.

PLP 37f. investigates why one might think that the claim 'It is possible to think such-and-such' is philosophically relevant. Many philosophers have conceived of grammar as reflecting the laws (and hence the possibilities) of thought. We cannot imagine, conceive such-and-such — and that is why we don't say it, why it is *senseless*; and if we *can* conceive it, then it makes sense! If this were the case, then grammar would have to be readjusted as people's conceivings improved. But this is absurd. The bounds of sense, and so of thought, are set by the rules of grammar, not vice versa.

(ii) 'the pneumatic conception of thinking': this is apparently a reference to the classical conception of thinking as a process involving *psychic pneuma* as its medium that is in question. W. tended to use 'ethereal' in this connection.

2.1   (i) '(The *pneumatic* conception of thinking)': MS 152, 94, immediately prior to a draft of PI §109, makes clear the target (I paraphrase): 'One just can think it', or 'Experience teaches that one just can think it', is revolting as long as thinking was the mental process // as long as one saw thinking as the mental process // by contrast with speaking, writing, etc. Logic must either dogmatically oppose such statements or withdraw from them and say it has nothing to do where such questions are raised.

The conception that W. is thinking of is one whereby the mind is conceived as a queer medium, and the mechanism of the mind, which we do not quite understand, can effect remarkable things by means of thinking (cf. BB 3f.), for 'thinking must be something unique' (PI §95).

(ii) 'may not advance any kind of theory': AWL 99 — 'It is characteristic of obsessions [in philosophy] that they . . . are attacked as scientific problems are, and treated perfectly hopelessly, as if we had to find out something new. The problems do not appear to concern questions about language but rather questions of fact of which we do not yet know enough. It is for this reason that you are constantly tempted to think that I am giving you some information, and that you expect from me a theory.'

(iii) 'Philosophy is a struggle . . .': MS 132, 7f., queries whether our concern is with mistakes and difficulties that are as old as language, as it were illnesses bound up with the very use of language, or whether they are of a special nature distinctive of our civilization? Or: is the preoccupation with the linguistic medium that runs through the whole of our philosophy an ancient struggle — or is it new, like our science? Or again, does philosophy always oscillate between metaphysics and critique of language?

(iv) 'Zusammenstellung': MS 117 (Vol. XIII), 220f., exemplifies both what W. means by 'assembling' or 'marshalling', and the difficulties encountered.

I don't know how to assemble things, what order I should give to the concepts. I don't know, for example, whether to count proof among experiments, mathematics among games, contradictions among confusions. Whether I should say that the difference between mathematical and experimental truths is a matter of degree, whether I should say that a new proof gives a proposition a new sense. I don't know my way around the human activities, the techniques of using words, mathematical propositions, proof. If I have to describe them, I cannot survey them at all. It is as if I had a minute visual field and a bad memory, and had to learn by looking back and forth on a huge map.[47]

[47] From the context it seems clear that this is not intended as a current autobiographical remark, but rather as an example of the nature of philosophical confusion, i.e. of not knowing one's way about.

It is important to realize that it is patent from W.'s writings that he had a very clear idea of how these concepts should be ordered. Moreover, the ordering is not optional and purpose-relative, let alone person-relative. Proofs should *not* be counted among experiments, mathematics should *not* be counted among games, nor contradictions among confusions — although in each case there are affinities; the difference between mathematical and experimental truths is *not* a matter of degree, and a proof *is* to be counted as giving a proposition a new sense.

SECTION 110

1   This is linked to §§93–5. Language seemed uniquely to show the essence of the world. The forms of the elements of language, the simple names, appeared to be the forms of the substance of the world, the simple objects. Thinking appeared uniquely to 'capture reality' (not to 'stop short of it'); there seemed to be a metaphysical, pre-established harmony between thought and reality (see Volume 4, 'Intentionality'). But these ideas, which obsessed the author of the *Tractatus*, are not *mistakes* — the negation of which would be true. For the denial that language reflects the logical structure of the world could be true only if it *made sense* to say of something that it did reflect such an a priori order. But if there is no such thing as 'the a priori order of the world', then there is no such thing as reflecting *or failing to reflect* it. So such ideas are, W. now declares, *superstitions*, not mistakes.

Why a superstition rather than nonsense? Perhaps because a superstition is associated with a particular *picture* or *conception*, which ramifies throughout one's reflections. Abandoning it is far more difficult than jettisoning something one comes to realize makes no sense (cf. CV 83). This is confirmed by W.'s referring to the mathematicians' fear of hidden contradictions as 'a superstition' (RFM 122).

What grammatical illusions produced this superstition? The very same illusions as are mentioned in §§93–5 and referred to as such in §96. Disabused of such illusions, the sublime character of the investigation disappears. We are not studying 'the a priori order of the world'. But now the impressiveness, the *Pathos*, retreats to the illusions themselves. The nature of philosophical illusion *is* extraordinary, and a fit subject for study.

1.1   'fällt nun das Pathos zurück': there is no English term that will do service for the German 'Pathos'. What W. means is that once the grand metaphysical vision of the *Tractatus* is destroyed, its *Pathos*, grandeur or aura is cast back onto the very illusions that gave rise to it. For the depth of the apparent insights into the logical structure of the world, of thought and of language is the depth of those illusions.

Section 111

1   Though philosophy is concerned with the illusions of reason, and though these have their roots in grammar, it is in no sense trivial. The problems are deep, since they are as deeply rooted in us as the forms of our language from which they stem. Elsewhere (e.g. BB 17f.) W. countenances other sources of philosophical confusion than the forms of our language (see 'Philosophy', sect. 2).

1.1   'Let us ask ourselves . . .': W. does not explain here why a grammatical joke is deep. But he did in MS 142, §112 (cancelled only in TS 227). He considered two jokes: Lewis Carroll's 'We called him "tortoise" because he taught us' (from *Alice in Wonderland*, ch. IX, and 'What the Tortoise Said to Achilles', *Mind* 1895)) and a joke from Lichtenberg's 'Letters from a Maid on Literature' in which one hundred is written '001'. W. stresses two points. The depth of a grammatical joke is lost if one thinks that since signs are arbitrary one could, e.g., use 'taught us' as a substantive (as with Czech forenames, e.g. 'Zaplatil' means 'he counted') or use '001' instead of '100'. The depth of absurdity is revealed only if one keeps in mind the correct use of the appropriate signs, sees what their consequences are, and notes the conflicts and incongruities which would stem from a change in notation, e.g. if '001' replaced '100', but everything else remained the same. We have the feeling of depth when we thus look at the system of language; it is as if we could see the whole world through its net.

Section 112

1   One kind of misinterpretation of forms of our language (§111) is produced by similes absorbed into language. W. does not give examples here. In MS 142, §113(c), he did: the substantive 'time' deceives us into conceiving of time as a *medium* [we speak of 'the river of time', of 'time passing']; we can *measure* the duration of an event [the simile here is the measurement of space], yet the event is never present; the rose is red, yet it is not (is not identical with) red; identity propositions say something, and yet they say nothing. One cannot find a way out, for language seems to leave none.

   §§112–15 arguably belong more properly in the previous discussion of §§89–108; they add little if anything to what has already been established.

1.1   (i)   '*this* isn't how it is' . . . 'Yet *this* is how it has to *be*': this sense of irresoluble conflict characterizes philosophical disquietude, especially W.'s. For example, 'On the one hand my theory of logical portrayal seems to be the only possible one, on the other hand there seems to be an insoluble contradiction in it' (NB 17). And, 'It keeps on looking as if the question "Are there simple things?" made sense. And surely this question must be nonsense!'

(NB 45). Hence his later remark: 'I try to make you see that "it isn't like that", but also that it *needn't* be like that' (LPP 47; see 'Surveyability and surveyable representations', sect. 3).

MS 119 (Vol. XV), 59f., recounts that Russell often said, in the course of their discussions, 'Logic's hell!' This, W. writes, expresses what they both experienced when thinking about logical problems. Each new aspect of language of which one might think seemed to render all the previous explanations useless (just as Socrates' arguments seemed to force constant revision of definitions). Language appeared continually to be making new and impossible demands. But Socrates' difficulties are only rendered more complicated when he tries to define a concept. For he continually gives up what he has achieved whenever he comes across a different application which does not fit. One says, W. concludes, 'But this isn't how it is! — But this is how it is!'

SECTION 113

1   A feature of the illusion is its irresistible, ineluctable, pressure (see 2.1 below).

2   In MS 142, §126, this occurs in a different context, in the discussion leading up to the claim that in philosophy we 'predicate of the thing what lies in the method of representation' (PI §104). It is thus preceded by PI §114, as well as by Z §443; so 'But this is how it is' was originally directed at the obsessive notion of the general propositional form. There it continued thus: 'For it seems to lie at the heart of the matter. Only when this optical illusion is dispelled can we simply see language as it is. The expression of this illusion is the metaphysical use of our words.' This was followed by a draft of PI §104.

In TS 239, §121, W. prefixed a generalizing remark: 'If we think about the nature of the proposition, of understanding, of private experience of which only I am conscious: "But *this* is how it is —" . . .' This was deleted in TS 227.

2.1   MS 158, 37r–v (in English):

In phil. puzzlement what plays a role besides disorder is a kind of mirage of a language which isn't there.

What is your disease? You ask the question again and again. — How can one make you stop doing this?

By drawing your attention to something else.

You are under the misapprehension that the phil. problem is *difficult* whereas it's hopeless.

I want you first to realise that you're under a spell.

If I leave the original example and pass to a different one I do it because in this example the philosophic pressure is not so high as in the original one.

The assertion that the philosophical problem is 'hopeless' is intended to indicate that it is hopeless to try to give an *answer* to such misbegotten questions,
as opposed to trying to dissolve them.

SECTION 114

2   This occurs in MS 142, §125, *before* PI §113, and *after* the following:

'Every proposition says: This is how things are.' Here is such a form which can mis-
lead us (and did mislead me).
Plato: 'Whoever means something, means something which is.' (*Theaetetus*.)
This is the kind of proposition . . . etc.

This is followed by Z §443: suppose one pointed at an object by describing
a circle in the air about the object pointed at. A philosopher might say that
all things are circular, for the table looks like *this*, the stove like *this*, the lamp
like *this* (each time describing a circle around the thing). See Exg. §104.

SECTION 115

1   In MS 142, §124(d), this precedes PI §114, which in turn precedes §113.
It is located towards the end of the discussion of the illusions of the *Tractatus*
(cf. Exg. §104). So *the* particular picture ('Das Bild' in MS 142) which held
him captive ('hielt mich gefangen' in MS 142) was the conception of the general propositional form — that every proposition says that things stand thus-
and-so (for the full context, see Exg. §104, 2).

SECTION 116

1   Knowledge, in the hands of Cartesians and their empiricist successors,
becomes something unachievable, for it seems that we *can* only really know
something not if all *actual* but only if all *possible* doubt is excluded.[48] Being
becomes, in the early Russell's hands, a property belonging to everything thinkable, whether it exists or not (if it did not 'have being', one *could* not think
of it). 'Object', for the young W., was transformed into a super-concept under
which properties, relations, times and spatial locations were included (TS 220,
§§108–10) — otherwise thought would *not be able* to reach right up to reality; for Frege, likewise, objects encompassed every 'referent' of singular referring expressions, including numbers, locations, simultaneous occurrences of
events[49] (cf. PR 137), etc. The first-person pronoun, in the hands of 'rational

---

[48]   To be sure, not even all actual doubt needs to be excluded for someone to know something.
That is a requirement for the legitimacy of *claiming* to know, not a condition of knowing.
[49]   See also Russell, TK 143.

psychologists', appeared to be the name of a spiritual entity, the real self, which
resides in the body but is quite distinct from it (since 'I' is not in general
substitutable for descriptions of the body (BB 69, 74)). For the idealization of
'proposition' and 'name', see Exg. §§104–5.

What does W. take to be a metaphysical use of words? Here only one mark,
with an implicit corollary, is given. That mark is: the quest for essences; the
corollary is: association with modality, with how things *must* or *cannot* be. This
obviously requires careful qualification, since taken in a suitably homely way,
W. too is concerned to clarify the nature or essence of language (PI §92), and
evidently does not hold, absurdly, that there are no essences at all. On the
contrary, he insists that *grammar* tells us the essence of a thing (PI §§371, 373).
And he does hold that if it is, in a humdrum sense, part of the essence of As
to be F, then, of course, if something is an A then it *follows* that it is F (but
not: it *must* follow; rather, it *does* follow; and not: it follows that it *must* be F;
rather, it follows that it *is* F (RFM 39–46)). How, then, does his current quest
differ from what he condemns? The conception of essence has shifted: essences
are not conceived *de re* but *de dicto*. Grammar tells us the essence of a thing,
not because it *reflects* the objective, language-independent, essential nature of
what is represented, but because it *determines* essence. For 'it is not the property of an object that is ever "essential", but rather the mark of a concept'
(RFM 64); i.e. we would not *count* this as a so-and-so unless it had *this* property. Grammar does not *describe* the essential nature of . . . , it determines what
is *called*. . . .

The metaphysical quest for essences is a misconceived attempt to disclose
how things *must be* in virtue of their essential nature (PR 86). Metaphysics
aspires to be a super-science of reality (BB 35): whereas physics describes how
things happen to be, metaphysics purports to describe how things must be. It
not only appears to describe the world, it also attempts to *explain* things on
the model of science (BB 18). So the *Tractatus* explained determinacy of sense
(which *must* obtain) by reference to the simple objects that constitute the
substance of the world. It explained the essence of thinking by reference to
simple names that *must* have isomorphic simple objects as their meanings, for
only thus can one explain how it is possible for thought to reach right up to
reality, which it *must* do, if it is to be possible to think what is not the case.
And so on.

It is evident that a 'metaphysical use of words' is the use of a certain word
(or phrase) in the context of a very specific philosophical endeavor, informed
by a very particular array of misconceptions. What W. does, he now declares,
is to bring words thus *misused*, back to their everyday use. One thing we must
do is to ask whether the word in question ('know', 'being', 'object', 'I', 'proposition', 'name') is ever actually used in the way the metaphysician is using it.
Our ordinary use of 'know' does not require the exclusion of all possible doubt;
we do not say that the square circle has being, or that the simultaneous occurrence of a court case and an eclipse of the moon is an object; and when we
say 'I am N.N.', we do not use the first-person pronoun to introduce an im-

material entity whose essence is thinking. These are but reminders, and are no more than the first step on the road back to sanity. There are many further steps that W. characteristically takes: he examines the consequences of the metaphysician's use (e.g. loss of an antithesis that is a condition of sense (BB 46)); unravels the confused crossing of the metaphysician's use with the ordinary use (e.g. in the solipsist's account (BB 55ff.)); discloses the misleading analogies or pictures that are at the roots of a metaphysical conception (e.g. the picture of analysis that lay behind logical atomism); clarifies the extent to which the metaphysician is *in effect* merely recommending an alternative form of representation, and shows that nothing is really achieved *here* by a mere change of notation (BB 57); etc.

1.1   (i)   'is the word ever actually used in this way . . . its original home': clearly, it is the everyday, ordinary language-game, not the metaphysical misuse of words, that wears the trousers. For it is in the language-game where the expression is at home that it has an established and intelligible sense. The apparent *super*-concepts characteristic of metaphysics in general, and a hallmark of the *Tractatus* in particular, are no more than *pseudo*-concepts, produced, in the *Tractatus*, by *sublimating* the ordinary concepts of name, sentence, proposition, language, word, inference, truth, experience, etc. But, W. now insists, if these 'words have a use, it must be as humble a one as that of the words "table", "lamp", "door"' (PI §97).

         (ii)   'back . . . to their everyday use': all the words listed are indeed everyday expressions, but the observation arguably applies equally to technical expressions, such as 'transfinite cardinal', when they are misused in philosophical reflection.

2   MS 157b, 14v–15r, notes that the remark that we bring words back from their metaphysical to their *ordinary* use belongs to the discussion of 'the Ideal name' and the source of the ideal, and cross-refers to this remark in BT 412. So one example of the metaphysical use of words is clearly meant to be W.'s own use of 'name' (and presumably 'proposition' (*Satz*), 'language', 'object', 'fact', 'world') in the *Tractatus*.

         The occurrence of §116(a) in 157b, 16v–17r, runs: If philosophy tries to grasp the essence of 'being', of reality, of knowledge, then one must always ask oneself . . . Note that W. himself had once thought that his whole task was to explain the essence of all being (NB 39).

2.1   (i)   'is the word ever actually used': MS 136, 94b (RPP II §289) reflects on the fact that many would dismiss W.'s discussion of the concept of knowledge as irrelevant, since the philosophers' use doesn't correspond to the everyday one, but is rather a more important and interesting concept constructed by sublimating the ordinary and not very interesting one. But in fact the philosophical concept arises from misunderstandings, which it duly fortifies. It is not in the least interesting, W. concludes, it is only a warning — presumably a warning to go down the paths suggested by such 'special philosophical senses' only with the greatest of care, knowing that they lead to quagmires of confusion.

BT 430 adds: 'Usually one will then find that it is not so, and that the word is being used against // contrary to // its normal grammar. ("Knowing", "Being", "thing".)'

(ii)   'bring words back from their metaphysical . . . use': MS 110 (Vol. VI), 34, has this in the context of a discussion of *alles fliesst* (*panta rea*). This is a metaphysical use of 'flows' (or 'in flux'). We bring words back from their metaphysical use to their correct use (*richtige Verwendung*) in the language. This is then followed (as in BT) by the remark that the man who says that one cannot step twice into the same river says something wrong; one can step twice into the same river.

It is noteworthy that in the same MS, on p. 10, W. had remarked that he would like to begin his book, as it were, with what is given to philosophy: namely, spoken and written sentences. And here one is up against the difficulty that 'everything flows (is in flux)' (*Alles fliesst*); and perhaps this is what one should begin with.

(iii)   'everyday use': BT 412 (derived from MS 110, 34) had here 'correct use' (*richtige Verwendung*) with wavy underlining indicating qualms, and 'normal' later added. Presumably the qualms were that normal use is the *standard of correctness*, and can no more be said to be correct than the standard metre can be said to be a metre long. Rather, use *in accordance* with normal use is correct (which does not exclude special technical uses in the sciences, as long as they are appropriately stipulated and explained).

(iv)   MS 127, 72f., queries whether the philosopher cannot use these words in a special technical sense, contrary to their ordinary use? Doesn't a scientist do so?[50] What is the difference? The scientist's new use of a received term is justified by his theory. If his theory is false, then the new use is abandoned. But that is not how it is in philosophy.

SECTION 117

1   In TS 239, §125 (where it was first inserted) this occurs between PI §116(a) and (b). In its source, in MS 127, 73, it occurs after the discussion of why philosophers, unlike scientists, cannot licitly use words contrary to their customary use (see Exg. §116, 2.1(iii)). This suggests that W. is responding to the wayward philosopher's saying: 'You understand the word "knowledge" ("object" or "name"), don't you? Well then, it is with that meaning, which you know, that I too am using it.' But the meaning of a word is not

---

[50]   W.'s example here is Freud, who called a nightmare (*Angsttraum*) 'a wish-fulfilment' (*Wunschtraum*).

something *attached* to it, and in a deviant application (as in the metaphysical use of words) the resultant sentence *lacks* a meaning, since the word is being misused.

§117(b) illustrates the circumstance dependence of sense. 'This is here', said while pointing to a present object, may seem to express a peculiarly secure kind of knowledge and to have a peculiarly 'solid' kind of meaning (Russell). But 'This is here' has an ordinary use (in rather special circumstances, e.g. leafing through documents in a drawer, and handing the relevant ones to a friend), and it is *not* to express an item of Cartesian knowledge.

1.1   (i)   For the use and misuse of 'I am here', see PI §514 and C §348.

(ii)   For repudiation of the view that the sense is an accompaniment of the sentence, see Z §139 (MS 116 (Vol. XII), 85).

SECTION 118

1   The importance of philosophy comes from clearing up the ground of language in order to dispel philosophical illusion. The misconceptions are anything but trivial, and infect the sciences (e.g. psychology, mathematics) too (PPF §§371–2 (p. 232)).

2.1   (i)   'Where does this investigation get its importance from . . .': PLP 78 elaborates: philosophy derives its grandeur from the significance of the statements it destroys. It overthrows idols, and it is the importance of those idols that makes philosophy important. BT 413 remarks that all philosophy can do is to destroy idols; and that also means not making an idol out of the absence of idols.

(ii)   'all that is great and important': everything involved in the 'sublime' conception of logic and philosophy, e.g. insights into the essence of the world (PI §89).

SECTION 119

1   The results of (decent) philosophy are the progressive disclosure of the nonsense latent in the 'houses of cards' that we (philosophers) construct in pursuit of 'all that is great and important', and the painful recognition of our own previous attempts to transgress the bounds of sense.

There is here both continuity and change relative to the *Tractatus*. There too W. claimed that 'Most of the propositions and questions to be found in philosophical works are not false but nonsensical' (TLP 4.003), *inter alia* because they transgress the rules of logical syntax by using formal concept-words as if they were material concept-words in the endeavor to say things that cannot be said but are shown by well-formed sentences of the language. For the same reason, he condemned the very propositions of the *Tractatus* itself as nonsensical (TLP 6.54). The later W. continued to think that the task of philosophy was to disclose the latent nonsense of putative philosophical propositions. But his conception of formal concepts changed, as did his conception of logical syntax. Words like 'language', 'experience', 'world' are not 'super-concepts' (PI §97), and words like 'colour', 'number', 'place' are not variables. He accepted that the family of propositions includes what he called 'grammatical propositions', such as 'Red is a colour' or '1 is a number' that he had previously excluded as nonsense. These are in effect rules for the use of the constituent expressions in the misleading guise of descriptions. Nevertheless, the putative propositions of philosophy (especially, but not only, of metaphysics) are either grammatical trivialities or nonsense that transgresses the grammar of the constituent expressions.

Is the 'plain nonsense' that philosophy discloses just like 'Ab sur ah', i.e. plain gibberish? It is *just as nonsensical* as gibberish (PI §§499f.; AWL 64), but not just like it.[51] For it is latent nonsense — difficult to detect, and difficult to demonstrate to be nonsense. Unlike gibberish, it is generated by the subtle *misuses* of significant words in our language, and there are many *different* kinds of misuses. There are deep reasons why we are tempted to misuse words thus — to 'run up against the limits of language'. This latent nonsense is transformed into patent nonsense (PI §§464, 524) by *operations* on the constituent expressions that show that they are being misused (AWL 64). One cannot and need not 'operate' on 'Ab sur ah' to reveal that it is nonsense. But if a philosopher thinks that *to mean something* is an act or activity of the mind, one can ask him how long it took to mean so-and-so by the name 'N.N.', or whether, when he said 'p' and meant by the sentence 'p' the state of affairs that p, he finished meaning it in good time, or whether he was interrupted in the middle, or how he acquired the skill to mean so much so quickly, and so on. These questions (operations on the problematic term or phrase) make it clear that the consequences of the thought that meaning is an act or activity are absurd. The argument is literally a *reductio ad absurdum* (unlike what traditionally goes by that name, which is strictly a *reductio ad contradictionem*), precisely because it transforms latent nonsense that looks like a sensible sentence into patent nonsense.

1.1   (i)   'and of bumps': the results of philosophy are, on the one hand, the disclosure of nonsense, and, on the other hand, the bumps the understanding incurs when transgressing the bounds of sense. The bumps are incurred in the course of the struggle against the bewitchment of our understanding (cf. §109),

[51]   As PI §282 remarks, 'Even a nonsense poem is not nonsense in the same way as the babbling of a child.' *A fortiori*, the fairy-tale in which the pots can see and hear is not nonsense 'in the same way' as a nonsense poem like Jabberwocky.

and they make us see the value of apprehending that what we thought and were inclined to say, was nonsense.

(ii)   'these bumps': the recognition of the conceptual illusions.

3   The metaphor 'Anrennen an die Grenze der Sprache' is similar to an aphorism of Karl Kraus: 'If I cannot get further, this is because I have banged my head against the wall of language. Then, with my head bleeding, I withdraw. And want to go on.'[52]

SECTION 120

1   Not only does the philosophy of logic speak about words and sentences in exactly the sense in which we ordinarily do (§108), but we speak about them *in* ordinary language. The questions raised, questions about the nature of the proposition, of naming, of logical consequence, etc., were all raised in ordinary language, and they are to be settled in ordinary language too. The scruples that one may have are in fact no more than misunderstandings.

One kind of scruple is that the words of ordinary language are too crude to incorporate the order which we think *must* be in language (§105). So it seemed that only analysis would reveal the real names, and *their* meanings would be the simple objects in reality that make representation possible and that constitute the substance of the world. Likewise, it seemed that only a phenomenological language could adequately account for the inner nature of material object statements. But such scruples are misunderstandings. Meanings of words are not objects correlated with them; and there is no need for a phenomenological language to render perspicuous the grammar of material object statements. If a word is compared with money, then its meaning is not comparable to *an object* that can be bought with money (e.g. a cow), but with the use of money.

1.1   (i)   'Is this language too coarse, too material . . .': directed against the *Tractatus* and the 1929 commitment to phenomenological analysis, but presumably also against advocates of an ideal language, such as Russell (e.g. in his Introduction to TLP, p. x) and Frege. Less general, but equally to the point, is William James's view, which W. criticized, that our language is inadequate to describe experiences (see Exg. §610; cf. PG 169, PI §436).

(ii)   'In giving explanations, I already have to use language full-blown'. These 'explanations' are the clarificatory remarks (grammatical explanations) of the *Investigations*, not the kind of (putatively metaphysical) explanations excluded

[52]   Karl Kraus, *Beim Wort genommen* (Kösel-Verlag, Munich, 1955), p. 326: cf. E. Heller, *The Artist's Journey into the Interior and Other Essays* (Secker and Warburg, London, 1966), p. 219.

from philosophy. MS 110 (Vol. VI), 231, adds after 'Dass ich beim Erklären der Sprache' the parenthesis '(in unserem Sinne)' ('(in our sense)').

(iii)   'dass ich nur Äusserliches über die Sprache vorbringen kann': 'Äusserliches' here contrasts with 'Wesentliches'. The legitimate explanations employ ordinary language — the genuine article, not something preparatory or provisional. Why does this show that one can adduce only externalities (*Äusserliches*) about language? 'Externalities' here are contrasted with putative truths about the hidden 'real names' and 'fully analysed propositions', or about the sublimated abstract sense of sentences (Frege), or 'the class of all equivalent sentences'.

(iv)   '(But contrast: money and its use.)': AWL 30 notes that money is not always used to buy things one can point at, e.g. when it buys permission to sit in a theatre, or a title, or one's life.

2   This first occurs in MS 110 (Vol. VI), 229f. There it is preceded by a discussion of how it is that one knows what one intends. The erroneous move W. was inclined to make in these reflections, he wrote, needs to be stated in its full generality. The mistake lay in the idea that the meaning of a word is an idea or representation (*Vorstellung*) that accompanies the word. This conception is connected with that of consciousness, i.e. with what he had always called 'the primary'. PI §120 follows immediately. In this context it seems that what he was criticizing was his earlier conception of a phenomenological language, i.e. a language consisting of names whose meanings were what is immediately given, which really would capture the nature of experience.

In *The Big Typescript* this remark occurs in section 16, entitled 'Logic speaks about sentences and words in an ordinary sense, not about sentences and words in some abstract sense'. The section opens with a variant of PI §108(b)–(d). After (c), W. continues (I paraphrase): we cannot attain greater generality in philosophy than that which we express in ordinary life and in science (i.e. here too we leave everything as it is (MS 114 (Vol. X) Um., 109, adds 'as in mathematics')). So an exciting new definition of number is not the business of philosophy. Philosophy is concerned with existing language, and shouldn't pretend it has to deal with an abstract one. But, in investigating language and meaning, we can easily come to think that we shouldn't really speak of words and sentences in a homely sense, but only in a sublimated, abstract, sense — as if a particular sentence were not really what someone uttered, but an ideal entity (the class of all equivalent sentences, or some such). But is the chess king that chess rules deal with such an ideal thing, an abstract entity? [Then follows §120.] We are not justified in having any more scruples about our language than the chess-player has about chess, namely none. This doesn't mean 'about the concept of language'; rather, it means, 'speak freely about it [language], as a chess-player plays — nothing can happen to you'. For your scruples are only misunderstandings, 'philosophical' propositions.

2.1   'your scruples are misunderstandings': MS 152, 92, reflects on the belief in the necessity of a phenomenological language. It seems as if our language is in some sense 'raw', an incomplete representation (*Darstellung*) of things. As if philosophy had to improve and refine it in order to be able to understand the structure of the world. . . . (But) the aim is not a novel clarity which the old language cannot provide, but the elimination of bewilderment, perplexities, riddles, etc. 'And your difficulties are misunderstandings' — if they weren't, if we really needed to analyse further in order to arrive at safe ground, then we should have to ask ourselves: into what more refined concept should we translate, for example, the ordinary concept of a word.

SECTION 121

1   This is linked with §120(e), but it is unclear against whom W. is arguing. It is not meant to block what would be a regress, but to undercut the view that metaphilosophy justifies or gives a foundation for philosophy, as Hilbert thought metamathematics gives the foundations of mathematics. But Hilbert's metamathematics is just another calculus (PG 296), and philosophical reflection upon the nature of philosophy is just more philosophy. In neither case do we 'give foundations' for, or justify, anything.

2   PG 116 (MS 111 (Vol. VII), 110; BT 67): the non-existence of meta-philosophy, W. claims, could be presented as a leading principle of all his philosophy.

Surveyability and surveyable representations
   1. Surveyability
   2. Precursors: Hertz, Boltzmann, Ernst, Goethe, Spengler
   3. The morphological method and the difficulty of surveying grammar
   4. Surveyable representations

SECTION 122

1   See 'Surveyability and surveyable representations'.

1.1   (i)   'übersehen': 'to survey', in the sense in which one can survey a scene from the heights.
       (ii)   'Our grammar is deficient in surveyability': for we are constantly deceived by similarities of form that mask deep differences in use.
       (iii)   'Zwischenglieder': 'intermediate links'; intermediate cases, actual or invented, sharpen our eyes to formal connections (GB 133), which need not

be by way of common properties — as is evident in the case of family-resemblance concepts. It is unclear whether the presentation of actual or invented intermediate cases is part of the 'surveyable representation' of the grammar of the problematic expression or merely that it facilitates it.

(iv) 'übersichtlichen Darstellung': 'surveyable representation'. For what might so count, see 2.1(iii) below and 'Surveyability and surveyable representations', sect. 4.

(v) 'Er bezeichnet unsere Darstellungsform': 'It characterizes the way we present things' (of philosophical issues). His philosophical method is neither theorizing on the model of science or explaining by means of inferences to the best explanation on the model of metaphysics that mimics science, nor analysing expressions into their depth grammar on the model of the *Tractatus* programme (cf. RLF). It is, rather, arranging the grammatical facts so that they are surveyable. The general form in which he presents matters (problems and their dissolution) is descriptive. And what is described is the grammar of problematic expressions. But it is to be described in a manner that makes it surveyable, easy to take in, so that the grammatical type of the expression will be easily recognized, the logical differences between it and expressions with which it is likely to be confounded will be evident, and the reasons for the confusion and conflation will spring to the eye. This is sometimes facilitated by finding or inventing intermediate cases to make clear formal connections and differences. W.'s 'way of looking at things' amounts to a morphological method in the tradition of Goethe (as W. interpreted his biological work) and prominent in Spengler (see 'Surveyability and surveyable representations', sect. 2).

(vi) '(Is this a "Weltanschauung"?)': this stems from 1931, MS 110 (Vol. VI), 257 (= BT 417 (cf. GB 133)) which mentions Spengler: '(Eine Art der "Weltanschauung", wie sie scheinbar für unsere Zeit typisch ist. Spengler.)' ('(A kind of "Weltanschauung" that seems to be typical of our time. Spengler.)'). This reference to Spengler remained in MS 142, §115, and TS 220, §100, and was removed only in TS 239, where the present query replaces the earlier, more emphatic suggestion. W. is querying whether the way *he* is looking at philosophical problems and their resolution is a feature of a kind of *Weltanschauung* typical of his times. Many of the thinkers to whom W. explicitly acknowledged an intellectual debt held that the deepest problems are solved not by scientific hypotheses, but by seeing connections, arranging what is known, looking at what is there in the right way (the 'morphological method'). This is typical of Hertz, Boltzmann, Ernst, Kraus and, of course, Spengler himself.[53] Support for this interpretation is given by W.'s remark written the previous year: 'Loos, Spengler, Freud and I all belong to the same class that is characteristic of these times' (MS 183, 29). W. held that Freud's

---

[53] Spengler acknowledges a debt to Goethe and Nietzsche. Of Nietzsche's 'outlook' (*Ausblick*) Spengler made an 'overlook' (*Überblick*) (O. Spengler, *Decline of the West*, tr. C. F. Atkinson (Allen and Unwin, London, 1932), vol. 1, p. xiv.).

real discovery was not scientific, but a new form of representing things (e.g. talk of unconscious motives as a way of describing familiar observations of behaviour in which action and avowal or admission are sincerely dissociated) warranted by the connecting links (formal similarities) between motivated behaviour and the deviant behaviour that Freud represents as 'unconsciously motivated'. It is less obvious what connection there is with Loos (whom he also cited as an influence). Perhaps it is that Loos, in his architecture, eschewed ornament in order to emphasize formal connections between elements. The only mention of Loos in a philosophical context is in association with the thought that inspired PI §217(b), in which W. points out that the demand for definitions is sometimes purely formal, comparable to the architectural requirement for a coping that has no function other than ornamental (see TS 302, 31).

2   This remark about the importance of a surveyable representation originates in W.'s discussion of Frazer's *Golden Bough* in MS 110 (Vol. VI), 256f. (cf. GB 133). It was transposed into a different context, and its significance generalized, in *The Big Typescript*. There it occurs in section 89, entitled 'THE METHOD OF PHILOSOPHY: THE SURVEYABLE REPRESENTATION OF GRAMMATICAL // LINGUISTIC // FACTS. THE GOAL: THE TRANSPARENCY OF ARGUMENTS. JUSTICE.'[54] There §122(b) precedes (a). It follows the observation that philosophical remarks are like combination locks on a safe — once the combination has been found, any child can open it. The draft of §122(a), lines 3–4, is followed by the remark 'A sentence is completely logically analysed when its grammar is laid out completely clearly. It might be written down or spoken in any number of ways. Above all, our grammar is deficient in *surveyability*.'

AWL 43 remarks that 'One difficulty with philosophy is that we lack a synoptic view.' This difficulty is compared to the difficulty one has finding one's way around a country when one has no map. The country here is language, and the geography its grammar. We don't know the country except by knowing the connections between the roads. Because these are manifold, and not readily surveyable, W. suggests repetition as a means of surveying them (hence the traveling 'over a wide field of thought, criss-cross in every direction' (Preface, p. ix)).

2.1   (i)   'Our grammar is deficient in surveyability': From MS 108 (Vol. IV), 31 — the grammatical rules for 'and', 'not', 'or', etc., W. wrote, are not exhausted by what he said in the *Tractatus*. There are rules about truth-functions that are also concerned with the simple constituents of the sentence. Our grammar is above all deficient in surveyability.

(ii)   'seeing connections': MS 134, 126, remarks that to survey the concept of feeling (fear, hope, etc.) and to clarify why one does not feel one's knowledge,

---

[54]   His term is 'Gerechtigkeit' — *doing justice* to the grammatical facts.

one must survey the concept. To do so, one must compare it differently from what is suggested by its surface grammar. One must conceive of different parts as homologous: what looks the same as a maxilla (perhaps a deliberate allusion to Goethe here) must be compared with a foot. Don't look only for similarities, W. advises, but also for connections. A father passes on his name to his son, even when the son is quite unlike him.

(iii) 'übersichtliche Darstellung': a relatively rare phrase in W.'s writing. The following are its most important occurrences (discussed in 'Surveyability and surveyable representations', sect. 4).

(a) The colour-octahedron is said to give a surveyable representation of the grammar of colour-words (PR 52; cf. VoW 135 (F 37)).

(b) MS 110 (Vol. VI), 257, observes that Frazer's collection of facts [about the Nemi rule of succession and related rituals] can be presented by means of an evolutionary hypothesis, or by means of a schema of a religious ceremony (functionally akin to Goethe's schema of the 'primal plant'), or simply by arranging the factual material in a 'surveyable representation'. [Then follows the draft of PI §122).] Hypothetical connecting links [of the kind Frazer postulates] function only to sharpen our eye to formal connections, not as developmental hypotheses [*pace* Frazer].

(c) In a letter to Schlick dated 30 November 1931, W. wrote that perhaps the main difference between his old and his new conception is that he now realizes that analysis of a proposition does not mean disclosing hidden things, but rather the tabulation, or surveyable representation, of the grammar of words (see 'Surveyability and surveyable representations', sect. 4).

(d) The *Diktat für Schlick* suggests that we can perspicuously represent the grammatical relationship between the content and intensity of belief if we replace the process of believing (*sic*) with the process of talking and the intensity of belief with the tone and strength of voice (TS 302, 21). The ring of conviction provides us with a simple and surveyable representation of the grammar of 'conviction'. W. explains by an analogy: imagine that chess was originally introduced not as a board game, but as a written game (as in reports of chess tournaments). Suppose someone then thinks of playing the game on a board. He will then also have produced a simple and easily surveyable way of presenting the rules of the game.

(e) MS 145, 25f., examines the nature of thinking and thoughts:

One could say that thinking is operating with symbols; but 'thinking' is a fluid concept, and what 'operating with symbols' is must, in every particular case, be examined separately.

I could also say that thinking is operating with language; but 'language' is a fluid concept and so too is what we call operating with it.

The thought is not essentially a mental process.

Different meanings of the word 'thought'.

The 'thought' as the sense of the sentence

The thought as psychological phenomenon

The thought as process of consciousness
The explanations that we // I // are trying to give of thinking and the thought are
only clarifications // surveyable representations // of the grammar of these words.

The opening remarks here primarily concern thinking conceived as reasoning
and inferring, rather than the ramified concept of thinking in general, which
encompasses much more. (One could hardly say that the surgeon, who is thinking what he is doing while undertaking an appendectomy, is operating with
symbols.) W.'s later, refined reflections on the general concept of thinking are
examined in 'Thinking: methodological muddles and categorial confusions' and
'Thinking: the soul of language' in Volume 3.

(f) BT 437, in the section entitled 'Phenomenology is grammar', observes
that the investigation of the rules of use of our language, the recognition of
these rules and [their?] surveyable presentation achieves the same as one often
wants to achieve by means of the construction of a phenomenological language. Each time we recognize that such-and-such a mode of representation
can be replaced by another, we take a step towards this goal.

(g) VoW 121ff., in a dictation entitled 'Philosophie', presents the 'method
of surveyable representations' as above all the method of resolving philosophical problems by *description* rather than *explanation*. Philosophical description
gets its importance from the fact that it gives us an overview of our grammar.
This guards us against adopting a *different* system of grammar [presumably
various forms of *Begriffsschriften*, or alternative 'languages', such as the 'phenomenological language' W. envisaged in 1929 or the languages Carnap advo-
cated in the 1930s]. It is because we lack a surveyable representation of our
grammar (in a given domain) that we are seduced into adopting some other
system of grammar (which W. characterizes as 'false'). Philosophy [in W.'s hands]
rescues us by offering us *the correct* surveyable representation of our 'system' ('und
nun erlöst uns die Philosophie dadurch dass sie uns die richtige übersichtliche
Darstellung anbietet'), so that we are no longer subject to such temptations.
'We provide a surveyable representation of a system of rules, namely of a system which does exclude our employing all those propositions which we have
always wanted to exclude, which have always aroused suspicion in us'[55] (VoW
125). By implication, we do not need Russell's Theory of Types and the
grammar of *Principia*, for example, to exclude as nonsense what is nonsense

[55] W.'s example (p. 125) is 'a = a', i.e. the so-called Law of Identity, which Frege held to be a
Law of Truth (a boundary stone 'set in an eternal foundation, which our thought can overflow
but never displace' (BLA i, p. xvi)). But 'A thing is identical with itself' is a very suspect proposition — 'There is no finer example of a useless proposition', he was to write in the *Investigations*
§216. In BT 412 (cf. MS 110 (Vol. VI), 164) he wrote: 'The Law (*Satz*) of Identity, for example, seems to have a fundamental significance. But the proposition (*Satz*) that this "law" (*Satz*)
is a nonsense has taken over this significance.' 'A thing is different from itself', he explained in
RFM 404 (cf. 89), is nonsense (*that* is why it is 'unthinkable'). Hence its negation 'A thing is
identical with itself' is nonsense too; it says nothing, delimits reality in no way.

anyway — and can be seen to be nonsense by a surveyable representation of the ordinary grammar of the relevant kind of self-referring propositions.

(h) VoW 129 (F 29) implies that the T/F notation of the *Tractatus* offers a surveyable representation of the rules of inference of the propositional calculus.

(i) MS 116 (Vol. XII), 55 (cf. Z §273) discusses Hardy's treatment of the infinite. The conception of the infinite that is to be found in the [Cantorian] calculus is worthy of investigation.

This may be compared to the way a chartered accountant precisely investigates and clarifies the management of a business undertaking. The aim is a surveyable comparative representation of all the applications, illustrations, conceptions of the calculus. An illumination *from all sides*. For every one-sided illumination also casts a shadow ~~& the stronger the illumination, the darker the shadow~~. The complete overview of everything that may produce unclarity. And this overview must extend over a wide space // a wide ~~field~~ domain //, for the roots of our ideas reach a long way. (MS 116 (Vol. XII), 55)

3   Spengler's book much impressed W. Other noteworthy mentions of Spengler are:

(i)   In MS 154, 16r (dated 1931), W. wrote that Spengler (together with Boltzmann, Hertz, Schopenhauer, Frege, Russell, Kraus, Loos, Weininger and Sraffa) had influenced him.

(ii)   MS 111 (Vol. VII), 119 (BT 259; CV 14) suggests that Spengler could have been better understood if he had said 'I *am comparing* different cultural periods to the lives of families; within a family there is a family resemblance, though you will also find a resemblance between members of different families; family-resemblance differs from the other sort of resemblance in such and such ways, etc.' More perspicuously, the object of comparison or prototype (*Urbild*), from which the way of looking at things is derived, must be given. (In Spengler's case, it is the life of an organism that progresses from childhood through youth and maturity to old age and decline.) Only thus can one avoid distorting the data that is presented by means of the prototype of the way of looking at things. For the danger comes from projecting what is true of the prototype on to the objects presented by its means.

(iii) Spengler is invoked in discussion of family resemblance in MS 113 (Vol. IX), 102v (see PG 299): proof is a family-resemblance concept — 'Like words such as "people", "king", "religion", etc., cf. Spengler.'

(iv)   MS 157(b), 16v, compares W.'s type of investigation with Spengler's, and criticizes Spengler for failing to see that the ideal (the archetypal life-cycle of a culture)[56] is the formal principle of the inquiry ('Prinzip der

---

[56]   e.g. Spengler's remark, 'beyond and above all, there stood out the fact that these great *groups of morphological relations*, each one of which symbolically represents a particular sort of mankind in the whole picture of world-history, are strictly symmetrical in structure' (*Decline of the West*, vol. 1, p. 47).

Betrachtungsform'). This remark follows a version of PI §131, which he associated with Spengler (see Exg.).

(v)   In MS 125, 30, written as late as 1942, W., in the course of remarks
on the philosophy of mathematics, jotted down: 'How very much I am influenced
by Spengler in my thought.'

SECTION 123

2   This originates in MS 112 (Vol. VIII), 24r, in the course of a discussion of
the question of whether a name is a representative of, or goes proxy for, its
bearer, and how this applies to the name of a name. Struggling with the complexities, W. remarked of himself 'I don't know my way about', and immediately added: 'This is the formulation of every philosophical problem.'

The remark was then selected for *The Big Typescript* (BT 421), where it is
preceded by: 'The philosophical problem is an awareness of disorder in our
concepts, and can be solved by ordering them.' It is followed by the remarks:
'As I do philosophy, its entire task consists in expressing myself in such a way
that certain troubles // problems // disappear. ((Hertz.)) If I am right, then
philosophical problems must really be completely solvable, by contrast with
all others.'

It was added to the TS only in TS 239, §133; its aptness being evident,
since not knowing one's way around is a corollary of lacking an overview of
the relevant grammar.

SECTION 124

1   The first of a series of remarks on the method and limits of philosophy.
Their rationale is given in the general discussions of language and (the autonomy of) grammar (see Volume 4, 'The arbitrariness of grammar and the bounds
of sense'). The justification of the method can be seen in the achievements of
the book in clarifying and dissolving fundamental philosophical problems.

Four points are made. (a) The method of philosophy involves describing
the use of language. (b) It may not *interfere* with the grammar of our language,
i.e. attempt to reform it for philosophical or supposedly 'scientific' purposes
(as Frege, Russell and Carnap thought it should do).[57] (c) It cannot give
language *foundations* (see 1.1(i)). (d) It also leaves mathematics as it is (LFM
13), and neither gives it 'foundations' nor solves its problems (see 2.1(ii)). This
conception is reflected in W.'s rejection of the logicist enterprise.

---

[57]   Of course, *scientists* may 'reform' language for scientific purposes, i.e. refine existing concepts
in various ways for purposes of their empirical theories.

Foundationalism is the mirror-image of reductionism, and both were ana-
thema to W. (Butler's 'Everything is what it is and not another thing' might
have been the motto for the *Investigations* had Moore not already used it.) Here
it is foundationalism with respect to language that is castigated, but foundationalism in mathematics, epistemology, ethics and aesthetics would be equally
good targets.

1.1   (i)   'it cannot give it any foundation either': as the *Tractatus* had tried to
do. It had argued that the foundations of language lie in the simple names the
meanings of which are the simple objects constituting the substance of the world.
Names connect language to the world, and the isomorphism of name and object
guarantees the pre-established harmony between language and reality that seemed
a condition for the possibility of representation. But this was illusion.

(ii)   'It leaves everything as it is': This does not intimate the impotence of
philosophy. It is a further gloss on the first sentence of §124. 'Everything' here
refers to what philosophy describes, i.e. the use of language. It is not the task
of philosophy to change the use (i.e. the grammar) of our language, but only
to describe it for the purpose of resolving philosophical problems. It does
not, of course, follow that philosophical clarification will have no effect. If,
'in psychology there are experimental methods and conceptual confusion'
(PPF §371 (p. 232)), philosophical investigation into psychological concepts
will affect empirical psychology, for it may show that some questions are senseless, that some experiments rest on incoherent presuppositions, and that some
experimental results do not prove what they are held to demonstrate.

(iii)   'It also leaves mathematics as it is': in mathematics there are 'conceptual confusion and methods of proof' (PPF §371 (p. 232)). An investigation
into 'the foundations of mathematics' is as little a mathematical investigation
as an examination of psychological concepts and theories is a psychological
one. 'It will not contain calculations, so it is not for example logistic' (ibid.).
It leaves mathematics unaltered in so far as its task is not to prove or disprove
theorems, nor even to resolve contradictions (see §125). But clarification of
conceptual confusion in mathematics will affect the reflections of mathematicians on their results (MS 154, 45v–46r). Mathematicians are inclined to
dismiss the philosopher who draws their attention to misleading forms of expression with a contemptuous 'Sure, we all know that, it isn't really very interesting'. But when a mathematician 'is troubled by philosophical questions it
is because of those very unclarities that he passed over earlier with a shrug of
the shoulders' (TS 219, 10).

Good philosophy of mathematics does not affect the theorems of mathematicians, but it *should* affect the *activities* of mathematicians.

What will distinguish the mathematicians of the future from those of today will
really be a greater sensitivity, and *that* will — as it were — prune mathematics; since
people will then be more intent on absolute clarity than on the discovery of new
games.

Philosophical clarity will have the same effect on the growth of mathematics as sunlight has on the growth of potato shoots. (In a dark cellar they grow yards long.) (PG 381)

(iv) 'no mathematical discovery can advance it': Mathematics is concept formation. Philosophy is the resolution of conceptual problems (confusions, unclarities) by description. The introduction of new conceptual connections by means of a new theorem cannot resolve conceptual unclarities in the pre-existing conceptual structures. So, W. did not think that Gödel's 'discoveries' had the *philosophical* implications for mathematics that are commonly attributed to them. Metamathematics, he held, is just more mathematics, and no new mathematical 'discovery' (proof) can clarify existing conceptual connections in mathematics, although it may throw up fresh conceptual problems for philosophy of mathematics that need disentangling — as does Gödel's incompleteness theorem.

2.1   (i)   LFM 103 comments on Hilbert's remark that no one is going to turn us out of the paradise which Cantor has created: 'I wouldn't dream of trying to drive anyone out of this paradise. I would try to do something quite different: I would try to show you that it is not a paradise — so that you'll leave of your own accord.'

(ii)   ' "a leading problem of mathematical logic" ': MS 110 (Vol. VI), 12 (PG 296): 'So there cannot be any "leading problems" of mathematical logic, if these are supposed to be problems whose solution would at long last give us a right to do arithmetic as we do.' MS 110, 189 (= BT 417f.) connects this phrase with Ramsey. MS 115 (Vol. XI), 71, observes:

One of the temptations that we must resist while philosophizing is to think that we must make our concepts more exact than they are, according to the current state of our insight. This deviation leads to a kind of mathematical philosophy that believes that it must solve mathematical problems to achieve philosophical clarity. (Ramsey). We need only a correct description of the status quo.

(iii)   RFM 378 remarks:

What does mathematics need a foundation for? It no more needs one, I believe, than propositions about physical objects — or about sense-impressions, need an *analysis*. What mathematical propositions do stand in need of is a clarification of their grammar, just as do those of other propositions.

The *mathematical* problems of what is called foundations are no more the foundations of mathematics for us than the painted rock is the support of a painted tower.

SECTION 125

1   This is linked directly to §124, as an addendum to 'Philosophy leaves mathematics as it is' (see 2 below), and indirectly to §§122–3. Philosophical

problems are resolved by surveying a segment of grammar, for philosophical difficulties arise through not 'knowing one's way about'. All philosophy does is *describe* the topography of the grammatical landscape, not *change* it. So too, in philosophy of mathematics: a problem in metamathematics is just another problem in mathematics, not in philosophy. Consequently, a contradiction in mathematics (or metamathematics) is not something which philosophy must resolve. Rather, it is the task of philosophy to describe the entanglement of rules which produces the contradiction.

In mathematics we lay down rules and determine connections between them by proofs. What is the significance of the emergence of a contradiction (e.g. in set theory)? That the calculus of mathematics was not really a calculus, that it was useless, had no application? A hidden contradiction is not like a malignant disease infecting the body mathematical (PR 319). If a contradiction between the rules of a game comes to light, that does not mean that the rules have hitherto been useless or that we have never really played the game, or any game at all.

The rules of a game, the axioms of a calculus, are in order until a case of their contradicting each other turns up (PG 303). Then a decision is called for — a clarification of the existing rules or the introduction of a further rule to resolve the contradiction. For we did not mean the rules to conflict, but to guide us in our transactions with them (in our various practices of applying them). If we do come across a contradiction, it can be sealed off (e.g. Russell's Theory of Types; see 2 below). *That* is not problematic (and that is why contradictions *per se* are not the catastrophes that mathematicians think they are (PR 319, 325)). After all, contradictions say the same as tautologies: namely, nothing.

It is the *civic* status of contradictions that is philosophically problematic. It is unclear what W. meant here. But one might conjecture as follows. The mathematical status of a contradiction is philosophically uninteresting. It is a mathematical, not a philosophical, task to find ways of restricting the rules so that the contradiction is prevented. But we are prone to think (as Turing did[58] (LFM, lecture XXII)) that a *hidden* contradiction may be responsible for bridges falling down, i.e. that outside mathematics, in 'civil life' (see 2.1 below), contradictions can cause practical harm. And *that* is a profound philosophical confusion.

1.1   'den Zustand der Mathematik . . . übersehbar zu machen': 'to render surveyable the state of mathematics', for that will enable us to see *how* we got entangled in our rules.

---

[58]   W. observed that a contradiction is not a germ showing a general illness. Turing replied that the 'real harm will not come in unless there is an application, in which case a bridge may fall down' (LFM 211).

2   §125 is a late remark, derived from MS 130, 12–15, written sometime between 1944 and 1946 (prior to composing *Bemerkungen I*). Here §125(a), which follows the draft of §125(b)–(e), is preceded by a note: 'For my remark "Philosophy leaves everything as it is. It also leaves mathematics as it is." ' It was entered into TS 227b, the successive paragraphs (a)–(e) being taken from B i §§582, 573, 574 and 578. In its origin in MS 130, it was a comment on Russell's Theory of Types and the contradiction it was introduced to deal with. What, W. queries, is the practical use of the Theory of Types? Russell draws our attention to the fact that in certain cases we must restrict the expression of generality in order to avoid drawing the unwanted consequences that would otherwise follow. [Then §125(b)–(d).] A contradiction, W. continues, is not a kind of catastrophe, but a wall that shows us that we cannot go further here. [Then §125(e).] The question, he goes on, is not what we must do to avoid a contradiction, but rather what we should do when we arrive at one. Why is a contradiction more to be feared than a tautology? Our motto could be: 'Let us not be bewitched!' [Then §125(a) as above.]

2.1   'Its status in civic life': RFM 257 remarks:

I want to say: it is essential to mathematics that its signs are also employed in *mufti* [im *Zivil*].

It is the use outside mathematics, and so the *meaning* of the signs, that makes the sign-game into mathematics.

SECTION 126

1   This is a further corollary of §124: namely, that philosophy may in no way interfere with the actual use of language. What is it that philosophy then puts before us? — *Descriptions* of the use of language (not recommendations for an 'ideal language'), reminders of the way we use words (§127), of the familiar grammar of our expressions. *That* lies open to view (cf. PI §89), although we commonly overlook it; but, to be sure, the appropriate *arrangement* of these grammatical facts is not evident, and it is this that the philosopher aims at. For this will render the relevant segment of grammar surveyable and dissolve the problems.

Why should the fact that everything lies open to view imply that there is nothing to explain? What lies open to view is the way we, competent speakers, use our words. The rules for the use of our words, understood in a homely sense (for detailed examination of W.'s conception of rules, see Volume 2, 'Rules and grammar'), are equally open to view — otherwise they could not fulfil their function: namely, to guide usage, to constitute stand- ards of correct use, and to provide explanations of meaning. Precisely because these are open to view, there is nothing that is relevant to philosophical questions here which demands or could be given explanations in the sense in which scientific theories explain phenomena (and which metaphysical theories misguidedly try to emulate).

What would there be to explain if, *per impossibile*, not everything lay open to view? It seemed to the author of the *Tractatus* that the depth grammar of language was 'hidden'. And it was by reference to what appeared to be thus hidden, e.g. the real simple names whose meanings are simple objects or the real elementary propositions, that he endeavoured to explain how a proposition can be false yet meaningful (i.e. describe what is *not* the case), and why there must be a pre-established harmony between language and reality (see Volume 4, 'Intentionality'). This, however, was illusion. 'It is all done in language' (not between language and reality); there is and could be no such thing as a hidden depth grammar of language. Such *metaphysical* explanations are chimerical.

However, *grammatical* explanations that call to mind how expressions are used (§127) and how they are interconnected are licit, and, appropriately arranged, they will dissolve the problems. Equally, explanations of how and why philosophers (including the author of the *Tractatus*), go wrong, build houses of cards, weave metaphysical and pseudoscientific webs of illusion, are in order. But neither of these kinds of explanation is in question here. Reminders of how expressions are used are not, in the requisite sense, explanations, and there is nothing hypothetico-deductive about them.

1.1   (i) 'Philosophy just puts everything before us': this may be contrasted with TLP 6.53, which laid down the future method of philosophy: namely, to say nothing except what can be said, i.e. propositions of natural science (i.e. empirical propositions), and to show that attempts to say anything metaphysical are futile. Now W. is willing to acknowledge that philosophy *can* put something before us that is not 'natural science', although it will be nothing new or interesting — only grammatical propositions (stale truisms (TS 219, 6) or ordinary and trivial answers (BT 412), which specify familiar rules for the use of words, of which we need to be reminded. But the *arrangement* of these rules will be of the greatest interest, in so far as it makes philosophical problems completely disappear (PI §133).

(ii) 'What is hidden . . . is of no interest to us': philosophy is concerned with describing the use of language, the grammar of the expressions of our language, for the purpose of dissolving philosophical difficulties. It is concerned with the network of conceptual connections within the language, connections that determine what makes sense (and which exclude certain combinations of words as nonsense). Nothing here *could* be hidden.

(iii) 'what is possible *before* all new discoveries': i.e. the bounds of sense — for what is logically possible just *is* what makes sense.

2.1   (i) 'puts everything before us, and neither explains nor deduces anything': MS 110 (Vol. VI), 217 (= BT 418) has this in the context of philosophy's presenting similes and comparisons, such as the simile of a picture (i.e. something that depicts how things stand) or the comparison of the application of language with the application of the calculus of multiplication. In that context philosophy simply compares and contrasts, but does not explain or deduce anything. MS 142, §117, and TS 220, §102, reproduce this context, but it is deleted in TS 239. Deleting it generalizes the remark, so that it is apparently no longer concerned merely with juxtaposing objects of comparison.

BT 437 observes that to try to resolve our dissatisfaction [in the face of conceptual unclarity] by explanation is the fault of metaphysics.

(ii) 'there is nothing to explain': MS 110, 90 (= BT 418) glosses this by reference to negation. In so far as we encounter philosophical puzzles concerning negation (as W. did (cf. NB 30: 'the mystery of negation')), that is not because we need to explain what 'not' means. In BT this is followed by the remark: 'We must know what *explanation* means. There is a constant danger of wanting to use this word in logic in a sense that is derived from physics.'

Section 127

1   What recollections do we have to assemble (marshall, arrange)? Descriptions of the ways in which we use words (cf. BT 419 below).

1.1   (i) 'Erinnerungen': not reminders, but things we recollect, viz. how we use words. Cf. §89(c); cp. MS 110 (Vol. VI), 131f. which links the thought with Socrates (the *Meno*).

(ii) 'for a particular purpose': viz. to resolve particular philosophical problems.

2   BT 419 (MS 111 (Vol. VII), 164) is more emphatic: 'To study philosophy is really to recollect. We remind ourselves that we really use words in this way.'

2.1   'assembling recollections': MS 153b, 36r, has 'truths' rather than 'recollections'. The remark is there followed by the English sentence 'We have to arrange evidence and do no more'.

Section 128

1   A controversial remark. What does W. mean by 'a thesis'? Arguably (see 2 below), theses would be debatable claims about the essence of things such as are advanced in the *Tractatus*. The possibility of *any* theses in philosophy is now rejected. Were it possible to advance any theses, they would have to be indisputable. Why so? Two different but compatible answers are possible. First, because what would be involved is insight into the essential nature of things (*Wesensschau*) — 'the essence of everything empirical' (§89) — that must

ultimately be perfectly transparent.[59] But there *cannot* be any such theses. For the very notion of objective, language-independent essences was chimerical. Second, because the only possible 'theses' would be grammatical propositions (to which everyone would have to agree), and they are not really theses at all.

Does W. in the *Investigations* not propound any theses? Not in the sense in question. He makes grammatical statements (e.g. 'Only of a living human being and what resembles (behaves like) a living human being can one say: it has sensations; it sees; is blind; hears; is deaf; is conscious or unconscious' (PI §281)). He reminds us of the ways in which we use words (e.g. 'the grammar of "knows" is related to that of "ability"' (§150); 'This is how things are', *pace* the *Tractatus*, is not the (illicit) expression of the (ineffable) general propositional form, but has a perfectly decent use as a propositional variable for purposes of anaphoric reference (§134)). He shows that certain combinations of words have no sense (e.g. there is no such thing as 'a private ostensive definition' (§258)). But these are not *theses* about the essential (language-independent) nature of things, but grammatical clarifications, reminders of how we use words, and arguments consequent upon them. 'Philosophy states only what everyone admits' (PI §599).

2   The earliest occurrence of this remark in the *Nachlass* appears to be in MS 110 (Vol. VI), 259, written on 2 July 1931. The context sheds no light on the matter. But on 9 December 1931, W. discussed the subject at length with Waismann (WWK 183f.), and refers to this remark. The example under discussion was Waismann's *Thesen* (WWK, Appendix B), written in 1930 and revised in 1931. It was apparently intended as an introduction to W.'s philosophy, which would give a simplified overview of the *Tractatus*, supplemented by some new material from W. on hypotheses and verification. So its theses consist of *Tractatus*-inspired pronouncements about essences such as 'Reality consists of facts not things', 'Every state of affairs is complex', 'What can exist or not exist is a configuration of elements'. This does, perhaps, give us a clue as to what W. here means by 'theses' — namely, apodictic pronouncements about the nature of things (including language). W. now holds that 'a rehash of such theses is no longer justified' (WWK 184; for discussion, see 'Philosophy', sect. 6). Those theses are disputable and lack the obviousness required of philosophical theses, if there were any. 'As long as there is a possibility of having different opinions and disputing about a question, this indicates that things have not yet been expressed clearly enough' (WWK 183). He also makes it clear that he did not think that perspicuously stating grammatical rules was advancing a thesis.

The denial of theses evidently went hand in hand with the denial of *opinions*. In AWL 97 (cf. LFM 22), W. remarked that 'On all questions we discuss I

---

[59]   Compare Descartes (a paradigmatic searcher after the essence of things) on his method.

have no opinion; and if I had, and it disagreed with one of your opinions, I would at once give it up for the sake of argument because it would be of no importance for our discussion. We constantly move in a realm where we all have the same opinions.' Clearly, the 'realm' is the realm of grammar. It is not *an opinion* that *this* colour ☞ ■ is black, that black is darker than white, that nothing can be both black all over and white all over simultaneously. But *if* there is any disagreement over the use of a word (which is *not* a disagreement in *opinion*), W. will follow the use the speaker proposes for the sake of the argument. For the speaker's philosophical difficulties stem from an entanglement *in the rules he is using,* and if these deviate from those we (or W.) is using, that, in itself, is of no consequence. We need to determine what *he* means by his words, and to show him how, by crossing the old use with the new, for example, he has become entangled (RPP I §548; cf. RPP II §289).

It is important to avoid the error of thinking that W.'s denial of opinions implies absence of any stand on philosophical questions. In MS 158, 39v–40r, in a remark evidently preparatory for a lecture, he jotted down (in English): ' "This expression misleads us to think that . . ." What sort of error does it leads us into? Does it lead us to think the impossible? — It leads us into puzzlement — or it leads you into admiring what I don't want you to admire, or it leads you into believing what is wrong or into doing what seems to me pernicious.' W. did indeed hold that it is wrong to suppose that we know of the mental states of others by analogy. He really did think that it is a mistake to suppose that the predicate calculus discloses the depth grammar of any possible language. He really did think that it is pernicious to attempt to establish the foundations of, for example, religious belief, morality, our knowledge of the empirical world around us, or of mathematics. And he did not want people to admire the theorems of mathematics as if they were phenomena of nature, wonderful crystals that have been discovered by mathematicians (CV 41 (MS 125, 2v), 57 (MS 134, 27)). He was anything but a philosophical quietist or relativist.

2.1   'everyone would agree with them': the general idea comes early in W.'s post-1929 works. PR 65 (MS 108 (Vol. IV), 104) notes that 'In philosophy we are always in danger of giving a mythology of symbolism, or of psychology: instead of simply saying what everyone knows and must admit'.

Section 129

1.1   (i)   'The aspects of things': What things? Probably aspects of language and its use (see 2.1(a) below).

    (ii)   'that are most important': What are these? Perhaps such things as the family-resemblance character of many of the concepts central to philosophical elucidation of language, or the fact that the samples we use in explaining the meanings of certain words are part of the means of representation and are not *described* by an ostensive definition, or that there is an internal relation between a rule and its extension. For these aspects of language are perfectly familiar and simple — we do often explain what a such-and-such is by a series of examples and a similarity-rider, we explain what colour-words mean by pointing at samples, we obviously think that nothing other than 1002 can follow 1000 in the series of even integers. But so familiar are we with such things that we are not struck by them and fail to notice their significance for the most fundamental questions in philosophy of language.

(iii) 'hidden': this only appears to contradict §126, since the aspects that are here said to be 'hidden' are in full view, and we do not notice them because of their familiarity.

(iv) 'The real foundations of his enquiry': The real foundations of enquiry are commonly precisely what is taken for granted at the outset and never questioned: for example, Augustine's picture of language (the thought that naming is the essence of language). Once it is pointed out, as it is in the *Investigations*, it is evident that it is a supposition (or array of suppositions) that is 'most striking and most powerful'.

2.1   BT 419 (derived proximately from MSS 110 (Vol. VI), 259, and 112 (Vol. VIII), 117v) has a similar remark.

(a) Instead of 'The aspects of things that are most important for us . . .', it has (derived ultimately from MS 153b, 24r): 'The philosophically most important aspects of things // of language . . .'. One may ask whether the change betokens a generalization, so that 'thing' (*Ding*) is not limited to aspects of language? This is not clear, especially since W. speaks of predicating of the thing (*Sache*) what lies in the method of presentation (§104), where the 'thing' evidently is such items as name, proposition, i.e. features of a language.

(b) After '. . . has at some time struck him', W. added '(Frazer, etc. etc.)'. Where Frazer sees terrible or awesome rituals and practices, he thinks to explain their character by reference to the natives' primitive scientific beliefs (GB). Where he sees depth in some folk practice (Beltane fire festivals), he thinks to explain the impressiveness by a historical hypothesis. These suppositions concerning the form of explanation appropriate to the phenomena were taken for granted by Frazer and never questioned. It may be these that W. is referring to as an example of 'the real foundations' of an enquiry. Once they are explicitly brought into view, they are very striking — and questionable. Ritual practices, W. argued, are often to be viewed as symbols, e.g. of what is terrible or awesome. The impressiveness of a (possibly residual, degenerate) ritual often does not lie in its highly conjectural past but in our recognition of its *possible* past and its relations to features of human history and characteristics, and our knowledge of ourselves.

Section 130

1   W. clarifies the purpose of his simple language-games. They are not a first step in a regimentation of language (i.e. in the design of an improved, more precise language), but rather objects for comparison to highlight specific features that we ordinarily fail to notice (§129).

It is striking that there are relatively few simple language-games in the *Investigations* (unlike the *Brown Book*), and they do not look like preliminary studies for a regimentation of language. Why is W. warning against such a temptation? The origins of this remark (see 2 below) suggest that this is perhaps a case of old wine which may have gone off. In his transitional phase, on his return to philosophy in 1929, W. indicated the construction of various fragmentary calculi, which he thought revealed the real logical forms underlying our natural languages (e.g. a phenomenological language, a language without personal pronouns, etc.). Subsequently he came to think that this was mistaken, and that these calculi, governed by rigorous rules, were merely models for comparison with ordinary language, the use of which was indefinitely fluid and fluctuating. So his model languages were not akin to Nicod's geometrical models (see below), i.e. they were not first approximations to natural language, nor were they preparatory for regimentation (cf. PI §81). Subsequently, the comparison of fragments of rigorous calculi with natural language disappears (and with it the conception of natural language as indefinitely fluid), to be replaced by the developed method of language-games (as exemplified in the *Brown Book*). Here in §130, it seems, W. issues a similar warning to the one in *The Big Typescript*: the clear and simple language-games are not first steps in building up a regimented (let alone 'ideal') language. But it is not evident, given the use of the language-game method in the *Investigations*, why anyone should think they are.

2   This occurs in MS 142, §133 (derived immediately from MS 157b, 17r–v, and mediately from BT 202r — so its roots are early). The preceding remark opened with PI §133(a): 'It is not our aim to refine or complete the system of rules for the use of our words in unheard-of ways.' This was followed by Z §440 (MS 115 (Vol. XI), 50), which reflects on the absence of any absolute conception of completeness of rules, and examines, by way of analogy, the regulation of traffic by rules and the senselessness of an ideal traffic ordering that tried to guide the totality of movements by prescription. Then comes the draft of PI §130, although with 'exact' instead of 'clear and simple' (altered only in TS 239, §145). After the first sentence, there is a different remark: 'This idea // conception // leads to distortions[60] (Nicod & Russell).' (This too was deleted only in TS 239.) Then follows the rest of the remark.

[60] 'Ungerechtigkeiten' — literally 'injustices'; Anscombe translated it as 'ineptness' in §131.

The reference to Nicod can be clarified (see 3). The moot question is what are the 'exact' language-games referred to.[61] For there is nothing especially *exact* about the language-games thus far introduced. It is, however, possible that some light is shed on the matter by the discussion of 'grammatical models' in PLP.

PLP 71–81 explains the 'method of grammatical models'. Waismann gives four examples. (i) In order to see what is right and what is wrong with the formalist claim (so contested by Frege) that arithmetic is a game with symbols, we should provide a model of a game with symbols to set beside arithmetic for purposes of comparison. (ii) In order to see what is right and what wrong about the claim that a material object is a collection of ideas, or that material object statements are analysable in terms of sense-data, we can construct a grammatical model. This would provide us with a precise formula for the derivation of the occlusion-shape of a certain material object from different distances and angles of view. Operating with these derivations in this simple and exact model can be compared with operating with our language. (iii) To examine the claim that ordinary observation-statements (such as 'There is a sphere') admit of definite verification, we can construct various systems of rules, some of which determine a conclusive verification, and others do not.[62] The former fix an equivalence-relation. The latter may lay down defeasibility conditions. But we may also introduce a model in which a material object statement simply refers to indefinitely many future observations. We can set these alternative, sharply determined models beside ordinary observation-sentences for comparison — our ordinary practices are, in some ways, similar to some of them, and in others to others. And there we let the matter rest — allowing the facts speak for themselves. (iv) If we are disquieted by the role of 'I'[63] in our language, we should invent a language in which it does not occur. In all these cases, Waismann concludes, we need not claim that such-and-such is the real meaning of a certain statement. We can avoid trying to force language into a pattern. Rather, we place our invented pattern beside language and let the one throw light on the other by way of similarities and differences. This method is similar to Boltzmann's method of describing a model for Maxwell's equations in the theory of electricity, without making any claim about its conformity with reality.[64]

---

[61] BT has here 'simple', with the reference to Nicod and Russell inserted in pen.

[62] One can see here the roots of Waismann's conception of verifiability, open texture and defeasibility that characterizes his later papers 'Verifiability' and 'Language Strata', in *Logic and Language*, ed. A. G. N. Flew, 1st and 2nd ser. (Blackwell, Oxford, 1951 and 1953). The view there defended is far removed from W.'s mature thought, and is influenced by W.'s 1929/30 conception of a hypothesis and his idea that empirical propositions are hypotheses that do not admit of conclusive verification. W. later abandoned this.

[63] Waismann has here 'the Ego'. It is plausible to associate these remarks with the invented language of PR ch. VI and the language of the oriental despot in WWK 49f.

[64] See W.'s remark on Boltzmann cited in Exg. §131, 2.1(ii).

There are two particularly striking features to this discussion. The first is that in some of these cases W. himself had once held the envisaged calculus to be the underlying depth grammar of ordinary language. Indeed, it is patent that Waismann's discussion is in part based on an antecedent of what is now published as Appendix 4B of the *Grammar*:

Formerly, I myself spoke of a 'complete analysis', and I used to believe that philosophy had to give a definitive dissection of propositions so as to set out clearly all their connections and remove all possibilities of misunderstanding. I spoke as if there was a calculus in which such a dissection would be possible. I vaguely had in mind something like the definition that Russell had given for the definite article, and I used to think that in a similar way one would be able to use visual impressions etc. to define the concept say of a sphere,[65] and thus exhibit once for all misunderstandings, etc. At the root of all this there was a false and idealized picture of the use of language. Of course, in particular cases one can clarify by definitions the connections between the different types of use of expressions. Such a definition may be useful in the case of the connection between 'visual impression' and 'sphere'. But for this purpose it is not a definition of the concept of a physical sphere that we need; instead we must describe a language-game related to our own, or rather a whole series of related language-games, and it will be in these that such definitions may occur. Such a contrast destroys grammatical prejudices and makes it possible for us to see the use of a word as it really is, instead of *inventing* the use for the word. (PG 211f.)

In his brief verificationist phase, W. had argued that primary statements of immediate experience are conclusively verifiable, and that material object statements are 'hypotheses' that do not admit of conclusive verification. And he had held that 'The word "I" belongs to those words that can be eliminated from language' (WWK 49), and that its elimination would 'show clearly what was logically essential in the representation' (PR 88). But he came to reject these views, and, initially at least, to think that such calculi as he had envisaged had a legitimate role in philosophy, not as revelations of depth grammar and logical form, but rather as objects of comparison. By juxtaposing such calculi governed by strict rules with a certain fragment of natural language, one will see clearly those features that are relevant to disentangling philosophical confusions. As he remarked in the *Blue Book*:

remember that in general we don't use language according to strict rules — it hasn't been taught us by strict rules, either. *We*, in our discussions, constantly compare language with a calculus proceeding according to exact rules.

This is a very one-sided way of looking at language. In practice we very rarely use language as such a calculus. . . . To suppose that there *must* be [strict rules and definitions] would be like supposing that whenever children play with a ball they play a game according to strict rules.

---

[65] Waismann uses the same example in his discussion of complete and incomplete verification.

. . . Why then do we in philosophizing constantly compare our use of words with one following exact rules? The answer is that the puzzles which we try to remove always spring from just this attitude towards language. (BB 25f.)

Again, it is striking that in the *Blue Book* W. did *not* systematically compare our uses of words with strict calculi at all. But many of the puzzles W. was trying to remove (many of his own puzzles when he wrote the *Tractatus*) did indeed stem from viewing language as having the deep structure of a calculus of logic.

Secondly, this method of juxtaposing strict calculi with ordinary language rapidly disappears from sight, and is replaced by the method of simple language-games (as exemplified paradigmatically in *The Brown Book*).

What is noteworthy with respect to present concerns is that in the *Investigations* there are no 'strict language-games' or 'calculi' in the sense Waismann is talking about. There are rather 'clear and simple language-games'. Evidently W. was still apprehensive that the language-game method might be seen as a device for gradually building up a full-scale model of, or indeed a regimentation of, natural language — hence the warning. However, unlike the *Brown Book*, where this warning might have been apt, it is not at all obvious, given the few language-games in the *Investigations* and their relatively unsystematic sequence, that this warning is really necessary.

2.1   'Not preliminary studies': BB 28 has 'Whenever we make up "ideal languages" it is not in order to replace our ordinary language by them; but just to remove some trouble caused in someone's mind by thinking that he has got hold of the exact use of a common word. That is also why our method is not merely to enumerate actual usages of words, but rather deliberately to invent new ones, some of them because of their absurd appearance.'

3   The conception of simplified, exact language-games that MS 142 discusses informs Nicod's methodology in *Geometry in the Sensible World*. Nicod's aim was to discover the formal structure of geometry 'in the book of nature'. Since this task is too great to be accomplished with a single effort, he recommends starting with the analysis of a simplified type of experience whose geometrical laws can be apprehended at a glance. This procedure mimics that of physical science. The physicist does not launch into the ocean of reality without the support of a lifebelt of the most utopian fictions of simplicity, and as he progresses in skill, he casts off these fictions one by one, and so his analysis gradually comes to approximate to nature more and more closely. This scientific method, paradoxically, is necessary for systematic, rigorous thought, for schematization facilitates the thorough examination of the objective consequences of hypotheses. The invention of simplified sensible geometries is parallel to studying the mechanics of point masses or the optics of light rays. Nicod is

content to outline this method and to mark out the beginning of the road which descends from schematic abstractions towards reality.[66]

SECTION 131

1   Viewing simplified language-games as no more than objects of comparison will ensure that we do not distort our account of the actual linguistic practices on which we wish to shed light. This remark, like the previous one, does not appear well adapted to its surroundings. The 'model' referred to seems to be a clear and simple language-game — it is this that is an 'object of comparison'. But it is not clear in what respect such language-games as (2), (8), (48) or (86) tempt us into thinking that language (or the world) *must* be thus-and-so. (Again, it may be that W. is thinking here of the exact language-games he had *earlier* envisaged (discussed in PLP, see Exg. §130, 2).)

If, however, we present a model as an ideal to which reality (the reality of our languages) *must* correspond (otherwise our propositions, those strange and unique entities (PI §§93f.), would not be able to do the remarkable thing they do), then we fall into dogmatism. What is the dogmatism? It is the insistence that things *must* be thus (even though they are not) — and we insist that although they are not so *on the surface*, they *must* be so on analysis (even though we cannot produce such a final analysis). And so we project into the supposed depth grammar features of forms of representing things that appeal to us (e.g. that every proposition has the form 'This is how things stand', that simple names have the form of '*this*', or that vague propositions are disjunctions of ones the sense of which is determinate) and think we *see* things with such forms 'as if from afar'.

1.1   (i)   'Ungerechtigkeit': unfairness or distortion — for the ordinary concepts of name, proposition, etc. were distorted by the misconceptions about names and propositions, about thinking, meaning and understanding, and about the role of the calculus of logic.

(ii)   'emptiness': like the claim that every proposition (no matter how vague) has a determinate sense (see Exg. §98, 2.1(ii)).

(iii)   'model': MS 157b, 16r, has 'ideal' here, referring to misconceptions about the role of 'the ideal', e.g. of arithmetic or geometry, or the calculus of logic, as a form (and sometimes norm) of representation, and to the spell of the ideal when projected on to language, as in the *Tractatus*. W. changed this to 'Vorbild' ('model') in MS 142, §122(d), although there it is still patently a discussion of how to free ourselves from this spell. Here, however, the remark has been stripped of these connections, and seemingly refers only to the role of the simple language-games referred to in the preceding remark.

[66]   His methodological remarks are concentrated in J. Nicod, *Foundations of Geometry and Induction*, tr. P. P. Wiener (Kegan Paul, Trench, Trubner, London, 1930), pp. 90–4, 189–92.

2.1   (i)   'as an object of comparison': AWL 99 comments

> Games or languages which we make up with stated rules one might call ideal languages, but this is a bad description since they are not ideal in the sense of being 'better'. They serve one purpose, to make comparisons. They can be put beside actual languages so as to enable us to see certain features in them and by this means to get rid of certain difficulties. Suppose I make up a language in which 'is' has two meanings.[67] Is it better? Not from the practical point of view. No ordinary person mixes up the meaning of 'is' in 'The rose is red' and '2 + 2 = 4'. It is ideal in the sense of having simply statable rules. Its only point is to get rid of certain obsessions . . .

The example is striking, since the simple language-games of the *Investigations* are very unlike an invented language in which two different signs do the service of 'is'.

(ii)   'dogmatism': In the early versions, W. added, after '*must* correspond': '(I am thinking here of Spengler's approach)'. In MS 157b, 16r–v, he added a further paragraph criticizing Spengler for the distortions consequent on his failure to realize that 'the ideal' (his conception of the life-cycles of cultures) loses none of its dignity if it is presented as the formal principle of the inquiry (*Betrachtungsform*). This criticism is elaborated in MS 111 (Vol. VII), 119f. (cf. MS 115 (Vol. XI), 56). Spengler would be better understood if he is seen as proposing an illuminating form of description. The dogmatism one is prone to fall into is to take characteristic features of the form of description, project them on to the object described, and then dogmatically to assert that things *must* be thus.[68] What he is here saying, W. remarks, is actually what Boltzmann said about the status of mechanical models in the theory of electricity (see PLP 77; Exg. §130, 2). For further discussion, see Volume 1, Part I, pp. 297f., 322f.

SECTION 132

1   §§130–1 concerned method. W. now shifts to purpose. We are competent language-users, and so know how to use words correctly. So it is not new knowledge that we aim at. (One might say that it is a certain kind of understanding; or that it is the kind of knowledge constituted by *realization* rather than given by new information.) What is the particular purpose (already mentioned in §127) aimed at? It is to break the spell by which we are bound by certain linguistic forms (MS 142, §131). What is the 'order' that we want to establish? It is an order that will make this possible. So it is an appropriate

---

[67]   One might suspect that W. said that instead of 'is' we had two different *signs*, viz. '=' and '∈', each with a different meaning.

[68]   So, presumably what is objectionable is the judgement that European civilization *must* decline (since it has reached 'old age').

arrangement of *grammatical* evidence (cf. MS 153b, 36r), obtained by assembling or marshalling familiar grammatical propositions (§109), grouped in such a way that we can obtain an overview that will dissolve the problem.

The order or arrangement is said to be one out of many possible orders. Does W. mean that there are many different ways, in any given case, of ordering the grammatical facts so as to dissolve the philosophical puzzlement in question? Or does he mean that the philosophical order that we seek is one order among others — so different, for example, from the grammarian's or comparative linguist's?

It is clear that he held the grammarian's (philologist's) order to be different from the philosopher's (BT 413). The end the grammarian has in view is altogether different from that of the philosopher.

It is evident (see 2.1(ii)) that the contrast he has in mind is between a 'super-order' (the depth grammar of every possible language) postulated by the *Tractatus* and the arrangement of grammatical facts that gives an overview. This does not, however, resolve the question of whether he envisaged many different, equally licit, *philosophical* orderings for a given problem.

Various remarks suggest that he did not have in mind radically different ways of ordering the same grammatical data. MS 120, 143v, queries what a philosopher's 'seeing' something consists in. It is that 'the right grammatical facts occur to him, the right picture, that is the picture that will order the things in our mind, make them easily accessible, and thereby relieves the mind'. MS 117 (Vol. XIII), 220f., gives examples of *not* knowing how to order one's concepts: e.g. not knowing whether to count proofs among experiments, mathematics among games, contradictions among confusions, whether to say that there is only a difference of degree between experimental and mathematical truths, whether a new proof gives a sentence a new sense. This is 'not knowing one's way around' — and when called upon to describe the techniques of the uses of words, of mathematical propositions, of proofs, one cannot survey them. This list (and W.'s resolutions of these difficulties elsewhere) suggest that finding an order is finding the *right* order for purposes of conceptual clarification.[69] So proofs should *not* be counted among experiments; the difference between factual and mathematical propositions is *not* a difference of degree; etc. Of course, different grammatical data will be relevant to different philosophical perplexities and confusions.

The concluding remark that the relevant confusions arise only when language is idling ('on holiday', MS 142, §131) is controversial. Worries about solipsism, idealism and realism, about Cartesian scepticism, etc. arise when language is idling. The solipsist, who insists that only his present experience is real, does not really think that his wife's pain is not real, and when she is in pain, he *does* call the doctor. The sceptic who denies that we can really know

---

[69]   This does not mean that there is *always* only *one* right order, for in some cases there may be an option that can be decided, if at all, only relative to a specific context and purpose.

anything beyond current subjective appearances *will* inform his guest that lunch is at 1.00 o'clock. But it is by no means obvious that conceptual confusions in psychology or neuroscience (such as the confusions involved in the supposition that visual recognition involves rotating mental images in mental space at constant velocity) occur when language is idling. Explanations of empirical phenomena are offered on the basis of this supposition, and experiments are conducted to discover the 'psychophysics' of mental images. Similarly, the confusions over the meaning of 'shock', with which W. was concerned in his work on wound shock during the war, did not arise when language was on holiday, but when it was hard at work.

1.1   (i)   'for a particular purpose' — as in §127.

(ii)   'language is . . . idling': cf. §271; this mechanical metaphor occurs in Hertz, *Principles of Mechanics*.

2.1   (i)   'an order': BT 421 has 'A philosophical problem is an awareness of disorder in our concepts, and can be solved by ordering them.' BT 415 gave a revealing analogy: a philosophical question is comparable to one about the constitution governing the meetings of a certain society. There are rules, but there is no arrangement for rendering the rules clear. 'Therefore we come along and create a clear order: we seat the president in a clearly identifiable spot, seat his secretary next to him at a little table of his own, and seat the other full members in two rows on both sides of the table, etc., etc.' This does not suggest a different arrangement for each meeting of the society.

(ii)   '. . . nicht *die* Ordnung': MS 142, §131, has '(Keine *Ueber*-Ordnung)' ('(Not a *super*-order)'), alluding presumably to the *Tractatus* conception of the hidden, ultimate order of language.

Section 133

1   This concludes the discussion of philosophy. It repudiates the conception of philosophy as the quest for the ideal ordering or regimentation of language. The clarity aimed at is indeed complete clarity, but that does not consist in a 'final analysis' of propositions of our language. Rather, it is attained when the problems are dissolved — by the various methods W. advocates.

The first sentence of (c) is obscure. Given that the 'real discovery' is the one that will legitimize philosophy, give it 'peace', i.e. enable us to cease calling it into question, why should this 'enable me to break off philosophizing when I want to'? This is a metaphor, clarified by the next sentence.[70] As long as

---

[70]   In conversation with Rhees, W. admitted that *he* could not stop (see R. Rhees, 'On Wittgenstein', *Philosophical Investigations* 24 (2001), p. 158), but this was transforming a metaphor into a literalism.

philosophy is tormented by questions that bring *itself* in question, the philosopher cannot 'stop doing philosophy when he wants', for the subject is under constant threat, his results may be called into question, the structure he has erected may collapse — so nothing solid is achieved, nothing can be 'put in the archives'.

Why is philosophy constantly called into question, and what discovery puts an end to these qualms? If the enterprise of philosophy is wrongly conceived, then both the activity and its outcome will be under constant challenge. This is a recurrent feature of the history of philosophy, especially of the various forms of foundationalism within philosophy. If the task of philosophy is thought to be the invention of an ideally complete and determinate language, the project may be undermined by revealing the logical incoherence of this ideal. Metaphysicians aim to reveal the ultimate nature of reality. But that project is undermined if this goal is chimerical — if what seems to be the essential, metaphysical structure of the world is no more than a shadow of grammar (or the recommendation of an alternative grammar, duly projected on to reality). Kant's philosophy was dedicated to explaining how knowledge of synthetic a priori propositions is possible (i.e. non-analytic propositions that are nevertheless necessary *and* hold true of reality). But if there are no such propositions, then his enterprise collapses. Epistemologists conceived of their subject as a search for the incorrigible foundations of empirical knowledge. This enterprise, too, is undermined — by arguments showing that the supposition that knowledge has incorrigible foundations is incoherent. The challenge may apply to the results of philosophy no less than to the general enterprise, if the results are conceived as uniquely philosophical propositions, e.g. proofs of the existence of God or the external world. Philosophy, thus conceived, constantly torments itself by questioning its own legitimacy. Both its presuppositions and its putatively cognitive results can be called into question. It is given peace only by 'the real discovery' of grasping the true nature of the philosophical enterprise, viz. the resolution of philosophical problems by methods which will yield, not philosophical knowledge, but an overview of the relevant segment of grammar that dissolves the problems. The result is not new knowledge, but a new understanding.

Why should the real 'discovery', i.e. insight into the nature of philosophical enquiry and the methodology appropriate to it, enable one to stop doing philosophy when one wants to? Precisely because one's results, i.e. surveyable representations of a segment of grammar that dissolve problems at hand, are no longer vulnerable to such undermining. Why so? Because there are no presuppositions comparable to the foundationalist ones of traditional philosophy (and of the *Tractatus*) that can be challenged. So we may investigate this or that example of a philosophical problem, and in resolving it, we demonstrate W.'s method. And we can break off when we please without the anxiety that no problem can be solved until all problems are solved and the presuppositions shown to be flawless.

2   MS 142, §134, follows the draft of PI §133(b)–(c) with Z §447, which amplifies the idea of disquietude in philosophy. Such disquietude arises from looking at philosophy wrongly, as if it has to grasp once and for all an infinite longitudinal strip (the perennial essence of language and the world). But in fact its task is that of describing finite latitudinal strips (a surveyable representation of a segment of the grammar of our present language, where it is causing us difficulties), a task which has no end, but each part of which can be achieved, piecemeal. Thus, 'problems are solved (difficulties eliminated), not a single problem'.

2.1   '. . . in unheard of ways': MS 115 (Vol. XI), 53, continues here: 'Calm in philosophy is produced when the redeeming word (*das erlösende Wort*) is found.' The conception of the redeeming or liberating word was important for W. It occurs frequently in his early notebooks (e.g. NB 54), is in the letter to von Ficker of 24 July 1915, and recurs in later writings. Philosophical bewilderment and disquiet are laid to rest only when the redeeming word is found (MS 110 (Vol. VI), 17; cf. MS 115, 66; MS 124, 218; MS 142, §121; etc.).

Boxed Remark Following §133

1.1   In the first three editions this occurred as §133(d)

(i) 'not a *single* problem': in contrast with the spirit of W.'s early work, e.g. 'My whole task consists in explaining the nature of the proposition. That is to say, in giving the nature of all facts, whose picture the proposition is' (NB 39).

(ii) 'Instead': Instead of trying to resolve one great problem (the essence of the proposition, the nature of the synthetic a priori, the foundations of knowledge) which will solve all problems, we tackle each philosophical problem as it arises and as it attracts our attention.

(iii) 'There is not a philosophical method . . .': this stands in superficial contrast with the remark in the 1930–3 lectures that *a* 'new method' has been found (M 322). For discussion of the various methods employed, see 'Philosophy', sect. 5.

(iv) 'different therapies': see §255; for discussion of the therapeutic analogy, see 'Philosophy', sect. 3.

Chapter 5

The general propositional form
(§§134–42)

INTRODUCTION

§§134–42 are not sharply separated from their antecedents and sequel. They both round off the discussion of the topics introduced in §§65ff. and introduce the examination of the nature of understanding which is the theme of §§143ff. §§134–6 are concerned with the subject of the general propositional form, which, in the early drafts, was more prominently interwoven with the reflections on the errors of the *Tractatus* and its preconceptions (§§89–108) and with the methodological remarks (§§b.r.f. 108–33) than it is in the final one. The *Tractatus* conception of the general propositional form expressed by the sentence 'Es verhält sich so und so' was misguided, obscuring the real role of such sentences, which is for anaphoric reference to something asserted. There is no such thing as 'the general propositional form' signifying common properties of all propositions, since the concept of a proposition is a family-resemblance concept. Of course, 'Es verhält sich . . .' indicates that we call 'a proposition' whatever is an argument of truth-functions in our language. But the concepts of truth and falsehood cannot be used to determine what is and what is not a proposition — they *belong to* but do not *fit* the concept of a proposition (similarly, the concept of checkmate *belongs* to the chess king, but does not *fit* it — whereas one cogwheel may *fit* another).

§§137–42 discuss objections to this conclusion which turn on an underlying picture of a 'meaning-body' (characteristic of the Augustinian conception) according to which grammar is determined by the entity that is correlated with an expression as its meaning. So the combinatorial possibilities of expressions in grammar merely reflect the fact that the underlying meanings fit. §138 raises a fresh puzzle: the meaning-body conception suggests that if one understands a sentence, then the meaning of a word in it fits the meaning of the sentence. But if the meaning of a word is its *use*, then it makes no sense to speak of such *fitting*. On the other hand, we understand the meaning of a word at a stroke. But if the meaning is the use, how can that be? For the use of a word seems to unfold only in successive applications over time, hence it is not something that can come before the mind at a stroke. So how is the thought that one can grasp the meaning of a word at a stroke be reconciled with the grammatical proposition that the meaning of a word is its use? What does come before one's mind in a flash when one understands? It cannot be a way of using a word. Can't it be a picture (as linguistic idealists supposed) — a mental image?

§§139–42 elaborate: a picture *might* come before our minds when we understand a word. But no picture *compels* any given use. Whether it *fits* a given use depends on the method of projection. A picture *suggests* a natural or normal method of projection, but is compatible with many possible ones. It is mistaken to suppose that a picture forces an application upon one. It is not *logically* compelling — indeed, there is no such thing, and to say that it is psychologically compelling is misleading. Even if the picture contains the schema of the method of application, a schema of an application is still just a picture containing lines of projection, and may itself be variously applied (cf. §86). §142 concludes with emphasis on the importance of normality conditions for the functioning and point of our language-games.

The structure of §§134–42.

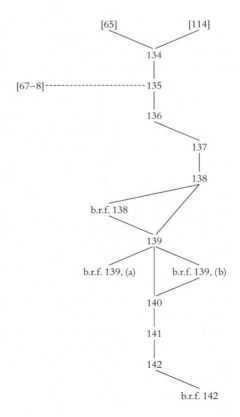

Sources

The numerical entries for MS 142 and TS 220 are Wittgenstein's. They are *in fact* miscounts by two.

PI§	MS 142§[1]	TS 220§[1]	TS 239§	Others
134	135	117	149	153a, 105v–107; 114 Um., 110f.
135	136	118	150	153a, 106r–108r; 114 Um., 99
136	137	119	151	PG 123f.; VoW 491–3
137	138	120	152	
138	139	121	153	
b.r.f. 138				116, 93; B i §82
139	140	122	154	
b.r.f. 139, (a)				129, 198f.; B i §363
b.r.f. 139, (b)				129, 175; B i §335
140	141	123	155	
141	142	124	156f.	PG 213
142			158	
b.r.f. 142				129, 194; B i §357

Truth and the general propositional form
1. The demands of the picture theory
2. 'That's the way the cookie crumbles'
3. '. . . do we have a *single* concept of proposition?' (PG 112)
4. '. . . the use of the words "true" and "false" . . . *belongs* to our concept "proposition" but does not "fit" it . . .' (PI §136)
5. Truth, correspondence and multi-valued logic

EXEGESIS §§134–42

SECTION 134

1   W. now reverts to the subject of the general propositional form, which he raised in §65. The determination of the general propositional form had been thought to provide an answer to the question of the essence of language; but the ensuing discussion (§§65–88) was designed to show that the concept of language is a family-resemblance concept, and has no essence constituted by common properties. §§89–108 illuminated the pressures and preconceptions that had driven W. to sublimate the ordinary concept of a proposition. 'What we call "proposition (*Satz*)" and "language" has not the formal unity' that he had once imagined, 'but is a family of structures more or less related to one another' (§108). §114 explicitly referred to the *Tractatus* 4.5, pointing out that the conception of the general propositional form there articulated was a form that he had *imposed* upon the presentation of propositions, not something he had *discovered* to be common to all propositions. Now, after a long detour encompassing a survey of the metaphysical temptations to which he had succumbed and a methodological excursus, he returns at last to probe further the illusion. How could he have thought that 'This is how things are' (*Es verhält sich so und so*) is the general form of a proposition?

It is itself a well-formed English sentence. Far from merely indicating what is common to all propositions, it has a distinctive use itself. So, how is it used in the language-game in which it is at home (cf. §116)? It is employed as a propositional schema to allude to some other statement. Other similar sentences, e.g. 'Such-and-such is the case' or 'Things are thus-and-so' (*so und so liegen die Sachen*) could do the same job. One might even imagine using a propositional variable '*p*' as in formal logic, but it would be absurd to say that the letter '*p*' is or expresses the general form of propositions — the common characteristic marks of everything we call 'a proposition'. 'This is how things are' is a sentence, which is indeed used only as a propositional schema *to refer to something already said*. It is not the expression of a form, without any genuine use at all (see 'Truth and the general propositional form', sect. 2). Furthermore, an important feature of many propositions — indeed a feature that the *Tractatus* had taken to be of the essence of all propositions with a sense — is that they agree (or disagree with reality). But it would obviously be nonsense to say that the proposition 'This is how things are' either agrees or disagrees with reality, since by itself it says nothing at all — it merely alludes to something already said by other propositions. But it *is* a proposition, for all that — which, W. remarks ironically, just illustrates the fact that *one* characteristic mark of our concept of a proposition (*Satz*, sentence) is that it has a propositional jingle (*Satzklang*, sentential jingle).

1.1   (i)   'Es verhält sich so und so', 'das und das ist der Fall', 'So und so liegen die Sachen': it is important to note the essential complexity of 'so und so' or 'das und das' which is, I suspect, meant also to capture the (erroneous) thought that the proposition is essentially complex, a combination of names depicting the concatenation of objects in a state of affairs (cf. PI §95). The thought that the proposition is essentially complex is common to the Aristotelian tradition of subject/predicate logic, to Frege's new function–theoretic logic and its Russellian variant, and to the *Tractatus*.

     (ii)   'To say that it agrees (or does not agree) with reality would be obvious nonsense': the role of 'Things are thus-and-so' is not to say something which agrees or disagrees with reality, but to allude anaphorically or cataphorically to something of which it can typically be said that *it* agrees or disagrees with reality.

2   (i)   MS 142, §135, opens with an explicit back–reference: 'Let us revert to the proposition: "Every proposition says: this is how things stand." ' W. remarks that one could imagine using a commonplace sentence, e.g. 'The sky is blue', as such a propositional variable: 'He described his financial situation, said that the sky is blue and asked for an advance.' But no one would say that 'The sky is blue' is the general form of propositions.

     If something sounds like a proposition, then we generally take it to be one (often wrongly, especially in philosophy). It would never have occurred to him, W. remarks, to take 'It so' (*Es so*) as an expression of the general propositional form, since it doesn't even sound like a proposition, but in a language without a copula (like Russian) it might be perfectly natural to do so.

     (ii)   MS 114 (Vol. X), 110f., notes that not everything that has an appropriate propositional jingle is actually a proposition (cf. MS 153a, 105v–107); and, conversely, we can readily imagine forms of words that lack such a propositional jingle, e.g. 'Sugar good', nevertheless expressing a proposition. So the moot question is whether, apart from this misleading propositional jingle, we have any general conception of a proposition at all.

     On p. 114, W. queries whether one can give the general form of a proposition. Why not? — he replies — as one can give the general form of a number by means of the sign '$[0, \xi, \xi + 1]$'. One is free to call only this 'number', and one can stipulate something similar for 'proposition'. (Of course, if one does so, one circumscribes something that by its nature is uncircumscribed.)

     On p. 115 he notes that in the schema 'Things stand thus-and-so', the 'things stand' ('Es verhält sich') is the point of contact of the truth-functions. It is an expression from the notation of the truth-functions, which shows what part of grammar enters into the function here. A general propositional form determines the proposition as a link in a calculation.

SECTION 135

1   §134, at first sight, appears to be denying that we have any general concept of a proposition at all — but what it denies is only that we have any
conception of common properties of everything that we call 'a proposition'.
Nevertheless, we *do* have a general concept of a proposition — as we have a
general concept of a game, or of a number (cf. §§67f.). The concept we have
is properly explained not by specification of characteristic marks, but by examples together with a similarity rider. For it is a family-resemblance concept.

2   (i)   MS 114 (Vol. X), 99–102, queries rhetorically whether the answer to
the question 'What is a proposition?' is meant to distinguish a proposition from
other elements within its grammatical system or from everything that we do
not call 'a proposition', including this chair, this watch, etc. (cf. MS 153a, 106r).
If someone asks 'How is the general concept of a proposition bounded?', one
must respond 'Do we have a single general concept of a proposition?' To this
they might reply that one surely has a particular concept of what one calls 'a
proposition'. To which the response is: how would one explain it to oneself
or to another? For what the concept is will be shown in this explanation.
One would explain it by examples. In which case the concept reaches just
as far as the examples. We can *give* our concept sharp boundaries, but it is
not actually sharply circumscribed. Furthermore, we can extend our concept
by admitting new elements — but this is done by analogy with existing
structures.

SECTION 136

1   The *Tractatus* claim that 'Es verhält sich so und so' encapsulates the general
form of the proposition really amounts to no more than that the proposition
is whatever can be true or false. Why so? Because instead of 'This is how
things stand' ('*Es verhält sich . . .*') one can just as well say 'This is true'. In
both cases there is an affirmatory reference to something already asserted (or
about to be asserted). And 'This is *not* how things stand' fulfils much the same
function as 'This is false'. So too, to assert ' "*p*" is true' serves merely to reaffirm
'*p*' and to assert ' "*p*" is false' is to deny '*p*' and is equivalent to asserting 'not-
p'. In short, to say that the general propositional form is 'Es verhält sich
so und so' is just to say that we call something 'a proposition' when *in our
language* we apply the calculus of truth-functions to it — it is what we negate,
what we conjoin by conjunction, disjunction and conditional.

      §136(b) moves quickly to block a misunderstanding. It may seem that one
has defined 'proposition' in terms of common properties: as if we could determine whether something is a proposition by reference to whether it can be
said to be true or false. This would mean that we had a concept of true and

false that can be grasped independently of the concept of a proposition, which we could use to determine whether something is a proposition, as we can use the concepts of *man* and *unmarried* to determine whether someone is a bachelor. But this is mistaken.

§136(c) clarifies why in terms of an analogy. We can say that the king in chess is the piece that one can check, but it is not as if we can determine which piece is the king by reference to this information. If we understand what it is to check a piece, then we already know what a chess king is, and vice versa. For being the piece that is checked is constitutive of being the chess king (it *belongs* to the concept; it does not *fit* it). So too, the concepts of truth and falsehood cannot be grasped independently of the concept of a proposition, and so cannot be used to determine whether something is or is not a proposition. The pertinent conclusion is summarized: what a proposition is, is in one sense determined syntactically (but not everything that sounds like a proposition is one (§134)), and in another sense by the use of the sign. We use the sign 'p' to affirm and the sign 'Not-p' to deny that something is so — hence the connection with truth and falsehood. But being true or being false cannot be represented as common properties *in virtue of which* something is a proposition. Being true and being false are not *criteria* for being a proposition (AWL 140).

1.1   (i) ' "p" is true $= p$': W. always cleaved to this formula (NB 9, cf. 94, 113). So, early and late, he insisted that ' "p" is true' says no more than the unvarnished 'p' (NB 9; MS 154, 31r; PLP 27–34). Similarly, already in his early work he invoked the formula commonly associated with Ramsey and subsequent deflationary theorists of truth: 'a proposition is then true when it is as we assert in this proposition' (NB 97), and 'a proposition is true if things are as we, by using it, say they are' (TLP 4.062, modified translation). Whether that is consistent with cleaving to the Correspondence Theory of Truth that is commonly ascribed to TLP is debatable (for discussion, see 'Truth and the general propositional form', sects 4–5).

The formula ' "p" is true $= p$' is unhappy. First of all, it is not the sign 'p' or the *sentence* 'p' that can be said to be true or false, but what is said by its use. W. himself had noticed this:

So is it correct to write ' "p" is true', ' "p" is false'; mustn't it be 'p is true' (or false)? The ink mark is after all not *true*; in the way in which it's black and curved. . . . (PG 123)

The proposition ' "p" is true' can only be understood if one understands the grammar of the sign 'p' as a propositional sign; not if 'p' is simply the name of a shape of a particular ink mark. In the end one can say that the quotation marks in the sentence ' "p" is true' are simply superfluous. (PG 124)

It is not just that the quotation marks are superfluous, they are mistaken. Secondly, the formula 'p is true' is also ungrammatical. The predicate '. . . is true'

demands a nominal — as in 'That p is true'. And so does the truth-operator
— as in 'It is true that p'.

(ii) 'apply the calculus of truth-functions to it': W. disregards here the extent
to which the use of the logical operators in the *calculus* of logic deviates from
the use of 'and', 'or' and 'if . . . then . . .' in natural language. For present purposes, that does not matter, since it is true that whatever we deem a proposition is also something we can operate on with the logical operators.

Whatever we call 'propositions' can indeed be conjoined by the connectives. This in no way affects the claim that the concept of a proposition is a
family-resemblance one. We conjoin with these particles propositions of such
diverse kinds as empirical propositions (in all their variety, including propositions of the world picture, avowals of experience, hypotheses, etc.), propositions of arithmetic and geometry, logical propositions, ethical and aesthetic
propositions, grammatical propositions, etc. that are members of the family.

However, we conjoin items that are not propositions by these connectives
— for example, imperatives ('Shut the door and open the window', 'Either
open the door or open the window', etc.) and interrogatives. On the other
hand, we do not ascribe truth and falsehood to these.

2   (i) MS 153a, 107v, remarks that one would like to say that a proposition
is anything with which one can mean something. But to explain what it is to
mean something, one would have to give examples. These are appropriate in
their own domain, but do not lend themselves to generalization.

(ii) PG 123 (MS 114 (Vol. X), 112) remarks in this context that 'A proposition is everything that can be true or false' means the same as 'a proposition is whatever can be negated'. After the two formulae 'p is true = p' and
'p is false = not-p', W. shows how to extend the account to truth-ascriptions
in which the proposition is not specified, as in 'Everything the Pope says is
true'. Instead of saying 'Whatever he says is true', W. points out, we can just
as well say 'Things are as he says'. BT 76 had similarly noted that 'What he
says is true' says the same as 'He says "p"' and p is the case'.

PG 124 (MS 114 Um., 114) denies that one can combine words with
'. . . is true (false)' by way of experiment to discover whether they constitute
a proposition. One could do that only if 'true' and 'false' had definite meanings independently of these test contexts. But for these words to have definite
meanings is for the possible contexts of their significant occurrence to be already
determined. So there is no possibility of 'experiment' (for detailed discussion,
see AWL 141).

(iii) In VoW 491, in a dictation entitled 'Truth', W. objects to the idea that
an answer to the question 'What is truth?' will inform us about the relationship between thought and reality. Indeed, the answer, 'truth is the agreement
of thought with its object', looks as if it is doing just that, for does it not tell
us that the proposition that p is true if the state of affairs that is meant obtains?
But it is an illusion that this is an expression of a metalogical insight. For all

it says is that the proposition that it will rain tomorrow, for example, is true if and only if it will rain tomorrow — i.e. the expression 'the state of affairs that is meant by p'[1] can be replaced by 'p'. To the question 'When is p true?', one can variously reply: if it is the case that p, if the state of affairs meant by p obtains, if the proposition agrees with reality, if things are as it says they are, if what it says is a fact, etc. Specifying this network of intersubstitutable expressions *is* the explanation of truth. It is a grammatical description (not a revelation about the relationship between thought and reality). 'The words "true", "agreement", etc. are only words within a specific calculus of language, like "yes" and "no", not words that set up a connection between this calculus and something else' (VoW 493). They are not, as he remarked elsewhere, metalogical (MS 113 (Vol. IX), 49v; MS 115 (Vol. XI), 85).

(iv)   PLP 372f. covers the same ground as PI §136, comparing the relation of the proposition to truth and falsehood with the relation of the chess king to checkmate. The error to be avoided is to think that saying that a proposition must be either true or false is a description of the essence of the proposition *to which the rules for the use of the word 'proposition' must conform*. This is as mistaken as the thought that the chess pieces must obey the rules of chess. The chess pieces are *defined* by the rules of chess.

2.1   'fitting' and 'belonging': for detailed discussion of this not very helpful simile, see AWL 144–6.

Section 137

1   This rebuts an objection to the conclusion that 'true' and 'false' do not *fit* but *belong* to the concept of a proposition. The previous section intimated (and PG 124 asserted) that one cannot combine words with '. . . is true' or '. . . is false' by way of experiment to see whether those words constitute (express) a proposition. The objection is that we teach children how to determine the subject of a sentence by asking 'Who or what?', exploiting the idea that the subject term *fits* the question. So surely we can determine whether a string of words expresses a proposition by asking ourselves whether we can say '. . . is true' after it, or '*This* is how things are . . .' before it.

The riposte is that in *this* sense of 'fit', the words 'true' and 'false' do fit propositions. But this is not the requisite sense. We 'find out' which letter of the alphabet succeeds 'K' by repeating the alphabet up to 'K' to ourselves, and we 'find ourselves' saying 'L' after 'K'. 'L' fits 'K' only in the sense that we have been trained to rehearse the alphabet in the order 'A, B, C . . . J, K, L . . .'. We don't *discover* the fit, as we discover that one cogwheel fits another (the metaphor of machinery and that of fitting belong together), we *remind* ourselves

1   The quotation marks around 'p' are missing, perhaps because this was a dictation.

of the predetermined series. Determining the subject of a sentence by the question 'Who or what . . . ?' is a move in syntax in which we remind ourselves of the form of the nominative case.

SECTION 138

1   This remark provides the transition from the discussion of the general propositional form to the discussion of instantaneous understanding and the relationships between meaning, understanding and use. W. picks up the notion of 'fitting' from §§136f. and raises the question of whether the meaning of a word does not fit the sense of a sentence which one understands. By implication, that one does not understand nonsensical sentences (word sequences that look like sentences but make no sense) is to be explained by reference to the fact that the meanings of the words in a nonsense sequence do *not* 'fit' each other. If this is intelligible, then the meaning of one word may fit the meaning of another, which is the case when the words can be combined. significantly. For example, one might think that colour-words have a meaning that fits the meanings of names of objects that are extended, but does not fit names of sounds or tastes — which is why 'black cat' makes sense and 'black twang' or 'reddish-salty' do not.

This picture of meanings fitting or failing to fit each other can reasonably be associated with the Augustinian conception of meaning. For if meanings are conceived to be entities correlated with words, it will be plausible to think that the meanings of some words fit together with the meanings of others, and that these fittings are reflected in grammar, in the rules for the use of words, and hence too in the rules of sentence-formation. This conception, W. noted, informs Frege's philosophy of language and mathematics (PG 40; BB 4; PLP 234; VoW 135). It is as if each word had behind it a *'meaning-body'* (PI §559; PG 54; PLP 234–9; TS 302, 4f.; VoW 133–41). Imagine various geometrical solids, e.g. squares, prisms, pyramids, etc., made of glass and invisible except for one painted surface. The visible forms that can be produced by their combination will be determined by the combinatorial possibilities of the invisible solids behind the visible surfaces. Analogously, the meaningful combinations of words are determined by the fit of the underlying meaning-bodies (see 3 below for the passages W. quotes from Frege). The rules for the use of words describe the combinatorial laws of the meaning-bodies. The *Tractatus* was equally guilty of this misconception, albeit in a different way. There W. argued that the constituents of reality (objects) are the meanings of names. Accordingly, one expression fits another if the object which is its meaning fits the object which is the meaning of the other. The rules of logical syntax merely reflect the combinatorial possibilities of objects.

W.'s reply here is swift: if the meaning of a word is its *use*, then, of course, it makes no sense to speak of such 'fitting' — the use of one word cannot intelligibly be said to *fit* the use of another word. But if that is right, a problem arises. We understand familiar words we hear in sentences immediately. If the meaning of a word were something like a meaning-body, that would be something one could grasp at a stroke, and it would determine the use of the word; i.e. it would determine with which other words it can or cannot combine. But if that is mistaken — as it is, if the meaning of a word is its use — how can the use of a word be something we understand at a stroke? For surely the use of a word is something spread out over time, exhibited in the manifold applications of the word in different sentential contexts and circumstances of utterance? The problem is unravelled in the next sections.

1.1   'mit einem schlag': 'at a stroke', i.e. immediately, without reflecting.

2   (i)   PPF §§12–14 (p. 176), §36 (p. 181), make the following points. (a) The difficulty in understanding how one can grasp the meaning of a word at a stroke is the dual reference to *a point in time* and to *the way of using a word*. It is this peculiar combination that we fail to grasp. (In this respect, grasping the meaning of a word at a stroke is akin to having meant something by what one said. For this too involves reference to a point in time but not to an action (other than the saying) performed at that time.)

(b) If we can grasp a meaning at a stroke, then it seems that what we grasp must be something which can occur, full-blown, in a moment, e.g. an image or picture. One reason why this is wrong has been examined: i.e. the multiple possibilities of application of such a representation. Other reasons are given here. (1) Instantaneous grasp of meaning cannot consist in having an image, since one can keep an image in mind over time (for five minutes, say), but not one's grasp of the meaning. Rather, once one has grasped the meaning, there is something one *can do*. (2) When one exclaims 'Now I have it', a picture may occur to one, and may remain in mind. But 'Now I have it' does not mean 'I have a picture before my mind', and one's joyous exclamation may prove premature if it turns out that one cannot . . . (3) Grasping a meaning at a stroke seems akin to experiencing a meaning, which in turn seems similar to experiencing a mental image. But the content of experiencing an image, of imagining (in this sense), is a picture or description. The 'experience of meaning', by contrast, has no 'content'. (4) Even if someone were able to do something only when, and as long as, he had a certain experience (image or picture), the ability he has is not the experience or its content.

(ii)   LFM 19–28 contains a lengthy discussion of understanding and application. One understands an expression when one knows how to use it. There is indeed such a thing as instantaneous understanding, but it does not involve having the whole use of the expression before one's mind. A picture or mental image may represent a rule, but not its application, or not its whole application, for the picture itself must be applied (cf. §141).

3   In BLA ii §91 Frege, arguing against the formalists, wrote:

> Whereas in meaningful arithmetic equations and inequations are sentences expressing
> thoughts, in formal arithmetic they are comparable with the positions of chess pieces,
> transformed in accordance with certain rules without consideration for any sense. For
> if they were viewed as having a sense, the rules could not be arbitrarily stipulated; they
> would have to be so chosen that from formulas expressing true propositions could be
> derived only formulas likewise expressing true propositions.

In BLA ii §158 he remarked that 'the rules follow necessarily from the meanings of the signs', and in §207 he adds, 'If one chose to go back to the meanings, then the rules would find their rationale in just these meanings.' All three
passages are quoted in W.'s dictation to Waismann (VoW 135).

    This conception of meaning also characterizes Frege's conception of the
analysis of sentences into argument-expression and function-name, and his
consequent conception of well-formedness. What makes sense in language is
a reflection of what is possible in reality, which is determined by the meanings
of the relevant expressions:

> An object, e.g. the number 2, cannot logically adhere to another object, e.g. Julius
> Caesar, without some means of connection. This, in turn, cannot be an object
> but rather must be unsaturated. A logical connection into a whole can come about
> only through this, that an unsaturated part is saturated or completed by one or more
> parts . . .
>   Now it follows from the fundamental difference of objects from concepts that an
> object can never occur predicatively or unsaturatedly; and that logically, a concept can
> never stand in for an object. (FG 372 (CP 281))

Boxed Remark Following §138 (p. 53n.)

1   Cut from B i §82, this originates in MS 116 (Vol. XII), 93, in a discussion
of understanding and ability. Its immediate context is an early version of
PI §181; however, the original version is not concerned with the sudden
dawning of understanding, but simply with an assertion of ability, followed by
failure to do what one said one could do. In what circumstances does it make
sense to say, 'When I said I could, I could, but now I can't' (cf. PI §182(a),
example (5))? The remark that follows explores self-knowledge of abilities and
degrees of understanding. To the questions 'Can you lift this weight?' and 'Can
you still play chess?', it makes sense to reply, 'I don't know; let's see'. But can
one reply in this way to 'Do you understand the word "tree"?'? One would
respond, 'You must surely know whether you understand it!' But this is too
hasty. If one were asked, 'Do you know how to move a pawn in chess?', and
the reply were 'Let's see', then we would be inclined to respond, 'You'll find

out whether you know or not.' On the other hand, if one were asked whether one knew what 'pure' and 'impure' mean in Jewish dietary laws, one could well answer, 'Let's see, such-and-such is called "pure", but whether *this is* called "pure", I do not know.' Here, and also with a question like 'Do you understand the word "integral"?', one can say, 'Up to a certain point I understand the word.' But now, can't one imagine circumstances in which one could say, 'Up to a certain point I understand the word "tree", but just how far, well, let's see'?

B.r.f. §138 follows this and is followed by Z §§193f. (= B i §§83, and 194; cf. MS 116 (Vol. XII), 270 and 93). Understanding words, like abilities, is capable of degrees. There are various criteria of understanding, and satisfaction of some and non-satisfaction of others may justify ascription of partial understanding. It makes sense for a person to think he understands, but be wrong. One may grasp the meaning of a word at a stroke; but equally, one may think wrongly that one has done so. The moot question is what are the criteria for someone's having grasped what a word means at a stroke. They lie in his avowal, his subsequent applications, and the explanations he gives of it. So the phenomenon of grasping the meaning at a stroke does not show that what is grasped is something different from the use. It is misleading to characterize the use as 'extended in time'. Rather, the way of using an expression is something that is manifest in practise over time — as is the ability to use a word correctly. To grasp the meaning of a word is to have acquired the ability to use it (not to have caught hold of an entity which 'fits' other similar entities). That ability may be acquired at a stroke, but it is exhibited over time, in one's applications of the word.

To this extent p. 53/46 n. is a riposte to the final sentence of §138, or an elaboration on §139(a).

SECTION 139

1   This section investigates the relation between grasping what a word means at a stroke and the idea that meaning is use. The meaning of a word *is* its use, but how can any object of instantaneous understanding either be, or accord with, a use — with *a way of using* an expression (PPF §7 (p. 175))? Suppose that what comes before one's mind when one understands the word 'cube' is a picture of a cube. How can the mental picture fit or fail to fit the use? One is inclined to say that it fits if one applies the word to objects of which the mental picture is a picture, i.e. to cubes and not to pyramids. But with a given method of projection a cube may well represent a pyramid. To be sure, the picture *suggests* a use, but it does not *determine* one. Consequently, instantaneous understanding, though it may be accompanied by mental pictures (images, ideas, mental representations), cannot consist in having mental images, since any such image is compatible with a misapplication of the word.

1.1   (i) 'isn't the meaning of the word also determined by this use?': In §43 W. asserted that for a large class of cases, the meaning of a word can be said to *be* its use. Is he now modifying this claim and holding that the use *determines* the meaning? This is doubtful, since here he is using the word 'determines' in such a manner that one can also say that meaning is determined by instantaneous understanding, since *what* one understands at a stroke is the meaning of a word. There is no reason to suppose that this is meant to be a qualification on the association of meaning and use.

(ii) 'And can these ways of determining meaning conflict': there cannot be a conflict between what is grasped in a flash when one grasps what the word means, and the way of using the word — which is its meaning. But, of course, there can be a conflict between one's sincere avowal that one has understood and what one goes on to do, which may show that one did not, after all, grasp correctly what the word means.

2   Z §§297f. (= B i §§48 and 15; cf. Vol. XII, 61f. and 19) pursues matters further. How do I manage always to use a word correctly? Not, indeed, by consulting a grammar. Is it then by *meaning* something by what I say? Of course, but that is not an explanation. My meaning something by the words consists in my knowing that I can apply them (and doing so), although I may believe that I can apply them and be wrong. Knowing that I can apply a word is knowing that I understand it. But understanding is not an *inner activity* (event or process), nor is it the outer manifestation of understanding (the criteria for understanding): it is not an event, process or activity at all (cf. 'Understanding and ability', sect. 4).

2.1   'can the whole *use* of the word come before my mind when I *understand* it in this way?': MS 114 (Vol. X) Um., 25 observes:

> If 'understanding the meaning of a word' means knowing the possibilities of its grammatical application, then this question can arise: 'How can I know what I mean by "sphere", for I cannot have whole way of applying the word in my head all at once?'
>
> In one sense one can say, I know the rules of chess ('have them in my head') while // when // I am playing. But isn't this 'having in the head' a hypothesis? Certainly, this knowing is only the hypothetical reservoir from which the water that is actually seen flows.

At this point various problems criss-cross: the relation between meaning and use, understanding at a stroke and knowing the application of a word, and the nature of understanding. The phenomenon of sudden understanding drives one to embrace the conception of understanding as a state that underlies performance. This is the main theme of §§146–155.

Boxed Remark Following §139 (p. 54), Note (a)

1   This is cut from B i §363. It is derived from MS 129, 198f., but that
context, concerning kinaesthetic sensations (cf. PI §§624f.) is unilluminating.
In the present context, in the vicinity of §139, the remark identifies another
source of the error of thinking of meanings as something that can be grasped
at a stroke, something that can come before the mind, from which the use of
a word *follows*. We sometimes choose between words, saying 'I believe the
right word in this case is . . .'. We are inclined to think that our choice is
based on something other than the words, e.g. a mental image — something
that comes before our mind, *as a result of which* we choose the right word.
This is particularly tempting precisely because we often choose between
words in a manner similar to choosing between pictures. But the temptation
should be resisted. What makes the word appropriate is not the image one
might have before one's mind, but the match between what the word means
(which is something one knows, since one has mastered the technique of its
use) and the phenomenon one is describing. (Cf. PI §335 and §597.)

Boxed Remark Following §139 (p. 54), Note (b)

1   This is cut from B i §335 (= MS 129, 175), but that reveals nothing. Is
this remark meant to illustrate the notion of a picture *suggesting* a use, even
though it is possible to use it differently (§139(e))? Or the related thought in
§140 that we are under a psychological but not a logical compulsion to take
the picture thus and not otherwise?

Section 140

1   The mistake in §139 lay in thinking that a mental picture *forces* an application on us. It then seems that if one has a picture of a cube before one's mind
and yet points at a triangular prism, saying 'That is a cube', one is confused.
We are tempted to say that the mental picture forces a use on one only in
a *psychological* sense. But this is misleading (LFM 184f.), for it suggests that
we can and do distinguish two kinds of case: that of *psychological* and that of
logical compulsion. In the sequel, and elsewhere (esp. RFM), W. argues against
the intelligibility of *logical* compulsion. The inexorability of logic is our inexorability in applying it as we do. Rules of inference, for example, do not
force us to do anything, but we 'force ourselves' to cleave to them.
    §139 showed that different uses of an expression could all, with justice, be
called 'applying the picture of a so-and-so'. The illusion that a picture forces
an application on us merely reflects the fact that by habit and training only
one application is naturally suggested to us. If, however, the same mental image
occurs to us in relation to different applications, we will not claim that the
word has the same meaning despite its different applications. Consequently,

the meaning of a word is not a picture in the mind, nor any other entity, and grasping the meaning of a word at a stroke does not consist in having such a picture come before one's mind.

The matters raised briefly here (§§138–41) are explored in the subsequent discussion of following a rule. Just as having a mental picture before one's mind does not guarantee its application, so too having a rule in mind (or even in print) does not guarantee applying it correctly. Likewise, just as a picture cannot 'logically compel' (since there is no such thing), neither can a rule; just as some applications of a picture come naturally and seem inexorable, so too do certain applications of rules.

1.1   'Then what sort of mistake did I make': a back-reference to §139(d) — the mistake of thinking that a picture that comes before the mind fits the use of a word independently of any method of projection, and therefore compels the particular application in question (for this seems to co-ordinate what one grasps at a stroke with the use that seems to be 'spread out over time').

Section 141

1   The argument thus far establishes that a mental picture does not carry its application with it, does not force an application on us. Any picture (mental or otherwise) can be applied in different ways, and the most that can be said *vis-à-vis* compulsion is that we may naturally think of one method of application, and others may not cross our minds. To this one might respond that what must come before our mind when we grasp the meaning of, e.g., 'a cube' at a stroke is the picture not only of the cube, but also of the method of projection (e.g. a picture of two cubes connected by lines of projection). Does *this* not force an application upon us? — Not so. It does not advance matters at all — as has already been made clear in §86. For this complex schema still has to be applied, and one can imagine different applications of it, none of which are compelled by the schema.

The response to this is the question, 'Can't an application come before one's mind?', to which the answer is, 'Of course' (anything that is thinkable can come before one's mind). But how do we apply the expression 'an application came before his mind'? We accept two different criteria for an application coming before someone's mind.[2] First, the picture that comes before his

---

[2]   The passage is confusing in that we begin with the argument that a representation of a method of projection does not carry with it its own application, to which the response is: 'Can't an application come before one's mind?' The answer is 'Yes', and the example examined is then of a *method of projection* coming before one's mind. The confusion dissolves once one realizes that *any representation* of an application is a representation, not an application. The most obvious representation of an application consists of delineating lines of projection. To be sure, this leaves room for erroneous application. But nothing, certainly no further schema, picture or representation, can bridge the 'gap' between the representation of an application (of a method of projection) and an application itself After all, there is not a *gap*, but a categorial difference.

mind, e.g. of the two cubes connected by lines of projection. What grounds do we have for saying that *this* picture comes before his mind? Surely, what he says in response to our question, 'How did you represent to yourself the application of this expression, or this picture?' And his answer may involve producing a description, a drawing, or a model. Consequently, for the person to have a method of projection before his mind, it is unnecessary that he imagine anything at all, he can look at a drawing or model we put before him.

The second criterion that we use is the application he makes of what he imagines (or of the pictorial or three-dimensional representation of the method of projection with which he is presented). If he goes on to use the expression correctly (as we do), then we will say that the correct method of application occurred to him.

The two criteria can conflict (although not *contradict* each other), but they normally do not. A person might picture cubes connected by lines of projection and go on to call a triangular prism 'a cube'. We would then take this to defeat the claim that the *application* came before his mind, and contend that he misapplied *the picture of the application*. But we allow the picture that occurs to him to constitute a criterion for an application occurring to him only in so far as normally people who have such a picture go on to apply the relevant expression in such-and-such a way.

The case is exactly the same with the avowal 'Now I understand' or (with respect to rules) 'Now I know how to go on'. We take such an avowal to be a criterion of understanding, but only in so far as people who exclaim that they understand normally go on to manifest their understanding in behaviour. If the regular correlation between avowal and performance did not obtain, our use of 'Now I understand' would lose its point.

1.1   'a *normal* case, and abnormal cases': the normal case of the application of the picture of a cube is to cubes, an abnormal one would be to a two-dimensional rectangle and two rhombi, for example.

2   (i)   LFM 23 points out that the use of 'understand' is based on the fact that in an enormous number of cases when we apply certain tests (criteria), we are able to predict that a person will use a word (which he is said, by those tests, to understand) in a certain way. If this were not so, there would be no *point* in using the word 'understand' at all.

(ii)   LFM 25 draws attention to similarities between 'understand' and 'intend'. People say 'I intend to play chess' (like 'Now I understand'). Since chess is a complex game defined by its rules, one might wonder how they know that it is chess that they are going to play. Do they have all the rules in mind when they declare their intention? Can they be uncertain about what it is that they intend to play? Could one say, 'I believe that I intend to play chess, but I don't know. Let's see'? It is intelligible that exceptionally people might say, 'I intend to play chess' and then do something quite different. But this could not be the norm. If people commonly avowed 'I intend to V' and never went on to V, then their use of 'intend' would differ fundamentally from ours, and the word would have a different sense. That the utterance 'I intend to V' is a criterion of people's intention depends on normal coincidence of that avowal of the intention to V and subsequent V -ing.

(iii)   W. once remarked that what was wrong with his conception of elementary propositions in the *Tractatus* was the confusion of the method of projection with the lines of projection.[3] It is noteworthy that TLP 2.1513–2.1515 explicitly includes the 'pictorial relationship', conceived as 'the correlations of the picture's elements with things', as part of the picture. It is surely apropos this that W. remarks, 'The lines of projection might be called "the connection between the picture and what it depicts"; but so too might the technique of projection' (Z §291). In the *Investigations*, W.'s adversary conceives of grasping a meaning as having a picture which includes its lines of projection, to which the response is that such a picture could still be misapplied.

PG 213f. remarks that a picture (proposition, blueprint, mental image) together with its lines of projection leaves room for different applications (as in the case of the cube here). So one may count the projection lines as part of the picture. But what of the method of projection? One conceives of it as a bridge between symbol and what it symbolizes. But if it is such a bridge, it is not built until the application is made (the symbol is not used until it is applied).[4] One hankers to incorporate the method of projection, the way the symbol is applied, into the symbol (picture) itself. But there is no such thing. One can only *describe* a method of application, and although one can incorporate the description into the picture (symbol), the description is still only a description, not itself an application, but something standing in need of an application.

SECTION 142

1   This remark was inserted into the text only in TS 239, §158, initially as a handwritten marginalium and then typed on to a separate page 101.1. It appears to hang on the last two paragraphs of §141, but the hook is not obviously well chosen to bear its weight. It is not clear whether this remark is meant to generalize the point made in §141(c), i.e. that *normally* people who share a common language apply a given picture uniformly, just as they normally read a chart uniformly (cf. §86) — even though there is no necessity of any kind to do so. This consideration is pivotal for the ensuing discussion of following rules, and of the relationship between the rule-formulation and the rule, on

---

[3]   See P. Winch, 'The Unity of Wittgenstein's Philosophy', in *Studies in the Philosophy of Wittgenstein*, ed. Winch (Routledge and Kegan Paul, London, 1969), p. 12.

[4]   Cf. MS 165, 82: 'Nicht die *Deutung* schlägt die Brücke zwischen dem Zeichen und dem Bezeichneten // Gemeinten //. Nur die Praxis tut das.' ('It is not the *interpretation* which builds the bridge between the sign and what is signified // what is meant //. Only the practice does that.')

the one hand, and the acts that accord with the rule, on the other. One might perhaps have expected W. to illustrate his point in this context by a remark on the regular concurrence between exclamations and avowals of sudden under- standing and manifestations of the ability to go on — for if people regularly exclaimed that they understood such-and-such (a word or sentence just uttered) but then went on to exhibit misunderstanding, then avowals of understanding would lose their point. But the two examples of §142 veer in a much more general direction than this.

The opening remark recapitulates a point already made in §80, apropos the disappearing chair. The rules for the use of words prescribe their use in normal cases. 'The signpost is in order — if, under normal circumstances, it fulfils its purpose' (§87). So the more abnormal the case, the more question- able the application of a word becomes — until we reach the point of simply not knowing what to say. W. now draws our attention to two categories of expressions the use of which patently depends on the obtaining of certain kinds of regularities — of very general facts of nature (p. 56/48 note) — namely, psychological concepts of the inner and concepts of measurement.

Psychological concepts would cease to be usable (and, one might add, there would cease to be consensus about their application), if pain, fear, joy, etc. did not have characteristic behavioural expression. If there ceased to be regu- lar coincidence between exclamations of pain and circumstances of injury, or if people's avowals of joy ceased to coincide with a joyful demeanour, or if avowals of fear were commonly associated with no avoidance behaviour, our normal language-games of expressions and ascriptions of pain, fear and joy would become pointless. Similarly, our concepts of measurement, and our practices of fixing the prices of commodities according to weight or length, would fall into desuetude if objects swelled and contracted unpredictably or if gravita- tional fields fluctuated constantly.

1.1   (i) 'our normal language-games would thereby lose their point': one might, of course, still ascribe pain or joy to people who exhibit pain- or joy- ous behaviour, and still weigh lumps of cheese. But it would be pointless, since a cry of pain might be followed by a bout of giggling, an exclamation of joy in joyous circumstances might be followed by behaviour of misery. In short, the regular convergence of the various criteria for the application of the con- cept would be radically disrupted. Similarly, a lump of cheese might halve its weight in a minute's time if it spontaneously shrank, or double its weight if it swelled, and our practices of weighing and pricing such goods according to weight would become pointless.

BOXED REMARK FOLLOWING §142 (p. 56n.)

1   TS 227(a) has this in handwriting on a separate slip of paper. A marginal note on p. 99 indicates that it is a footnote to the penultimate sentence of

§142. This suggests that W.'s point is that part of the explanation of the importance to us of, for example, weighing, consists in such very general facts of nature as the relative stability of the weights of material things and quantities of stuffs. For in a world in which things expanded and contracted randomly and frequently (and accordingly registered a different weight on scales), our concept of the weight of a thing would lose its importance.

This note is cut from B i §357, where W. added '(Hierher die Bemerkung von den "kuriosen Beiträgen")' ('(Here the remark about "curious contributions")'). The allusion is to PI §415 (cf. RFM 92), which suggests that the general facts of nature W. has in mind are not curiosities, but facts so obvious that we do not notice them (e.g. that objects do not significantly expand and shrink with great and unpredictable frequency, that people who cry out on injuring themselves generally nurse their injury). B i §357 is derived from MS 129, 194, where it is preceded by the following observation: 'It is possible to call us nominalists if we are not conscious that the boundary drawn by a definition is only drawn for the sake of the importance of this boundary. And the propositions which explain this importance are not propositions about language.' In that context, the very general facts of nature bear on explaining the importance of drawing a sharp boundary circumscribing a concept by means of a definition. Hence, they also bear on the importance of having sharply defined measures of weight and length (breadth and height).

2.1   'general facts of nature': cf. MS 130, 136f.:

The *facts* of human natural history which cast light upon our problem are difficult to see // find //, for our language // discourse // *passes them by*, being busy with other matters. (Thus we say to someone, 'Go to the shop and buy . . .' — not — 'Put the left foot in front of the right foot, etc. etc., then put money on the counter, etc.')

Chapter 6

Understanding and ability (§§143–84)

INTRODUCTION

§§138–42 raised an apparent difficulty for W.'s conception of meaning. How is it possible, on the one hand, for the meaning of an expression to be its use, and, on the other hand, for one to understand something at a stroke? The ramifications of this question guide the investigation throughout the next hundred sections, leading to clarification of the concepts of understanding, following a rule, the relation between a rule and its applications, and so forth. Meaning, W. has argued, is what is given by an explanation of meaning. Explanations of meaning belong to grammar; they are rules for the use of words. Giving a correct explanation of what an expression means is one criterion for understanding that expression, for knowing what it means. Using it correctly, in accordance with the rules for its use, is another. Understanding a language is mastery of a rule-governed technique. Each of the connections is complex and has multiple consequences, which W. explores. §§143–84 are an examination of the concept of understanding and its kinship with the concept of an ability. So the concept of an ability and the irreducibility of abilities to states or processes are investigated too.

The chapter divides into three parts: A §§143–55, B §§156–78, C §§179–84.

Part A is concerned with the nature of understanding, in particular with knowing how to act in accordance with a rule. The example which dominates the discussion is grasping the rule of an arithmetical series. This provides a model for understanding what an expression means, which is specified by an explanation of what it means, which is a rule for its use. If one knows the rule of a series, then one can apply the rule and produce a segment of the infinite series. Similarly, if one knows the meaning of 'W', the rule for its use, one can apply 'W' in the appropriate circumstances. Part A can be subdivided into three groups.

(α) §§143–7 introduce the problem. Conceptual abilities rest on brute, pre-conceptual abilities. Inasmuch as conceptual abilities are, with us, acquired, they rest on training. Training is only possible given standard natural reactions of trainees. It is important to look at our complex conceptual abilities as resting upon brute preconceptual ones and to see that the hierarchical structure of conceptual abilities is, in one sense, contingent. For example, our ability to survey is such-and-such, but could be more or less. If it were different, the conceptual structures we would create (the language-games we would engage in) would be different (§144). Explanation itself presupposes possession of abilities which, with us, are acquired through training. But it too rests upon standard normal reactions and abilities (e.g. recognition of recurrent patterns, discriminatory abilities). Mastery of a technique, however, is, in general, a matter of degree, and there is no sharp borderline between partial and complete mastery. Since understanding (like an ability) is distinct from its behavioural manifestations, one is inclined to think of it as their source, to see understanding as a *state* (e.g. of having the rule before one's mind) from which one's applications of the rule flow. But no matter what one has before one's mind, it is the application that is the criterion of understanding. §147 raises an objection that provides the transition to the next group of remarks. Although application is the criterion of understanding here, one is inclined to say that when one exclaims 'Now I understand', when one knows that one understands, one's knowledge is not an inductive inference from one's past performance. Understanding, one thinks, is an inner state (or process) which, in one's own case, one recognizes introspectively. That is how one knows that one understands.

(β) §§148–50 explore this false picture. If one thinks of understanding as a state, then not as a mental state like being in a state of intense excitement or feeling depressed. For one does not cease to know the rule of the series '2, 4, 6, 8, . . .' when one is not thinking about it or even when one is asleep. Mental states, such as feeling cheerful or being in a state of intense concentration, have 'genuine duration'; they take time, can be interrupted by distraction of attention and later continued, and are terminated by sleep or loss of consciousness. But being able to do something does not take time (unlike learning to be able to do something). Knowing, understanding and being able to do something are closely related. They lack genuine duration and are categorially different from mental states in this sense. So if one insists that knowing the alphabet, for example, is a state of mind, one is conceiving of it as a state of a mental *apparatus* (perhaps a dispositional state of the brain) the operation of which *explains* the manifestations of knowledge (§149). But then one criterion for knowing should be the presence of the apparatus, irrespective of performance. However, it is the performance that is the criterion of knowing or understanding.

(γ) §§151–5 revert to the phenomenon of sudden understanding ('Now I know!'), mooted in §§138f., which may incline one to think that understanding is an event or performance. So W. describes what happens when one suddenly understands, specifying various accompanying processes. Now one might think that understanding is one of these, or some further hidden process. But none of these accompanying processes is either necessary or sufficient for understanding. Understanding is not a mental process at all. What warrants a person's utterance 'Now I understand!' is not an inner state or process that he observes *in foro interno*, but the circumstances of the utterance (including his past learning and practice). This theme is resumed at §179.

The structure of Part A:

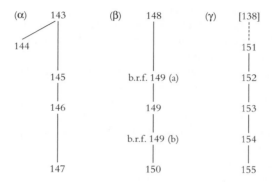

| (α) | 143 | (β) | 148 | (γ) | [138] |

144

145   b.r.f. 149 (a)   151

146   149   152

     b.r.f. 149 (b)   153

147   150   154

       155

Part B (§§156–78) consists of a detailed examination of reading, conceived simply as mapping signs or sounds on to sounds or signs (irrespective of understanding what is read). The point of this interpolation is to destroy misconceptions of rule-guided behaviour. The philosophical examination of reading is intended to illuminate the nature of understanding, conceived of as akin to an ability, in particular the nature of understanding a rule. It illuminates what it is to be following, applying, conforming, or intending to conform, to a rule. It is complementary to §§185–242, which are concerned with what it is for a certain consequence to be determined by, follow from, be derived from, a rule.

Five kinds of misconception typically characterize reflection in this area. First, our craving for the *essence* of a phenomenon drives us to look for a defining characteristic beneath the multiplicity of circumstances that justify the application of a term. Like Peer Gynt, we strip the onion of its skins in search of its essence, discarding them successively, and when we fail to find a heart, we think we are confronted by something singularly mysterious and elusive. Secondly, the inner/outer picture of the mind, rooted in the grammatical asymmetry between certain first- and third-person present-tense psychological verbs, holds us in thrall. The 'inner' seems hidden to all but its owner, whose access to it is privileged; others must make do with mere outward behaviour. I know whether I understand, am reading, can do thus-and-so; others can only conjecture. Thirdly, we are prone to construe verbs of ability as signifying states of the possessor of the ability in question. In the special case of such distinctively human abilities as being able to read or to sing a tune, we construe them as dispositional states of an apparatus of the mind, e.g. the brain. Fourthly, we tend, when philosophizing, to search for (and to postulate) intermediate, explanatory links. Since reading is not mere utterance of phonemes subsequent to seeing the appropriate words, we search for a special connecting experience or mechanism that will, we think, distinguish reading from pretending to read, and also explain the reading. We dimly apprehend categorial differences, e.g. between rule and application, ability and its exercise, psychological states or experiences and their manifestation, but, failing to apprehend the grammatical nature of a categorial distinction, we think we perceive a logical gap that must be bridged. So we look for, or postulate, a connecting mechanism. Finally, a wide range of misconceptions surround the notion of normativity. Following a rule is not merely acting in accordance with it. It is being guided by it, acting because of it, deriving what is required from the rule. And here, under the impact of previous pressures, we search for the essence of guidance or derivation. We think that we can find it in a causal nexus or the feeling of one, in the experience of guidance or the feeling of motivating force, in a peculiar intimation given by a rule. And as the various attempts are seen to be unsatisfactory, we think that the 'experience of normativity' is quite particular, but indescribable, elusive and mysterious.

The examination of reading, conceived as mastery of (i.e. knowing or understanding) the rule of the alphabet, investigates these misconceptions. In so doing it further clarifies the nature of understanding and ability. §§156–78 consist of fairly consecutive exposition (being derived largely from MS 115 (Vol. XI), the reworking of the *Brown Book* (EPB), which is among the most continuous of W.'s writings). It can roughly be divided into three groups: (α) §§156–61; (β) §§162–4; (γ) §§165–78.

(α) §156 introduces the example of reading and lays bare the temptation to think that reading (like understanding in one of its aspects) is a special conscious activity of the mind. It also shows how, under pressure, alternative pictures are substituted, e.g. that reading is an unconscious activity of the mind or an activity of the brain. §§157–8 briefly dismiss the mechanical (neural) picture. §§159–61 return to the theme of §156, i.e. reading *qua* conscious activity. No matter what experiences accompany reading, they are neither necessary nor sufficient conditions for reading, nor are they criteria for reading.

The structure of Part B, group α:

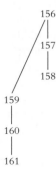

156

157

158

159

160

161

(β) In §§162ff. a new departure is made. (β) and (γ) could be treated as one continuous grouping. They have been separated because (β) does not emphasize the experiential component of normativity, which is prominent in (γ).

Thus far both a mechanistic connection and a mentalistic, associationist one have been suggested to mediate between the operative facts (the letters) and the rule-guided action (reading), and both have been duly rejected. §162 attempts to introduce a normative component into the analysis of reading; i.e. one reads only when one *derives* the copy from the original. This is the first of many similar gambits. Deriving, it is argued in §§163–4, is no less a family-resemblance concept than reading itself. Recourse to it does not disclose the essence of reading in any conscious mental activity.

The structure of Part B, group (β):

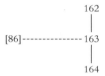

(γ) §165 returns to the original suggestion of §156: i.e. to the thought that reading is a particular process, a special conscious activity of the mind. The words one reads (as opposed, say, to those one repeats from memory while pretending to read) *come* in a special way, 'of themselves' (for, to be sure, one doesn't make them up). But again, no *experiences* of the way they come are either individually necessary, or jointly or disjunctively sufficient for reading. The fiction of the special way the words come, and the idea that reading is a quite particular but elusive process, are examined in §§165–8.

§§169–78 attempt various related moves which might seem to illuminate the putative nexus which the idea of 'the special way the words come' failed to capture. Which way do they come? Do the signs cause the utterance, or constitute a reason for them, so that one feels the causation or justification (§169)? One is inclined to say that one *feels the influence* of the operative facts, or that one is *guided* by them, that the letters *intimate* the sounds to be uttered. The experience of guidance, influence, deliberation, 'experiencing the because', are severally examined up to §178. In each case the same general points hold: reading (following the rule of the alphabet) is a rule-guided activity, but its essence is not to be found in any accompanying experiences. Being able to read is an ability, not a mental state or reservoir, from which the overt performance flows. Reading is the exercise of that ability; it is something defined not by inner processes, but rather by the public criteria in the various circumstances, that justify application of the term. The structure of Part B, group γ is, by and large, linear.

Part C returns to the theme of §151: the utterance 'Now I can go on (understand)' and the problems it raises. The utterance is akin to a signal (§180); thus used, it is an avowal, not a report upon an inner observation, or a description of the circumstances in which it is correctly employed. Indeed, the avowal may be correctly used even though the subsequent performance may not be forthcoming, for though the failure defeats the criterial support given by a sincere avowal, special circumstances (e.g. an interruption between avowal and performance) may defeat the defeating force of the failure (§181). §182 is a compressed discussion of abilities and their criteria. §183 touches on different conditions of possibility, and §184 discusses again the reservoir picture associated with ability and its avowal.

The structure of Part C:

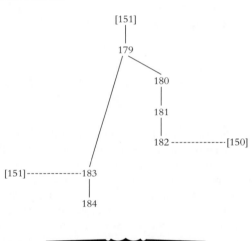

Sources

PI§	BrB	MS 115 (EPB)	MS 142§	TS 220§	TS 239§[1]	Others
143			143[2]	125[2]	159	
144			144	126	160	
145			145	127	161	
146			146	128	162–3	
147			147	129	164	
148			148	130	165	
b.r.f. 149(a)						116, 88; B i §79
149	117–18	192–3 (170)	149(a)–(b)	131(a)	166	110, 236–7; 111, 26; 140, 11; 302, 1; BT 143–69
b.r.f. 149(b)						116, 97; B i §86; 110, 235; 153a, 8v; 114, Um., 23; 302, 1
150			149c	131c	167	
151	112–13	182–3 (163–4)	150	132	168	
152	113	184 (164–5)	151(a)–(b)	133(a)–(b)	169	
153	113–14	184 (165)	151(c)	133c	170	
154(a)–(c)	114	185–6 (165–6)	152(a)–(c)	134(a)–(c)	171[3]	
155	114	185–6 (165–6)	152(e)	134(e)	173	
156	119–20	195–7 (172–3)	152(f)–153	134(f)–135	173(b)–174	
157	120–1	197–8 (173)	154	136–9	175	
158			158	140	176	
159	121	199–200 (174–5)	159	137[4]	177	
160	122	200–1 (175–6)	160–1	138	178	
161	122	201 (176)	162	139	179	
162	122–3	201–2 (176–7)	163	140	180	
163	123–4	202–3 (177–8)	164	141(a)–(c)	181	
164	125	204 (179)	165	141(d)–(e)	182	
165		205–6 (179–80)	166	142	183	152, 5
p. 66/56		10				B i §395
166		206–8 (180–1)	167	143	184	
167		208–9 (181–2)	168	144	185	152, 6–7
168		209 (182)	169	145	186	
169		209–10 (182–3)	170	146	187	152, 7–8[5]

PI§	BrB	MS 115 (EPB)	MS 142§	TS 220§	TS 239§[1]	Others
170		210–11 (183–4)	171	147	188	152, 8–9
171		211–12 (184)	172	148	189	
172		213 (185)	173	149	190	
173		213–14 (185–7)	174	150	191	
174			175	151(a)–(b)	192	152, 9
175		216–17 (187–8)	176	151(c)–(d)	193	
176		217 (188)	177	152(a)	194	152, 11
177		218 (188–9)	179	152(d)	195	
178		218–19 (189)	180	153	196	
179	114–15	185–6 (165–6)	181(a)–(c)	154(a)–(c)	197	
180			181(d)	154(d)	198	
181	115–16	187–8 (167)	182	155	199	116, 92
182						119, 49–59; 121, 58r–59v; ZF §181
183	114–15	186–8 (166–7)	183	156	200	
184			184	157	201	

[1] The section numbers in the Intermediate Draft (ZF) coincide with the final section numbers, and so are not included.
[2] The numbered sections are those assigned by Wittgenstein. Due to double counting, they are, at this point, in fact two less than they should be. But to facilitate locating the sections, only Wittgenstein's numbers are cited.
[3] Paragraphs (d)–(e) added only in ZF.
[4] At this point Wittgenstein's enumeration errs by six; i.e. §137 in the MS ought to be numbered §143, and all subsequent numbers are six short of the actual count. But, as before, to facilitate finding the relevant remark, the numbers in the above list are not corrected.
[5] Paragraphs (b) and (c) only.

> Understanding and ability
>   1. The place of the elucidation of understanding in the *Investigations*
>   2. Meaning and understanding as the soul of signs
>   3. Categorial misconceptions of understanding
>   4. Categorial clarification
>   (a) Understanding is not an experience
>   (b) Understanding is not a process
>   (c) Understanding is not a mental state
>   (d) Understanding is neither a dispositional state of the brain nor a disposition
>   5. Powers and abilities
>   6. Understanding and ability

EXEGESIS §§143–84

1   §§138–42 have prepared the ground for the investigation of understanding, following a rule and being guided by a rule, the relationships between a rule and its extension, between understanding a rule and applying it, and between meaning and understanding. This investigation runs from §143 to §242. The first part (§§143–84) focuses upon the nature of understanding a rule. The ability to apply predicates, no less than the ability to expand a series according to a rule, is normative. One might question whether the arithmetical example of learning to expand a series is the most illuminating model for learning how to use words correctly. Perhaps the arithmetical example was given pride of place partly because W. was waging a campaign on two fronts. The early draft (TS 220) continued after §189 with what is now RFM I (but in a different arrangement (TS 221)).

W.'s first point is that the ability to understand the formation rule rests upon a brute reaction to training: namely, repetition. The teaching, at this level, is not a matter of cognition and calculation, or of explanation, but only of training aimed at producing a regularity of behaviour. Secondly, the possibility of this training and subsequent training, teaching and explanation rests on brute reaction which is *normal* (cf. §142). Thirdly, understanding, misunderstanding and not understanding are distinguished by the difference between reacting correctly to training, making systematic mistakes, and making random mistakes. Fourthly, the borderline between random and systematic error is fuzzy, and hence, by implication, the borderline between misunderstanding and not understanding. The close and complex connections between ability, performance and understanding are intimated here.

1.1   (i)   '(Do not baulk at the expression "series of numbers")': presumably a warning against the unwarranted pedantry of insisting that what one writes down is a series of *numerals*. But that is not how we use the term 'number', nor is it the correct way of differentiating numbers from numerals. We give our telephone *number* (not numeral) to a friend and write down the licence *number* (not numeral) of a car.[1]

(ii)   '. . . die *Möglichkeit der Verständigung* . . .': 'the *possibility of communication*'.

(iii)   'And then communication stops at *that* point': i.e. random mistakes betoken lack of understanding, hence one cannot progress. If the pupil cannot

---

[1]   For discussion, see B. Rundle, *Grammar in Philosophy* (Clarendon Press, Oxford, 1979), §31.

copy out the series in anything but a random order, the teacher can do nothing with him. But a systematic mistake (§143(d)) may provide the basis for further development, although here too the capacity to learn may come to an end (cf. Exg. §144).

2   (i)   LFM 27 draws the same kind of distinction between misunderstanding and not understanding, and gives examples such as responding to '+ 2' correctly up to 100, and then adding threes, and beyond 1,000 fours, etc. There W. moves directly on to the two central questions: (a) Does it follow that we can never be sure that others understand? (b) *More importantly*, can we really know that we ourselves understand?

(ii)   MS 116 (Vol. XII), 35: 'Missverständnis — Unverständis. Gegen das Missverständnis hilft Erklärung, gegen das Unverständnis — Abrichtung. — Wenn er sich abrichten läßt.' ('Misunderstanding — non-understanding. Explanation will help against misunderstanding, against non-understanding — training, — If he lets himself be trained.') Cf. Z §419 (MS 136, 135): 'Any explanation has its foundation in training. (Educators ought to remember this.)'

SECTION 144

1   This discusses the last line of §143. The remark that the ability to learn may come to an end is based neither on one's own experience (e.g. of finding that one just cannot master a certain branch of learning), nor simply on the fact that one can imagine a pupil's learning capacity ending here, there or elsewhere. Rather, W. is drawing our attention to a logical possibility, reminding us of a particular contingency, in order to reorient our way of looking at things. At what things? At the phenomena associated with understanding and meaning. He aims, in particular, at getting us to conceive of understanding quite differently from the way we are tempted to construe the concept: namely, as akin to an ability rather than as a mental state or process. If we compare understanding with abilities and think of manifestations of understanding as exercises of abilities rather than as causal consequences of inner states, we shall look quite differently at the phenomenon of sudden understanding, and also cease to conceive of understanding as a reservoir from which applications of understanding flow.

The fact that one can imagine, i.e. that it is possible, that learning capacities should cease at a given point is of importance in a reorientation of one's overall conception of language, meaning and understanding. First, that we do have certain elementary abilities (to imitate, react in standard ways, recognize shapes and colours, continue activities in a common pattern, etc.) is a general brute fact of human nature (b.r.f. §142 (p. 56n.)), which is crucial for our having the kind of language we have. Secondly, that many abilities are hierarchically ordered is an important factor underlying our linguistic competence and partly determines the kinds of language-games we can and do engage in.

1.1   (i)   'I wanted to put that picture . . .': this is a reply to the question, 'Then what am I doing with that proposition?'

(ii)   'compare it with *this* rather than *that* set of pictures': It is not clear what *picture* or *pictures* W. has in mind. Perhaps he means no more than comparing understanding with abilities and their exercise rather than with states and their causal consequences.

(iii)   '(Indian mathematicians: "Look at this.")': in MS 142, §126 (= Z §461) this was sufficiently long to be intelligible: 'I once read somewhere that a geometrical figure, with the words "Look at this!", serves as a proof for certain Indian mathematicians. This looking too effects an alteration in one's way of seeing (*Anschauungsweise*).' In TS 239, §160, W. added in the margin, apropos 'somewhere', the single word query 'Hardy?'.[2] Noteworthy in W.'s discussions of mathematics is the frequent appeal to stroke diagrams and the like as surveyable proofs (which look like, but are not, experiments, and seem to be, but are not, appeals to a common intuition).

Cf. also MS 161, 6:

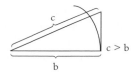

Wie überzeugt mich dieser Beweis? It convinces my eyes.' ('. . . How does this proof convince me? . . .')

2.1   MS 142, §144 (= TS 220, §126) opens this remark with 'Nun, lass mich diese Betrachtung für einen Augenblick unterbrechen und fragen:' ('Let me break off this investigation for a moment and ask:')

---

[2]   The point which W. is making is discussed in Eduard von Hartmann, *Philosophy of the Unconscious: Speculative Results according to the Inductive Method of Physical Science*, with a preface by C. K. Ogden (Kegan Paul, Trench and Trubner, London, 1931), pp. 320f.:

It is in ethno-psychological respects extremely characteristic that the treatment of geometry among the Greeks aims at a rigorous discursive mode of proof, and sedulously ignores the most obvious intuitive demonstrations; whereas that of the Hindoos, in spite of an endowment for arithmetic far surpassing the Greeks, is yet entirely based on direct intuition, and is usually confined to an artificial construction in support of intuition, to which the one word 'see!' is appended.

The general principle of intuitively perceptible proof is propounded by Schopenhauer (whom von Hartmann also discusses) in *The World as Will and Representation*, tr. E. F. J. Payne (Clarendon Press, Oxford, 1974), vol. 1, §15.

SECTION 145

1   This continues §143. Four main points are made. First, if a person *V*s,
it does not follow that he has the ability to *V*, since we distinguish a fluke
(beginner's luck) from the exercise of an ability. Secondly, the grounds for
ascription of an ability are, in a sense, partly indeterminate. Whether A can *V*
is determined by his usual success in *V*-ing, but there is no sharp ratio of success to failure, and no lower bound to the number of trials necessary. Thirdly,
the role which explanation can play in teaching depends upon the pupil's reactions. Such things as using particular emphases, underlining figures, writing
them in columns to draw attention to regularities, all have a role in teaching
and explaining here. But if, for example, the pupil suffers from various mental
deficiencies, such as an inability to distinguish certain patterns of recurrence
of written symbols, some such explanations will be out of the question. The
acquisition of the hierarchy of abilities involved in mastering a language
depends upon brute or trained reactions. Moreover, this genetic point is
mirrored analytically to the extent that such reactions are, in the appropriate
circumstances, elements in the complex criteria for the possession of various
abilities. Fourthly, in §145(b) the central issue of the subsequent debate is raised
again. The criterion for having understood a rule with limitless application is
not the successful completion of an infinite set of tasks. One cannot state a
determinate limit to the number of times the pupil must apply the rule '+ 1'
before he can be said to be able to count, or to the number of things he must
identify as red before he can be said to know what 'red' means. But it does
not follow that we can never know whether he has understood.

1.1   'this will only be the case when he is often successful': MS 142, §127, adds
'(Aber wie oft ist "*oft*"?)' ('(But how often is "*often*"?)').

2   (i) BB 89f. elaborates the role of encouragement in training. Imagine that
one is training a pupil to use a table correlating words and pictures, with the
object of enabling him to use new tables or even to construct them for himself. Acts of encouragement will play a central role in the training, but they
are only possible, only have a role, given certain responses. One can train a
dog to retrieve, and in the course of training use gestures or sounds of encouragement. But they only have a point because of the way the dog reacts to
them. A cat does not respond to such encouragements, and so such acts are
pointless (cf. Z §87).
       (ii) LA 2 stresses the importance of exaggerated gestures and facial grimaces
in teaching a child (especially words like 'good'). The child understands, reacts
appropriately, to these gestures and grimaces. If he did not, he could understand *nothing*.
       (iii) MS 116 (Vol. XII), 33f., makes explicit the relation of explanation to
a hierarchy of abilities. How can one ask for explanations of word-meanings?

Compare (1) What colour is called 'chrome-yellow'? (2) What is C‴?[3] (3) What does the (Latin) word *nefas* mean? The first, and possibly the second, can be answered by pointing or showing. The third can be answered by a translation or by examples of its application. But what if someone who has not learnt mathematics asks, 'What does "integral" mean?'? One can only answer: 'It is a mathematical expression which I cannot explain to you until you have learnt more mathematics.'

Section 146

1   This begins the examination of the false pictures of understanding which we are inclined to entertain. §145 argued that there is no specific limit to the numbers the pupil must write down to qualify as having grasped the rule of the series. So, confronted with the question, 'Has he understood the system if he continues up to the *n*th place?', one is inclined to distinguish under-standing the system from applying one's understanding. (And this is right, for an ability is not identical with its exercise.) So one thinks of understanding as a *state* which is the *source* of correct use.

What then is this state? One is thinking of grasping the rule of the series as a mental state from which one's applications of the rule flow. But, W. remarks, this is where we were before. As intimated in §141, one can think of different 'projection lines' for any rule, and any application can, with an appropriate interpretation, be brought into line with a given rule. It is the *application*, not the occurrence of the formula of the series in the imagination, that is the criterion of understanding. Understanding no more contains its mani-festations *in nuce* than an ability contains its exercise, or a rule its applications.

1.1   'Understanding itself is a state which is the *source* of the correct use': since we commonly understand an expression at a stroke and then go on to use it correctly, it may well seem that understanding consists in grasping something from which the use flows (cf. §§138–40).

2   PG 44 gives further reasons that tempt us to adopt this false picture of under-standing: namely, that understanding is something *inner*, spiritual or mental, that we can only *manifest* it in its exercise, but cannot *exhibit* it (just as one cannot exhibit one's pain). Here understanding is surrounded by the standard mythology of the mental (cf. PG 82f.).

2.1   (i)   'The understanding itself is a state which is the *source* of the correct use': PG 49 discusses the parallel moves with respect to knowledge and ability. We misconceive knowledge as 'the hypothesized reservoir out of which the visible water flows'.

[3]   'Das dreigestrichene C': C three octaves above middle C.

Tracing the metaphor back to BT 150f. reveals the ramifications of the model. When I use words, I do not know when or how I learnt them. But if grammar, the rules for the use of these words, is essential to their meaning, then must I not have these rules in my mind if the words are to have any meaning for me? Or is it as in a piece of machinery: the cogwheels do not know the laws that determine the movements they can make when engaged. Do the rules of grammar determine what I do with the words I use? (If the calculus model of language is one of axioms, formation and transformation rules that will 'mechanically' generate all meaningful sentences of the language, is the speaker of the language a biological mechanism, a sentence-generating machine?) For, to be sure, I do not have the whole use (all the rules of use) of a word before my mind when I use it. So how can I know what I mean by a word when I use it (cf. MS 116 (Vol. XII), 98f.)?

Similarly, one can say that when I play chess I know the rules ('have them in my head'). But is not this 'having them in my head' just a hypothesis, since I only 'have them' in so far as I apply them in playing? So this 'knowing' is merely a hypothesized reservoir out of which the visible water flows.

BB 143 calls the 'reservoir' model a 'general disease of thinking', and gives as a further example: 'The fashion changes because the taste of people changes': here the taste is pictured as the mental reservoir from which changes of style and fashion flow.

(ii)   'Isn't one thinking of the derivation of a series from its algebraic formula?': Cf. PG 55:

Here it can easily seem as if the sign [in this case the formula] contained the whole of the grammar; as if the grammar were contained in the sign like a string of pearls in a box and he had only to pull it out. (But this kind of picture is just what is misleading us.) As if understanding were an instantaneous grasping of something from which later we only draw consequences which already exist in an ideal sense before they are drawn.

One here treats understanding as an inner state from which its manifestations flow in a way analogous or parallel to the conception of meaning as *determining* application and correct use (the 'meaning-body' conception). Different 'pictures' interlock here, or succeed each other kaleidoscopically, each dragging in its wake a host of misconceptions.

Section 147

1   This picks up the last sentence of §146, and presents an objection resting on first-/third-person asymmetry in respect of psychological verbs. When I say understand, I do not say so on the basis of my past applications. My past applications are *not* my criterion for saying that I understand. I know which

series I mean to be developing, even if I have only written down a few steps in it.

(b) strengthens this objection: my knowledge of the rule (how to apply it) must surely be independent of my remembered applications, since the latter are finite and the series infinite. But *I know how to go on* (and, of course, I do).

These two issues are further pursued in the sequel. Saying 'I understand' in such contexts is commonly an avowal, not a description. Ascribing understanding to others rests on criteria. Possible applications of a rule may be infinite, but ascription of understanding to another is fully justified by a finite number of applications.

1.1   'I surely know that I mean such-and-such a series': §146 reminded us that 'every mode of application can in turn be formulated algebraically'. So no matter how many steps in the expansion of a given series the learner writes down, it seems that it may still be that he is actually developing a quite different series from the one we asked him to expand. So he may have misunderstood the rule of the series, even though he has continued the series to a hundred places. (This theme is developed in §§185ff.) But in my own case, if I write down '2, 4, 6, 8, . . . 102, 104, 106, . . .' *I* surely know that the series I am developing is the series of even numbers, specified by the rule 'Add 2'. My developments of it flowed from my understanding — which is an inner state and the source of the correct applications (§146). This is the target of W.'s criticisms in the next few sections.

SECTION 148

1   This questions the categorial classification of knowledge and understanding as states of the mind. For the reservoir model of understanding and knowledge that is proposed by the interlocutor in §§146f. presupposes that understanding and knowledge of the rules of the series are mental states from which applications flow.

Mental states, such as occurrent moods and emotions, being in pain, thinking of something, have what W. elsewhere calls 'genuine duration' (Z §§71–85, 472; for discussion, see Volume 4, 'Methodology in philosophical psychology', sect. 3). They are continuous, having reasonably determinate beginnings and endings. They do not persist through periods of sleep or loss of consciousness. They can be interrupted through distraction of attention and then subsequently resumed. They may be contrasted with abilities and ability-like conditions, which have duration, but not, in this technical sense, 'genuine duration', since abilities do not lapse during sleep.

So, *when* does one know the rule of a series? — Continuously, day and night? Or only when one thinks about it? Is one's knowledge akin to one's knowledge of the alphabet and multiplication tables — i.e. akin to an ability, and therefore lacking genuine duration? Or is it a state of consciousness or mental process, like thinking about something, which has genuine duration? We are left to answer for ourselves, but it is obvious enough where the answer lies. Knowing the rule of a series, like knowing the alphabet or multiplication tables, does not have genuine duration, and so is not a mental state in the sense in which one may say that feeling cheerful or depressed are (occurrent) mental states.

2   (i)   MS 142, §148 (TS 220, 130) adds a paragraph: if you now know various tunes by heart, how is it that they do not together make a frightful cacophony? If you know the alphabet now, it does not mean that you are running through it in your mind, or that you are in a state of mind that is somehow equivalent to reciting it.

      (ii)   MS 116 (Vol. XII), 101 (cf. MS 180a, 7r) discusses Mozart's remark in a letter[4] that when composing he sometimes could behold the whole composition simultaneously in advance of writing it down. Does this not provide empirical confirmation of the reservoir 'picture'? But Mozart cannot have meant that he 'heard' the whole composition in a moment, as if all the notes were being struck together, or as if the piece were being played at a great speed. The question is: what does the combination of words ('I saw (heard) the whole piece in a moment') mean? Under what circumstances is it correctly used, and when incorrectly? W.'s implication is that the whole development's occurring to Mozart in a flash is not his suddenly doing something at high speed, but his suddenly being able to do something at normal speed: namely, write down or play the piece.

Boxed Remark Following §149 (p. 59n.), (a)

1   This note and note (b) were typed on separate snippets and inserted between pp. 103 and 104 of TS 227(a) with a handwritten addendum (not in W.'s hand) '103(1)' and '103(2)'.[5] It would be plausible to locate them between §149 and §150, or between §148 and §149, or note (a) between §148 and §149 and note (b) between §149 and §150 (as in the tree diagram on p. 307). Note (a) was cut from B i §79, which was typed from MS 116 (Vol. XII), 88. It reinforces the argument by comparing understanding with genuine mental states like depression, excitement and pain. The continuity ('genuine duration') of mental states is not paralleled by continuity of understanding, for

---

[4]   This notorious letter is quoted in various writings on Mozart: e.g. Edward Holmes, *The Life of Mozart*, reprinted in Everyman's Library (J. M. Dent and Sons, London, 1921), pp. 254ff. It is almost certainly a forgery (cf. Emily Anderson, *The Letters of Mozart* (Macmillan, London, 1966) vol. i, p. xvii), but this does not affect W.'s point.

[5]   In TS 227(b) between pp. 102 and 103.

although I may say that I have understood such-and-such since yesterday, it makes no sense to add 'continuously'. One can say 'I have understood the meaning of "W" since yesterday's lesson', but not 'I have understood it all day' (or 'continuously'), let alone 'I have been understanding it all day'. Mental states can be interrupted (e.g. being in pain, by taking an analgesic), but an 'interruption' of understanding consists in no longer being able to do something, and subsequently being able to do it again, perhaps after being reminded or having matters explained again. Such a temporary loss of an intellectual ability, unlike the interruption of a genuine mental state, does not normally have precise temporal location (compare 'When did you cease to understand integration?' with 'When did you cease to concentrate?').

1.1   'a state. But a *mental* state?': Curiously, this apparently concedes that understanding may be conceived as a state, only not a mental one. What state then? A state of what? — Judging by the source (MS 116, 88), a state of an underlying mechanism of the mind, a mechanism postulated by a mind-model in psychological theory or a mechanism of the brain (cf. Exg. §149 and 2(i) below). But this is the position criticized in §149: namely, of taking predicates of powers and abilities to signify such states (see also the criticisms from BrB 117f. quoted in Exg. §149, 2.1(iii)). So probably the point is to be construed rhetorically: if understanding is a state, then at any rate not a mental one — and the refutation of the reduction of understanding to the state of what W. calls 'a mental apparatus', i.e. of a mind-model or of the brain, is discussed in §149.

2   (i)   MS 116, 88, and its typed version B i §79 begin 'Ist "ein Wort verstehen" ein seelischer Zustand?' ('Is "understanding a word" a mental state?'). The apparently concessive rephrasing 'ein Zustand. Aber ein *seelischer* zustand?' occurs in W.'s hand as an addition to the snippet cut from B i and inserted into TS 227.

After 'We also say "Since yesterday I have understood this word" ', the MS continues:

If, perhaps, it was explained to me yesterday; — but have I understood it uninterruptedly? Yes, one could talk of an interruption of understanding if I had at some time forgotten it and had then learnt it again;[6] but does it make sense to ask: 'At what time did you cease understanding it?' as one can ask: 'At what time did your pains get less?'?
'I have understood the word "valve" since yesterday.' — did you sense the understanding the whole time? You have been able to use the word since yesterday; as you can also use thousands of other words — since long ago. If one wants to call understanding words a mental state, then in the sense of certain *abilities*, e.g. the ability to calculate, to speak a language, to play chess, to recite a poem.

[6]   But cf. Z §85.

On p. 89 W. remarks that he wants to call pains, sadness, rage, 'states of consciousness', by contrast with knowing the multiplication tables, being able to play chess, to integrate, to use the symbols of chemistry and the ordinary words of German: these, he says, he wants to call 'hypothetical states of the mind'. One could also call them hypothetical states of a mind-model. And the brain and nervous system can also function as mind-models. He then emphasizes how misleading it would be to assimilate this distinction to the distinction between conscious and unconscious states.

(ii)   MS 116, 96, shows W. hesitating between different views (cf. AWL 92–5). He was tempted to distinguish between different uses of 'understand', in some of which it *does* signify a mental state and in others not. One does say, he noted, 'At that moment I understood which facial expression he meant — I saw it before me.' Here understanding is a state of consciousness or process. It is akin to 'When I listened to this quartet afresh, I understood it'. Interestingly, W. later changed tack and added the sentence: 'No; one says "I listened to it with understanding", but not "I was understanding it the whole time".'

(iii)   Numerous texts emphasize the differences, with respect to duration, continuity, interruption and attention, between occurrent mental states such as being in pain, moods and occurrent emotions, on the one hand, and abilities and ability-like conditions such as knowledge and understanding, on the other (e.g. PG 48; MS 116, 89; Z §§71ff.). I can attend to the course of my pains, but not in the same way to that of my belief or knowledge. I can be in pain continuously, but not know continuously. I can feel pain, anger, sadness, but not knowledge or understanding. States of consciousness do not persist through periods of loss of consciousness or distraction of attention, but knowledge and understanding do.

SECTION 149

1   §148 offered us two alternative construals of knowing the application of the rule of a series: it is either akin to knowing the alphabet or multiplication tables, i.e. an ability to do something (mastery of a technique), or it is a state of consciousness, like thinking about something. It was evident that the conclusion was meant to be that such knowledge is akin to the former kinds of case. §149 now explores a further alternative, an alternative to which a defender of the view that knowledge and understanding are states of the mind from which the application flows may still have recourse.

Granted that knowing the alphabet is not a state of consciousness, one might argue that it is an *unconscious* state of the mind that explains the manifestations of knowledge. After all, although this knowing does not have 'genuine duration', like conscious mental states, it does have duration. One knows the alphabet even when one is not thinking about it or reciting it, and one does not cease to know it when one falls asleep. *If* we think of knowledge of the alphabet as such an enduring state, then we shall think of it as a state of 'an apparatus of the mind' — an underlying mechanism subservient to the mind, perhaps *a state of the brain*. This unconscious, perhaps neural, mechanism is hypothesized as underlying the application of the knowledge ('the *source* of the correct use' (§146)).

W. now observes that such a state, i.e. the hypothesized state of the *apparatus* of the mind, is called 'a disposition'. It might be conceived to be what is sometimes called 'a dispositional state of the brain',[7] i.e. a neural state that is held to cause the agent, under appropriate stimuli, to manifest the knowledge of the ABC by reciting it, or correcting mistakes in its recitation, etc. But this move is not without objections. To call *this* 'a state of the mind' would be misleading. For, unlike genuine states of mind, it ought to have two distinct kinds of criteria. We should be able to ascribe such knowledge (the putative state of mind) to a person if we know that his brain (the apparatus of the mind) is in a given neural configuration, *quite independently of what this apparatus does*, i.e. independently of the manifestations of knowledge that it produces. But that is precisely what we do *not* do — and not merely through ignorance. Even if we knew the neural concomitants of knowing the alphabet or understanding the rule of a series, those neural configurations would not be what knowing or understanding consists in. Nor would their obtaining (as established by positron emission tomography or functional magnetic resonance imaging) be *criteria* of knowledge. The criteria for knowing or understanding are the behavioural manifestations alone.

The parenthesis is a warning. If we think of knowing and understanding as states of the apparatus of the mind, then, to be sure, we shall concede that they are not 'conscious mental states' like feeling happy or excited, thinking of this or that, or having a headache. They are, we may insist, *unconscious* ones. (We might hold that when one 'exercises' one's knowledge or understanding — for example, in reciting the alphabet or expanding the series of numbers — then one's knowledge is a conscious state, but when one does not, it 'lapses', as it were, into the unconscious.) But this is quite wrong. The contrast between states of consciousness and dispositions is not the same as the contrast between conscious and unconscious states.

---

[7]   W.'s statement in the opening two sentences is excessively brief. However, the confusion he is pointing out with such compactness is not uncommon — for example: 'the belief that [*p*] is a genuine mental state, even though it happens to be a mental state that most of the time is not present to consciousness', and when a person is asleep, 'it is true to say of him that he has a number of unconscious mental states. For example, he believes that [*p*, that *q*] etc. But *what fact about him makes it the case that he has these unconscious beliefs?* Well, the only facts that could exist while he is completely unconscious are neurophysiological facts.' So, 'Unconscious beliefs are indeed dispositional states of the brain, but they are dispositions to produce conscious thoughts and conscious behaviour' (J. R. Searle, *The Rediscovery of the Mind* (MIT Press, Cambridge, Mass., 1992), pp. 156, 159, 161).

There are two unclarities here. First, it is not clear from the remark whether W. is still speaking of the so-called disposition or dispositional state of the mental apparatus, e.g. the brain, alluded to in line 4, or whether he is here committing himself to the thought that knowledge (e.g. of the alphabet) *is* a disposition in the ordinary sense of the word. Ancestral remarks suggest the former, even though there was a phase in W.'s thought in which he did construe understanding as a disposition (see 1.1(iv) and 2(iii) below). Secondly, it is not clear what conception of the contrast between conscious and unconscious states he is invoking. It could be the psychoanalytic one, or it could be the naive contrast between things of which one is conscious, e.g. because they catch and hold one's attention, as opposed to things of which one is not conscious, e.g. because they are occluded. The sources suggest the latter (see 1.1(iv)).

The contrast between conscious states and dispositional states of the brain, i.e. states that cause the agent to behave in certain ways in response to certain stimuli, is not the same as the contrast between conscious and unconscious states of mind. For here we conceive of the latter contrast as akin to that between an object that is in view and an object that is out of view. In this sense, what is unconscious can become conscious (as an occluded chair might become visible). But one could not become conscious of or apprehend one's neural dispositional state, let alone become aware of it *as a dispositional state*.

Knowledge, mastery of a technique, is a power — an ability to do certain things (§150) — and a power that is not being exercised is not at all like an object that is not being apprehended but might be.

1.1   (i)   'knowing the ABC is a state of mind': MS 142, §149, continues here: 'so kann // könnte // das nur ~~heisen~~ einen //den // Zustand eines hypothetischen Mechanismus // Seelenapparates // bedeuten, etwa ~~oder~~ einen Zustand unsres Gehirns . . .' ('then it can // could // only mean a // the // state of a hypothetical mechanism // apparatus of the mind //, perhaps a state of our brain').

(ii)   'Such a state is called a disposition': it is important to note that the 'state' in question is the hypothesized state of a 'mental apparatus', such as the brain. In MS 142, §149, W. wrote, perhaps more appropriately, ''Einen seelischen Zustand in diesem Sinne will ich eine Disposition nennen' ('A mental state in this sense I want to call a disposition'). For, to be sure, this is *not* what we ordinarily call 'a disposition'. Human dispositions, in the ordinary sense of the word, are traits of character, pronenesses and tendencies of the person (not the causal powers of certain states of his brain).

(iii)   'there would then have to be two different criteria': W.'s drafting is poor here. The two criteria would have to be (a) that the mind's apparatus (e.g. the neural state) obtains, and (b) the manifestations of understanding that are caused by the operations of the mind's apparatus. W. stresses that on this (objectionable) conception, the former criterion should be independent of the latter, so that if we know that the apparatus is there (that the appropriate neural state obtains), then we can say of the person that he understands, irrespective of what he actually goes on to do.

(iv) 'the contrast between states of consciousness and dispositions': What dispositions does W. have in mind here? The sources show that he is still speaking of dispositional states of the 'apparatus of the mind', construed either as a mental model or as a neurological state of the brain.

This remark seems to be based on ideas that appear clearly in MS 140, 11 (= PG 48), the 'Zweite Umarbeitung' of *The Big Typescript* (there are earlier, but less explicit occurrences). There W. first gives a series of examples (namely, having a toothache, expecting, knowing, being able to) that exemplify the differences between states of mind that have genuine duration, on the one hand, and knowledge and ability, on the other hand, that do not. Then he observes that *if* knowledge *is* called 'a state', then it must be a state in a physiological sense (or, he writes, 'in the sense used in a psychology that talks about unconscious states of a mind-model' (see 2.1(iii) below)). This, he there says, is unobjectionable. But, he notes immediately, we have moved from the realm of conscious states into a different grammatical domain. For if a state in the physiological sense is to be called 'unconscious', then the expression 'a conscious state' does not stand to the expression 'an unconscious state' as 'the chair I see' stands to 'the chair I don't see because it is behind me'. MS 116 (Vol. XII), 90f., is even clearer: 'But "conscious state" and "unconscious state" are for us inevitably associated with the picture: a thing that we see, and the same kind of thing that we do not see because it is behind us. But this comparison is completely misleading.'

2   W.'s struggle with the categorization of knowledge and understanding was prolonged. Some of the milestones on his journey are as follows.

(i)   In MS 110 (Vol. VI), 236, W. remarked: 'Das können & Verstehen wird scheinbar als Zustand beschrieben wie die Zahnschmerz, & das ist die falsche Analogie unter der ich laboriere.' ('Being able to and understanding are apparently described as states, like toothache, and that is the false analogy under which I am labouring.') The struggle to sort out the relationships between these concepts took considerable time and underwent various changes and development. The early ideas are incorporated in *The Big Typescript* §§35–9 (pp. 143–69), which contains significant errors that were subsequently rectified (the *Grammar* here is very misleading, since, due to the editing, the opening remarks on understanding post-date the later ones, with which they are indeed sometimes inconsistent.)

(ii)   MS 111 (Vol. VII), 26, remarks: 'If one conceives of understanding, knowing, etc. as *states*, then only hypothetical ones in the sense of a psychological disposition, which stands on the same level as a physiological disposition.' This is henceforth a recurrent theme in W.'s reflections on the question of the status of understanding, which culminates in the current remark.

(iii)   In dictations to Waismann, W. committed himself to the view that understanding is a disposition (not a dispositional state of the apparatus of the mind):

Understanding is a disposition to use [a] word. But that does not mean that in this capacity all the future applications of the word are already stored up; this is no more true than that the multiplications are already performed in the calculating machine, and in this sense the conception of a disposition as a reservoir from which the applications flow is decidedly misleading. (VoW 359)

This was repeated in another dictation (VoW 369): 'Understanding a word is a disposition to make use of it, this disposition is a possibility, and possibilities are taken for an image of reality. In this way the idea arises that in the understanding of a word all of its future applications are pre-existent or dormant.' So we think that the dispositional state of the mind-model contains *in nuce* all the future applications. The thought that knowing the meaning of a word is a disposition recurs in VoW 441.

It was only much later that he realized that although it was perfectly correct to deny that knowing and understanding are states or processes, it is mistaken to conceive of them as dispositions. In MS 135, 180 (= RPP II §45) he wrote cautiously: 'I want to say that believing, understanding, knowing, intending and others, are not states of consciousness. If for the moment I call these latter "dispositions", then an important difference between dispositions and states of consciousness consists in the fact that a disposition is not interrupted by a break in consciousness or a shift in attention.' But he rightly withdrew even from this tentative classification in MS 136, 90b: 'Why don't I want to say that knowing is a disposition? Because "I know that . . ." at any rate does not say, I am thus and so disposed. Knowing means something like possessing. Or rather, that is the picture that is there used. "I am in possession of all the facts."' (For discussion of understanding and its categorial status, see 'Understanding and ability', sects 4–6).

2.1   (i)   'one is thinking of the state of an apparatus of the mind (perhaps of the brain)': MS 110 (Vol. VI), 237, observes that having an intention, or an ability, or a wish is treated as a continuous state (like being pleased, happy or sad). But one can speak of a persistent state in such cases only if one is concerned with a disposition, i.e. a property, of the body.

(ii)   'there would then have to be two different criteria for such a state': cf. PG 82, where two moves are made. (a) We are inclined to call understanding 'a mental state' or 'process', and this allocates the concept to the wrong grammatical category: namely, a hypothesized (inductively inferred) state or process. (b) This is exacerbated since there *are* similarities between mental states or processes (even though understanding is not a state or process) and, say, brain-processes which are (often) hypothesized processes. *But* it makes sense to conduct a direct (observational) check on a brain-process. By contrast, there is no such thing (it is senseless) in the case of mental processes. (Here the 'direct check' is observation of the behavioural manifestations of the continuing process.)

(iii)   BrB 117f. notes that there are various reasons that incline us to think of possessing a power or an ability as being in a kind of state. 'He *is* capable of . . .', 'He *is* able to . . .', and 'he *can* . . .' all employ the verb in the present tense, which suggests that the phrases describe states that exist at the moment of speaking.

The same tendency shows itself in our calling the ability to solve a mathematical problem, the ability to enjoy a piece of music, etc., certain states of mind; we don't mean by this expressions 'conscious mental phenomena'. Rather, a state of mind in this sense is the state of a hypothetical mechanism, a mind-model meant to explain the conscious mental phenomena. (Such things as unconscious or subconscious mental states are features of the mind-*model*.) In this way also we can hardly help conceiving of memory as of a kind of storehouse. Note also how sure people are that to the ability to add or to multiply or to say a poem by heart, etc., there *must* correspond a peculiar state of the person's brain, although on the other hand they know next to nothing about such psycho-physiological correspondences. We regard these phenomena as manifestations of this mechanism, and their possibility is the particular construction of the mechanism itself.

For discussion of why this reduction of a power to its vehicle, i.e. to the structures that make it possible for the agent to exercise its powers, is misguided, see 'Understanding and ability', sect. 5.

Boxed Remark Following §149 (p. 59n.), (b)

1   This clarifies further the difference between the duration of mental states ('genuine duration') and of abilities. If I know (have mastered) a system of rules (e.g. chess or arithmetical rules, or rules of grammar), then that knowledge is possessed even when it is not being exercised (as my ability to run does not terminate when I sit down). The question 'When can you . . . ?' is misleading in suggesting that being able to (knowing how) . . . is a process, event or state. Since it bears a *kinship* to each, one is inclined to say both that one knows 'all the time', and that one knows at any given time when exercising the ability. *Then* it *does* seem odd that being able to play takes so little time and playing so long. But 'being able to do something' does not take time; it is not a process, state or event, although acquiring the ability may take time, the sudden dawning of a method of doing something may be a momentary event, and one may have an ability for a time (between certain ages).

This snippet comes from B i §86. Its source is MS 116 (Vol. XII), 97, where it occurs in a discussion of understanding and ability. Shortly before it is a section (cf. Z §672) which points out that the fact that the conditions (extraneous circumstances) for exercising an ability may be clockable exacerbates our inclination to think that an ability is a state or process, especially if we conflate ability with opportunity. Thus, if it is true that so long as the temperature of the rod does not fall below . . . then it can be forged, it would make sense to say, e.g., that I can forge it from 5.00 to 6.00. Or — so long as my pulse doesn't fall below . . . I can do the calculation, which takes two minutes. One can rid oneself of the wrong picture not by asking, misleadingly, 'When can you . . . ?', which is normally a question about *opportunity*, yet slides readily into 'When do you know?', but by asking 'How long does being able to . . . take?', which is obviously nonsense.

1.1   (i)   'Wann *kannst* du Schach spielen?': 'When *can* you play chess?' In B i §86, W. added to the remark: '(Und nun überlege Dir den *alltäglichen* Gebrauch von "Wann kannst Du Schach spielen?"!)'. ('(And now consider the everyday use of "When can you play chess?"!)'). The *everyday use* of 'When can you play chess?' is to make an appointment for a game. It concerns opportunity, not ability.

     (ii)   'that being able to play chess should take so short a time': To acquire an ability typically takes time, and so does exercising it. But possession of an ability does not *take* time, but *lasts for* a time.

2   MS 114 (Vol. X) Um., 23 (cf. PG 50) compares the confusion about 'When can you . . . ?' with Augustine's confusion about '*When* do I measure a period of time?'

SECTION 150

1   There are affinities between the grammar of 'knows' and of 'can', 'is able to' and 'understands'. Juxtaposing 'knows' with these verbs helps to disabuse us of the illusion that knowing is, as it were, a reservoir from which the correct performances flow, on the one hand, and of the error of conceiving of understanding as a state or process, on the other.

     There are also differences. That a person can V is manifest in his V-ing. But if a person knows that p, there is no specific act that correlates with his knowing as V-ing is correlated with the ability to V. The abilities with which knowing that p are bound up are multiple and diffuse. They include being able to answer questions as to whether it is the case that p, and other WH-questions related to the fact that p. If one knows that p, one can cite the fact that p as a reason for various things,[8] and perhaps (in certain cases) explain something else by reference to the reason that p. Like knowing that p, so too, if a person knows chess or knows the multiplication tables, then he is able to do a diffuse range of things. He can play chess and recite the tables, but also watch a game of chess with understanding, teach others how to play, explain

[8]   One *can*, but this is *a possibility*, not *an ability*.

the strategy he is pursuing in his game, etc. Similarly, if someone knows how to add, then he can also correct errors of addition, check his shopping bills or bank statements, and so on.

Being able to V is not the same as knowing how to V. Plants can, are able to, grow in the shade and climb walls, but they do not know how to do what they can do. There are many things *we* can do that we cannot be said to know how to do — for example, to breathe, hear, see, move our limbs. And we often know how to do things, e.g. lose weight, which we cannot do or, as we grow old and frail, may no longer be able to do, e.g. ice-skate or play tennis. Nevertheless, it is true that 'The grammar of "know" and of "can" runs for a stretch over parallel tracks (PLP 346).'

Similarly, knowing is closely related to understanding. Both involve multiple abilities. But they differ. To understand French may fall short of knowing (and being able to speak) French. To be able to understand French (e.g. when spoken slowly) has no parallel in 'being able to know' French, and to be able to learn French (a second-order ability) is not at like being able to understand it. To know what someone said does not imply understanding what he said, and to understand what he said is distinct from knowing that what he said is true.

1.1   The last parenthetical remark was added only in the Intermediate Draft (ZF). It is unclear why 'mastered' is in scare-quotes.

2.1   (i)   MS 142, §149c (and TS 220, §131c) add here: 'For I have understood, for years, how a steam engine works, as I have, for many years, known the ABC and been able to play chess.'

(ii)   'also closely related to that of "understands" ': MS 166, 29r, notes: 'The technique of the use of the verb "understanding" is most similar to the technique of the use of the verb "to be able to". In particular in such cases as "to be able to play chess".' W. then queries: 'Aren't you trying to make the distinction between understanding as a disposition & u. as an action?' To which he typed 'No' as an answer, and then crossed it out and began a new paragraph. Actually, understanding is never an action. It is not something we do, and what may appear to be an act of understanding is no more than the transition from a condition of incomprehension to understanding, and is therefore the inception of an ability.

VoW 357 remarks:

understanding the meaning of a word is comparable with what we call an ability [*ein Können*] or capacity. I.e. there is a kinship between the grammar of the words 'can' [*können*], 'is capable of' and the phrase 'understanding the meaning'. One could indeed explain that understanding the meaning is the capacity to apply the word correctly. Only this explanation does not protect us from further philosophical dangers, for the same difficulties hold for the word 'can' as for the word 'understanding'. One is tempted to ask: isn't an ability merely a hypothetical reservoir from which the applications flow? (modified translation)

Section 151

1   Hitherto the error of subsuming understanding under the category of state has been examined. Now that the affinities between 'know', 'can' and 'understand' have been elicited, W. reverts to the puzzles of instantaneous understanding (§§138f.). Two confusions are prominent: (a) that sudden understanding is some event or process underlying the manifestations of understanding; and (b) that saying 'Now I understand' describes, and rests on the apprehension of, this inner event or process of understanding. These confusions support the reservoir picture of understanding already discussed.

A further affinity between the uses of 'know', 'can' and 'understand' is that with all three one can *exclaim*, 'Now I know (can do it, understand)!' This makes it look as if understanding is an event, 'something that occurs in a moment'. There is a temptation to think that what happens when one suddenly understands, that specific event, is precisely what makes it possible to go on. It seems that this occurrence enables one to identify the rule of the series, or, more generally, to do those things that exhibit an understanding of the problem the solution to which one has suddenly come to understand. So, what is it that suddenly happens? W. describes various *very different* things that *might* happen. But, as the sequel makes clear, none of them is either necessary or sufficient for understanding. However, the natural response is not to relinquish the preconception of what suddenly understanding something consists in, but rather to jump to the conclusion that such understanding (from which performance flows) is some inner event or activity hidden *behind* these outward symptoms of understanding.

(§151 is picked up again at §§179ff. and §§321ff.)

1.1   'something occurs in a moment': MS 115 (Vol. XI), 182, remarks here that the example is especially instructive because *being able to go on* seems to be a specific occurrence, and if we investigate it, we think, we shall be able to pin down exactly what it is.

2   This and the following remarks are derived from MS 115, 182f., i.e. the failed attempt to redraft the *Brown Book* (cf. EPB 163f. = BB 112f.).

Section 152

1   The characteristic accompanying processes of sudden understanding are not what understanding consists in, and we are therefore inclined to think that 'He understands' must be something *more* than any or the sum of these processes. Actually, it is not *more* than, but something *other* than: namely, an ability rather than a further process.

2   MS 115 (Vol. XI), 184 (EPB 164f.; BB 113), which discusses here *being able to go on* rather than *understands*, adds further points. First, it is irrelevant whether the accompanying processes described are overt or covert, e.g. whether the formula of the series appears before my mind's eye, or whether I select it out of a list of formulae written on a blackboard before me. Second, understanding the rule of the series does not mean that such-and-such formula occurred to a person. Nor is the production of the formula sufficient for understanding — if a parrot uttered the right formula, we would not say that it understood. Third, the thought that 'He can continue' *contains more* than just uttering the formula (or than any of the accompaniments) inclines us to think that these various possible occurrences are merely *symptoms* of being able to go on, and not the ability itself. Then we think that the ability itself is something (some further process or event) hidden behind the symptoms.

Section 153

1   Even if we were to find some occurrence that accompanies all cases of suddenly understanding something (perhaps a certain kind of neural activity), *that* would obviously not be the understanding. It would be a mere *symptom* of understanding, which presupposes the criteria of understanding. For since it would be discovered inductively by correlating understanding with this constant accompaniment, we must be able to determine when a person understands something independently of any such correlation.

Furthermore, *one* reason for thinking that understanding is an inner process is that the person who suddenly understands something can say that he does — it is he who exclaims 'Now I understand'. It seems that he does so *because* he understands and notes that the process of understanding has taken place within his mind. It is this process, it seems, that he describes when he says, 'Now I understand'. But if so, how can the process be *hidden*? For if it is hidden, how can a person *know* that he understands?

The disentangling of this muddle is not completed until §§321–3 (see Exg.). 'Now I know how to go on!', thus uttered, is typically an exclamation — a signal of understanding, not a description of an inner process that has taken place. One can indeed know that one understands, but not because one has observed a process of understanding *in foro interno*.

Section 154

1   'Now I understand the system' does not mean the same as 'The formula . . . occurs to me' (etc.). But it does *not* follow that the avowal of understanding describes a process behind uttering the formula, as if the latter were a mere symptom of understanding.

The idea of a hinterland misleads us here. It is not a hidden process that justifies saying 'I can go on'. If there has to be anything 'behind the utterance of the formula', it is the *circumstances* that warrant it. This is unclear. The circumstances, together with the fact that the formula has occurred to me, do not constitute *justifying grounds* for my utterance (cf. §§179f., 323). On the other hand, it is the circumstances, e.g. of having been taught algebra (§179), having used such formulae before (§179) and having learnt to compute such functions (§320), and now being asked 'Who can continue?', together with the fact that the formula has occurred to me, which makes it *appropriate* to utter, 'I can go on'. It is such circumstances which make it appropriate to *signal* one's comprehension (cf. PI §§179–83), although, of course, one may be mistaken. They are not a justification but a warrant.

The idea that understanding is a mental process of *any* kind misleads one here. One should rather look at the 'language-game' in which these expressions are used, how one is taught to use them (cf. §179). There are characteristic processes, including mental ones, that accompany sudden understanding (being able to go on); but understanding is categorially distinct from mental processes.

1.1   (i)   'circumstances': note that W. does not mean only current circumstances or current facts about oneself (see §§179, 320).

(ii)   '(A pain's growing more and less . . .)': the waxing and waning of pain may be called 'a mental process', but the examples of listening to a tune or a sentence are poorly chosen. Better examples would be such things as reciting the alphabet or composing a sonnet or a sonata in one's imagination.

2   MS 142, §152 (= TS 220, §134) does not contain §154 (d)–(e), but has instead Z §446(b) (Z §446(a) = PI §154(c)). The point made is that our means of representation (grammar) produces an illusion. 'To understand' is a *verb*, so we think it must stand for an *activity* of the mind. (Cf. BB 117: our inclination to think that abilities are *states* stems, *inter alia*, from the fact that we use the present-tense static verbs 'is capable of, 'is able to', 'can' when talking of abilities, thus suggesting that the phrases describe occurrent states.)

BB 113: Noting that the manifestations of being able to go on are neither necessary nor sufficient for being able to go on, we mistakenly think they are mere symptoms. This misleads us into thinking that being able to go on is hidden *behind* the symptoms. But this is a metaphorical use of 'behind'. 'Behind' the utterance of the formula of the series which the person who suddenly understands the rule of the series utters may lie only the *circumstances* of the utterance. W. compares the error of someone who notes that being able to go on is not uttering the formula and so thinks that it is some *other* activity with that of someone who is told that 'chair' does not mean *this* ☞ chair and therefore looks around the room or *inside* the chair for the object that it really means.

SECTION 155

1   This remarks rounds off the discussion for the time being, before the digression that follows. The investigation is resumed at §179.

Suddenly knowing how to go on, suddenly understanding, may be accompanied by an experience of illumination, but the experience is not the ability or the understanding.

1.1   (i) 'for us it is *the circumstances* under which he had such an experience that warrant him . . .': a slightly clumsy formulation. Understanding is not an experience, and someone who exclaims, 'Now I understand' is not reporting an experience in virtue of which he knows that he understands. Rather, having such an experience (an 'Aha' experience) in the circumstances (of having learnt algebra, etc.) warrants saying, 'I've got it'. That, however, does not mean that if the person does not have such an experience, yet nevertheless says, 'Now I can go on', he is misusing this signal (cf. §180) of understanding. For one may sometimes suddenly see the solution to a problem and say so without any particular experience or sense of illumination (§179).

(ii) 'berechtigt': 'warrant', since the circumstances here are not *justifying grounds*. The point is picked up in §181 (see Exg.), where W. raises the question of whether a person who says he can go on, and then finds that he cannot, has *wrongly* (*mit Unrecht*) said so.

SECTION 156

1   This begins the examination of reading (§§156–78). Its purpose is to illuminate further the nature of understanding, discussion of which is resumed at §179. It also anticipates, and bears on, questions concerning following a rule discussed in the sequel (§§185ff.).

§156 introduces themes later considered in detail. (i) 'Reading' is deliberately *detached* from understanding, since this example is to be used to illuminate understanding, and hence must not invoke understanding of what is read (but only mastery of the technique of 'mapping' written words on to spoken or copied words, or dictated words on to written ones). (ii) The variety of 'inner' and 'outer' accompaniments of reading is stressed. This parallels the preceding discussion of understanding the rule of a series (§151). (iii) The inclination to think that reading is a 'special conscious activity of the mind' (just as understanding is conceived as a special state of the mind, and sudden understanding as a special mental process or event) is argued to be derived particularly from distorted reflection upon the reading of a beginner, where phenomenological accompaniments are pronounced (cf. §146(a)). (iv) The temptation to think that only the pupil 'really knows' whether he is reading is mentioned, parallel to the suggestion that an agent has privileged access to his own understanding (§147). (v) The alternative move to (iii) is raised: i.e. that reading is a hypothesis based on behaviour, since it really is an activity of the 'unconscious mind' or of the brain. On this conception, it is the operation of such mechanisms that distinguishes really reading from pretending to read (cf. §149; BB 120).

1.1   (i) 'This will become clearer . . .': What is 'this' is meant to be? BrB 119 (EPB 172 = MS 115 (Vol. XI), 195) introduces the discussion of reading explicitly to clarify the meaning of 'being guided by'. However, since the order there is somewhat different, and the discussion of reading succeeds a discussion of being guided by signs, all this shows is that W. put the example of reading to work for different purposes in the different contexts. More importantly, the final paragraph of MS 142, §152, says that this digression will clarify what the circumstances alluded to in the previous remark (PI §155) are, and what role they play in the use of the words 'understand' and 'know'. TS 239 says that *this*, i.e. the observation of PI §155, will become clearer if we break off the investigation of 'understand' and 'know' and interpolate an examination of the word 'to read'.

(ii) 'We have yet to discuss these propositions "Only he knows . . .'": a promise redeemed in §§246f.

2   PG 72 discusses reading *with* understanding in the context of a discussion of understanding. Reading with understanding is contrasted with reading without understanding, compared with following a melody, seeing the pattern of decorative ornament, etc. The later discussions (BB, EPB and MS 142) separate reading from understanding.

SECTION 157

1   The point is analogous to §145(b) and §146.

1.1   (i) 'So this concept was quite independent of . . .' (§157 (d)): the *concept* of reading is independent of any reference to an internal mechanism. What neural mechanisms may be involved in reading is an empirical question, and of no direct philosophical concern. The *criteria* for reading are obviously independent of any such mechanisms.

(ii) 'Nor can the teacher here say . . . "Perhaps he was . . ."': it would make sense to conjecture that *perhaps* he read a particular word only if reading were an inner mechanism and emitting words counted as reading only if such-and-such connections were set up and operative. But in the case of the 'living reading-machine', 'reading' means reacting to signs thus-and-so. It is not a matter of our not being able to *tell* which is the first word he read, but rather it makes no sense to speak of 'a first word in his new state' (of being able to react appropriately to the written signs).

(iii) 'a change in his *behaviour*': he starts reading fluently, but there is no *point* at which he makes the transition from hesitant to fluent reading.

2   (i) '. . . a certain experience of transition': BB 120f. has 'when a particular conscious process of spelling out the words takes place in a person's mind . . .'.

(ii) '. . . a change in his *behaviour* . . .': BB 121 argues that there is no sense in asking at what point did the pupil change from not being able to read to being able to read. The case is compared with the following: a row of dots with large intervals gradually succeeds a row of dots with small ones [this is wrongly printed in BrB], but one cannot say which is the last dot of the first sequence and the first of the second (or, in the case of a siren, when the low pitch ceases and the high pitch begins). The change in behaviour when a pupil begins to read is analogous. '. . . we have in this case not given a meaning to the expression "the first word in the new era".'

Section 158

1   This contains the 'mechanist's' riposte to the preceding argument, and W.'s parry. That it makes no sense to speak of 'a first word in his new state' does not stem from our ignorance of neurophysiology. Neither the ability to read nor its exercise are states of the brain. Whatever neural connections may underpin the ability, they play no role in the grammar of 'can read'. Indeed, an investigation into the neural foundations of the ability presupposes that grammar. If we feel that there *must be* a neural 'reading connection', this merely shows that this is a form of representation which appeals to us. This appeal rests on our inclination to assimilate abilities to states; our disposition to confuse philosophical questions with scientific ones; our hankering, in philosophy, for explanation (on the model of science), rather than realizing that our questions are resolved only by an overview of grammar; the charms of reductivism and the attractions of psychophysical parallelism.

1.1   'a form of representation which is very appealing . . .': as is, e.g., representing our body as something we possess. With the advent of fMRI and PET the mesmerizing character of this form of representation has become almost irresistible.

2.1   MS 119 (Vol. XV), 21ff., contains an interesting parallel discussion of the attraction of a form of representation. W. considers two quite different kinds of plants the seeds of which, after exhaustive examination, cannot be found to differ. But the seeds of the one type produce only plants of that type, and those of the other only plants of the other type. If we say that there must be a difference in the seeds, otherwise they *could not* produce different plants, that their previous history *could not* cause their subsequent development without leaving traces in the seeds, this merely means that we *refuse* to call this a 'causal connection'. So our insistence that there *must* be a difference only shows how firmly we cleave to the picture or schema of cause and effect. (Graphology, in a similar fashion, insists that character *must* express itself in handwriting.) It would by no means be pointless to say, W. concludes, that philosophy is the study of the grammar of 'must' and 'can', for it shows what is *a priori*, what *a posteriori*.

This lengthy discussion of the strength of our commitment to the schema of causality, and our particular interpretation of it, surfaces in Z §608 side by side with W.'s repudiation of the view that thought processes *must* be mirrored by, correlated with, brain-processes. 'The prejudice in favour of psychophysical parallelism is a fruit of primitive interpretations of our concepts' (Z §611).

SECTION 159

1   This picks up the thread from §156(e). The mechanical model having been, for the moment, disposed of, we return to the mentalist one. The mentalist is tempted to say that the *real* criterion of reading is private and mental (hence that only the reader *really* knows whether he is reading or merely pretending to read). Clearly, W. replies, there are feelings characteristic of reading, and different feelings or experiences characteristically accompanying pretending to read. But suppose that A wants to make B believe he can read Cyrillic and tells us so. We teach him to pronounce a Russian sentence. He then says it in front of B while looking at the printed words. Here we may certainly say that A knows that he is not reading, and we know it too. But our criteria for saying that he is not reading are quite independent of his alleged 'conscious act of reading'. We may also be in a position to say that A had characteristic experiences of pretence, but these are not criteria for reading or for not reading either (cf. §160).

1.1   (i)   '. . . the one real criterion . . .': Of course, this 'conscious act of reading' is not even a *possible* criterion of reading. If there is such a thing as a conscious act or experience of reading, the concept of such an experience presupposes the concept of reading. So the criteria for reading must be independent of experiences or feelings of reading. Furthermore, criteria must be public and capable of being embodied in explanations of the meaning of 'to read'.

(ii)   'und er wird etwa eine Reihe von Empfindungen haben . . .': since nine lines earlier W. has asserted 'und er empfinde, während er zu lesen vorgibt, eben dies', this would be better translated 'and will for instance have a number of experiences . . .'. The use of 'sensation' here is misleading, and does not occur in the *Brown Book* (English) version.

SECTION 160

1   The feelings that accompany reading (or the feeling that one is reading) are neither necessary nor sufficient for reading. They are not criteria for reading,

and their absence is not a criterion for not reading. The criterion for a person's reading is that the sounds he produces are appropriately correlated with the text before him, *in the circumstance* that he has learnt to read. §160(b) shows that even if the sounds produced correlate idiosyncratically with a set of marks, we might say that the person was reading if the regularity is adequate.

Section 161

1   There is no sharp boundary between cases of reading and cases of repeating from memory. This is made clear by §161(b). Evidently one does not *do* anything to make it into reading, apart from looking at the dial *in the circumstance* of having learnt to read numbers.

Section 162

1   Here a new line is explored: namely, that one reads if and only if one *derives* the 'reproduction' from the 'original' (the 'copy' from the 'model' (BrB 122)). A parallel move with respect to expanding a series is to say that A is expanding a given series if and only if every number he writes down is *derived* from the formula for the series.

But what do we mean by 'deriving'? What is the nature of the normative guidance of a rule? In the primary case we teach the pupil the rule of the Cyrillic alphabet, i.e. tell him how each letter is to be pronounced. Then he goes on to read. Here we are inclined to say that he *derived* the spoken words from the script by means of the 'rule of the alphabet'. But what does the 'deriving' consist in? How did the rule 'enter into' the activity of reading? We taught him, and then he read correctly. What shows that he used the rule?

A case which would meet our requirement that the use of the rule be *manifest*, and hence that we know of a process of derivation mediating between teaching and execution, would be one in which the pupil has to copy from print into cursive script by using a correlating table. Here the 'deriving' manifests itself in his consulting the table or trying to visualize it from time to time. (Note the similarity here between the table and a chart of colour samples.)

2   PG 99f. (cf. PI §156) repudiates the view that no outward observation can distinguish reading from mere reproduction of noises when viewing a text. On the contrary, deriving a reproduction from an original may be a visible process, like what takes place on paper in carrying out a particular calculation. Here in PI §162(b), derivation from a table is perfectly overt. However, derivation that is not overt, as in PI §162(a), is not covert either.

PG 101 clarifies this point: every case of following a rule, 'deriving' an action from a command, is the same kind of thing as writing down the steps that lead to the answer of a sum or pointing to a table correlating signs. The implication is that we can say that the pupil 'derives' his act from the rule if he *justifies* it by reference to the rule.

SECTION 163

1   The example §162(a) seemed clearly one of deriving, but one in which the deriving appeared to be concealed, unclear. In the example of §162(b) deriving was manifest, in that the rule 'entered into' the activity. But if this seemed to be the *real* deriving, our illusion is rapidly swept away by reflection on further cases. The pupil might use the table according to the second schema of §86. That would still be a case of deriving; and so would an even more irregular schema of correlating arrows. But what are we to say if the schema of correlation changes at each application? Where is the boundary between this and a random procedure? After all, we could *impose* an interpretation on his transcription *no matter what he wrote* (as we can represent a sequence of numbers as part of a series of many different rules). What then remains of 'deriving', in so far as it is invoked to *explain* reading?

2   PG 93f. explores the theme of interpretation according to a chart, i.e. the insertion of an intermediary rule between rule and application. The conclusion is that one can insert as many intermediary rules as one wishes, but one still has to make the transition from the rule to its application. Explanations come to an end somewhere — and then one has to *act*.

BrB 123ff. adds these points: (i) in the case of deriving according to the second schema of PI §86, the pupil, when actually looking up the table, nevertheless passes his eyes (or finger) horizontally from left to right. The gap between the intermediary overt derivation and the product still remains. (ii) In the case of interpretation according to the second schema of §86, one might say, 'He understood the table differently, not in the normal way.' To this objection W. responds, 'What do we call "understanding the table in a particular way"?' Whatever process one imagines understanding to be, it is only another link interposed between deriving (as described, whether outward or inner) and transcription. In any particular case, we could say that the pupil looked up the table thus:

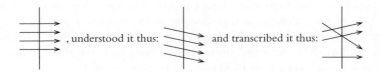

What, here, is the value of the intermediate step that is meant to represent understanding? And what, here, is the deriving? Does anything he does with the table count as deriving? Does anything he does count as understanding 'in a particular way'? Cf. TS 211, 514: 'One can now ask: but is it still a game, when someone sees the letters a b b c and does *something or other*? And where does the game cease, and where does it begin? The answer, naturally, is: it is a game if it is in accord with a rule. But what is still a rule and what no longer one?'

Section 164

1   §162(b) produced a manifest case of deriving (following a table by horizontal interpretation), but nevertheless a special case (for not all deriving need be thus). But as more examples were examined, the apparent essence of deriving dissolves, for 'deriving' is applied to a family of cases, linked by overlapping similarities.

In the same way 'reading' applies to a family of cases. Moreover, in different circumstances different criteria justify its application. Hence, invoking 'deriving' to capture the essence of reading is doubly futile: reading is not defined by characteristic marks, and neither is deriving. Nevertheless, the description of examples is not a hint at an explanation, which could be better done in some other way. 'It is not an indirect means for producing a certain image or idea in a person's mind' (BB 125; cf. PI §73). It is a grammatical explanation.

2   BrB 125 elaborates the family-resemblance point. It makes clear that the reference to §162 is to paragraph (b), not (a); and that the family-resemblance explanation of deriving applies in general to 'being guided by symbols' (and hence to expansion of a series too).

Section 165

1   Invoking 'deriving' proved futile, so another mentalist strategy is explored, a variant on the theme examined in §§159–61. The difference between reading and merely uttering the right words while looking at the text must surely consist of a quite particular process or experience — the experience of the words *coming in a quite particular way.*

But if the real reading consists of a specific experience, then it surely becomes unimportant whether one reads according to any recognizable alphabetic rule correlating letters and sounds. As long as this 'distinctive experience' occurs, it seems that the actual sounds uttered are irrelevant — which is absurd.

Second, what is this 'distinctive' experience? That the words *come* in a special way — of themselves? But the right sounds may occur to one while looking at the printed words even though one was not reading. Is it that the written sign *reminds* one of the correlated sound? No — the sound comes irresistibly. So both arbitrary occasionalism and mnemonic association are rejected; but *coming in a special way* needs further probing.

2   MS 152, 5, introducing a version of §165, comments: 'One could say, if you want to see what reading consists in, read, and attend to what happens. Well, what happens? I see words and say them aloud. But it is difficult to say what really happens, it is all so quick. I should see it better if I read Cyrillic, for then it is slower. (Cf. BrB 149f.)

An example of this confusion occurs in James:

> Reading exemplifies this kind of cohesion even more beautifully. It is an uninterrupted and protracted recall of sounds by sights which have always been coupled with them in the past. I find that I can name six hundred letters in two minutes on a printed page. Five distinct acts of association between sight and sound . . . must then have occurred in each second in my mind. In reading entire words the speed is much more rapid. Valentin relates in his *Physiology* that the reading of a single page of the proof, containing 2629 letters, took him 1 minute and 32 seconds. In this experiment each letter was *understood* in 1/28 of a second . . .[9]

Clearly Cyrillic should slow things down.

Boxed Remark Following §165 (p. 66n.)

1   This boxed remark was inserted on a separate snippet between p. 115 and p. 116 (which straddle §165) of TS 227a. The slip was cut from B i §395 (= MS 115 (Vol. XI), 10 = PG 169). Paragraph (b) was typed on it, and paragraph (a) was added in W.'s hand. The remark is clearly associated with the first sentence of §165 (also §167 and §§173−4).

When we delve, rather than survey, we are frequently driven to the point of thinking that we are trying to capture, in the 'crude' net of language, something too delicate to be expressible, but absolutely specific nevertheless (cf. PI §§106, 120, 436, 606−10). So, in the case of reading, we are inclined to think that it is a 'quite particular' process, but cannot describe it. It has to be experienced, we think, it cannot be put into words.

Further contexts in the book in which the idea of the 'quite specific' or the 'quite particular' are invoked and critically examined are §§184, 417, 542, 595, 606, 645.

1.1   (i)   '(atmosphere)': cf. BB 150, 155–7, 159f., 177f.; see Exg. §§607–9.

          (ii)   '*particular* expression': cf. BB 170–7; see Exg. §§606–8.

---

[9]   W. James, *The Principles of Psychology* (Dover, New York, 1950). vol. 1, p. 557.

2   (i) In MS 115 (Vol. XI), 10, paragraph (b) is immediately followed by
PI §436 (without the Latin quotation), which coheres with MS 152, 5 (cf.
Exg. §165, 2). To believe that the difficulty of philosophy is the description
of the ineffable or the perception of 'an indescribably rapid succession of inner
experience' (as James so often insists) is a dead end.

Section 166

1   This dispels the fiction that in reading words come 'in a distinctive way'.
The difference between reading and not reading in the envisaged circumstances
does not lie in the 'peculiar experience of reading', but in the difference of
situation (circumstances).

1.1   The final parenthesis: This empiricist idea (Hume, Russell, James) is discussed by W. elsewhere (see Volume 4, 'Memory and recognition', sects 1–3).
Just as the differentiation of reading from the mere utterance of the right sounds
seems to be due to the presence of a distinctive experience, so too what distinguishes a memory-image from what is not a memory-image seems to be a
special accompanying experience, such as a feeling of familiarity. But in both
cases, that is an illusion.

2   (i) EPB 181: after 'ein umgekehrtes Sigma' ('a reversed sigma') it continues: 'And if you say, the letter A does not "remind" you of the sound, in
the way the sight of a crocodile does of the word "devour", nevertheless there
are transitions; you could, for example, see an A-shaped trestle or roof-truss,
without the sound "a" occurring to you; or else the sight could remind you
of an A and you then utter the sound.'
     (ii) PPF §296 (p. 219) contains a further move: How am I to see 'how a
word comes'? By attending carefully? But that is no use, for what am I to
attend to? I ought to have to wait until a word occurs to me again, but it is
distinctive that it seems that I do not have to do so; I can, it seems, exhibit
to myself how it comes, even when it is not happening. I *act* it! Namely, I
produce certain characteristic accompaniments, gestures, faces, tones of voice.
That shows something about the 'field of force' of a word — which is important — but nothing about the myth of the words 'coming in a special way'.

Section 167

1   Having disposed of 'the distinctive way' words allegedly come, W. returns
to the formula 'reading is a "quite particular process"' (§165a). What lies behind
it? On the one hand, the mental processes may differ greatly (as between, e.g.,
reading print and transcribing into Morse code (bearing in mind that for

present purposes transcribing into Morse, writing from dictation, or copying, all count as reading (PI §156(a))). So to this extent it is wrong to think that, when one reads, one particular, introspectively identifiable process occurs. On the other hand, the experience of reading draws a certain uniformity from the more or less uniform process of reading (the overt production of sounds or signs). Moreover, the experience of arbitrary association at the sight of doodles, or the reaction to misspelling *is* distinctive, and different from normal reading.

By implication, our error is this. We infer from the distinctive and unusual experiences of association with arbitrary marks or reactions to misspellings that ordinary reading is accompanied by normal familiar and uniform experiences which constitute the truth-grounds or criteria for reading. One might say that the feeling of familiarity consists largely in the absence of feelings of unfamiliarity. But this 'familiarity' of the appearance of a word is not what reading it consists in, nor is it necessary, sufficient or a criterion for reading.

2.1   Z §184 discusses the import of our sensitivity to orthography; cf. Exg. §171.

Section 168

1.1   Various experiences *may* accompany reading, but none is either necessary or sufficient for reading. Furthermore, none of these possible accompaniments is a *criterion* for reading.

Section 169

1   This section, though linked with §168 (in EPB the counterpart of line 4 is a row of arbitrary pothooks and squiggles, as in its version of §168), branches out in a new direction. The nature of reading has been variously probed. We have explored the idea that reading, in the preferred sense of simply producing sounds or signs from sounds or signs according to a set of rules, is a matter of neural mechanisms or of mental experiences. The latter alternative has been explored from various angles: (i) accompanying experiences; (ii) deriving the reproduction from the original; (iii) that the words 'come in a particular way'; (iv) that the inner process of reading is special and peculiar. All these proved futile.

The new line to be pursued is causal, in the spirit of Russell's causal theory of meaning.[10] Why should we not argue that reading (as opposed to emitting

---

[10]   Cf. AM ch. X, with which W. was familiar; also IMT. For more thorough criticism see PLP ch. VI.

arbitrary sounds on looking at signs) is a process that occurs when the signs *cause* the corresponding utterance, and that knowing that one is reading (as opposed to knowing that one is not) is a matter of feeling the causal connection between seeing the signs and uttering the words? One might even think that in inner experience one has a more direct access and insight into causal connectedness than by mere outer observation of concomitance.

W.'s response, here, is telescoped. To the extent that causation is something established by experiment, e.g. by observation of regular concomitance, one cannot say that one *feels* the causing. To the extent that a causal connection in a particular case implies a causal generalization, it is unclear how any *feeling* could show that that particular case is an instance of a causal generalization. (And this point, if correct, holds even though observation of regular concomitance is not the only way to establish that a causal nexus obtains.) Finally, what feature of a *feeling* could indicate that C (seeing a sign) caused E (uttering a sound). Any *feeling* would merely be the interposition of a further element between C and E.

One might better say that the letters are the *reason* for my uttering such-and-such, since I would justify my utterance by reference to the letters ('justify', not 'causally explain'). But this, though correct, will not salvage the appeal to a *feeling of* connectedness, whether causal or justificatory. For while there is such a thing as feeling justified, there is no such thing as feeling a justification; my justification is something I say or think, something I appeal to, not something I feel.

W. pays out still more rope; one wants to say that one feels a kind of influence when one reads, but not when one scans a doodle. W.'s first move is to admit a phenomenological difference, *when one engages in such experiments*, between saying the sound 'i' aloud or silently, in response to seeing the letter, and in response to seeing a doodle.

Section 170

1   This is W.'s riposte. We do notice a difference between reading and associating sounds with doodles. In the context of our endeavour to fathom the essence of reading according to the rule of the alphabet, we misguidedly identify *this* difference with the difference between being influenced and not being influenced.

This 'phenomenological' interpretation (so attractive to James and other empiricists) is especially powerful when, under the spell of a *misconception* of our philosophical task, we read especially slowly (e.g. Cyrillic), in order better to observe what really happens when we read (fast). It seems then that we let ourselves be *guided* by the letters. But this amounts to no more than, say, looking carefully at the letters, and enunciating very deliberately.

§170(c) notes how the mechanistic model intertwines with the mentalist one.

SECTION 171

1   Yet another variant to capture the illusory essence of reading: the experience one has when reading is the experience of the written word *intimating*
the sound. Or it is to experience the sound and letter as forming a unity. To
feel this unity is to *see or hear the sound in the written word*.

The riposte is to emphasize that these experiences characteristically occur
when one is thinking about the concept of reading, not when one is reading.
If they do occur when one reads while *thinking about the concept of reading*, then
to describe these feelings is not to describe what occurs when one normally
reads, i.e. without thinking about the concept of reading.

1.1   (i) 'the written word *intimates* the sound': §§222ff. has a parallel discussion of intimation in the context of following rules.

(ii) 'I see or hear the sound in the written word': this phenomenon is akin
to 'aspect-seeing' and 'experiencing the meaning of a word'. What is this queer
experience? It is not stranger than others, but rather differs in kind from some
which we regard as fundamental, e.g. sense-impressions (PI p. 215/183). Thus
what we describe by 'I feel hot' or 'I hear a noise' are different in kind from
what we describe by 'I feel as if I knew the city lay over there' or 'I feel as
if the name "Schubert" fitted Schubert's works and Schubert's face'. The
latter experiences presuppose the mastery of a technique (cf. p. 208/178); we
are dealing here with a different, though related, concept of experience. For
having such experience, unlike having a toothache, presupposes conceptual
abilities, presupposes mastery of techniques of rule-following. W. goes so far
as to say that the concept of seeing (in such cases) is modified: the experience
is infused with a concept, soaked with a rule. 'It is only if someone can do,
has learnt, is master of, such-and-such, that it makes sense to say that he has
had this experience' (PI p. 209/178).

Seeing or hearing the sound in the word exemplifies the normative irradi-
ation of an experience characteristic of one kind of aspect-seeing. Various considerations support this conclusion. First, the Schubert example is pertinent here
('a similar fusion occurs, e.g. the faces of famous men and the sound of their
names' (see 2 below)). Secondly, the peculiar phrase 'seeing the x in the y' is
prominent in the various discussions of seeing aspects. Thirdly, the unity of
letter and sound is an analogue of 'experiencing the meaning of a word' (cf.
PPF §294 (p. 218): 'The familiar face of a word, the feeling that it has assimilated its meaning into itself, that it is a likeness of its meaning'). Finally, Z
§184 correlates orthography and seeing aspects. Sensitivity to orthographical
change is not a kind of piety; if one treats spelling as merely a practical
matter, 'the feeling you are lacking in is not unlike the one that a "meaning-
blind" man would lack'.

If so, the attempt to pin down the essence of the experience of reading by
reference to this feeling of unity of sound and letter can be rejected on the

ground that the experience appealed to presupposes what it is meant to explain. For only someone who can read can have that peculiar experience.

2   (i)   EPB 184 continues after '. . . dem Klang ihrer Namen' ('. . . the sound of their names'):

> When you, for example, say to yourself names like Schubert, Haydn, Mozart, and simultaneously imagine the faces of these men, it can appear to you as if those names were the correct expression of these faces; that this face, for instance, is correctly described by the name Schubert. When I have this experience of unity, it is as if I could not, for example, while reading the word 'yes' distinguish the written and spoken word. I could say that the utterance is a part of the perception of the sign itself.

(ii)   EPB 185 strengthens the argument of PI §171:

> I could, to be sure, say that whoever reads is guided by the letters; and that someone who utters a sentence while looking along a row of flourishes is not guided. This is an explanation for someone who understands the expression 'being guided by letters' before he understands the word 'read'. But it would be wrong to say 'whoever reads has the feeling, the experience, of being guided'. (Unless we are simply to give the name 'experience of being guided' to any experience had while reading.

3   'A similar fusion occurs . . . between the faces of famous men and the sound of their names': the thought is related to a passage in *Dichtung und Wahrheit* which impressed W. In response to a rude letter from Herder which punned on Goethe's name, Goethe wrote:

> It was not polite, indeed, that he should have permitted himself this jest on my name; for a man's name is not like a mantle, which merely hangs about him, and which, perchance may be safely twitched and pulled, but is a perfectly fitting garment which has grown over and over him like his very skin, at which one cannot scratch and scrape without wounding the man himself.[11]

W. referred to this passage in connection with proper names (e.g. MS 131, 141; Z §184).

SECTION 172

1   The proposal still under consideration is that what distinguishes reading from haphazard utterances which accompany looking at arbitrary doodles or at words

---

[11]   Goethe, *The Autobiography of Johann Wolfgang von Goethe*, tr. S. Oxenford (Sidgwick and Jackson, London, 1971), vol. 2, p. 14.

which one is not reading is the experience of being guided (§170). The riposte here resembles the previous one: cast around for further cases. Then it will become clear that although there are similarities between cases of being guided, there is no experience common to them all.

2   (i)   EPB 185 (cf. Exg. §171) clarifies the link between §171 and §172.

(ii)   BrB 99 discusses being guided in the context of a rule which correlates signs (dots and dashes) with hops and steps. What does being guided by an order, say ' — . . .', consist in? There are various possibilities: a person is guided by the signs if he 'reads' the order sign by sign (perhaps pointing at each sign, and then hopping or stepping as appropriate); or he is guided if he goes through a conscious process connecting the pointing at the sign and the correspond-ing action (which process might be an overt consulting of the table correlat-ing the signs with pictures of hopping and stepping, or consulting a memory image of it); or he is guided if he experiences a peculiar strain of 'trying to remember what the sign means' and a relaxation when the meaning comes to mind. These alternatives seem unsatisfactory, and we are taken into a long digres-sion which examines the concept of an ability. Once the illusions surround-ing the idea of being able to do something are dispelled, W. returns to the problem of being guided (BrB 118). For it becomes clear that the first attempts to answer the question of what being guided consists in were tacitly dominated by a picture of a mechanism (in the mind or brain) *connecting* see-ing the signs with acting according to them (akin to the mechanism of a pianola). But no such mechanisms are involved in the grounds for saying of a person that he is guided by signs (following a rule). The mechanical picture of being guided, in the sense in which the hammers of the pianola are guided by the perforations in the pianola roll, is only one kind within a family of kinds of guidance.

Section 173

1   This runs roughly parallel to §164. We can imagine many features charac-teristic of being guided *in certain cases*. But none of them, on closer scrutiny, *is* the experience of being guided. So we look for the real 'being guided' (the real artichoke) behind its 'mere outward' manifestations.

1.1   'a particular experience': cf. Exg. b.r.f. §165 (p. 66n.).

Section 174

1   Being guided, one wants to say, is 'surely a particular [distinctive] experience' (§173). When one draws a line parallel to an arrow, one does so deliberately

— one is guided by the arrow (and equally deliberately one may draw a line at right angles to the arrow). The essential nature of *deliberately* doing something must surely be *some specific experience*. For doing something deliberately is obviously quite different from doing the same thing unintentionally (cf. PG 98f.). Just as in §173, so too, when we try to envisage deliberately doing something, we think of a look or gesture. But that is no 'inner experience', so we think that there *must be* some 'quite particular' experience behind the careful movements that makes them deliberate.

1.1 Final parenthesis: What is the connection? As intimated in §176 and discussed in §§611–28, just as we are inclined to think that willing must be an experience (since raising one's arm is surely a quite different experience from one's arm's rising without one's raising it), and yet also that it cannot be an experience (since surely willing is something we *do*, not something that happens to us), so too we are inclined to think that doing something deliberately (drawing the line parallel to the arrow, and so being guided by it) must be, and also cannot be, an experience. (For discussion of the predicament with regard to the will, see Volume 4, 'Willing and the nature of voluntary action').

2 (i) EPB 187 and MS 152, 9, add meaning and understanding to intention and willing. In all these cases we are inclined to look for an experience, and hence to misconstrue the verbs and their cognates.

SECTION 175

1 When one copies a doodle, one is, of course, being guided. It is only when one reflects on the matter, that the *guidance* seems to become elusive. It does so partly because one wrongly demands that corresponding to the various nouns one chooses (e.g. 'guidance', 'influence') there must be some entity (an experience, for example). But the role of these expressions is not to stand for some correlative object.

2.1 EPB 188 (MS 115, 216f.) notes a connection with voluntary action and alludes to W. James's account[12] of the role of the will in getting out of bed on a freezing morning: 'Now how do we *ever* get up under such circumstances? If I may generalize from my own experience, we more often than not get up without any struggle or decision at all. We suddenly find that we *have* got up . . .' (cf. BrB 151; EPB 234; PI §§611ff.).

---

[12] James, *Principles of Psychology*, vol. 2, p. 524.

Section 176

1   When one reflects on following a paradigm, as when one copies something, one is inclined to think that what is essential about so doing is an experience of being influenced or guided. But now something puzzling emerges, which W. has already hinted at in connecting the current discussion with willing (§174). For on further reflection, one would not want to call *any* kind of experience 'the *experience* of being influenced'. For following a paradigm is something *one does*, not something that *happens to one*.

1.1   (i)   'Hence the idea that the will is not a *phenomenon*': a Schopenhauerian preoccupation (see NB 89), discussed in §§611ff. (see Volume 4, 'Willing and the nature of voluntary action').

(ii)   'I do not want to call . . .': Why not? Presumably because doing something for a reason is not an experience.

Section 177

1   The inclination to suppose that one *experiences* the 'because', *feels* the influence of the model, is due to the fact that one does indeed do what one does *because* the model or paradigm is as it is, and one is following it (no matter whether in drawing the line or in reading, or in any other case of following a rule). But one is prone, in philosophical reflection, to conflate doing something *for a reason* (one's reason for drawing a line thus is that the line one is copying *is* thus) with a form of causation. This, in turn, is articulated as a feeling, for how else would one know that one was being guided by the model, and what else could distinguish *being guided* from doing the same act *without being guided*? (For discussion of W.'s explanation of the contrast between reasons and causes, see Volume 4, 'Inductive reasoning', sect. 2.)

1.1   'even though this in turn is not in general essential to being guided': failing to draw the line parallel to the model does not mean that one was not being guided (cf. PG 98).

Section 178

1   §178(a) shifts the discussion from the first to the third person, hence from §177 back to §§173f., away from the idea of *an experience* as being what determines the difference between *being guided in one's* V-*ing* and V-*ing without being guided* and back to the question of what the overt manifestations of being guided are.

W. does not answer his question, but turns in §178(b) to an expressive gesture of guidance. But the gesture is not guiding anyone — it is emblematic. Although it guides nothing, we insist on calling it 'a movement of guiding'. It is a single *form* of guidance, which is compelling. But it does not contain 'the essence' of guidance. Guidance, it is becoming evident, has no essence. What needs to be done is to scout around and describe the environs of guidance — which is what W. has done. There are various criteria for being guided. Sometimes guidance may be evident, in many different forms, to observation. On other occasions it may be only what a person says afterwards that shows that he was being guided.

2   EPB 189 (MS 115 (Vol. XI), 218f.) strengthens the argument against conceiving of guidance as an experience.

> But it can also be what I say about the event after it has happened that makes this being guided; for example, that I say 'I was guided'. — This sounds strange, for how can something be made true subsequently by the fact that I say things were thus-and-so. — The use of the past tense here is however similar to that of the verb '*to mean*' in sentences like 'When I spoke of Henry IV, I meant the King of France'. (This must be discussed later.) We will, in certain circumstances also say that someone was guided because he subsequently viewed his action as falling under the concept of being guided. (This is also connected with the fact that we say that someone can know the reason for his action with certainty but not its cause.)

W. stresses the deceptiveness of the past tense of 'to mean' in PI §187 (see Exg.), and comprehensively examines the puzzles surrounding the concept of meaning something in §§661–93 (for a detailed account, see Volume 4, 'The mythology of meaning something'). 'When I said "...", I meant ...' refers to a moment of time (namely, the time of the saying), but not to an action performed at that time (other than the act of saying). 'I meant ...' does not signify an action I performed. *But a criterion that I meant such-and-such is that I later say that I did.* Similarly, a criterion for being guided is that one subsequently explains that one did thus because the paradigm or model was thus. And this is indeed related to acting for a reason. So, 'I am leaving the room because you tell me to' does not *describe* the connection between my action and his order, but *makes it* (PI §487, see Exg. and Volume 4, 'Inductive reasoning', sect. 2; see also §§681–7 and Exg.).

                              SECTION 179

1   Having closed the long digression into reading, W. returns to the theme of §§151–5 for the illumination of which it was introduced. The problems introduced at §151 were those presented by the sudden dawning of understanding, expressed by the exclamation, 'Now I know (can do it, understand)!'

The moot questions were: What constitutes the understanding? What event is the speaker reporting? What are the grounds for his utterance? How does he know that he understands?

§179 summarizes and expands some of the conclusions previously reached. (a) makes two points. (i) B's right to say 'Now I know!' depends upon B's having learnt to use such locutions and grasping the point of using them. The mere thought of the formula does *not* justify B's saying, 'Now I can go on!' Eccentric decorators who used formulae of arithmetical series to decorate the wall might have the experience of a particular formula occurring to them, but that would not mean that they knew what to do with it other than decorate the wall. Clearly, there *is* a connection between thinking of, writing down, or pointing at a formula, and knowing how to go on, *if B has learnt algebra and has used such formulas before.* Then, if the formula occurs to him when faced with a segment of a series, he typically can, and usually does, go on to expand it correctly. (ii) Nevertheless, 'I can go on' is not *a report* by B of an internal process which he has inductively correlated with his subsequently continuing a given series. This is not what B means by his utterance (any more than the schoolchild who raises his hand to answer a question *means*, by his gesture, that he has had an experience which he inductively correlates with subsequent answering).

§179(b) elaborates these points: the exclamation is correctly used in this complex context, but is not a description of it.

§179(c) repeats §151(c): namely, that B might utter 'Now I know' without anything at all crossing his mind and, in certain contexts, still have used the expression quite correctly.

1.1   (i)   'namely under certain circumstances. For example, . . .': note that the circumstances incorporate more than what is present at the time of the utterance.

(ii)   'that does not mean that his statement is only short for a description . . .': cf. §§321f. — the question 'What happens when one suddenly understands?' is misleading. If it asks for the meaning of 'sudden understanding', it misleads us into thinking that it is answered by a description of (possible) concurrent mental processes. It might mean, 'What are the tokens of sudden understanding?' One's face lighting up, change in breathing, etc., are such tokens, but the agent is not commonly aware of these, and they are not the grounds of his exclamation. It might mean, 'What are the characteristic mental accompaniments of sudden understanding?' But these too are not grounds for the use of 'Now I know!'

The moot question we forget when we describe these various experiences is: what is the criterion of identity *for them*, i.e. on what grounds do we say that these experiences are experiences (accompaniments) of sudden understanding?

(iii)   'in what family of language-games we learn their use': obviously in the wide range of language-games in which we are instructed in a technique. And one use of the utterance in those contexts is *to indicate that one needs no further explanation or assistance.*

2   (i)   BrB 114:

To say the phrase 'B can continue . . .' is correctly used when prompted by such occurrences . . . but that these occurrences justify its use only under certain circumstances
(e.g. when experience has shown certain connections) is not to say that the sentence
'B can continue . . .' is short for the sentence which describes all these circumstances,
i.e. the whole situation which is the background of our game.

   (ii)   Z §136 links the thought of §179 and §180:

Think of putting your hand up in school. Need you have rehearsed the answer silently
to yourself, in order to have the right to put your hand up? And *what* must have gone
on inside you? — Nothing need have. But it is important that you usually know an
answer when you put your hand up; and that is the criterion for one's *understanding*
of putting one's hand up.
   Nothing need have gone on in you; and yet you would be remarkable if on such
occasions you never had anything to report about what went on in you.

Section 180

1   It is best to view 'Now I know how to go on!', used in the circumstances
described in §179(c), as akin to a signal (like raising one's hand at school).
We judge whether it was correctly used (as we judge the schoolchild) by what
happens subsequently, not by reference to any grounds or evidence that justify the utterance. But note that in other circumstances, its point may be not
to herald a confirming performance, but to forestall any further explanations.
And even if one silently works out the next few steps in the expansion of the
series before saying 'Now I can go on', the utterance is still not a description
of any mental process.

1.1   '*This is how these words are used*': i.e. not as a description of an event to which
one is privy, nor as the expression of a conclusion from evidence, but as a
reaction of understanding.

2   PI §323: ' "Now I know how to go on!" is an exclamation; it corresponds
to an instinctive sound, a glad start.' PPF §293 (p. 218):

'Now I know!' What went on here? — So did I not know, when I declared that
now I knew?
   You are looking at it in the wrong way.
   (What is the signal for?)
   And could the 'knowing' be called an accompaniment of the exclamation?

W.'s strategy may induce the question: 'How do you suddenly *know* that you
can do it, can answer the question, etc.?' To this the reply is — not *any* how!

(How do I know that this colour is green? When I am drowning and shout 'Help!', how do I know what 'Help' means? Cf. RFM 337.)

Section 181

1   We use phrases like 'I can!', 'Now I know', etc., and gestures such as raising one's hand, like signals (in certain contexts and in certain respects). We judge the correctness of their use by subsequent behaviour. But 'Now I can go on' is not a prediction that is falsified if one then fails. It may happen that someone who indicates his ability and readiness is then unable carry out the task in question. This does not always mean that he has misused the 'signal'. For in some cases, when he said that he could go on, he could — but then something happened, and he was unable to continue.

1.1   '(Consider both kinds of case.)': the point is elaborated in §182. Cf. PI §323: it does not follow from my feeling (conviction) that I know how to go on that I shall not find myself unable to when I try. In some cases, as when an unforseen interruption occurs (a distraction of attention, etc.), I might be justified in claiming that when I avowed that I could go on, I could, but now I cannot. On the other hand, what is unforeseen must not simply be that I get stuck and cannot go on. My getting stuck *simpliciter* is a criterion for my not being able to go on. But it does not follow that my getting stuck after an unforeseen interruption is such a criterion.

2.1   'different things in different cases': BrB 115f. gives a rich range of examples. Suppose that when B says 'I can continue the series' (and is then unable to), (i) he visualizes the formula, but when asked to continue the series, he has forgotten it; (ii) he says to himself the next five terms of the series, but when asked, they do not come to mind; (iii) he still remembers the next five terms as in (ii), but has forgotten how he calculated them; (iv) he says, 'I felt I could, now I can't.' The various examples demonstrate subtle variations between different kinds of cases. In some instances we will firmly assert that when he said he knew, he knew. In others we will equally firmly deny it. In yet others we will hesitate; we may say (of a pupil) that he 'almost got it' (but was interrupted), or that he thought he could do it and, if not for the interruption, he probably would have done it, etc.

Section 182

1   This seems to elaborate §181, yet it is not concerned with the dawning of understanding and its avowal, but with more general features of abilities and inanimate powers. Early versions (MS 119 (Vol. XV), 49ff.; MS 121 (Vol. XVII), 58r–59v) occur in a different context, and §182 does not obviously fit well

here. It links up tenuously with the brief §150, but the thorough examinations of ability in the *Brown Book* and various MSS are omitted.

The exercises: (i) When is a cylinder C said to fit into a hollow cylinder H? Only when C is stuck into H? That would involve an illegitimate Humean reduction of power to its exercise (BrB 116f.; MS 119, 49ff.). (ii) What criteria are used for saying that C ceased to fit into H at t? Various: e.g. H contracted, or was damaged by a blow, at t; C expanded, or was likewise distorted at t. (iii) What are the criteria for a body changing weight at t (although not on scales at t)? Various: e.g. loss or accession of some constitutive matter at t, very rapid acceleration. These in turn may be determined by various criteria, some by ordinary non-theoretical observation, others by theory-laden scientific observation.

(i)–(iii) are cases of inanimate powers. All are directed at Humean reductionism, and the moral is given in §182(b). W. then switches to human abilities. (iv) When does it make sense to assign a time to the loss of an ability? Primarily when one can associate the loss of ability with a temporally identifiable cause (a blow on the head, a sudden shock, etc.). Note that 'to forget' is *not* generally used to designate instantaneous loss of abilities by causal interference. (We would not say, 'I was hit in the head by a bullet, and at that moment forgot how to speak French', nor even '. . . and that made me forget French', but more likely '. . . and I was not able to speak French thereafter', or '. . . and that deprived me of the ability to . . .'.) (v) The weight-lifting example is the nearest we get to the issue of §181, but it is still different. BrB 116 gives one answer: when I said I could lift it, my arm did not hurt, now it does! Many variants can be imagined.

1.1   (i)   'is more involved . . . than we are tempted to think': The investigation of abilities, introduced by Aristotle, fell out of fashion after Descartes, who was prone to reduce powers to their vehicles, as Hume was later to reduce them to their exercise. The study of powers was revived as a result of Wittgenstein's work, and many of the complexities concerning first- and second-order powers, the relation of powers to their vehicle and to their exercise, of abilities to opportunities, and of wants and reasons to abilities have been clarified over the past fifty years.

(ii)   'This role is what we need to understand': the role of verbs of powers (including an inanimate power such as fitting) and of abilities (animate and inanimate), as well as of tendency, proneness and disposition verbs, needs to be investigated, in order to shake the grip of the idea that they signify states of an apparatus of the mind, such as the brain (cf. §149 and Exg.). Definitions here are unlikely to resolve the puzzles that arise, and recourse to indefinability is no more than a tacit confession of bafflement). Rather, we must look at the occasion for the use of such verbs, the point of using them in such contexts, and what can be achieved by their use. Some indication of the direction of investigation is given in §183.

2   MS 121 (Vol. XVII), 58r–59v, is the immediate source. On 25 December 1938, W. indicated in TS. 239 that this remark should be inserted from MS 121, between TS 239, §199 (PI §181) and §200 (PI §183) and and did so in the Intermediate Draft (ZF §181).

MS 119 (Vol. XV), 49–59, is a more remote source. It is preceded (26–44) by a version of PI §§193–7, followed (44–9) by a version of PI §§215f. The conclusion is a version of PI §182(b).

Section 183

1   This, explicitly linked to §151, resumes the theme of §179. It is slightly curious inasmuch as W. has already argued at length that the two sentences do not have the same meaning. The point is perhaps this: the previous arguments have shown that 'B understands, can go on, etc.' does not mean 'The formula of the series has occurred to B' (§152), and equally that 'Now I understand' and 'The formula has occurred to me' differ in meaning (for I may use the former in circumstances in which it would be incorrect to use the latter (§154)). The argument of §183 is that in certain circumstances both sentences amount to much the same. For when, in the appropriate circumstances, the formula occurs to me, it is indifferent whether I say, 'I can go on!', or 'The formula has occurred to me!' Both exclamations achieve the same purpose — and to that extent W. is willing to say that in *these circumstances*, they have the same sense.

'We do say: "Now I can go on, I mean I know the formula"' introduces an analogous point. Different kinds of conditions are relevant to whether someone can do something. The question 'Can A *V*?' may, in different contexts, be an enquiry into the logical possibility of A's *V*-ing, the physical possibility, the legal or moral possibility, into A's *ability* to *V*, into the circumstantial possibility or opportunity for A's *V*-ing, and many other conditions. Normally the context of the question will make clear its purpose. *Pari passu*, a speaker declaring that he can *V* (e.g. continue a series) may make explicit what type of possibility or condition for *V*-ing he is alluding to. He may say, 'Now I can go on, I mean . . .' and add such qualifiers as 'the formula has occurred to me', 'I have sharpened my pencil', 'the pain has passed', etc. Thus we can introduce 'the formula has occurred to me' in this sentence as a condition for being able to go on, in contrast with other conditions. To this extent, we would, *in certain contexts*, be willing to replace the question 'Can he go on?' by 'Has the formula occurred to him?' But it does not follow that the two interrogative sentences have the same meaning.

What is the warning given in the last sentence? Certainly there is no set of conditions of the type in question such that, if they are satisfied, a person cannot but walk; the most that a totality of such conditions will give is an 'all-in' *possibility* of walking. Even if all circumstantial conditions and agential powers obtain, it is still up to the agent whether he will take advantage of the opportunity and exercise his ability. But the analogue with 'Now I can go on' is not whether, given the satisfaction of various conditions, the agent cannot but walk, but whether the satisfaction of certain conditions entails that he *can* walk.

1.1   (i)   'the one sentence has the same sense (comes to the same thing) as the other. But also that in *general* . . .': cf. PI §61.

        (ii)   'We do say: "Now I can go on, I mean I know the formula"': i.e. *this* condition of the possibility of continuing is satisfied.

2   The section is derived from BrB 114f. (EPB 166). The question of identity of meaning of 'He can continue . . .' and 'He knows the formula' (i.e. can point it out, write it down, etc.) can, W. argues, be variously answered. He compares this case to a notional language in which two different sentences are used to say that a person's legs are in working order, the one being used only when a person is about to go on an expedition, walking tour, etc., the other when this is not so. We will be undecided whether the sentences do or do not have the same meaning. In general such questions can only be decided by examination of details of usage. But it is clear that if we decide to say that the expressions differ in meaning we cannot do so on the grounds that the fact that makes the first true differs from the fact that makes the second true. We are justified in saying that our pair of sentences differ in meaning, but not because 'He can continue . . .' refers to a particular state of affairs on a different level from the events that take place overtly or mentally (realizing what the formula is, imagining further terms, etc.). What determines the meaning of the sentence is not a state of affairs to which it refers.

SECTION 184

1   W. switches from the example of being able to develop an arithmetical series to being able to sing a tune. Here, similarly, one may try to remember the tune, and suddenly exclaim, 'Now I know it' (cf. §151). And here too, one may be tempted, in Jamesian fashion, by the reservoir model of the mind. For singing the tune seems to be the unfolding of something that 'in some sense' is already *there*, in one's mind. But clearly, being 'there' does not mean that one heard the whole tune in one's mind in a flash (cf. the Mozart example, Exg. §148, 2(ii)). W. offers the interlocutor an alternative construal: knowing the tune is a *particular* feeling, *as if* the tune were there. Rather than probing the idea of 'a feeling as if', W. puts pressure on the object of the putative feeling. For might one not have the feeling, and then find, after one begins singing, that one *cannot* go on, after all (cf. §182)? But one may have been absolutely certain, when one said 'Now I know it', that one could go on — and indeed,

maybe *then*, for a moment, one could have gone on (parallel to §182, example (5)). So, was it *there* after all? Now W. puts pressure on the phrase 'it was there'. What does it mean? One might use it if someone successfully sang the tune through, or rehearsed it right through in his imagination (and told us). Thus used, it is no more than a picturesque way of saying that he knows the tune — not an *explanation* of how it is that he can sing it through. (To be sure, W. concedes, one might give the phrase a quite different use, viz. to say that the tune is written down before one.) So now, what does the being certain, the knowing, consist in? W. leaves us to answer (but see §§323ff.) — the knowing consists in the *ability* to sing the tune, not in any inner state or process (the reservoir model is to be rejected). And the being certain? Well, people often feel certain that they can do something — and say so, or raise their hand to indicate that they know how to do it. And *usually* they can go on to do what they signal that they can do.

The conclusion is ironic: of course, one could say that when someone says with conviction that he now knows the tune, then it is present (in some sense) in its entirety in his mind. But this is an *explanation* of the meaning of the phrase 'it is present to his mind in its entirety' — which now means 'he is convinced that he knows it'. What is important is that the 'presence of the tune to the mind' is not the *ground* of, and *explanation* of, the certainty or the exercise of the ability.

This concludes the discussion of abilities, of knowledge and understanding, which was needed as a preparation for the discussion of following a rule, which is the theme of §§185–242.

2.1   BB 130 compares 'He must know the tune before he can sing it' with 'He must understand an order before he can obey it' and 'He must know where his pain is before he can point to it'. In all these cases we are driven to demand an intermediate step — between wanting to remember the tune and being able to sing it, between having a pain and pointing at it, between hearing the order and obeying it. This in turn is related to our demand to interpose between perception and utterance (e.g. 'that's red') an act of recognizing a similarity between cases, which is supposed to explain why we use the same word.

Index

(*Since this is a volume of textual exegesis, this index should be used in conjunction with Wittgenstein's text and its index*)